The Strategy and Tactics of Pricing

A Guide to Profitable Decision Making

THIRD EDITION

The Strategy and Tactics of Pricing

A Guide to Profitable Decision Making

THOMAS T. NAGLE

Strategic Pricing Group, Inc.

REED K. HOLDEN

Strategic Pricing Group, Inc.

Prentice
Hall

Upper Saddle River, NJ 07458

Library of Congress Cataloging-in-Publication Data
Nagle, Thomas T., 1951–
    The strategy and tactics of pricing: a guide to profitable decision making / Thomas T.
Nagle, Reed K. Holden.
        p. cm.
    Includes bibliographical references and index.
    ISBN 0-13-026248-X
    1. Pricing. 2. Marketing—Decision making. I. Holden, Reed K. II. Title.

HF5416.5 .N34 2002
658.8'16—dc21
                                                                    2001036857

Acquisitions Editor: Whitney Blake
Editor-in-Chief: Jeff Shelstad
Assistant Editor: Anthony Palmiotto
Editorial Assistant: Melissa Pellerano
Media Project Manager: Michele Faranda
Marketing Assistant: Christine Genneken
Managing Editor (Production): John Roberts
Production Editor: Renata Butera
Production Assistant: Diane Falcone
Permissions Coordinator: Suzanne Grappi
Associate Director, Manufacturing: Vinnie Scelta
Production Manager: Arnold Vila
Manufacturing Buyer: Diane M. Peirano
Art Director: Jayne Conte
Cover Design: Bruce Kenselaar
Manager, Print Production: Christy Mahon
Composition: Carlisle Communications, Ltd.
Full-Service Project Management: Carlisle Communications, Ltd.
Printer/Binder: Phoenix Color Corp.

Credits and acknowledgments borrowed from other sources and reproduced, with permission, in this textbook appear on appropriate page within the text.

10 9 8 7
ISBN 0-13-026248-X

The Prentice Hall International Series in Marketing
Philip Kotler, Series Editor

Anderson/Narus	*Business Market Management*
Armstrong/Kotler	*Marketing: An Introduction,* Fifth Edition
Ballou	*Business Logistics Management,* Fourth Edition
Batra/Myers/Aaker	*Advertising Management,* Fifth Edition
Berman/Evans	*Retail Management,* Eighth Edition
Best	*Market-Based Management,* Second Edition
Burns/Bush	*Marketing Research,* Third Edition
Coughlan/Anderson/ Stern/El-Ansary	*Marketing Channels,* Sixth Edition
Cutlip/Center/Broom	*Effective Public Relations,* Eighth Edition
Hair/Anderson/Tatham/ Black	*Multivariate Data Analysis,* Fifth Edition
Johnson/Wood/Wardlow/ Murphy	*Contemporary Logistics,* Seventh Edition
Keegan	*Global Marketing Management,* Seventh Edition
Keller	*Strategic Brand Management*
Kerin/Peterson	*Strategic Marketing Problems,* Ninth Edition
Kotler	*Marketing Management,* Tenth Edition
Kotler/Andreasen	*Strategic Marketing for Nonprofit Organizations,* Fifth Edition
Kotler/Armstrong	*Principles of Marketing,* Ninth Edition
Lovelock	*Services Marketing,* Fourth Edition
Malhotra	*Marketing Research,* Third Edition
Manning/Reece	*Selling Today,* Eighth Edition
Nagle/Holden	*The Strategy and Tactics of Pricing,* Third Edition
Russell/Lane	*Kleppner's Advertising Procedure,* Fifteenth Edition
Sawhney	*PhotoWars: A Strategy Simulation CD*
Schiffman/Kanuk	*Consumer Behavior,* Seventh Edition
Solomon	*Consumer Behavior,* Fifth Edition
Strauss/Frost	*E-Marketing,* Second Edition
Urban/Hauser	*Design and Marketing of New Products,* Second Edition
Wells/Burnett/Moriarty	*Advertising,* Fifth Edition

To Dan Nimer,
Who labored alone
with vision and persistence
until others sought to share his wisdom

Brief Contents

Contents

CHAPTER 12   Competitive Advantages   305

CHAPTER 13   Measuring Perceived Value and Price Sensitivity   332

Preface

"Pricing is the moment of truth—all of marketing comes
to focus in the pricing decision."

When Raymond Corey wrote these words at the Harvard Business School in the early 1960s, marketing was just coming into its own as a strategic discipline that could drive the direction of a business. Unfortunately, few marketing practitioners actually took Corey's words to heart. Enjoying their new prestige and power to influence corporate strategy, they were reluctant to let financial considerations constrain their "strategic" thinking.

Instead, they focused on achieving market share and customer satisfaction, believing that high profitability would somehow naturally follow. Marketing academics also slighted pricing, offering little research and few courses on the subject. Whenever the subject of pricing problems did arise, professors assured their students that all could be solved indirectly by redoubling efforts to differentiate products and services.

These attitudes toward pricing changed radically when marketers encountered the challenges of the 1980s. Companies with leading brand names saw brand loyalty and their power over distribution erode from years of price "promotion" to defend market share. Even large companies often found profits unattainable, as smaller firms targeted and lured away the most profitable customers (a practice labeled "cream skimming" by the victims). Successful corporate raiders then showed that they could increase cash flow and profits, often by raising prices, even as they lost some share. In the 1990s, a brief counterrevolution took place, as e-competitors bought market share from more efficient bricks and mortar competitors. By the end of 2000, most e-competitors went bankrupt, while the remainder looked for ways to charge prices consistent with financial viability.

Not only marketing practitioners are now under the gun to show that their efforts can ultimately pay off at the bottom line. So also are marketing theorists. Companies have become almost maniacal in their focus on increasing shareholder value. Strategies defined in terms of market share or customer satisfaction alone get short shrift. For marketers to achieve respect and influence, the key is to show how their ideas can generate profitability. As a result, creative thinkers are integrating marketing thought with financial concepts.[1]

Successfully making that integration requires understanding not only what creates value for customers, but also how and when that value can be transformed into earnings per share. This does not mean that companies should regress to the days when they naively tried to increase profits by marking up costs with higher margins. It means understanding that strategic pricing is about much more than setting prices. It is about targeting markets that can be served profitably, communicating information that justifies price levels, and managing pricing processes and systems to keep prices aligned with value received.

These are not skills that have traditionally resided in finance or marketing departments. Strategic pricing is becoming a profession in its own right that bridges marketing, finance, sales, and top management. The Professional Pricing Society[2] reported in a survey of its members that pricing decisions were principally made by a pricing manager in 25 percent of the companies and by a cross-functional team in another 20 percent. Others cited were the marketing department (15 percent) and product manager (15 percent). Decentralized pricing by the sales organization was practiced in only 11 percent of these companies, and none had pricing principally made by finance. Although this is a biased sample, it is indicative that price in the most sophisticated companies is being proactively managed.

As in the first edition, the primary objective of this edition is to develop a practical and readable manager's guide to pricing, not a textbook. Our references are not necessarily to the seminal articles on the subject, but to those that are most managerially relevant and accessible. Professors will be happy to learn that an expanded Instructor's Manual for this edition includes new classroom exercises. We expect that the combination of clear writing and current, relevant examples will continue to make this the most popular reference on pricing for managers[3] as well as the most popular text in the classroom.

---

[1] Eugene W. Anderson, Claes Fornell, and Donald R. Lehmann, "Customer Satisfaction, Market Share, and Profitability: Findings from Sweden," *Journal of Marketing,* 58 (July 1994), pp. 53–66; Rolan Rust, Anthony J. Zahorik, and Timothy L. Keiningham, "Return on Quality: Making Service Quality Financially Accountable," *Journal of Marketing* 58 (April 1995), pp. 58–70; Rajendra K. Srivastava, Tasadduq A. Shervani, and Liam Fahey, "Market-Based Assets and Shareholder Value: A Framework for Analysis," *Journal of Marketing* 62(*1*), (January 1998), pp. 2–18.

[2] Professional Pricing Society, *PPS Members 2001 Current Practices Survey* (Atlanta, GA: 2001). For additional information about PPS and the survey, go to www.pricingsociety.com.

[3] As measured by amazon.com.

Acknowledgments

W e cannot practically enumerate all those people to whom we owe a debt of gratitude, but collectively they have contributed substantially to the content of this work. We wish to renew our thanks to all who contributed to the first and second editions and whose specific contributions were acknowledged there. The success of those earlier works gave us access to client companies and managers from whom we have learned much more about pricing strategy and implementation than would have been possible from purely academic research. Many thanks to our students and seminar participants whose probing questions and challenging problems continue to keep our work interesting and relevant.

We gratefully acknowledge the advice of numerous experts in marketing, pricing, and business management whose published and unpublished insights we have incorporated into this text. While we could never enumerate them all, we wish to acknowledge our special debt to George Cressman, Kent Monroe, Dan Nimer, and Mike Marn. Richard Harmer has contributed immensely to our thinking about pricing over the past fifteen years. His work is defining "value segments," and his concepts of "segmentation fences" and "price metrics" are now widely adopted by pricing practitioners. He also contributed to our thinking about the role of income and affordability in pricing. Gerald (Jerry) Smith of Boston College coauthored two chapters in the second edition that have been revised and integrated into this edition, and he also added numerous examples and scholarly references to this edition. Jerry's exceptional intellect added much to our own insights. Barry Margeson added an insightful section to Chapter 12. Eugene Zelek, an antitrust attorney and believer in creatively managing within rather than reacting to legal constraints, wrote the section in Chapter 14 on the law.

It is easy to underestimate how much work beyond writing is involved in publishing a book. Allison Bray edited the revised chapters. Evelyn Hennessey managed manuscript preparation. Susanna Barmakian and Bonnie Walsh secured permissions. We would like to thank our colleagues at Strategic Pricing Group who were understanding and supportive of our need for "writing time" and who accepted additional management and project responsibilities to give us that time.

Finally, Tom Nagle thanks his wife Leslie for her patience and spiritual guidance.

Reed Holden thanks his fiance Carolyn Ruech, his children, Mark and Rebecca, and his parents Carl and "Bunny" Holden for their unwavering support over the years.

CHAPTER

1

Strategic Pricing

The Harvest of Your Profit Potential

Few managers, even those specializing in marketing, think strategically about pricing. Consider your experiences and observations. Were the pricing decisions you encountered made in reaction to a pricing problem, or were they planned to exploit an opportunity? Did the company arrive at those decisions by analyzing only the immediate impact on profitability, or did it also consider how the reactions of customers or competitors might change the picture? Did the decisions focus purely on price, or did they involve alignment of a marketing program to support the pricing decision? Few companies proactively manage their businesses to create the conditions that foster more profitable pricing.

WHY PRICING IS OFTEN INEFFECTIVE

The difference between price setting and strategic pricing is the difference between reacting to market conditions and proactively managing them.[1] It is the reason why companies with similar market shares and technologies often earn such different rewards for their efforts. Strategic pricing is the coordination of interrelated marketing, competitive, and financial decisions to set prices profitably. For most companies, strategic pricing requires more than a change in attitude; it requires a change in when, how, and who makes pricing decisions. For example, strategic pricing requires anticipating price levels before beginning product development. The only way to ensure profitable pricing is to reject early those ideas for which adequate value cannot be captured to justify the cost. Strategic pricing also requires that management take responsibility for establishing a coherent set of pricing policies and procedures, consistent with its strategic goals for the company. Abdicating responsibility for pricing to the sales force or to the distribution channel is abdicating responsibility for the strategic direction of the business.

Perhaps most important, strategic pricing requires a new relationship between marketing and finance. Strategic pricing is actually the interface between marketing and finance. It involves finding a balance between the customer's desire to obtain good value and the firm's need to cover costs and earn profits.

1

Unfortunately, pricing at most companies is characterized more by conflict than by balance between these objectives. If pricing is to reflect value to the customer, specific prices must be set by those best able to anticipate that value—presumably marketing and sales managers. But their efforts will not generate sustainable profits unless constrained by appropriate financial objectives. Rather than attempting to "cover costs," finance must learn how costs change with changes in sales and must use that knowledge to develop appropriate incentives and constraints for marketing and sales to achieve their objectives profitably.

With their respective roles appropriately defined, marketing and finance can work together toward a common goal—to achieve profitability through strategic pricing. Before marketing and finance can attain this goal, however, they must discard the flawed thinking about pricing that leads them into conflict and that drives them to make unprofitable decisions. Let's look at these flawed paradigms and destroy them once and for all.

The Cost-Plus Delusion

Cost-plus pricing is, historically, the most common pricing procedure because it carries an aura of financial prudence. Financial prudence, according to this view, is achieved by pricing every product or service to yield a fair return over all costs, fully and fairly allocated. In theory, it is a simple guide to profitability; in practice, it is a blueprint for mediocre financial performance.

The problem with cost-driven pricing is fundamental: In most industries it is impossible to determine a product's unit cost before determining its price. Why? Because unit costs change with volume. This cost change occurs because a significant portion of costs are "fixed" and must somehow be "allocated" to determine the full unit cost. Unfortunately, since these allocations depend on volume, which changes with changes in price, unit cost is a moving target.

To "solve" the problem of determining unit cost, cost-based pricers are forced to make the absurd assumption that they can set price without affecting volume. The failure to account for the effects of price on volume, and of volume on costs, leads managers directly into pricing decisions that undermine profits. One particularly tragic example, for the company and its customers, was Wang Laboratory's experience in pricing the world's first word processor. Introduced in 1976, the product was an instant success, enabling Wang to grow rapidly and dominate the market. By the mid-1980s, however, personal computers with word-processing software were becoming credible competitors. As competition increased and growth slowed, the company's cost-driven pricing philosophy began killing its market advantage. Unit costs were repeatedly recalculated and prices raised to reflect the rising overhead allocation. As a result, sales declined even further. Before long, even Wang's most loyal customers began making the switch to cheaper alternatives.

A price increase to "cover" higher fixed costs reduces sales further and causes unit cost to rise even higher. The result is often that price increases actually reduce profits. On the other hand, if a price cut causes sales to increase, fixed costs are spread over more units, making unit costs decline. The result is often increased profit. Instead of pricing *reactively* to cover costs and profit objectives, managers need to price *proactively*. They need to acknowledge that pricing affects sales volume, and that volume affects costs.

The dangers of cost-based pricing are not limited to products facing increasing competition and declining volume. In fact, cost-based pricing is even more insidious when applied to strong products since there are no signals (such as declining market share) to warn of the potential damage. For example, an international telecommunications company with many leading technologies uses cost-based pricing only as a "starting point" for pricing. Product and sales managers review the cost-based "target prices" for consistency with market conditions and then argue for adjustments to reflect market conditions. Everyone in the organization finds this system fair and reasonable.

But does the system foster profitability? During the three years this system has been in place, marketing has frequently requested and received permission to charge prices less than the cost-based "target" in order to reflect market conditions. Now, how many times during those three years do you think marketing argued that a target price should be raised to reflect market conditions? Never, despite the fact that the company often has large backlogs of orders on some of its most popular products. At this company, as at many others, cost-based target prices have become cost-based "caps" on profitability for the most valuable products.

Cost-plus pricing leads to overpricing in weak markets and underpricing in strong ones—exactly the opposite direction of a prudent strategy. The financial questions that should drive proactive pricing are "How much more sales volume must we achieve to earn additional profit from a lower price?" and "How much sales volume can we lose and still earn additional profit from a higher price?" The answers to these questions depend on how the cost of the product changes with volume. They do not depend on whether the current price of a product, at current volume, covers the cost and profit objectives.

How, then, should managers deal with the problem of pricing to cover costs and achieve profit objectives? They shouldn't. The question itself reflects an erroneous perception of the role of pricing, a perception based on the belief that one can first determine sales levels, then calculate unit cost and profit objectives, and then set a price. Once managers realize that sales volume (the beginning assumption) depends on the price (the end of the process), the flawed circularity of cost-based pricing is obvious. The only way to ensure profitable pricing is to let anticipated pricing determine the costs incurred rather than the other way around. Value-based pricing must begin *before* investments are made.

Exhibit 1-1 illustrates the flawed progression of cost-based pricing and the necessary progression for value-based pricing. Cost-based pricing is product driven. Engineering and manufacturing departments design and make what they consider a "good" product. In the process, they make investments and

Cost-Based Pricing

PRODUCT ⟶ COST ⟶ PRICE ⟶ VALUE ⟶ CUSTOMERS

Value-Based Pricing

CUSTOMERS ⟶ VALUE ⟶ PRICE ⟶ COST ⟶ PRODUCT

EXHIBIT 1-1 Cost-Based Versus Value-Based Pricing

incur costs to add features and related services. Finance then totals these costs to determine "target" prices for the various versions of the product that they might offer. Only at this stage does marketing enter the process, charged with the task of demonstrating enough value in these products to justify the prices to customers.

If cost-based prices prove unjustifiable, managers may try to fix the process by allowing "flexibility" in the markups. Although this tactic may minimize the damage, it is not fundamentally a solution since the financial return on the product remains inadequate. Finance blames marketing for cutting the price, and marketing blames finance for excessive costs. The problem keeps reoccurring as the features and costs of new products continue to mismatch the needs and values of customers. Moreover, when customers are rewarded with discounts for their price resistance, this resistance becomes more frequent even when the product has value to them. Solving the problems of cost-based pricing requires more than a quick fix. It requires completely reversing the process—starting with customers. The target price is based on estimates of value and the portion that the firm can expect to capture given the competitive alternatives. The job of financial management is not to insist that prices recover costs. It is to insist that costs are incurred only to make products that can be priced profitably given their value to customers.

Designing products that can be sold profitably at a target price has gone in the past two decades from being unusual to being the goal at most successful companies.[2] From Marriott to Boeing, from medical technology to automobiles, profit-leading companies now think about what market segment they want a new product to serve, determine the benefits those potential customers seek, and establish a price those customers can be convinced to pay. Then companies challenge their engineers to develop products and services that can be produced at a cost low enough to make serving that market segment profitable. It wasn't always so. The first companies to adopt such a strategy in their industries gained huge strategic advantage (see Box 1-1). The laggards now have to learn value-based pricing for new products just to survive.

BOX 1-1

The Story of the Mustang

Four decades ago, Lee Iacocca saved Ford Motors from extinction by building the first sports car to sell at a price point that middle-class people could afford. From an engineering perspective, it was hardly a good sports car. From the customers' perspective, it represented a better value than they ever thought they could afford. From a sales and profit perspective, it was the most successful car in history.

In the early 1960s, America was young, confident, and in love with sports cars. Many popular songs of the era were odes to those cars. Unfortunately for Ford, the cars arousing the greatest passion were products of General Motors and European manufacturers. Hoping to remedy this situation, Ford set out to build a sports car that would woo buyers to its showrooms. Had Ford followed the traditional approach for developing a new car, management would have begun the process by sending a memo to the design department, instructing it to develop a sports car that would top the competition. Each designer would then have drawn on individual preconceptions of what makes a good sports car in order to design bodies, suspensions, and engines that would be better. In a few weeks, management would have reviewed the designs and picked out the best prospects. Next, manage-

ment would have turned those designs over to the marketing research department. Researchers would have asked potential customers which they preferred and whether they liked Ford's designs better than the competition's, given prices that would cover their costs and yield the desired rate of return. The best choice would ultimately have been built and would have evoked the adoration of many, but it would have been purchased by only the few who could have afforded it.

Fortunately, Ford's general manager had a better idea. Unlike most top auto executives, he was not an expert in finance, accounting, or production. He was Lee Iacocca, a marketer. He did not begin looking for a new car in the design department. He began by researching what customers wanted. Iacocca found that a large and growing share of the auto market longed for a sports car, but that most people could not afford one. He also learned that most buyers did not really need much of what makes a "good" sports car to satisfy their desires. What they craved was not sports-car performance—a costly engine, drive train, and suspension—but sports-car excitement—styling, bucket seats, vinyl trim, and fancy wheel covers. Nobody at

(continued)

BOX 1-1 (*continued*)

the time was selling excitement at a price most customers could afford: less than $2,500.

The challenge for Ford was to design a car that looked sufficiently sporty to satisfy most buyers, but without the usual mechanical elements of a sports car that drove its price out of reach. To meet that challenge, Ford built its sports car with the mechanical workings of an existing economy car, the Falcon. Many hard-core sports-car enthusiasts, including some at Ford, were appalled. The car was obviously no match for GM's Corvette, but it was what many people seemed to want, at a price they could afford.

In April 1964, Ford introduced its Mustang sports car, at a base price of $2,368. More Mustangs were sold in the first year than any other car Ford ever built. In just the first two years, net profits from the Mustang were $1.1 billion, in 1964 dollars.* That was far more

than any of Ford's competitors made selling their "good" sports cars, priced to cover costs and achieve a target rate of return.

Ford began with the customers, asking what they wanted and what they were willing to pay for it. Their response determined the price at which a car would have to sell. Only then did Ford attempt to develop a product that could satisfy potential customers at a price they were willing to pay, while still permitting a substantial profit.

Costs played an essentially important role in Ford's strategy; they determined what Ford's product would look like. Cost considerations determined what attributes of a sports car the Mustang could include and what it could not, while still leaving Ford with a profit. For what they would pay, customers could not afford everything they might have liked. At $2,368, however, what they got in the Mustang was a good value.

*Lee Iacocca (with William Novak), *Iacocca: An Autobiography* (Bantam Books, Toronto, 1984), p. 74.

Customer-Driven Pricing

Most companies now recognize the fallacy of cost-based pricing and its adverse effect on profit. They realize the need for pricing to reflect market conditions. As a result, many have taken pricing authority away from financial managers and given it to sales or product managers. In theory, this trend is clearly consistent with value-based pricing, since marketing and sales are that part of the organization best positioned to understand value to the customer. In practice, however, the misuse of pricing to achieve short-term sales objectives often undermines perceived value and depresses profits even further.

The purpose of value-based pricing is not simply to create satisfied customers. Customer satisfaction can usually be bought by discounting sufficiently, but marketers delude themselves if they believe that the resulting sales represent marketing successes. The purpose of value-based pricing is to price more profitably by capturing more value, not necessarily by making more sales. When marketers confuse the first objective with the second, they fall into the trap of pricing at whatever buyers are willing to pay, rather than at what the product is really worth. Although that decision enables marketers to meet their sales objectives, it invariably undermines long-term profitability.

Two problems arise when prices reflect the amount buyers seem willing to pay. First, sophisticated buyers are rarely honest about how much they are actually willing to pay for a product. Professional purchasing agents are adept at concealing the true value of a product to their organizations. Once buyers learn that sellers' prices are flexible, the former have a financial incentive to conceal information from, and even actively mislead, the latter. Obviously, this tactic undermines the salesperson's ability to establish close relationships with customers and to understand their needs.

Second, there is an even more fundamental problem with pricing to reflect customers' willingness to pay. The job of sales and marketing is not simply to process orders at whatever price customers are currently willing to pay but rather to raise customers' willingness to pay a price that better reflects the product's true value. Many companies underprice truly innovative products because they ask potential customers, who are ignorant of the product's value, what they would be willing to pay. But we know from studies of innovations that the "regular" price has little impact on customers' willingness to try them. For example, most customers initially perceived that photocopiers, mainframe computers, and food processors lacked adequate value to justify their prices. Only after extensive marketing to communicate and guarantee value did these products achieve market acceptance. *Forget what customers who have never used your product are initially willing to pay!* Instead, understand the value of the product to satisfied customers and communicate that value to others. Low pricing is never a substitute for an adequate marketing and sales effort.

Competition-Driven Pricing

Lastly, consider the policy of letting pricing be dictated by competitive conditions. In this view, pricing is a tool to achieve sales objectives. In the minds of some managers, this method is "pricing strategically." Actually, it is more analogous to "letting the tail wag the dog." Why should an organization want to achieve market-share goals? Because more market share usually produces greater profit. Priorities are confused, however, when managers reduce the profitability of each sale simply to achieve the market-share goal. Prices should be lowered only when they are no longer justified by the value offered in comparison to the value offered by the competition.

Although price-cutting is probably the quickest, most effective way to achieve sales objectives, it is usually a poor decision financially. Since a price cut can be so easily matched, it offers only a short-term competitive advantage at the expense of permanently lower margins. Consequently, unless a company has good reason to believe that its competitors cannot match a price cut, the long-term cost of using price as a competitive weapon usually exceeds any short-term benefit. Although product differentiation, advertising, and improved distribution do not increase sales as quickly as price cuts, their benefit is more sustainable and thus is usually more cost-effective.

The goal of pricing should be to find the combination of margin and market share that maximizes profitability over the long term. Often, the most profitable price is one that substantially restricts market share relative to the competition. Godiva chocolates, BMW cars, Peterbilt trucks, and Snap-on tools would no doubt all gain substantial market share if priced closer to the competition. It is doubtful, however, that the added share would be worth forgoing their profitable and successful positioning as high-priced brands.

Although the fallacy of competition-driven pricing is most obvious for high-priced products, the principle can be applied more generally. Many companies that were recapitalized in the 1980s learned that they could substantially increase cash flow simply by scaling back their market-share objectives. One low-margin, industrial company increased price by 9 percent and suffered a 20 percent loss of market share—proof, some might argue, that its market was price sensitive. On the other hand, this company retained four out of five sales. Apparently, most customers valued the product by at least 9 percent more than they had been paying! The company had been prevented from capturing that value by its market-share goal. Although some capacity was idled, the company's contribution to profit increased by more than 70 percent.

Asking the Right Questions

Strategic pricing involves recognizing that not all pricing problems involve changing price as the best solution. The reason why pricing is ineffective is frequently not that the pricers have done a poor job. It is that decisions were made about costs, customers, and competitive strategy without correctly thinking through their broader financial implications. Since the fallacy in those decisions is frequently not revealed until the product is launched and the pricing proves unprofitable, it is the pricer's job to work back from the price to understand the problem. Is the price unprofitable because there is a better price to charge, or because the value has been ineffectively communicated? Is the market share goal too high, or is the market inadequately segmented? Is the product and service offering overbuilt (and therefore too expensive) for the value it delivers, or has the seller simply enabled customers to avoid paying for the value they get?

The pricer's job is often less to set prices than to structure a pricing process that gets everyone to think about how best to address pricing problems. Recall the tactical questions about costs, customers, and competition that we argued often lead to poor pricing decisions. Whenever they come up, it is the pricer's job to reframe the discussions to consider overall financial profitability. Exhibit 1-2

EXHIBIT 1-2 Strategic Pricing: Asking the Right Questions

Reactive, tactical questions commonly asked	*Proactive, strategic questions that should be asked*
What price do we need to cover our cost and profit objectives?	What sales changes would be necessary or tolerable for us to profit from a price change?
	Can we deploy a marketing strategy that will keep those sales changes within acceptable ranges?
	What costs can we afford to incur, given the prices achievable in the market, and still earn a profit?
What price is this customer willing to pay?	Is our price justifiable given the objective value of our product or service to the customer?
	How can we better communicate that value, thus justifying the price?
How can we discount to price-sensitive customers without others finding out?	How can we convince the customer that our pricing has integrity and was measured against value?
	How can we better segment the market to justify pricing differently when the value is different?
What prices do we need to meet our sales or market-share objectives?	What level of sales or market share can we most profitably achieve?
	What marketing tools should we use to win market share most cost-effectively?

lists the reactive, tactical questions commonly asked, and the questions that the pricing manager should be guiding the organization to ask instead.

Note that a key difference between the two types of questions is the ambiguity of the answers. The tactical answers to pricing problems are clear. To increase the margin, raise the price. To make the sale, cut the price. As with most marketing decisions, the answers to strategic questions about pricing are more open-ended. Pricing is an art. It depends as much on good judgment as on precise calculation. But the fact that pricing depends on judgment is no justification for pricing decisions based on hunches or intuition. Good judgment requires that one ask the right questions and comprehend the factors that make some pricing strategies succeed and others fail.

Good judgment also requires integrating information. The danger in the tactical approach to pricing is the narrow focus of the decisions. Profitable prices cannot be driven by a cost number with little or no understanding of how customers might respond, or by a customer's demands with little or no information about how competitors might respond, or by a market-share goal with little or no understanding of the company's ability to win a price war. The value in asking strategic questions is that they force one to integrate information across functional lines.

Note that implementing answers to strategic questions on the right side of Exhibit 1-3 may involve marketing decisions other than changes in price levels. Profitable pricing may require changing the product, communicating the relationship between price and value, or managing competitive interactions differently to preserve value. In short, strategic pricing requires that a company's entire marketing strategy become profit-focused. That is why pricing goals and objectives must become one of the first steps in formulating a marketing strategy, even though setting the final price may be the last part of the strategy to be executed.

THE DISCIPLINE OF STRATEGIC PRICING

Pricing should play an integrative role in business strategy. Pricing is not only part of marketing, but also part of finance and competitive strategy. Done correctly, pricing is the interface between those activities—the glue that holds them together. Superior profitability is achievable only by finding and exploiting synergies between customer needs and seller capabilities—synergies that produce high value for both parties. Finding and exploiting such synergies is what we call "strategic pricing."

Exhibit 1-3 illustrates the integrating role that pricing decisions play in a company that is committed to creating value cost-effectively and being rewarded with profit for doing so. Section I depicts the external factors (customer needs and competitor's capabilities and intentions) and internal constraints (corporate capabilities, product markets chosen, cost structures) that are the inputs to pricing strategy. The decisions that determine these constraints are strategic issues that drive the long-run health and success of the firm.[3]

The focus of pricing strategy is more limited. Given the markets and the firm's capabilities to serve them, how can it serve them most profitably? The integrative role of pricing strategy is illustrated in Section II of Exhibit 1-3. The three arrows that cross from Section I are the informational inputs to pricing. Chapters in this book are devoted to understanding that information and its implications for the profitability of alternative pricing decisions. Chapter 2, on costs, explains how to analyze cost structures so as to understand the true profitability of a product or service. In an ideal world, this might not be part of a marketer's job. In the real world, marketers who do not understand costs unwittingly make bad decisions for their companies because they unknowingly work with misleading cost numbers. Chapter 4 defines customer value and its role in pricing strategy. Chapter 4 also identifies the major factors that influence buyers' price sensitivity and explains how those factors can be used to segment customers and to influence the role of price in their purchase decisions. Chapter 5 explains the process of price competition and how to manage it dispassionately and proactively to minimize the damage that it can cause. Building competitive advantages, while not part of pricing strategy per se, is covered

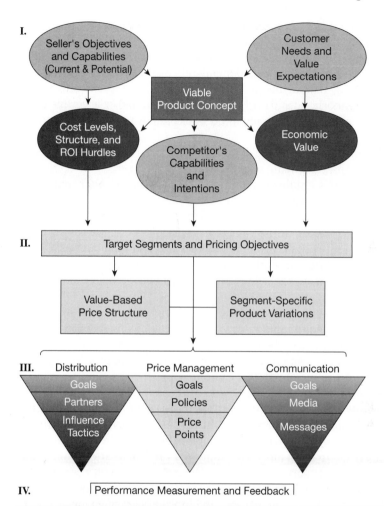

I.

II.

III.

IV.

EXHIBIT 1-3 Formulating a Profit-Driven Business Strategy

in Chapter 12 for the reader who wants to understand the causes of a company's capabilities that are constraints on its pricing options.

With these inputs, it is possible to formulate pricing objectives. In the parlance of business strategy, objectives are general aspirations toward which all activities will be directed.[4] The choice of target segments and specific pricing objectives is completely intertwined, which is why it is shown as one step in Exhibit 1-3. If a company is going to set prices based on value, important strategic questions must be answered before one can set a price. Different segments of customers will value the same product features very differently. Will the company choose to serve only customers willing to pay the most for its differentiation (high-end watches, leading-management consulting firms, BMW automobiles), or will it try to serve multiple segments at different price points

(Toyota automobiles)? If the latter, will the different prices be maintained by creating different product bundles (different car models such as Toyota's Avalon, Camry, and Corolla), by relying on different channels of distribution (own stores like Gateway computer stores, own independent stores like CompUSA, or sell direct like Dell), or by making the product available at lower prices only in certain locations (neighborhood and off-brand gasoline stations) or at certain times (discount airline tickets available only three weeks in advance with a Saturday-night stay).

Chapter 6, on pricing strategy, describes the trade-offs that lead to decisions to adopt alternative pricing objectives. Among them might be a decision to "skim" a market by maintaining a market position as the premier supplier to the high-priced segment. Another might be to "penetrate" a market to maintain a low-cost position and deter entry by higher-cost competitors. Chapter 6 also introduces the concept of the value-based price structure, which is often supported by segment-specific product-service variations that support different pricing goals for different market segments. Chapter 7 explains how pricing objectives, and the tactics to achieve them, must change over the life cycle of a product category.

Section III of Exhibit 1-3 focuses on the tactical implementation of pricing decisions, as do the remaining chapters. Note that tactical implementation involves more than just management of the pricing function. It also involves coordinating distribution and market communication to support price objectives. An objective may be to maintain a dominant market share to support a cost advantage in research and development (Intel's strategy in semiconductors). If the objective is to be maintained with low prices, distribution must add minimally to the cost and market communication must minimize the importance of anything but price. It may also require communication to potential competitors that the firm has the capability and intention to repel any threat to its low-price market position. However, the same dominant-share objective could be maintained with a campaign to saturate distribution channels and use intense market communication to create a preference for the brand (for example, the "Intel Inside" campaign), which could support higher pricing without risking the competitive advantage.

This vision of pricing as central to the practice of marketing is not descriptive of how marketing is widely practiced. Traditional marketing often focuses on a single objective—customer satisfaction—to achieve a single goal: market share. This assumes that the result will be profitable, but profitability is not the criteria for judging the appropriateness of a decision. We believe that when marketing focuses on customers alone, pricing becomes reactive and short-term. Rather than actively managing customer information and choices to maximize profitability, pricing becomes an afterthought driven by whatever customers will pay. As a result, companies are often successful when measured by market share but not when measured by the return they generate on the assets they invest.

The antidote to this problem is to replace customer-driven marketing, with its short-term focus on satisfying all customers and winning every sale, with value-based marketing. Value-based marketing focuses on creating, communicating, and capturing value. Because a company may not cost-effectively create the same value for all customers, value-based marketing requires that a firm carefully select which customers it will serve—implying that other potential customers will be left unserved and unsatisfied. It involves proactive management of customer perceptions rather than reactive adaptation to their perceived needs. It also involves making judicious decisions about when to respond in kind to price competition and when a nonprice response, or no response at all, is a more prudent alternative.

Strategic pricing imposes financial discipline—an optimizing constraint—on marketing and sales decisions. It says that a firm should satisfy customers, but only up to the point where the incremental increase in value created exceeds the incremental increase in the product's cost. It dictates that a firm should satisfy customers when doing so is consistent with its competitive position and complements its core competencies. Without this discipline, top-line revenue is pursued indiscriminately, without constraints regarding which customers to serve and how to serve them. Indeed, sales and customer satisfaction achieved by giving ever more while asking ever less in return is, more often than not, a recipe for financial mediocrity.

SUMMARY

Progressive companies have begun doing more than just worrying about pricing. To increase profitability, many are abandoning traditional reactive pricing procedures in favor of proactive strategies. More than ever before, successful companies are building products and marketing strategies to support pricing objectives, rather than the other way around. In the past decade, traditional industry leaders in marketing and sales, such as Procter and Gamble and General Electric, made explicit corporate decisions to change their focus from growth in top-line sales to growth in profitability. In many industries, the current profit leader is a company with a very explicit pricing strategy supported by its product and promotional strategies. Southwest in airlines, Intel in semiconductors, Dell in computers, Wal-Mart in retailing, Quad in printing, Sony in consumer electronics, and the *New York Times* in publishing have all adopted pricing models that drive which customers they will serve and how they will serve them.

It is not surprising that pricing has taken its place as a major element in marketing strategy in the last decade. After all, marketing itself has been in the midst of a revolution. The meaning of marketing has been transformed from "selling what the company produces" to "producing what the customer wants to buy." Marketing has become the means by which firms identify unmet needs in the marketplace, develop products to satisfy those needs, promote them honestly, and follow with postpurchase support to ensure customer satisfaction. As selfless as all this may sound, though, the ultimate goal of marketing is not to convert the firm into a charitable organization for the sole benefit of consumers. The ultimate goal is profits for the stockholders, jobs for the employees, and growth for the organization.

Perhaps it is reasonable that marketers have only recently begun to focus seriously on effective pricing. Only after managers have mastered the techniques of creating value do the techniques of capturing value become important. When companies were totally financially driven and internally focused, it was marketing's sole job to become an advocate for the customer's perspective. Today, however, marketers have won the power to make business decisions, not just advocate perspectives. With that responsibility, they must understand not only customer needs but also how and when to profitably satisfy those needs. The true test of a successful marketing strategy is its ability to create value profitably. As one marketing expert aptly stated, "For marketing strategists, [pricing] is the moment of truth—all of marketing comes to focus in the pricing decision."[5] The purpose of this book is to make sure that when you reach that moment, you know what to do.

Notes

1. The bias toward a reactive concept of "market orientation" has been described by Bernard Jaworski, Ajay Kohli, and Arvind Sahay, in "Market-Driven Versus Driving Markets," *Journal of the Academy of Marketing Science,* 28(1) (Winter 2000), pp. 45–54.

2. Peter F. Drucker, "The Information Executives Truly Need," *Harvard Business Review* (January–February 1995), p. 58.

3. In the past two decades, serious theoretical work has replaced simplistic, anecdotal guidelines for how to create a sustainably successful business. See Michael E. Porter, *Competitive Advantage* (The Free Press, New York, 1985); Gary Hamel and C. K. Parhalad, *Competing for the Future* (Harvard Business School Press, Cambridge, MA, 1994); Adrian Slywotzky and David Morrison, *The Profit Zone* (Random House, New York, 1997); Robert Kaplan and David Norton, *The Strategy-Focused Organization* (Harvard Business School Press, Cambridge, MA, 2001).

4. Most likely, pricing objectives will be subsidiary to general corporate objectives. Thus if the corporate objective is to establish a market presence in Brazil leading to eventual manufacture there, the corporate objective may not be to maximize profitability. It may be, rather, to build volume or name recognition quickly. For purposes of this book and the analysis of pricing strategies, we will usually assume that sustainable profitability is the pricing objective, although we will see how there are often reasons to trade off near-term on one product's profitability to maximize the longer-term return from an entire product line.

5. Raymond Corey, *Industrial Marketing: Cases and Concepts,* 3rd ed. (Prentice-Hall, Inc., Englewood Cliffs, NJ, 1983), p. 311.

CHAPTER

Costs

How Should They Affect Pricing Decisions?

In most companies, there is ongoing conflict between managers in charge of covering costs (finance and accounting) and managers in charge of satisfying customers (marketing and sales). Accounting journals warn against prices that fail to cover full costs, while marketing journals argue that customer willingness-to-pay must be the sole driver of prices. The conflict between these views wastes company resources and leads to pricing decisions that are imperfect compromises. Profitable pricing involves an integration of costs and customer value. To achieve that integration, however, both need to let go of misleading ideas and form a common vision of what drives profitability.[1] In this chapter and the next, we explain when costs are relevant for pricing, how marketers should use costs in pricing decisions, and the role that finance should play in defining the price-volume trade-offs that marketers should use in evaluating pricing decisions.

THE ROLE OF COSTS IN PRICING

Costs should never determine price, but costs do play a critical role in formulating a pricing strategy. Pricing decisions are inexorably tied to decisions about sales levels, and sales involve costs of production, marketing, and administration. It is true that how much buyers will pay is unrelated to the seller's cost, but it is also true that a seller's decisions about which products to produce and in what quantities depend critically on their cost of production.

The mistake that cost-plus pricers make is not that they consider costs in their pricing, but that they select the quantities they will sell and the buyers they will serve before identifying the prices they can charge. They then try to impose cost-based prices that may be either more or less than what buyers will pay. In contrast, effective pricers make their decisions in exactly the opposite order. They first evaluate what buyers can be convinced to pay and only then choose quantities to produce and markets to serve.

Firms that price effectively decide what to produce and to whom to sell it by comparing the prices they can charge with the costs they must incur.

Consequently, costs affect the prices they charge. A low-cost producer can charge lower prices and sell more because it can profitably use low prices to attract more price-sensitive buyers. A higher-cost producer, on the other hand, cannot afford to underbid low-cost producers for the patronage of more price-sensitive buyers; it must target those buyers willing to pay a premium price. Similarly, changes in costs should cause producers to change their prices, not because that changes what buyers will pay, but because it changes the quantities that the firm can profitably supply and the buyers it can profitably serve. When the cost of jet fuel rises, most airlines are not naive enough to try passing on the fuel cost through a cost-plus formula while maintaining their previous schedules. But some airlines do raise their average revenue per mile. They do so by reducing the number of flights they offer in order to fill the remaining planes with more full-fare passengers. To make room for those passengers, they eliminate or reduce some discount fares. Thus the cost increase for jet fuel affects the mix of prices offered, increasing the average price charged. However, that is the result of a strategic decision to reduce the number of flights and change the mix of passengers served, not of an attempt to charge higher prices for the same service to the same people.

Such decisions about quantities to sell and buyers to serve are an important part of pricing strategy for all firms and the most important part for many. In this chapter, we discuss how a proper understanding of costs enables one to make those decisions correctly. First, however, a word of encouragement: Understanding costs is probably the most challenging aspect of pricing. You will probably not master these concepts on first reading this chapter. Your goal should be simply to understand the issues involved and the techniques for dealing with them. Mastery of the techniques will come with practice.

DETERMINING RELEVANT COSTS

One cannot price effectively without understanding costs. To understand one's costs is not simply to know their amounts. Even the least effective pricers, those who mechanically apply cost-plus formulas, know how much they spend on labor, raw materials, and overhead. Managers who really understand their costs know more than cost levels; they know how their costs will change with the changes in sales that result from pricing decisions.

 Not all costs are relevant for every pricing decision. A first step in pricing is to identify the relevant costs: those that actually determine the profit impact of the pricing decision. Our purpose in this section is to set forth the guidelines for identifying the relevant costs once they are measured. In principle, identifying the relevant costs for pricing decisions is actually fairly straightforward. They are the costs that are incremental (not average) and avoidable (not sunk). In practice, identifying costs that meet those criteria can be difficult. Consequently, we will explain each distinction in detail and illustrate it in the context of a practical pricing problem.

Why Incremental Costs?

Pricing decisions affect whether a company will sell less of the product at a higher price or more of the product at a lower price. In either scenario, some costs remain the same (in total). Consequently, those costs do not affect the relative profitability of one price versus another. Only costs that rise or fall (in total) when prices change affect the relative profitability of different pricing strategies. We call these costs incremental because they represent the increment to costs (positive or negative) that results from the pricing decision.

Incremental costs are the costs associated with changes in pricing and sales. The distinction between incremental and nonincremental costs parallels closely, but not exactly, the more familiar distinction between variable and fixed costs. *Variable costs,* such as the costs of raw materials in a manufacturing process, are costs of doing business. Since pricing decisions affect the amount of business that a company does, variable costs are always incremental for pricing. In contrast, *fixed costs,* such as those for product design, advertising, and overhead, are costs of being in business.[2] They are incremental when deciding whether a price will generate enough revenue to justify being in the business of selling a particular type of product or serving a particular type of customer. Since fixed costs are not affected by how much a company actually sells, most are not incremental when management must decide what price level to set for maximum profit.

Some fixed costs, however, are incremental for pricing decisions, and they must be appropriately identified. Incremental fixed costs are those that directly result from implementing a price change or from offering a version of the product at a different price level. For example, the fixed cost for a restaurant to print menus with new prices or for a public utility to gain regulatory approval of a rate increase would be incremental when deciding whether to make those changes. The fixed cost for an airline to advertise a new discount service or to upgrade its planes' interiors to offer a premium-priced service would be incremental when deciding whether to offer products at those price levels.

To further complicate matters, many costs are neither purely fixed nor purely variable. They are fixed over a range of sales but vary when sales go outside that range. The determination of whether such *semifixed costs* are incremental for a particular pricing decision is necessary to make that decision correctly. Consider, for example, the role of capital equipment costs when deciding whether to expand output. A manufacturer may be able to fill orders for up to 100 additional units each month without purchasing any new equipment simply by using the available equipment more extensively. Consequently, equipment costs are nonincremental when figuring the cost of producing up to 100 additional units. If the quantity of additional orders increased by 150 units each month, though, the factory would have to purchase additional equipment. The added cost of new equipment would then become incremental and relevant in deciding whether the company can profitably price low enough to attract that additional business.

To understand the importance of properly identifying incremental costs when making a pricing decision, consider the problem faced by the business manager of a symphony orchestra. The orchestra usually performs two Saturday evenings each month during the season with a new program for each performance. It incurs the following costs for each performance:

Fixed overhead costs	$1,500
Rehearsal costs	$4,500
Performance costs	$2,000
Variable costs (e.g., programs, tickets)	$1 per patron

The orchestra's business manager is concerned about her very thin profit margin. She has currently set ticket prices at $10. If she could sell out the entire 1,100-seat hall, total revenues would be $11,000 and total costs $9,100, leaving a healthy $1,900 profit per performance.[3] Unfortunately, the usual attendance is only 900 patrons, resulting in an average cost per ticket sold of $9.89, which is precariously close to the $10 admission price. With revenues of just $9,000 per performance and costs of $8,900, total profit per performance is a dismal $100.

The orchestra's business manager does not believe that a simple price increase would solve the problem. A higher price would simply reduce attendance more, leaving less revenue per performance than the orchestra earns now. Consequently, she is considering three proposals designed to increase profits by reaching out to new markets. Two of the proposals involve selling seats at discount prices. The three options are:

1. *A "student rush" ticket priced at $4 and sold to college students one-half hour before the performance on a first-come, first-served basis.* The manager estimates she could sell 200 such tickets to people who otherwise would not attend. Clearly, however, the price of these tickets would not cover even half the average cost per ticket.

2. *A Sunday matinee repeat of the Saturday evening performance with tickets priced at $6.* The manager expects she could sell 700 matinee tickets, but 150 of those would be to people who would otherwise have attended the higher-priced Saturday performance. Thus net patronage would increase by 550, but again the price of these tickets would not cover average cost per ticket.

3. *A new series of concerts to be performed on the alternate Saturdays.* The tickets would be priced at $10, and the manager expects that she would sell 800 tickets but that 100 tickets would be sold to people who would attend the new series instead of the old one. Thus net patronage would increase by 700.

Which, if any, of these proposals should the orchestra adopt? An analysis of the alternatives is shown in Exhibit 2-1. The revenue gain is clearly smallest for the student rush, the lowest-priced alternative designed to attract a fringe market, while the revenue gain is greatest for the new series, which attracts

	I *Student* *Rush*	II *Sunday* *Matinee*	III *New* *Series*
Price	$4	$6	$10
x Unit sales	$200	$700	$800
= Revenue	$800	$4,200	$8,000
– Other sales forgone	(0)	($1,500)	($1,000)
Revenue gain	$800	$2,700	$7,000
Incremental rehearsal cost	0	0	$4,500
Incremental performance cost	0	$2,000	$2,000
Variable costs	$200	$550	$700
Incremental costs	$200	$2,550	$7,200
Net profit contribution	$600	$150	($200)

EXHIBIT 2-1   Analysis of Three Proposals for the Symphony Orchestra

many more full-price patrons. Still, profitability depends on the incremental costs as well as the revenues of each proposal. For the student rush, neither rehearsal costs nor performance costs are incremental. They are irrelevant to the profitability of that proposal since they do not change regardless of whether this proposal is implemented. Only the variable per-patron costs are incremental, and therefore relevant, for the student-rush proposal. For the Sunday matinee, however, the performance cost and the per-patron cost are incremental and affect the profitability of that option. For the totally new series, all costs except overhead are incremental.

To evaluate the profitability of each option, we subtract from revenues only those costs incremental to it. For the student rush, that means subtracting only the $200 of per-patron costs from the revenues, yielding a contribution to profit of $600. For the Sunday matinee, it means subtracting the performance cost and the variable per-patron costs for those additional patrons (550) who would not otherwise have attended any performance, yielding a profit contribution of $150. For the new series, it means subtracting the incremental rehearsal, performance, and per-patron costs, yielding a net loss of $200. Thus, the lowest priced option, which also happens to yield the least amount of additional revenue, is in fact the most profitable.

The setting out of alternatives, as in Exhibit 2-1, clearly highlights the best option. In practice, opportunities are often missed because managers do not look at incremental costs, focusing instead on the average costs that are more readily available from accounting data. Note again that the orchestra's current average cost (total cost divided by the number of tickets sold) is $9.89 per patron and would drop to $8.27 per patron if the student-rush proposal were adopted. The student-rush tickets, priced at $4 each, *cover less than half the average cost per ticket.* The manager who focuses on average cost would be misled into rejecting a profitable proposal in the mistaken belief that the price would be inadequate. Average cost includes costs that are not incremental and are therefore irrelevant to evaluating the proposed opportunity. The adequacy of any price can be ascertained only by looking at the incremental cost of sales and ignoring those costs that would be incurred anyway.

Although the orchestra example is hypothetical, the problem it illustrates is highly realistic. Scores of companies profit from products that they price below average cost when average cost includes fixed costs that are not true costs of sales.

- Packaged goods manufacturers often supply generic versions of their branded products at prices below average cost. They can do so profitably because they can produce them with little or no incremental costs of capital, shipping, and selling beyond those already incurred to produce their branded versions.
- A leading manufacturer of industrial cranes also does milling work for other companies whenever the firm's vertical turret lathes would not otherwise be used. The price for such work does not cover a proportionate share of the equipment cost. It is, however, profitable work since the equipment must be available to produce the firm's primary product. The equipment cost is therefore not incremental to the additional milling work.
- Airlines fly weekend flights that do not cover a proportionate share of capital costs for the plane and ground facilities. Those costs must be incurred to provide weekday service and so are irrelevant when judging whether weekend fares are adequate to justify this service. In fact, weekend fares often add incrementally more to profits precisely because they require no additional capital.

In each of these cases, the key to getting the business is having a low price. Yet one should never be deceived into thinking that low-price sales are necessarily low-profit sales. In some cases, they make a disproportionately large contribution to profit because they make a small incremental addition to costs.

Why Avoidable Costs?

The hardest principle for many business decision makers to accept is that only avoidable costs are relevant for pricing. *Avoidable costs* are those that either have not yet been incurred or can be reversed. The costs of selling a product, delivering it to the customer, and replacing the sold item in inventory are avoidable, as is the rental cost of buildings and equipment that are not covered by a long-term lease. The opposite of avoidable costs are *sunk costs*—those costs that a company is irreversibly committed to bear. For example, a company's past expenditures on research and development are sunk costs since they cannot be changed regardless of any decisions made in the present. The rent on buildings and equipment within the term of a current lease is sunk, except to the extent that the firm can avoid the expense by subletting the property.[4]

The cost of assets that a firm owns may or may not be sunk. If an asset can be sold for an amount equal to its purchase price times the percentage of its remaining useful life, then none of its cost is sunk since the cost can be entirely recovered through resale. Popular models of commercial airplanes often retain their value in this way, making avoidable the entire cost of their continued use. If an asset has no resale value, then its cost is entirely sunk even though it may have much useful life remaining. A neon sign depicting a company's corporate logo may have much useful life remaining, but its cost is entirely sunk since no other company would care to buy it. Frequently, the cost of assets is partially avoidable and partially sunk. For example, a new truck could be resold for a substantial portion of its purchase price but would lose some market value immediately after purchase. The portion of the new price that could not be recaptured is sunk and should not be considered in pricing decisions. Only depreciation of the resale value of the truck is an avoidable cost of using it.

From a practical standpoint, the easiest way to identify the avoidable cost is to recognize that it is the *future cost,* not the *historical cost,* associated with making a sale. What, for example, is the cost for an oil company to sell a gallon of gasoline at one of its company-owned stations? One might be inclined to say that it is the cost of the oil used to make the gasoline plus the cost of refining and distribution. Unfortunately, that view could lead refiners to make some costly pricing mistakes. Most oil company managers realize that the relevant cost for pricing gasoline is not the historical cost of producing a gallon of gasoline, but rather the future cost of replacing the inventory when sales are made. Even LIFO (last-in, first-out) accounting can be misleading for companies that are drawing down large inventories. To account accurately for the effect of a sale on profitability, managers need to adopt NIFO (next-in, first-out) accounting for managerial decision making.[5]

The distinction between the historical cost of acquisition and the future cost of replacement is merely academic when supply costs are stable. It becomes very practical when costs rise or fall.[6] When the price of crude oil rises, companies quickly raise prices, long before any gasoline made from the more expensive crude reaches the pump. Politicians and consumer advocates label this practice *price gouging,* since companies with large inventories of gasoline increase their reported profits by selling their gasoline at higher prices than they paid to produce it. So what is the real incremental cost to the company of selling a gallon of gasoline?

Each gallon of gasoline sold requires the purchase of crude oil at the new, higher price for the company to maintain its gasoline inventory. If that price is not covered by revenue from sales of gasoline, the company suffers reduced cash flow from every sale. Even though the sales appear profitable from a historical cost standpoint, the company must add to its working capital (by borrowing money or by retaining a larger portion of its earnings) to pay the new, higher cost of crude oil. Consequently the real "cash" cost of making a sale rises immediately by an amount equal to the increase in the replacement cost of crude oil.

What happens when crude oil prices decline? If a company with large inventories held its prices high until all inventories were sold, it would be undercut by any company with smaller inventories that could profitably take advantage of the lower cost of crude oil to gain market share. The company would see its sales, profits, and cash flow decline. Again, the intelligent company bases its prices on the replacement cost, not the historical cost, of its inventory. In historical terms, it reports a loss. However, that loss corresponds to an equal reduction in the cost of replacing its inventories with cheaper crude oil. Since the company simply reduces its operating capital by the amount of the reported loss, its cash flow remains unaffected.

Unfortunately, even level-headed businesspeople often let sunk costs sneak into their decision making, resulting in pricing mistakes that squander profits. The case of a small Midwestern publisher of esoteric books illustrates this risk. The publisher customarily priced a book at $20 per copy, which included a $4 contribution to overhead and profit. The firm printed 2,000 copies of each book on the first run and normally sold less than half in the first year. The remaining copies were added to inventory. The company was moderately profitable until 1980 when, due to a substantial increase in interest rates, the $4 contribution per book could no longer fully cover the interest cost of its working capital.

Recognizing a problem, the managers called in a pricing consultant to show them how to improve the profitability of their prices in order to cover their increased costs. They were, however, quite resistant to the consultant's suggestion that they run a half-price sale on all their slow-moving titles. The publisher's business manager pointed out that half price would not even cover the cost of goods sold. He explained to the consultant, "Our problem is that our prices are not currently adequate to cover our overhead. I fail to see how cutting our prices even lower—eliminating the gross margin we now have so that we cannot even cover the cost of production—is a solution to our problem."

The business manager's logic was quite compelling, but his argument was based on the fallacy of looking at sunk costs of production as a guide to pricing rather than looking at the avoidable cost of holding inventory. No doubt, the firm regretted having printed many of the books in its warehouse, but since the production cost of those books was no longer avoidable regardless of the pricing strategy adopted, and since the firm did not plan to replace them, historical production costs were irrelevant to any pricing decision.[7] What was relevant was the avoidable cost of working capital required to hold the books in inventory.

If, by cutting prices and selling the books sooner instead of later, the publisher could save more in interest than it lost from a price cut, then price-cutting clearly would increase profit even while reducing revenue below the cost of goods sold. In this case, the publisher could ultimately sell all books for $20 if it held them long enough. By selling some books immediately for $10, however, the company could avoid the interest cost of holding them until it could get the higher price. Exhibit 2-2 shows the cumulative interest cost of holding a book in inventory, given that it could be sold immediately for $10 and that the cost of capital at the time was 18 percent. Since the interest cost of holding a book longer than four years exceeds the proposed $10 price cut, any book for which the firm held more than four years of inventory could be sold more profitably now at half price than later at full price.[8]

Years Inventory Held	1	2	3	4	5	6	7	8
Interest cost to hold inventory*	$1.80	$3.90	$6.43	$9.39	$12.88	$16.99	$21.85	$27.59

*Interest cost to year $n = \$10(1.18^n - 1)$.

EXHIBIT 2-2   The Cumulative Interest Cost of Holding a Book in Inventory

The error made by the business manager was understandable. It is a common mistake among people who think about pricing problems in terms of a traditional income statement.

AVOIDING MISLEADING ACCOUNTING

Unfortunately, accounting statements can often be misleading. One must approach them with care when making pricing decisions. Let us further examine the publisher's error presented above, and others, to better understand the pitfalls of accounting data and how to deal with them. By accounting convention, an income statement follows this form:

Sales revenue

−Cost of goods sold
= Gross profit

−Selling expenses
−Depreciation
−Administrative overhead
= Operating profit

−Interest expense
= Pretax profit

−Taxes
= Net profit

This can lead managers to think about pricing sequentially, as a set of hurdles to be overcome in order. First managers try to get over the *gross profit* hurdle by maximizing their sales revenue and minimizing the cost of goods sold. Then they navigate the second hurdle by minimizing selling expenses, depreciation, and overhead to maximize the *operating profit.* Similarly, they minimize their interest expense to clear the *pretax profit* hurdle and minimize their taxes to reach their ultimate goal of a large, positive *net profit.* They imagine that by doing their best to maximize income at each step, they will surely then reach their goal of a maximum bottom line.

Unfortunately, the road to a profitable bottom line is not so straight. Profitable pricing often calls for sacrificing gross profit in order to reduce expenses further down the line. The publisher in our last example could report a much healthier gross profit by refusing to sell any book for less than $20, but only by bearing interest expenses that would exceed the extra gross profit, leaving an even smaller pretax profit. Moreover, interest is not the only cost that can be reduced profitably by trading off sales revenue. Discount sales through direct mail often save selling expenses that substantially exceed a reduction in sales revenue. While such discounts depress gross profit, the greater savings in selling expenses produce a net increase in operating profit. Discounting for a sale prior to the date of an inventory tax may also save more on tax payments than the revenue loss.

Effective pricing cannot be done in steps. It requires that one approach the problem holistically, looking for each trade-off between higher prices and higher costs, and cutting gross profit whenever necessary to cut expenses by even more. The best way to avoid being misled by a traditional income statement is to develop a managerial costing system independent of the system used for financial reporting,[9] as follows:

focus 1st on costs that are truly incremental & avoidable

Sales revenue
−Incremental, avoidable variable costs
= Total contribution (in dollars)

−Incremental, avoidable fixed costs
= Net contribution

−Other fixed or sunk costs
= Pretax profit

−Income taxes
= Net profit

The value of reorganization is that it first focuses attention on costs that are incremental and avoidable and only later looks at costs that are nonincremental and sunk for the pricing decision. In this analysis, maximizing the *profit contribution* of a pricing decision is the same as maximizing the net profit, since the fixed or sunk costs subtracted from the profit contribution are not influenced by the pricing decisions and since income taxes are determined by the pretax profit rather than by unit sales.

One could not do such a cost analysis simply by reorganizing the numbers on a traditional income statement. The traditional income statement reports quarterly or annual totals. For pricing, we are not concerned about the cost of all units produced in a period; we are concerned only with the cost of the units that will be affected by the decision to be made. Thus, the relevant cost to consider when evaluating a price reduction is the cost of the additional units that the firm expects to sell because of the price cut. The relevant cost to consider when evaluating a price increase is the avoided cost of units that the firm will not produce because sales will be reduced by the price rise. For any managerial decision, including pricing decisions, it is important to isolate and consider only the costs that affect the profitability of that decision.

ESTIMATING RELEVANT COSTS

The essence of incremental costing is to measure the cost incurred because a product is sold, or not incurred because it is not sold. Here we cannot delve into all the details of setting up a useful managerial accounting system. That task occupies an entire literature on "activity-based costing," to which we refer the reader interested in the details of cost management.[10] For our purposes, it will suffice to caution that there are four common errors that managers frequently make when attempting to develop useful estimates of true costs.

1. **Beware of averaging total variable costs to estimate the cost of a single unit.** The average of variable costs is often an adequate indicator of the incremental cost per unit, but it can be dangerously misleading in those cases where the incremental cost per unit is not constant. The relevant incremental cost for pricing is the actual incremental cost of the particular units affected by a pricing decision, which is not necessarily equal to average variable cost. Consider the following example:

   A company is currently producing 1,100 units per day, incurring a total materials cost of $4,400 per day and labor costs of $9,200 per day. The labor costs consist of $8,000 in regular pay and $1,200 in overtime pay per day. Labor and materials are the only two costs that change when the firm makes small changes in output. What then is the relevant cost for pricing? One might be tempted to answer that the relevant cost is the sum of the labor and materials costs ($13,600) divided by total output (1,100 units), or approximately $12.36 per unit. Such calculation would lead to serious underpricing when demand is strong, since the real *incremental* cost of producing the last units is much higher than the *average* cost. A price increase, for example, could eliminate only sales that are now produced on overtime at a cost substantially above the average.

   What is the cost of producing the last units, those that might not be sold if the product's price was raised? It may be reasonable to assume that materials costs are approximately the same for all units, so that average materials cost is a good measure of the incremental materials cost for the last units. Thus a good estimate of the relevant materials cost is $4 per unit ($4,400/1,100). We know, however, that labor costs are not the same for all units. The company must pay time-and-a-half for overtime, which are the labor hours that could be eliminated if price is increased and if less of the product is sold. Even if workers are equally productive during overtime and regular hours, producing approximately 100 units per day during overtime hours, the labor cost is $12 per unit ($1,200/100), resulting in a labor and materials cost for the last 100 units of $16 each, substantially above the $12.36 average cost.[11]

2. **Beware of accounting depreciation formulas.** The relevant depreciation expense that should be used for all managerial decision making is the change in the current value of assets. Depreciation of assets is usually calculated in a number of different ways depending upon the intended use of the data. For reporting to the Internal Revenue Service, depreciation is accelerated to minimize tax

BOX 2-1

Peak Load Pricing: An Application of Incremental Costing

The adverse financial impact of average costing is greatest for those companies, such as service providers, whose products are not storable. Such companies face the problem of having to build capacity to serve temporary but predictable "peaks" in demand. This creates the interesting situation where the cost of capacity goes from being incremental to sunk, and back to incremental again, over the period of a year, a month, a week, or even a day. Airlines face peaks at the beginning and ends of weeks but have excess capacity midweek and on weekends. Telecom companies face peaks in the middle of each weekday but have excess capacity in the evenings and on weekends. Restaurants, car rental companies, marketers of advertising space, commercial printers, health clubs, resorts, electric utilities, and landscape maintenance companies all face substantial peaks and valleys in demand for nonstorable products or services. One way to manage capacity in those cases, and to thus maximize profitability, is with price.

The key to using price to manage capacity profitably is to understand how to allocate the capacity costs over time. Most companies make the mistake of averaging the capacity cost over all of the units produced. If an electric utility sells 40 percent of its kilowatts during a few peak hours, and 60 percent during the other twenty-one hours in the day, then 40 percent of the capacity cost (the depreciation and maintenance cost for the power plants) would be allocated to the peak hours. This results in each kilowatt being assigned the same capacity charge. Although this is the usual approach (utilities have even been required to cost and price this way by regulation), it makes no sense in principle and undermines profitability in practice. Why? Because the need for the capacity is created entirely by the peak period demand. Off-peak demand can be satisfied without the additional capacity, so capacity costs are not incremental to decisions that affect the volume of off-peak sales. Consequently, the cost of capacity above what is necessary to meet off-peak demand should be allocated entirely to the peak period sales.

One effect of allocating those costs only to sales in the peak period is to raise the hurdle required to justify peak-period investment. The way to ensure that capacity costs are covered is to make no capacity investments that cannot be entirely justified by the revenue from peak demand. If

BOX 2-1 (*continued*)

additional capacity really is required only for a few hours a day, a few days a week, or a few months a year, then prices in those periods should be covering all the cost of the capacity, or the capacity should not be built. The other effect is to reveal the surprisingly high profitability of the lower-price, lower-margin sales in off-peak periods. Because the contribution from off-peak sales is not required to cover the cost of capacity, which will be there whether or not the capacity is used, that contribution falls directly to the bottom line. Companies that fail to realize this overinvest for peak demand and then are forced either to cut their prices to fill their off-peak capacity or to suffer even greater losses during off-peak periods. On net, they invest themselves into unprofitability.

As a company moves toward pricing differently for the peaks and valleys, its average price decreases, but its profit and return

on capital invested will increase. For companies with a peak capacity problem, it is usually far more important that they earn a high return per unit of capacity than it is for them to earn a high contribution margin per sale. For many years, hotels mismeasured their success by their ability to command and increase their "average daily rate." Of course, one way to increase average daily rate is simply to rent no rooms except at times of peak demand when the hotel can ask for and get its highest rates. That is unlikely, however, to yield a good return on assets. When hotels began being managed more rationally, the industry adopted a new measure, "revenue per available room," that changed the incentive to manage capacity. The bottom line became "Get all you can get at peak, but make sure you fill the room and earn something at off peak."

liability. For standard financial reporting, rates of depreciation are estimated as accurately as possible but are applied to historical costs.[12] For pricing and any other managerial decision making, however, depreciation expenses should be based on forecasts of the actual decline in the current market value of assets as a result of their use.

Failure to accurately measure depreciation expenses can severely distort an analysis of pricing options. For example, the author of one marketing textbook wrote that a particular airline could price low on routes where its older planes were fully depreciated, but had to price high on routes where new planes were generating large depreciation charges. Such pricing would be quite senseless. Old planes obviously have a market value regardless of their book value.

The decline in that market value should either be paid for by passengers who fly on those planes or the planes should be sold. Similarly, if the market value of new planes does not really depreciate as quickly as the financial statements indicate, excessive depreciation expenses could make revenues appear inadequate to justify what are actually profitable new investments. The relevant depreciation expense for pricing is the true decline in an asset's resale value.

3. **Beware of treating a single cost as either all relevant or all irrelevant for pricing.** A single cost on the firm's books may have two separate components—one incremental and the other not, or one avoidable and the other sunk—that must be distinguished. Such a cost must be divided into the portion that is relevant for pricing and the portion that is not. Even incremental labor costs are often not entirely unavoidable.

During the recession of 1981–82, some steel producers found when they considered laying off high-seniority employees that the avoidable portion of their labor costs was only a small part of their total labor costs. Their union contracts committed them to paying senior employees much of their wages even when laid off. Consequently, those companies found that the prices they needed to cover their incremental, avoidable costs were actually quite low, justifying continued operations at some mills even though those operations produced substantial losses when all costs were considered.

4. **Beware of overlooking opportunity costs.** Opportunity cost is the contribution that a firm forgoes when it uses assets for one purpose rather than another. Opportunity costs are relevant costs for pricing even though they do not appear on financial statements. They should be assigned hard numbers in any managerial accounting system, and pricers should incorporate them into their analyses as they would any other cost. In the earlier example of the book publisher, the cost of capital required to maintain the firm's inventory was the cost of borrowed funds (18 percent). It therefore generated an explicit interest expense on the firm's income statement. A proper analysis of the publisher's problem would have been no different had we assumed that the inventory was financed entirely with internally generated funds. Those internally generated funds do not create an interest expense on the publisher's income statement, but they do have alternative uses. Internally generated funds that are used to finance inventories could have been used to purchase an interest-bearing note or could have been invested in some profitable sideline business such as printing stationery. The interest income that could have been earned from the best of these alternatives is an incremental, avoidable cost of using internally generated funds, just as the interest paid explicitly is an incremental, avoidable cost of using borrowed funds.

The same argument would apply when costing the use of a manufacturing facility, a railroad right-of-way, or the seat capacity of an airline. The historical cost of those assets is entirely irrelevant and potentially a very misleading guide to pricing. There is often, however, a current cost of using those assets that is very relevant. That cost occurs whenever capacity used either could be used to

BOX 2-2

Opportunity Costs: A Practical Illustration

An airline's most important cost for pricing is the "opportunity cost" of its capacity. Incremental costs other than capacity costs (e.g., food, ticketing) are literally trivial in comparison. An airline that took the historical cost or even the replacement cost of buying planes would miss many opportunities for profitable pricing and, in a competitive market, would soon go bankrupt because most of the profitability of an airline comes from the "incremental" revenue that it generates selling some seats at prices below the average cost per seat. The key to making such a strategy profitable is to understand on an ongoing basis the expected opportunity cost of selling a seat at any particular time on any particular flight.

What is the opportunity cost of a seat? On Saturday afternoon to nonresort locations, it is probably zero since there is no way that the plane will ever be filled. At most times, however, a plane could easily be filled by offering a low discount price during the month before the flight. The opportunity cost of selling such a seat is the contribution that could be earned from a full-fare passenger, usually a business traveler, times the probability that such a price-insensitive passenger will in fact buy the seat before the plane departs. For example, if a plane currently has empty seats one month before the flight, the airline uses historical booking patterns to estimate that it has a 70 percent probability that the plane will depart with at least one empty seat. That means that there is a 30 percent probability that a seat would not be available to a last-minute passenger willing to pay full fare. If the contribution from a full-fare ticket for the flight is \$500, then the "opportunity cost" to sell a discount ticket in advance is $0.3 \times \$500 = \$150$, to which we add the cost of ticketing, food, and incremental fuel, to estimate the total cost of offering the ticket.

This costing system explains why the price of a discount ticket on the same flight might go up or down many weeks before a flight departs, while there are still many seats available. Airlines have sophisticated "yield management" systems that use historical booking patterns to estimate the probability of an empty seat at departure. If a plane is not filling up as rapidly as historically expected, the probability of an empty seat goes up, the opportunity cost of selling more discounted seats goes down, so the airline's management system may offer some tickets at an exceptionally low price. If, however, a group of seven businesspeople suddenly books onto the flight, the probability of filling the flight jumps substantially, the opportunity cost goes up, and the airline's yield management system automatically blocks additional sales of the cheapest tickets.

make and sell some other product, or could be rented or sold to some other company. Even though the historical cost is sunk, the relevant cost of using those assets is positive whenever there are competing profitable uses. That opportunity cost is the contribution that must be forgone if the assets are not sold or used to produce the alternative product or service. It can easily exceed not only the historical cost but even the replacement cost of the capacity.

Even if a company has current excess capacity but there is some probability that future business might have to be turned away, the capacity should be assigned an opportunity cost for pricing. Airlines, for example, stop selling discounted seats for a particular flight long before the flight is full. The opportunity cost of selling a discounted seat is near zero only if that seat would otherwise certainly be empty at flight time. As a plane's capacity fills, however, the probability increases that selling a discounted seat will require turning away a passenger who would have paid full fare on the day of the flight. The probability of such a passenger wanting the seat, times the contribution that would be earned at full price, is the opportunity cost of selling a discounted seat in advance.

Obviously, moving beyond these costing principles to estimating the true cost of a sale is not easy. Too often, however, managers shrink from the task because of the cost and complexity of measuring true costs on an ongoing basis. Usually, in our experience, it is possible to get much closer to true costs by doing even a simple point-in-time study of cost drivers. We have, for example, worked with a company that charged every item produced the same amount for paint, even though some items were produced in large lots and others in small lots. By doing a simple statistical regression, using prior year data, paint purchases by color as a function of production of that color product and average lot size, we rationally reallocated paint costs to reflect the higher costs of small batches. In other cases, we have relied on cost drivers as subjective as a plant foreman's judgment about the relative difficulty of making different types of products. Are such judgments highly accurate? Probably not. That is not a reason to avoid making them if that is the best you can do with the time and money available. *It is better to make pricing decisions based on rough approximations of the true costs of products or services than on precise accounting of costs that are sure to be, at best, irrelevant and, at worst, highly misleading.*

PERCENT CONTRIBUTION MARGIN AND PRICING STRATEGY

There are three benefits to determining the true unit cost of a product or service for pricing. First, it is a necessary first step toward controlling costs. The best way to control variable costs is not necessarily appropriate for controlling fixed costs. Second, it enables management to determine the minimum price at which the firm can profitably accept incremental business that will not affect the pricing of its other sales. Third, and most important for our purposes, it enables management to determine the contribution margin for each product sold, which, as will be seen in the next chapter on financial analysis, is essential for making informed, profitable pricing decisions.

The size of the contribution as a percentage of the price has important strategic implications. It is the share of price that adds to profit or reduces losses. It is not the return on sales, which is used by financial analysts to compare the performance of different companies in the same industry. The return on sales indicates the average profit as a percentage of the price after accounting for all costs. Our concern, however, is not with the average, but with the added profit resulting from an additional sale. Even when variable costs are constant, the added profit from a sale exceeds the average profit because some costs are fixed or sunk. The share of the price that adds to profit, the contribution margin, is everything above the share required to cover the incremental, variable cost of the sale.

When variable cost is constant for all units affected by a particular pricing decision, it is proper to calculate the percent contribution margin from aggregate sales data. After calculating the sales revenue and total contribution margin resulting from a change in sales, one can calculate the percent contribution margin, or %*CM*, as follows:

$$\%\,CM = \frac{\text{Total contribution margin}}{\text{Sales revenue}} \times 100$$

When variable costs are not constant for all units (for example, when the units affected by a price change are produced on overtime), it is important to calculate a dollar contribution margin per unit for just the units affected by the price change. The dollar contribution margin per unit, $*CM*, is simply

$$\$CM = \text{Price} - \text{Variable cost}$$

where variable cost is the cost per unit of only those units affected by the price change and includes only those costs that are avoidable. With the dollar contribution margin, one can calculate the percent contribution margin without being misled when variable costs are not constant. The formula for this calculation of the percent contribution margin is

$$\%\,CM = \frac{\$CM}{\text{Price}}$$

which gives the percent contribution margin in decimal form.

The percent contribution margin is a measure of the leverage between a firm's sales volume and its profit. It indicates the importance of sales volume as a marketing objective. To illustrate, look at Exhibit 2-3. A company sells two products, each with the same net profit on sales, but with substantially different contribution margins. A company using full-cost pricing would, therefore, treat them the same. However, the actual effect of a price change for these two products would be radically different because of their varying cost structures.

Product A has high variable costs equal to 80 percent of its price. Its percent contribution margin is therefore 20 percent. Product B has low variable

	Product A	Product B
Percentage of setting price accounted for by:		
Variable costs	80.0	20.0
Fixed or sunk costs	10.0	70.0
Net profit margin	10.0	10.0
Contribution margin	20.0	80.0
Breakeven sales change (%) for a:		
5% Price reduction/advantage	+ 33.3	+ 6.7
10% Price reduction/advantage	+100.0	+14.3
20% Price reduction/advantage	∞	+33.3
5% Price increase/premium	− 20.0	− 5.9
10% Price increase/premium	− 33.3	−11.1
20% Price increase/premium	− 50.0	−20.0

[handwritten annotations: "To benefit by 5% price reduction" with "required sales increase →" pointing to + 33.3]

EXHIBIT 2-3   Effect of Contribution Margin on Breakeven Sales Changes

costs equal to 20 percent of its product's price. Its percent contribution margin is therefore 80 percent. Although at current sales volumes each product earns the same net profit, the effect on each of a change in sales volume is dramatically different. For product A, only $0.20 of every additional sales dollar increases profit or reduces losses. For product B, that figure is $0.80.

The lower part of Exhibit 2-3 illustrates the impact of this difference on pricing decisions. In order for product A, with its relatively small percent contribution margin, to profit from a 5 percent price cut, its sales must increase by more than 33 percent, compared with only 6.7 percent for product B with its larger percent contribution margin. To profit from a 10 percent price cut, product A's sales must increase by more than 100 percent, compared with only 14.3 percent for product B. Clearly, this company cannot justify a strategy of low pricing to build volume for product A nearly as easily as it can for product B. The opposite conclusion follows for price increases. Product A can afford to lose much more sales than product B and still profit from higher prices. Consequently, it is much easier to justify a premium price strategy for product A than for product B.

SUMMARY

Costs are central considerations in pricing. Without understanding which costs are incremental and avoidable, a firm cannot accurately determine at what price, if any, a market can profitably be served. By erroneously looking at historical costs, a firm could sell its inventory too cheaply. By mistakenly looking at nonincremental fixed costs, a firm could overlook highly profitable opportunities where price is adequate to more than cover the incremental costs. By overlooking opportunity costs, successful companies frequently underprice their products. In short, when managers do not understand the true cost of a sale, their companies unnecessarily forgo significant profit opportunities. They tend to overprice when they have excess capacity, while underpricing and over-investing when sales are strong relative to capacity.

Having identified the right costs, one must also understand how to use them. The most important reason to identify costs correctly is to be able to cal-culate an accurate contribution margin. The contribution margin is a measure of the leverage between a product's profitability and its sales volume. An ac-curate contribution margin enables management to determine the amount by which sales must increase following a price cut or by how little they must de-cline following a price increase to make the price change profitable. Under-standing how changes in sales will affect a product's profitability is the first step in pricing the product effectively.

It is, however, just the first step. Next, one must learn how to judge the likely impact of a price change on sales. That requires understanding how buyers are likely to perceive a price change and how competitors are likely to react to it.

Notes

1. Gerald Smith and Thomas Nagle, "Fi-nancial Analysis for Profit-Driven Pricing," *Sloan Management Review,* 35(3) (Spring 1994).

2. Beware of costs classified as "over-head." Often costs end up in that classification, even though they are clearly variable, simply because "overhead" is a convenient dumping ground for costs that one has not as-sociated with the products that caused them to be incurred. A clue to the existence of such a misclassifica-tion is the incongruous term "vari-able overhead."

3. Revenue = 1,100 × $10. Cost = $1,500 + $4,500 + $2,000 + ($1 × 1,100).

4. Most economics and accounting texts equate avoidable costs with variable costs, and sunk costs with fixed costs, for theoretical conven-ience. Unfortunately, those texts usu-ally fail to explain adequately that this is an assumption rather than a necessarily true statement. Conse-quently, many students come away from related courses with the idea that a firm should always continue producing if price at least covers variable costs. That rule is correct only when the variable costs are en-tirely avoidable and the fixed costs are entirely sunk. In many industries (for example, airlines) the fixed costs are often avoidable since the assets can be readily resold. Whenever the fixed costs are avoidable if a decision is not made to produce a product, or to produce it in as large a quantity, they should be considered when de-ciding whether a price is adequate to serve a market.

5. LIFO and NIFO costs are the same in any accounting period when a firm makes a net addition to its inventory. In periods during which a firm draws down its inventory, LIFO will under-state costs after the firm uses up the portion of its inventory values at cur-rent prices and begins "dipping into old layers" of inventory valued at un-realistic past prices.

6. Neil Churchill, "Don't Let Inflation Get the Best of You," *Harvard Busi-ness Review,* March–April 1982.

7. The forward-looking production cost of replacing the book in inventory would have been relevant if the firm intended to maintain its current inventory levels.
8. We are assuming here that the half-price sale will not reduce the rate of sales after the sale is over. When it will, then one must add the discounted value of those lost sales to the price discount and compare that figure with the interest cost of holding the inventory. In other industries (for example, hotels and theaters), the cost of capacity is variable (you can build a hotel with any number of rooms or a theater with any number of seats), but this cost becomes sunk after capacity is built.
9. Robert S. Kaplan, "One Cost System Isn't Enough," *Harvard Business Review,* 66 (January–February 1988), pp. 61–66.
10. Robin Cooper and Robert S. Kaplan,"Activity-Based Systems: Measuring the Costs of Resource Usage," *Accounting Horizons* (September 1992), pp. 1–13; James P. Borden, "Review of Literature on Activity-Based Costing," *Cost Management,* 4 (Spring 1990), pp. 5–12; Peter B. B. Turney, "Ten Myths About Implementing an Activity-Based Cost System," *Cost Management,* 4 (Spring 1990), pp. 24–32; George J. Beaujon and Vinod R. Singhal,"Understanding the Activity Costs in an Activity-Based Cost System," *Cost Management,* 4 (Spring 1990), pp. 51–72; Robert Kaplan and Robin Cooper, *Cost and Effect* (Cambridge, MA: Harvard Business School Press, 1997).

11. The calculation of the portion of output produced on overtime (assuming equal productivity) is as follows: $1,200 overtime is the equivalent in hours of $800 regular time ($1,200/1.5) and is 9.1 percent of the total hours worked ($800/[$8,000 + $800]). Multiplying 9.1 percent times 1,100 units shows that 100 units are produced on overtime if production is at a constant rate.
12. Since 1979, however, the Financial Accounting Standards Board (FASB) has required that large, publicly held corporations also report supplemental information on increases or decreases in current costs of inventory, property, plant, and equipment, net of inflation. See FASB Statement of Financial Standards No. 33, "Financial Reporting and Changing Prices," 1979.

CHAPTER

Financial Analysis

Pricing for Profit

Internal financial considerations and external market considerations are, at most companies, antagonistic forces in pricing decisions. Financial managers allocate costs to determine how high prices must be to cover costs and achieve profit objectives. Marketing and sales staff analyze buyers to determine how low prices must be to achieve sales objectives. The pricing decisions that result are politically charged compromises, not thoughtful implementations of a coherent strategy. Although common, such pricing policies are neither necessary nor desirable. An effective pricing decision should involve an optimal blending of, not a compromise between, internal financial constraints and external market conditions.

Unfortunately, few managers have any idea how to facilitate such a cross-functional blending of these two legitimate concerns. From traditional cost accounting, they learn to take sales goals as "given" before allocating costs, thus precluding the ability to incorporate market forces into pricing decisions. From marketing, they are told that effective pricing should be entirely "customer driven," which ignores costs except as a minimum constraint below which the sale would become unprofitable. Perhaps along the way, these managers study economics and learn that, in theory, optimal pricing is a blending of cost and demand considerations. In practice, however, they find the economist's assumption of a known demand curve hopelessly unrealistic.

Consequently, pricing at most companies remains trapped between cost- and customer-driven procedures that are inherently incompatible. This chapter suggests how managers can break this tactical pricing deadlock and infuse strategic balance into pricing decisions. Many marketers argue that costs should play no role in market-based pricing. This is clearly wrong. Without perfect segmentation (the ability to negotiate independently a unique price for every customer),

---

This chapter is coauthored by Professor Gerald E. Smith of Boston College with Dr. Thomas Nagle.

pricers must make trade-offs between charging higher margins to fewer customers and lower margins to more customers. Once the true cost and contribution of a sale are understood, managers can appropriately integrate costs into what is otherwise a market-driven approach to pricing strategy.

[handwritten margin note: Evaluate Price change] This chapter describes a simple, logically intuitive procedure for quantitatively evaluating the potential profitability of a price change. First, managers develop a baseline, or standard of comparison, to measure the effects of a price change. For example, they might compare the effects of a pending price change with the product's current level of profitability, or with a budgeted level of profitability, or perhaps with a hypothetical scenario that management is particularly interested in exploring. Second, they calculate an incremental "breakeven" for the price change to determine under what market conditions the change will prove profitable. Marketing managers must then determine whether they can actually meet those conditions.

The key to integrating costs and quantitatively assessing the consequences of a price change is the incremental breakeven analysis. Although similar in form to the common breakevens that managers use to evaluate investments, incremental breakeven analysis for pricing is quite different in practice. Rather than evaluating the product's overall profitability, which depends on many factors other than price, incremental breakeven analysis focuses on the incremental profitability of price changes. Consequently, managers start from a baseline reflecting current or projected sales and profitability at the *current price*. Then they ask whether a change in price could improve the situation. More precisely, they ask:

- How much would the sales volume have to increase to profit from a price reduction?
- How much could the sales volume decline before a price increase becomes unprofitable?

Answers to these questions depend on the product's contribution margin.

The sample problems in this chapter introduce the four equations involved in performing such an analysis and illustrate how to use them. They are based on the experience of Westside Manufacturing, a small company manufacturing pillows for sale through specialty bedding and dry cleaning stores. Although the examples are, for simplicity, based on a small manufacturing business, the equations are equally applicable for analyzing any size or type of business that cannot negotiate a unique price for each customer.[1] If customers can be somewhat segmented for pricing, the formulas apply to pricing within a segment.

Following are Westside Manufacturing's income and costs for a typical month:

Sales	4,000 units
Wholesale price	$10.00 per unit
Revenue	$40,000
Variable costs	$5.50 per unit
Fixed costs	$15,000

Westside is considering a 5 percent price cut, which it believes would make it more competitive with alternative suppliers, enabling it to further increase its sales. Management believes that the company would need to incur no additional fixed costs as a result of this pricing decision. How much would sales have to increase for this company to profit from a 5 percent cut in price?

BREAKEVEN SALES ANALYSIS: THE BASIC CASE

To answer Westside's question, we calculate the breakeven sales change. This, for a price cut, is the minimum increase in sales volume necessary for the price cut to produce an increase in contribution relative to the baseline. Fortunately, making this calculation is simple, as will be shown shortly. First, however, it may be more intuitive to illustrate the analysis graphically (see Exhibit 3-1).

In this exhibit it is easy to visualize the financial trade-offs involved in the proposed price change. Before the price change, Westside receives a price of $10 per unit and sells 4,000 units, resulting in total revenues of $40,000 (the total area of boxes a and b). From this Westside pays variable costs of $5.50 per unit, for a total of $22,000 (box b). Therefore, *before* the price change, total contribution is $40,000 minus $22,000, or $18,000 (box a). In order for the proposed price cut to be profitable, contribution after the price cut must exceed $18,000.

After the 5 percent price reduction, Westside receives a price of only $9.50 per unit, or $0.50 less contribution per unit. Since it normally sells 4,000 units, Westside would expect to lose $2,000 in total contribution (box c) on sales that

EXHIBIT 3-1 Finding the Breakeven Sales Change

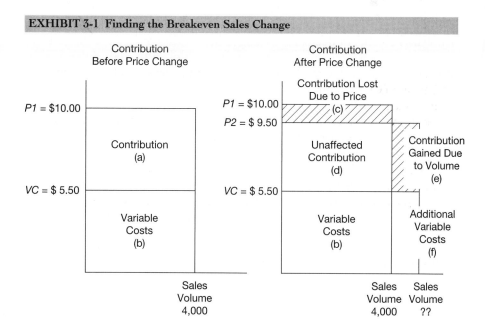

it could have made at a higher price. This is called the *price effect*. Fortunately, the price cut can be expected to increase sales volume.

The contribution earned from that increased volume, the *volume effect* (box e), is unknown. The price reduction will be profitable, however, when the volume effect (the area of box e) exceeds the price effect (the area of box c). That is, in order for the price change to be profitable the gain in contribution resulting from the change in sales volume must be greater than the loss in contribution resulting from the change in price. The purpose of breakeven analysis is to calculate the *minimum* sales volume necessary for the volume effect (box e) to balance the price effect (box c). When sales exceed that amount, the price cut is profitable.

So how do we determine the breakeven sales change? We know that the lost contribution due to the price effect (box c) is $2,000, which means that the gain in contribution due to the volume effect (box e) must be at least $2,000 for the price cut to be profitable. Since each new unit sold following the price cut results in $4 in contribution ($9.50 – $5.50 = $4), Westside must sell at least an additional 500 units ($2,000 divided by $4 per unit) to make the price cut profitable.

The minimum sales change necessary to maintain at least the same contribution can be directly calculated by using the following simple formula (see Appendix 3A for derivation):

$$\% \text{ Breakeven sales change} = \frac{-\text{ Price change}}{CM + \text{ Price change}}$$

$$= \frac{-\Delta P}{CM + \Delta P}$$

In this equation, the price change and contribution margin may be stated in dollars, percents, or decimals (as long as their use is consistent). The result of this equation is a decimal ratio that, when multiplied by 100, is the percent change in unit sales necessary to maintain the same level of contribution after the price change. The minus sign in the numerator indicates a trade-off between price and volume: Price cuts increase the volume and price increases reduce the volume necessary to achieve any particular level of profitability. The larger the price change—or the smaller the contribution margin—the greater the volume change necessary to generate at least as much contribution as before.

Assume for the moment that there are no incremental fixed costs in implementing Westside's proposed 5 percent price cut. For convenience we make our calculations in dollars (rather than in percents or decimals). Using the contribution margin equation (Chapter 2), we derive the following:

$$\$CM = \$10 - \$5.50 = \$4.50$$

Given this, we can easily calculate the breakeven sales change as follows:

$$\% \text{ Breakeven sales change} = \frac{-(-\$0.50)}{\$4.50 + (-\$0.50)} = 0.125 \text{ or } 12.5\%$$

Thus, the price cut is profitable only if sales volume increases more than 12.5 percent. Relative to its current level of sales volume, Westside would have to sell at least 500 units more to maintain the same level of profitability it had prior to the price cut, as shown below:

$$\text{Unit breakeven sales change} = 0.125 \times 4{,}000 = 500 \text{ units}$$

If the actual increase in sales volume exceeds the breakeven sales change, the price cut will be profitable. If the actual increase in sales volume falls short of the breakeven sales change, the price change will be unprofitable. Assuming that Westside's goal is to increase its current profits, management should initiate the price reduction only if it believes that sales will increase by more than 12.5 percent, or 500 units, as a result.

If Westside's sales increase as a result of the price change by more than the breakeven amount—say, by an additional 550 units—Westside will realize a gain in profit contribution. If, however, Westside sells only an additional 450 units as a result of the price cut, it will suffer a loss in contribution. Once we have the breakeven sales change and the profit contribution, calculating the precise change in contribution associated with any change in volume is quite simple: It is simply the difference between the actual sales volume and the breakeven sales volume, times the new contribution margin (calculated *after* the price change). For Westside's 550-unit and 450-unit volume changes, the change in contribution equals the following:

$$(550 - 500) \times \$4 = \$200$$
$$(450 - 500) \times \$4 = -\$200$$

The $4 in these equations is the new contribution margin ($9.50 − $5.50). Alternatively, you might have noticed that the denominator of the percent breakeven formula is also the new contribution margin.

We have illustrated breakeven analysis using Westside's proposed 5 percent price cut. The logic is exactly the same for a price increase. Since a price increase results in a gain in unit contribution, Westside can "absorb" some reduction in sales volume and still increase its profitability. How much of a reduction in sales volume can Westside tolerate before the price increase becomes unprofitable? The answer is this: until the loss in contribution due to reduced sales volume is exactly offset by the gain in contribution due to the price increase. As an exercise, calculate how much sales Westside could afford to lose before a 5 percent price increase becomes unprofitable.[2]

BREAKEVEN SALES INCORPORATING A CHANGE IN VARIABLE COST

Thus far we have dealt only with price changes that involve no changes in unit variable costs or in fixed costs. Often, however, price changes are made as part of a marketing plan involving cost changes as well. A price increase may be made along with product improvements that increase variable cost, or a price cut might be made to push the product with lower variable selling costs. Expenditures that represent fixed costs might also change along with a price change. We need to consider these two types of incremental costs when calculating the price–volume trade-off necessary for making pricing decisions profitable. We begin this section by integrating changes in variable cost into the financial analysis. In the next section, we do the same with changes in fixed costs.

Fortunately, dealing with a change in variable cost involves only a simple generalization of the breakeven sales change formula already introduced. To illustrate, we return to Westside Manufacturing's proposed 5 percent price cut. Suppose that Westside's price cut is accompanied by a reduction in variable cost of $0.22 per pillow, resulting from Westside's decision to use a new synthetic filler to replace the goose feathers it currently uses. Variable costs are $5.50 before the price change and $5.28 after the price change. By how much would sales volume have to increase to ensure that the proposed price cut is profitable?

When variable costs change along with the price change, managers simply need to subtract the cost change from the price change before doing the breakeven sales change calculation. Unlike the case of a simple price change, managers *must* state the terms on the right-hand side of the equation in currency units (dollars, pounds, French francs, and so forth) rather than in percentage changes:

$$\% \text{ Breakeven sales change} = \frac{-(\$\Delta P - \$\Delta C)}{\$CM + (\$\Delta P - \$\Delta C)}$$

where Δ indicates "change in," P = price, and C = cost. Note that when the change in variable cost ($\$\Delta C$) is zero, this equation is identical to the breakeven formula previously presented. Note also that the term ($\$\Delta P - \$\Delta C$) is the change in the contribution margin and that the denominator (the original contribution margin plus the change) is the new contribution margin. Thus, the general form of the breakeven pricing equation is simply written as follows:

general form

$$\% \text{ Breakeven sales change} = \frac{-\$\Delta CM}{\text{New }\$CM}$$

For Westside, the next step in using this equation to evaluate the proposed price change is to calculate the change in contribution margin. Recall that the change in price is $9.50 − $10 or –$0.50. The change in variable costs is –$0.22. Thus, the change in contribution can be calculated as follows:

$$\$\Delta CM = (\$\Delta P - \$\Delta C) = -\$0.50 - (-\$0.22) = -\$0.28$$

Previous calculations illustrated that the contribution margin before the price change is $4.50. We can therefore calculate the breakeven sales change as follows:

$$\% \text{ Breakeven sales change} = \frac{-(-\$0.28)}{\$4.50 + (-\$0.28)} = 0.066, \text{ or } +6.6\%$$

In units, the breakeven sales change is 0.066 × 4,000 units, or 265.

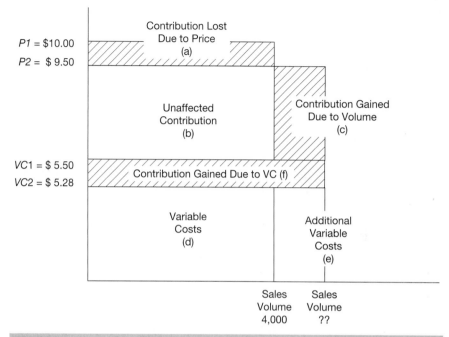

EXHIBIT 3-2   Finding the Breakeven Sales Change Given a Change in Variable Costs

Given management's projection of a $0.22 reduction in variable costs, the price cut can be profitable only if management believes that sales volume will increase by more than 6.6 percent, or 265 units. Note that this increase is substantially less than the required sales increase (12.5 percent) calculated before assuming a reduction in variable cost. Why does a variable cost reduction lower the necessary breakeven sales change? Because it increases the contribution margin earned on each sale, making it possible to recover the contribution lost due to the price effect with less additional volume. This relationship is illustrated graphically for Westside Manufacturing in Exhibit 3-2. Westside can realize a gain in contribution due to the change in variable costs (box f), in addition to a gain in contribution due to any increase in sales volume.

BREAKEVEN SALES WITH INCREMENTAL FIXED COSTS

Although most fixed costs do not impact the incremental profitability of a pricing decision (because they do not change), some pricing decisions necessarily involve changes in fixed costs, even though these costs do not otherwise change with small changes in volume. The management of a discount airline considering whether to reposition as a higher-priced business travelers' airline would probably choose to refurbish its lounges and planes. A regulated utility would need to cover the fixed cost of regulatory hearings to gain approval for a higher price. A fast-food restaurant would need to advertise its promotionally priced "special-value" meals to potential customers. These are incremental fixed costs, necessary for the success of a new pricing strategy but unrelated to the sales volume actually gained at those prices. Recall also that semifixed costs remain fixed only within certain ranges of sales. If a price change causes sales to move outside that range, the level of semifixed costs increases or decreases. Such changes in fixed and semifixed costs need to be covered for a price change to be justified, since without the price change these incremental costs can be avoided.

Fortunately, calculating the sales volume necessary to cover an incremental fixed cost is already a familiar exercise for many managers evaluating investments independent of price changes. For example, suppose a product manager is evaluating a $150,000 fixed expenditure to redesign a product's packaging. The product's unit price is $10, and unit variable costs total $5. How many units must be sold for the firm to recover the $150,000 incremental investment? The answer, as found in most managerial economics texts, is given by the following equation:

$$\text{Breakeven sales volume} = \frac{\$ \text{ Change in fixed costs}}{\$CM}$$

Remembering that the $\$CM$ equals price $-$ variable cost, the breakeven sales volume for this example is:

$$\text{Breakeven sales volume} = \frac{\$150,000}{\$10 - \$5} = 30,000 \text{ units}$$

How can the manager do breakeven analysis for a change in pricing strategy that involves both a price change and a change in fixed cost? He simply adds the calculations for (a) the breakeven sales change for a price change and (b) the breakeven sales volume for the related fixed investment.

The breakeven sales change for a price change with incremental fixed costs is the basic breakeven sales change plus the sales change necessary to cover the incremental fixed costs. Since we normally analyze the breakeven for a price change as a *percent* and the breakeven for an investment in *units*, we need to multiply or divide by initial unit sales to make them consistent. Consequently, the *unit* breakeven sales change with a change in fixed costs is as follows:

$$\frac{\text{Unit breakeven}}{\text{sales change}} = \frac{-\ \$\Delta CM}{\text{New } \$CM} \times \frac{\text{Initial}}{\text{unit sales}} + \frac{\$ \text{ Change in fixed costs}}{\text{New } \$CM}$$

The calculation for the *percent* breakeven sales change is as follows:

$$\frac{\text{Breakeven}}{\text{sales change}} = \frac{-\ \$\Delta CM}{\text{New } \$CM} + \frac{\$ \text{ Change in fixed costs}}{\text{New } \$CM \times \text{Initial unit sales}}$$

In both cases, if the "$ change in fixed costs" is zero, we have the breakeven sales change equation for a simple price change.

To illustrate the equations for a price cut, return again to the pricing decision faced by Westside Manufacturing. Westside is considering a 5 percent price cut. We already calculated that it can profit if sales increase by more than 12.5 percent. Now suppose that Westside cannot increase its output without incurring additional semifixed costs. At the company's current rate of sales—4,000 units per month—it is fully utilizing the capacity of the equipment at its four work stations. To increase capacity enough to handle 12.5 percent more sales, the company must install equipment for another work station, at a monthly cost of $800. The new station raises plant capacity by 1,000 units beyond the current capacity of 4,000 units. What is the minimum sales increase required to justify a 5 percent price reduction, given that it involves an $800 increase in monthly fixed costs? The answer is determined as follows:

$$\frac{\text{Unit breakeven}}{\text{sales change}} = 0.125 \times 4{,}000 \; units + \frac{\$800}{\$4} = 700 \; units$$

$$\frac{\%\text{ Breakeven}}{\text{sales change}} = 0.125 + \frac{\$800}{\$4 \times 4{,}000 \; units} = 0.175, \; or \; 17.5\%$$

The company could profit from a 5 percent price reduction if sales increased by more than 700 units (17.5 percent), which is less than the 1,000 units of added capacity provided by the new work station. Whether a prudent manager should actually implement such a price decrease depends on other factors as well: How likely is it that sales will increase substantially more than the breakeven minimum, thus adding to profit? How likely is it that sales will increase by less, thus reducing profit? How soon could the decision be reversed, if at all, if sales do not increase adequately?

Even if management considers it likely that orders will increase by more than the breakeven quantity, it should hesitate before making the decision. If orders increase by significantly less than the breakeven minimum, this company could lose substantially, especially if the cost of the new work station is largely sunk once the expenditure has been made. On the other hand, if orders increase by significantly more, the most the company could increase its sales without bearing the semifixed cost for further expansion is 25 percent, or 1,000 units. Consequently, management must be quite confident of a large sales increase before implementing the 5 percent price reduction.

Consider, however, if the company has already invested in the additional capacity and if the semifixed costs are already sunk. The monthly cost of the fifth work station is then entirely irrelevant to pricing, since that cost would have to be borne whether or not the capacity is used. Thus, the decision to cut price rests entirely on management's judgment of whether the price cut will stimulate unit sales by more than 12.5 percent. If the actual sales increase is more than 12.5 percent but less than 17.5 percent, management will regret having invested in the fifth work station. Given that this cost can no longer be avoided, however, the most profitable course of action is to price low enough to use the station, even though that price will not fully cover its cost.

BREAKEVEN SALES ANALYSIS FOR REACTIVE PRICING

So far we have restricted our discussion to *proactive price changes,* where the firm contemplates initiating a price change ahead of its competitors. The goal of such a change is to enhance profitability. Often, however, a company initiates *reactive price changes* when it is confronted with a competitor's price change that will impact the former's sales unless it responds. The key uncertainty involved in analyzing a reactive price change is the sales loss the company will suffer if it fails to meet a competitor's price cut, or the sales gain the company will achieve if it fails to follow a competitor's price increase. Is the potential sales loss sufficient to justify cutting price to protect the sales volume? Or is the potential sales gain enough to justify forgoing the opportunity for a cooperative price increase? A slightly different form of the breakeven sales formula is used to analyze such situations.

To calculate the breakeven sales changes for a reactive price change, we need to address the following key questions: (1) What is the minimum potential sales loss that justifies meeting a lower competitive price? (2) What is the minimum potential sales gain that justifies *not* following a competitive price increase? The basic formula for these calculation is this:

$$\frac{\text{\% Breakeven sales change}}{\text{for reactive price change}} = \frac{\text{Change in price}}{\text{Contribution margin}} = \frac{\Delta P}{CM}$$

To illustrate, suppose that Westside's principal competitor, Eastside, has just reduced its prices by 15 percent. If Westside's customers are highly loyal, it probably would not pay for Westside to match this cut. If, on the other hand, customers are quite price sensitive, Westside may have to match this price cut to minimize the damage. What is the minimum potential loss in sales volume that justifies meeting Eastside's price cut? The answer (calculated in percentage terms) is as follows[3]:

$$\frac{\text{\% Breakeven sales change}}{\text{for reactive price change}} = \frac{-15\%}{45\%} = -0.333, \text{ or } 33.3\%$$

Thus, if Westside expects sales volume to fall by more than 33 percent as a result of Eastside's new price, it would be less damaging to Westside's profitability to match the price cut than to lose sales. On the other hand, if Westside expects that sales volume will fall by less than 33 percent, it would be less damaging to Westside's profitability to let Eastside take the sales than it would be to cut price to meet this challenge.

This analysis has focused on minimizing losses in the face of a competitor's proactive price reduction. However, the procedure for analysis is the same when a competitor suddenly raises its prices. Suppose, for example, that Eastside raises its price by 15 percent. Westside might be tempted to match Eastside's price increase. If, however, Westside does not respond to Eastside's new price, Westside will likely gain additional sales volume as Eastside's customers switch to Westside. How much of a gain in sales volume must be realized in order for no price reaction to be more profitable than a reactive price increase? The answer is similarly found using the breakeven sales change formula with a reactive price change. If Westside is confident that sales volume will increase by more than 33.3 percent if it does not react, a nonreactive price policy would be more profitable. If Westside's management does not expect sales volume to increase by 33.3 percent, a reactive price increase would be more profitable.

Of course, the competitive analysis we have done is, by itself, overly simplistic. Eastside might be tempted to attack Westside's other markets if Westside does not respond to Eastside's price cut. And Westside's not matching Eastside's price increase might force Eastside to roll back its prices. These long-run strategic concerns might outweigh the short-term profit implications of a decision to react. In order to make such a judgment, however, the company must first determine the short-term profit implications. Sometimes long-term competitive strategies are not worth the short-term cost.

CALCULATING POTENTIAL FINANCIAL IMPLICATIONS

To grasp fully the potential impact of a price change, especially when the decision involves incremental changes in fixed costs, it is useful to calculate the profit impact for a range of potential sales changes and to summarize them with a breakeven table and chart. Doing so is relatively simple after having calculated the basic breakeven sales change. Using this calculation, one can then simulate what-if scenarios that include different levels of actual sales volume following the price change.

The top half of Exhibit 3-3 is a summary of the basic breakeven sales change analysis for Westside's 5 percent price cut, with one column summarizing the level of contribution before the price change (the column labeled "Baseline") and one column summarizing the contribution after the price change (the column labeled "Proposed Price Change"). The bottom half of Exhibit 3-3 summarizes nine what-if scenarios showing the profitability associated with changes in sales volume ranging from 0 percent to 40 percent given incremental semifixed costs of $800 per 1,000 units. Columns 1 and 2 show the actual change in volume for each scenario. Columns 3 through 5 calculate the change in profit that results from each change in sales.

To illustrate how these breakeven sales-change scenarios are calculated, let us focus for a moment on scenario 6, where actual sales volume is projected to

Breakeven Sales Change Summary	*Baseline*	*Proposed Price Change*
Price/unit	$10.00	$9.50
% Price change		–5%
$ Contribution/unit	$4.50	$4.00
% Contribution	45%	42%
Breakeven sales change (%)		12.5%
Breakeven sales change (units)		500
Total sales volume (units)	4,000	4,500
Total contribution	$18,000	$18,000

Breakeven Sales Change Simulated Scenarios

		% Change in Actual Sales Volume	*Unit Change in Actual Sales Volume*	*Change in Contribution After Price Change*	*Incremental Fixed Costs*	*Total Change in Profit After Price Change*
	1	0.0	0	–2,000	800	–2,800
	2	5.0	200	–1,200	800	–2000
Simulated Scenarios	3	10.0	400	–400	800	–1,200
	4	12.5	500	0	800	–800
	5	17.5	700	800	800	0
	6	20.0	800	1,200	800	400
	7	25.0	1,000	2,000	800	1,200
	8	30.0	1,200	2,800	1,600	1,200
	9	40.0	1,600	4,400	1,600	2,800

EXHIBIT 3-3 Breakeven Sales Analysis and Breakeven Sales Simulated Scenarios: Westside Manufacturing Proposed 5% Price Reduction

increase 20 percent. A 20 percent change in actual sales volume is equivalent to an 800-unit change in actual sales volume, since 800 units is 20 percent of the baseline sales volume of 4,000 units. How does this increase in sales translate into changes in profitability? Column 3 shows that a 20 percent (or an 800-unit) increase in sales volume results in a change in contribution after the price change of $1,200. This is calculated by taking the difference between the actual unit sales change (800 units) and the breakeven sales change shown in the top half of the exhibit (500 units) and multiplying by the new contribution margin after the price change ($4). However, the calculations made in column 3 do not take into account the incremental fixed costs required to implement the price change (shown in column 4). Column 5 shows the change in profit after subtracting the change in fixed costs from the incremental contribution generated. Where there is inadequate incremental contribution to cover the incremental fixed costs, as in scenarios 1 through 4, the change in profit is negative. Scenario

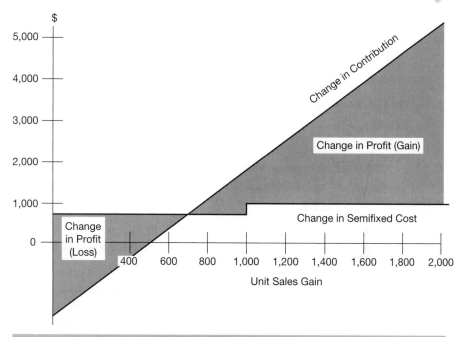

EXHIBIT 3-4 Breakeven Analysis of a Price Change

5 illustrates the breakeven sales change. Scenarios 6 through 9 are all profitable scenarios since they result in greater profit after the price change than before.

The interrelationships among contribution, incremental fixed costs, and the sales change that results from a price change are often easier to comprehend with a graph. Exhibit 3-4 illustrates the relationships among the data in Exhibit 3-3. Appendix 3B (at the end of this chapter) explains how to produce breakeven graphs, which are especially useful in comprehending the implications of price changes when many fixed costs become incremental at different sales volumes.

BREAKEVEN SALES CURVES

So far we have discussed breakeven sales analysis in terms of a single change in price and its resultant breakeven sales change. In the example above, Westside Manufacturing considered a 5 percent price reduction, which we calculated would require a 17.5 percent increase in sales volume to achieve enough incremental contribution to cover the incremental fixed cost. However, what if the company wants to consider a range of potential price changes? How can we use breakeven sales analysis to consider alternative price changes simultaneously? The answer is by charting a breakeven sales curve, which summarizes the results of a series of breakeven sales analyses for different price changes.

Price Change	Price	Breakeven Sales Change	Unit Breakeven Sales Change	Unit Breakeven Sales Volume	Incremental Fixed Costs	Breakeven Sales Change with IFC
25%	$12.50	−35.7%	−1,429	2,571	0	−35.7%
20%	$12.00	−30.8%	−1,231	2,769	0	−30.8%
15%	$11.50	−25.0%	−1,000	3,000	0	−25.0%
10%	$11.00	−18.2%	−727	3,273	0	−18.2%
5%	$10.50	−10.0%	−400	3,600	0	−10.0%
0%	$10.00	0.0%	0	4,000	0	0.0%
−5%	$9.50	12.5%	500	4,500	$800	17.5%
−10%	$9.00	28.6%	1,143	5,143	$1,600	40.0%
−15%	$8.50	50.0%	2,000	6,000	$2,400	70.0%
−20%	$8.00	80.0%	3,200	7,200	$4,000	120.0%

Exhibit 3-5   Breakeven Sales Curve Calculations (with Incremental Fixed Costs)

Constructing breakeven sales curves requires doing a series of what-if analyses, similar to the simulated scenarios discussed in the last section. Exhibits 3-5 and 3-6 show numerically and graphically a breakeven sales curve for Westside Manufacturing, with simulated scenarios of price changes ranging from +25 to −20 percent. Note in Exhibit 3-6 that the vertical axis shows different price levels for the product, and the horizontal axis shows a volume level associated with each price level. Each point on the curve represents the sales volume necessary to achieve as much profit after the price change as would be earned at the baseline price. For example, Westside's baseline price is $10 per unit, and baseline sales volume is 4,000 units. If, however, Westside cuts the price by 15 percent to $8.50, its sales volume would have to increase 70 percent to 6,800 units to achieve the same profitability. Conversely, if Westside increases its price by 15 percent to $11.50, its sales volume could decrease 25 percent to 3,000 units and still allow equal profitability.

The breakeven sales curve is a simple, yet powerful tool for synthesizing and evaluating the dynamics behind the profitability of potential price changes. It presents succinctly and visually the dividing line that separates profitable price decisions from unprofitable ones. Profitable price decisions are those that result in sales volumes in the area to the right of the curve. Unprofitable price decisions are those that result in sales volumes in the area to the left of the curve. What is the logic behind this? Recall the previous discussion of what happens before and after a price change. The breakeven sales curve represents those sales volume levels associated with their respective levels of price, where the company will make just as much net contribution *after* the price change as it made before the price change. If the company's sales volume after the price change is greater than the breakeven sales volume (that is, actual sales volume is to the right of the curve), the price change will add to profitability. If the company's sales volume after the price change is less than the breakeven sales vol-

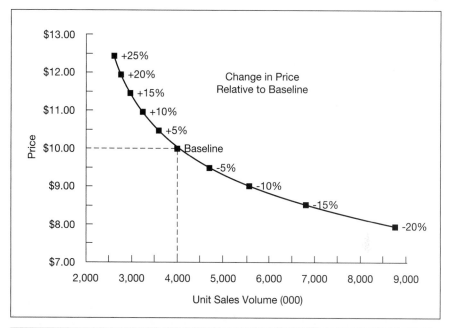

EXHIBIT 3-6 Breakeven Sales Curve Trade-off Between Price and Sales Volume Required for Constant Profitability

ume (that is, the area to the left of the curve), the price change will be unprofitable. For example, for Westside a price of $8.50 requires a sales volume of at least 6,800 units to achieve a net gain in profitability. If, after reducing its price to $8.50, management believes it will sell more than 6,800 units (a point to the right of the curve), then a decision to implement a price of $8.50 per unit would be profitable.

The breakeven sales curve also clearly illustrates the relationship between the breakeven approach to pricing and the economic concept of price elasticity. Note that the breakeven sales curve looks suspiciously like the traditional downward-sloping demand curve in economic theory, in which different levels of price (on the vertical axis) are associated with different levels of quantity demanded (on the horizontal axis). On a traditional demand curve, the slope between any two points on the curve determines the elasticity of demand, a measure of price sensitivity expressed as the percent change in quantity demanded for a given percent change in price. An economist who knew the shape of such a curve could calculate the profit-maximizing price.

Unfortunately, few firms use economic theory to set price because of the unrealistic expectation that they first have to know their demand curve, or at least the demand elasticity around the current price level. To overcome this shortcoming, we have addressed the problem in reverse order. Rather than asking "What is the firm's demand elasticity?" we ask, instead, "What is the

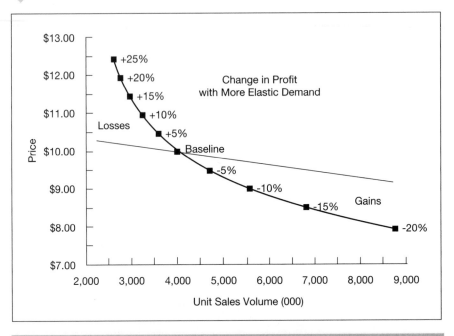

EXHIBIT 3-7 Breakeven Sales Curve Relationship Between Price Elasticity of Demand and Profitability

minimum demand elasticity required?" to justify a particular pricing decision. Breakeven sales analysis calculates the minimum or maximum demand elasticity required to profit from a particular pricing decision. The breakeven sales curve illustrates a set of minimum elasticities necessary to make a price cut profitable, or the maximum elasticity tolerable to make a price increase profitable. One is then led to ask whether the level of price sensitivity in the market is greater or less than the level of price sensitivity required by the firm's cost and margin structure.

This relationship between the breakeven sales curve and the demand curve is illustrated in Exhibits 3-7 and 3-8, where hypothetical demand curves are shown with Westside's breakeven sales curve. If demand is more elastic, as in Exhibit 3-7, price reductions relative to the baseline price result in gains in profitability, and price increases result in losses in profitability. If demand is less elastic, as in Exhibit 3-8, price increases relative to the baseline price result in gains in profitability, and price reductions result in losses in profitability. Although few, if any, managers actually know the demand curve for their product, we have encountered many who can comfortably make judgments about whether it is more or less elastic than is required by the breakeven sales curve. Moreover, although we have not found any market research technique that can estimate a demand curve with great precision, we have seen many (described

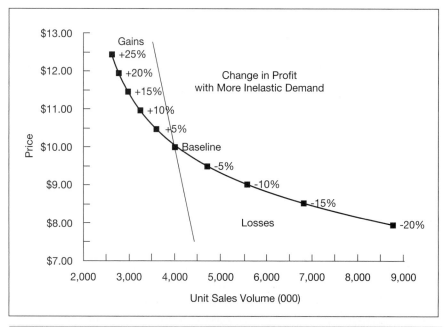

EXHIBIT 3-8 Breakeven Sales Curve Relationship Between Price Elasticity of Demand and Profitability: Changes in Profit with More Inelastic Demand

in Chapter 13) that could enable management to confidently accept or reject a particular breakeven sales level as achievable.

Watching Your Baseline

In the preceding examples, the level of baseline sales from which we calculated breakeven sales changes was assumed to be the current level. For simplicity, we assume a static market. In many cases, however, sales grow or decline even if price remains constant. As a result, the baseline for calculating breakeven sales changes is not necessarily the current level of sales. Rather, it is the level that would occur if no price change were made.

Consider, for example, a company in a high-growth industry with current sales of 2,000 units on which it earns a contribution margin of 55 percent. If the company does not change its price, management expects that sales will increase by 20 percent (the projected growth of total industry sales) to 2,400 units. However, management is considering a 5 percent price cut in an attempt to increase the company's market share. The price cut would be accompanied by an advertising campaign intended to heighten consumer awareness of the change. The campaign would take time to design, delaying implementation of the price change until next year. The initial sales level for the constant contribution analysis, therefore, would be the projected sales in the future, or 2,400 units. Consequently, the breakeven sales change would be calculated as follows:

$$\% \text{ Breakeven sales change} = \frac{-(-5\%)}{55\% + (-5\%)} = 0.10, \textit{ or } 10\%$$

or

$$0.10 \times 2,400 = 240 \text{ units}$$

If the current sales level is used in the calculation, the unit breakeven sales change is calculated as 200 units, understating the change required by 40 units.

Covering Nonincremental Fixed and Sunk Costs

By this point, one might be wondering about the nonincremental fixed and sunk costs that have been ignored when analyzing pricing decisions. A company's goal must surely be to cover all of its costs, including all fixed and sunk costs, or it will soon go bankrupt. This concern is justified and is central to pricing for profit, but it is misguided when applied to justify higher prices.

Note that the goal in calculating a contribution margin and in using it to evaluate price changes and differentials is to set prices to maximize a product's profit contribution. Profit contribution, you will recall, is the income remaining after all incremental, avoidable costs have been covered. It is money available to cover nonincremental fixed and sunk costs and to contribute to profit. When managers consider only the incremental, avoidable costs in making pricing decisions, they are not saying that other costs are unimportant. They simply realize, that the level of those costs is irrelevant to decisions about which price will generate the most money to cover them. Since nonincremental fixed and sunk costs do not change with a pricing decision, they do not affect the relative profitability of one price versus an alternative. Consequently, consideration of them simply clouds the issue of which price level will generate the most profit to cover them.

All costs are important to profitability since they all, regardless of how they are classified, have to be covered before profits are earned. At some point, all costs must be considered. What distinguishes value-based pricing from cost-driven pricing is *when* they are considered. A major reason that this approach to pricing is more profitable than cost-driven pricing is that it encourages managers to think about costs when they can still do something about them. *Every cost is incremental and avoidable at some time.* For example, even the cost of product development and design, although it is fixed and sunk by the time the first unit is sold, is incremental and avoidable before the design process begins. The same is true for other costs. The key to profitable pricing is to recognize that customers in the marketplace, not costs, determine what a product can sell for. Consequently, before incurring any costs, managers need to estimate what customers can be convinced to pay for an intended product. Then they decide what costs they can profitably incur, given the expected revenue.

Of course, no one has perfect foresight. Managers must make decisions to incur costs without knowing for certain how the market will respond. When their expectations are accurate, the market rewards them with sales at the prices they expected, enabling them to cover all costs and to earn a profit. When they overestimate a product's value, profit contribution may prove inadequate to cover all the costs incurred. In that case, a good manager seeks to minimize the loss. This can be done only by maximizing profit contribution (revenue minus incremental, avoidable costs). Shortsighted efforts to build nonincremental fixed and sunk costs into a price that will justify past mistakes will only reduce volume further, making the losses worse.

CASE STUDY: RITTER & SONS

The Westside Manufacturing example illustrates the principles of costing and financial analysis in the context of one product with easily defined costs. Applying these analysis tools in a more typical corporate setting is usually much more complex. The following case study illustrates how one company dealt with more complex incremental costing issues, and then used the financial analysis tools presented in this chapter to develop well-reasoned proposals for more profitable pricing. Note how, even in the absence of complete information, these tools enable managers to fully integrate the information they have, cross-functionally, to make better decisions.

Ritter & Sons is a wholesale producer of potted plants and cut flowers. Ritter's most popular product is potted chrysanthemums (mums), which are particularly in demand around certain holidays, especially Mother's Day, Easter, and Memorial Day, but they maintain a high level of sales throughout the year. Exhibit 3-9 shows Ritter's revenues, costs, and sales from mums for a recent fiscal year. After attending a seminar on pricing, the company's chief financial officer, Don Ritter, began to wonder whether this product might somehow be priced more profitably. A serious examination of the effect of raising and lowering the wholesale price of mums from the current price of $3.85 per unit was then begun.

Ritter's first step was to identify the relevant cost and contribution margin for mums. Looking only at the data in Exhibit 3-9, Don was somewhat uncertain how to proceed. He reasoned that the costs of the cuttings, shipping, packaging, and pottery were clearly incremental and avoidable and that the cost of administrative overhead was fixed. He was far less certain about labor and the capital cost of the greenhouses. Some of Ritter's work force consisted of longtime employees whose knowledge of planting techniques was highly valuable. It would not be practical to lay them off, even if they were not needed during certain seasons. Most production employees, however, were transient laborers who were hired during peak seasons and who found work elsewhere when less labor was required.

After consulting with the production manager for potted plants, Don concluded that about $7,000 of the labor cost of mums was fixed. The remaining $44,850 (or $0.52 per unit) was variable and thus relevant to the pricing decision.

Crop *Preparer: DR*	6" Mums *Total*	*Per Unit*
Unit sales	86,250	1
Revenue	*$332,063*	*$3.85*
Cost of cuttings	34,500	0.40
Gross margin	*297,563*	*3.45*
Labor	51,850	0.60
Shipping	26,563	0.31
Package foil	9,056	0.10
Package sleeve	4,312	0.05
Package carton	4,399	0.05
Pottery	14,663	0.17
Capital cost allocation	66,686	0.77
Overhead allocation	73,320	0.85
Operating profit	$46,714	$0.54

EXHIBIT 3-9 Cost Projection for Proposed Crop of Mums

Don also wondered how he should treat the capital cost of the greenhouses. He was sure that the company policy of allocating capital cost (interest and depreciation) equally to every plant sold was not correct. However, when Don suggested to his brother Paul, the company's president, that since these costs were sunk, they should be entirely ignored in pricing, Paul found the suggestion unsettling. He pointed out that Ritter used all of its greenhouse capacity in the peak season, that it had expanded its capacity in recent years, and that it planned further expansions in the coming year. Unless the price of mums reflected the capital cost of building additional greenhouses, how could Ritter justify such investments?

That argument made sense to Don. Surely the cost of greenhouses is incremental if they are all in use, since additional capacity would have to be built if Ritter were to sell more mums. But that same cost is clearly not incremental during seasons when there is excess capacity. Ritter's policy of making all mums grown in a year bear a $0.77 capital cost was simply misleading since additional mums could be grown without bearing any additional capital cost during seasons with excess capacity. Mums grown in peak seasons, however, actually cost much more than Ritter had been assuming, since those mums require capital additions. Thus, if the annual cost of an additional greenhouse (depreciation, interest, maintenance, heating) is $9,000, and if the greenhouse will hold 5,000 mums for three crops each year, the capital cost per mum would be $0.60 ($9,000/[3 × 5,000]) only if all greenhouses are fully utilized throughout the year. Since the greenhouses are filled to capacity for only one crop per year, the relevant capital cost for pricing that crop is $1.80 per mum ($9,000/5,000), while it is zero for pricing crops at other times.[4]

	With Excess Capacity	At Full Capacity
Price	$3.85	$3.85
– Cost of cuttings	0.40	0.40
– Incremental labor	0.52	0.52
– Other direct costs	0.68	0.68
= Dollar contribution margin	$2.25	$2.25
– Incremental capital cost	0	1.80
= Profit contribution	$2.25	$0.45

EXHIBIT 3-10 Relevant Cost of Mums

As a result of his discussions, Don calculated two costs for mums: one to apply when there is excess capacity in the greenhouses and one to apply when greenhouse capacity is fully utilized. His calculations are shown in Exhibit 3-10. These two alternatives do not exhaust the possibilities. For any product, different combinations of costs can be fixed or incremental in different situations. For example, if Ritter found itself with excess mums after they were grown, potted, and ready to sell, the only incremental cost would be the cost of shipping. If Ritter found itself with too little capacity and too little time to make additions before the next peak season, the only way to grow more mums would be to grow fewer types of other flowers. In that case, the cost of greenhouse space for mums would be the opportunity cost (measured by the lost contribution) from not growing and selling those other flowers. The relevant cost for a pricing decision depends on the circumstances. Therefore, one must begin each pricing problem by first determining the relevant cost for that particular decision.

For Ritter, the decision at hand involved planning production quantities and prices for the forthcoming year. There would be three crops of mums during the year, two during seasons when Ritter would have excess growing capacity and one during the peak season, when capacity would be a constraint. The relevant contribution margin would be $2.25, or 58.5 percent ($2.25/3.85), for all plants. In the peak season, however, the net profit contribution would be considerably less because of the incremental capital cost of the greenhouses.

Don recognized immediately that there was a problem with Ritter's pricing of mums. Since the company had traditionally used cost-plus pricing based on fully allocated average cost, fixed costs were allocated equally to all plants. Consequently, Ritter charged the same price ($3.85) for mums throughout the year. Although mums grown in the off-peak season used the same amount of greenhouse space as those grown during the peak season, the relevant incremental cost of that space was not always the same. Consequently, the profit contribution for mums sold in an off-peak season was much greater than for those sold in the peak season. This difference was not reflected in Ritter's pricing.

Don suspected that Ritter should be charging lower prices during seasons when the contribution margin was large and higher prices when it was small. Using his new understanding of the relevant cost, Don calculated the

5% Off-Peak Season Price Cut

$$\text{Breakeven sales change} = \frac{-(-5.0)}{58.5 - 5.0} = +9.3\%$$

10% Peak Season Price Increase

$$\text{Breakeven sales change} = \frac{-10.0}{58.5 + 10.0} = -14.6\%$$

$$\text{Breakeven sales with incremental fixed costs*} = -14.6\% + \frac{-\$9,000}{\$2.635 \times 45,000}$$

$$= -22.2\%$$

*The new dollar contribution margin is $2.635 after the 10% price increase.

EXHIBIT 3-11 Breakeven Sales Changes for Proposed Price Changes

breakeven sales quantities for a 5 percent price cut during the off-peak season, when excess capacity makes capital costs irrelevant, and for a 10 percent increase during the peak season, when capital costs are incremental to the pricing decision. These calculations are shown in Exhibit 3-11.

Don first calculated the percent breakeven quantity for the off-peak season, indicating that Ritter would need at least a 9.3 percent sales increase to justify a 5 percent price cut in the off-peak season. Then he calculated the basic breakeven percentage for a 10 percent price increase during the peak season. If sales declined by less than 14.6 percent as a result of the price increase (equal to 6,570 units, given Ritter's expected peak season sales of 45,000 mums), the price increase would be profitable. Don also recognized, however, that if sales declined that much, Ritter could avoid constructing at least one new greenhouse. That capital cost savings could make the price increase profitable even if sales declined by more than the basic breakeven quantity. Assuming that one greenhouse involving a cost of $9,000 per year could be avoided, the breakeven decline rises to 22.2 percent (equal to 9,990 units). If a 10 percent price increase caused Ritter to lose less than 22.2 percent of its projected sales for the next peak season, the increase would be profitable.

Judging whether actual sales changes were likely to be greater or smaller than those quantities was beyond Don's expertise. He calculated a series of "what if" scenarios, called breakeven sales change simulated scenarios, and then presented his findings to Sue James, Ritter's sales manager (see Exhibit 3-12).

Sue felt certain that sales during the peak season would not decline by 22.2 percent following a 10 percent price increase. She pointed out that the ultimate purchasers in the peak season usually bought mums as gifts. Consequently, they were much more sensitive to quality than to price. Fortunately, most of Ritter's major competitors could not match Ritter's quality since they had to ship their plants from more distant greenhouses. Ritter's local competition, like Ritter, would not have the capacity to serve more customers during the peak season. The high-quality florists who comprised most of Ritter's customers were, therefore, unlikely to switch suppliers in response to a 10 percent peak-period price

With Excess Capacity
5% Off-Peak Season Price Cut

Scenario	% Change in Actual Sales Volume	Unit Change in Actual Sales Volume	Change in Contribution After Price Change
1	0%	—	$ (16,504)
2	5%	4,313	$ (7,631)
3	10%	8,625	$ 1,242
4	15%	12,938	$ 10,115
5	20%	17,250	$ 18,988
6	25%	21,563	$ 27,861
7	30%	25,875	$ 36,734

Baseline price	$ 3.85
Baseline contribution margin	$ 2.25
New price	$ 3.66
New contribution margin	$ 2.06

At Full Capacity
10% Peak Season Price Increase

Scenario	% Change in Actual Sales Volume	Unit Change in Actual Sales Volume	Change in Contribution After Price Change
1	0%	0	$ 50,454
2	–5%	–4313	$ 39,090
3	–10%	–8625	$ 27,727
4	–15%	–12938	$ 16,363
5	–20%	–17250	$ 5,000
6	–25%	–21563	$ (6,364)
7	–30%	–25875	$ (17,727)

Baseline price	$ 3.85
Baseline contribution margin	$ 2.25
New price	$ 4.24
New contribution margin	$ 2.64

EXHIBIT 3-12 Breakeven Sales Change Simulated Scenarios

increase. If peak season sales remained steady, profit contribution would increase significantly, by about $50,000. If peak season sales declined modestly, the change in profit contribution would still be positive.

Sue also felt that retailers who currently bought mums from Ritter in the off-peak season could probably not sell in excess of 9.3 percent more, even if they cut their retail prices by the same 5 percent that Ritter contemplated cutting the wholesale price. Thus, the price cut would be profitable only if some retailers who normally bought mums from competitors were to switch and buy from Ritter. This possibility would depend on whether competitors chose to defend their market shares by matching Ritter's price cut. If they did, Ritter would probably gain no more retail accounts. If they did not, Ritter might capture sales to one or more grocery chains whose price-sensitive customers and whose large expenditures on flowers make them diligent in their search for the best price.

Don and Sue needed to identify their competitors and ask "How does their pricing influence our sales, and how are they likely to respond to any price changes we initiate?" They spent the next two weeks talking with customers and with Ritter employees who had worked for competitors, trying to formulate answers. They learned that they faced two essentially different types of competition. First, they competed with one other large local grower, Mathews Nursery, whose costs are similar to Ritter's. Because Mathews's sales area generally overlapped Ritter's, Mathews would probably be forced to meet any Ritter price cuts. Most of the competition for the largest accounts, however, came from high-volume suppliers that shipped plants into Ritter's sales area as well as into other areas. It would be difficult for them to cut their prices only where they competed with Ritter. Moreover, they already operated on smaller margins because of their higher shipping costs. Consequently, they probably would not match a 5 percent price cut.

Still, Sue thought that even the business of one or two large buyers might not be enough to increase Ritter's total sales in the off-peak season by more than the breakeven quantity. Don recognized that the greater price sensitivity of large buyers might represent an opportunity for segmented pricing. If Ritter could cut prices to the large buyers only, the price cut would be profitable if the percentage increase in sales to that market segment alone exceeded the breakeven increase. Perhaps Ritter could offer a 5 percent quantity discount for which only the large, price-sensitive buyers could qualify.[5] Alternatively, Ritter might sort its mums into "florist quality" and "standard quality," if it could assume that its florists would generally be willing to pay a 5 percent premium to offer the best product to their clientele.

Don decided to make a presentation to the other members of Ritter's management committee, setting out the case for increasing price by 10 percent for the peak season and for reducing price to large buyers by 5 percent for the two off-peak seasons. To illustrate the potential effects of the proposed changes, he calculated the change in Ritter's profits for various possible changes in sales. To illustrate the profit impact for a wide range of sales changes, he presented the results of his calculations graphically. The graph he used to illustrate the effect of a 10 percent price increase at various changes in sales volume is reproduced in Exhibit 3-13. After Don's presentation, Sue James explained why she believed that sales would decline by less than the breakeven quantity if price were raised in the peak season. She also felt sales might increase more than the breakeven percent if price were lowered in the off-peak seasons, especially if the cut could be limited to large buyers.

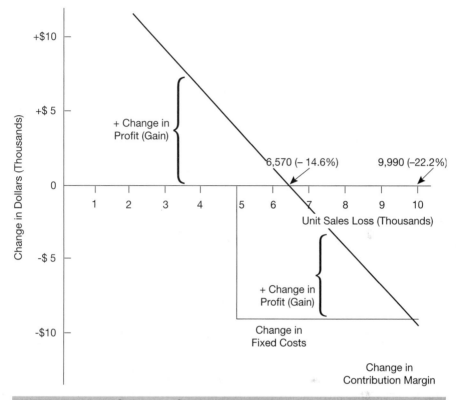

EXHIBIT 3-13 Profit Impact of a 10 Percent Increase

Since Ritter has traditionally set prices based on a full allocation of costs, some managers were initially skeptical of this new approach. They asked probing questions, which Don and Sue's analysis of the market enabled them to answer. The management committee recognized that the decision was not clear-cut. It would ultimately rest on uncertain judgments about sales changes that the proposed price changes would precipitate. If Ritter's regular customers proved to be more price-sensitive than Don and Sue now believed, the proposed 10 percent price increase for the peak season could cause sales to decline by more than the breakeven quantity. If competitors all matched Ritter's 5 percent price cut for large buyers in the off-peak season, sales might not increase by as much as the breakeven quantity.

The committee accepted the proposed price changes. In related decisions, they postponed construction of one new greenhouse and established a two-quality approach to pricing mums based on selecting the best for "florist quality" and selling the lower-priced "standard quality" mums only in lots of 1,000. Finally, they agreed that Don should give a speech at an industry trade show on how this pricing approach could improve capital utilization and efficiency. In the speech, he would reveal Ritter's decision to raise its price in the peak season. (Perhaps the Mathews management might decide to take such information into account in independently formulating its own pricing decisions.) He would also let it be known that if Ritter were unable to sell more mums to large local buyers in the off-peak season, it would consider offering the mums at discount prices to florists outside of its local market. This plan, it was hoped, would discourage nonlocal competitors from fighting for local market share, lest the price-cutting spread to markets they found more lucrative.

At this point, there was no way to know if these decisions would prove profitable. Management could have requested more formal research into customer motivations or a more detailed analysis of nonlocal competitors' past responses to price-cutting. Since past behavior is never a perfect guide to the future, the decision would still have required weighing the risks involved with the benefits promised. Still, Don's analysis ensured that management identified the relevant information for this decision and weighed it appropriately.

SUMMARY

The profitability of pricing decisions depends largely on the product's cost structure and contribution margin and on market sensitivity to changes in price. In Chapter 2 we discussed the importance of identifying the costs that are most relevant to the profitability of a pricing decision, namely, incremental and avoidable costs. Having identified the right costs, one must also understand how to use them. The most important reason to identify costs correctly is to be able to calculate an accurate contribution margin. An accurate contribution margin enables management to determine the amount by which sales must increase following a price cut, or by how little they may decline following a price increase, to make the price change profitable. Understanding how changes in sales will affect a product's profitability is the first step in pricing the product effectively.

It is, however, just the first step. Next one must learn how to judge the likely impact of a price change on sales, which requires understanding how buyers are likely to perceive a price change and how competitors are likely to react to it. We consider these subjects in the next two chapters.

Notes

1. The rule for analyzing the profitability of independently negotiated prices is simple: A price is profitable as long as it covers incremental costs. Unfortunately, many managers make the mistake of applying that rule when prices are not independent across customers. They assume, mistakenly, that because they negotiate prices individually, they are negotiating them *independently*. In fact, because customers talk to one another and learn the prices that others pay, prices are rarely independent. The low price you charge to one customer will eventually depress the prices that you can charge to others.

2. $$\frac{-\$0.50}{\$4.50 + \$0.50} =$$

-0.10, or -10%

3. This equation can also accommodate a change in variable cost by simply replacing the "change in price" with the "change in price minus the change in variable cost." One can also add to it the breakeven necessary to cover a change in fixed costs.

4. We are assuming that a greenhouse depreciates no more rapidly when in use than when idle. If it did depreciate faster when used, the extra de-preciation would be an incremental cost even for crops grown during seasons with excess capacity.

5. This option could expose Ritter to the risk of a legal challenge if Ritter's large buyers compete directly with its small buyers in the retailing of mums. Ritter could rebut the challenge if it could justify the 5 percent discount as a cost saving in preparing and shipping larger orders. If not, then Ritter may want to try more complicated methods to segment the market, such as offering somewhat different products to the two segments.

Appendix 3A

Derivation of the Breakeven Formula

A price change can either increase or reduce a company's profits, depending on how it affects sales. The breakeven formula is a simple way to discover at what point the change in sales becomes large enough to make a price reduction profitable, or a price increase unprofitable.

Exhibit 3A-1 illustrates the breakeven problem. At the initial price P, a company can sell the quantity Q. Its total revenue is P times Q, which graphically is the area of the rectangle bordered by the lines $0P$ and $0Q$. If C is the product's variable cost, then the total profit contribution earned at price P is $(P - C)Q$. Total profit contribution is shown graphically as the rectangle bordered by the lines CF and $0Q$.

If this company reduces its price from P to P', its profits will change. First, it will lose an amount equal to the change in price, ΔP, times the amount that it could sell without the price change, Q. Graphically, that loss is the rectangle labeled A. Somewhat offsetting that loss, however, the company will enjoy a gain from the additional sales it can make because of the lower price. The amount of the gain is the profit that the company will earn from each additional sale, $P' - C$, times the change in sales, ΔQ. Graphically, that gain is the rectangle labeled B. Whether or not the price reduction is profitable depends on whether or not rectangle B is greater than rectangle A, and that depends on the size of ΔQ.

EXHIBIT 3A-1 Breakeven Sales Change Relationships

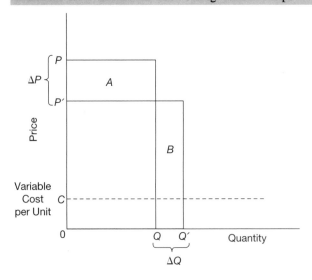

The logic of a price increase is similar. If P' were the initial price and Q' the initial quantity, then the profitability of a price increase to P would again depend on the size of ΔQ. If ΔQ were small, rectangle A, the gain on sales made at the higher price, would exceed rectangle B, the loss on sales that would not be made because of the higher price. However, ΔQ might be large enough to make B larger than A, in which case the price increase would be unprofitable.

To calculate the formula for the breakeven ΔQ (at which the gain from a price reduction just outweighs the loss or the loss from a price increase just outweighs the gain), we need to state the problem algebraically. Before the price change, the profit earned was $(P - C)Q$. After the change, the profit was $(P' - C)Q'$. Noting, however, that $P' = P + \Delta P$ (we write $+ \Delta P$ since ΔP is a negative number) and that $Q' = Q + \Delta Q$, we can write the profit after the price change as $(P + \Delta P - C)(Q + \Delta Q)$. Since our goal is to find the ΔQ at which profits would be just equal before and after the price change, we can begin by setting those profits equal algebraically:

$$(P - C)Q = (P + \Delta P - C)(Q + \Delta Q)$$

Multiplying this equation through yields

$$PQ - CQ = PQ + \Delta PQ - CQ + \\ P\Delta Q + \Delta P\Delta Q - C\Delta Q$$

We can simplify this equation by subtracting PQ and adding CQ to both sides to obtain

$$0 = \Delta PQ + P\Delta Q + \Delta P\Delta Q - C\Delta Q$$

Note that all the remaining terms in the equation contain the "change sign" Δ. This is because only the changes are relevant for evaluating a price change. If we solve this equation for ΔQ, we obtain the new equation

$$\frac{\Delta Q}{Q} = \frac{-\Delta P}{P + \Delta P - C}$$

which, in words, is

$$\% \text{ Breakeven sales change} = \frac{-\text{ Price change}}{CM + \text{ Price change}}$$

To express the right side in percentages, multiply the right side by

$$\frac{\left(\dfrac{1}{P}\right)}{\left(\dfrac{1}{P}\right)}$$

Appendix 3B

Breakeven Analysis of Price Changes

Breakeven analysis is a common tool in managerial accounting, particularly useful for evaluating potential investments. Unfortunately, the traditional forms of breakeven analysis appropriate for evaluating investment decisions are often misleading when applied to pricing decisions. Individual investments (should the company buy a new computer? should it develop a new product? should it field a sales force to enter a new market?) can often be evaluated apart from other investments. Consequently, it is appropriate to use traditional breakeven analysis, which compares the total revenue from the investment with its total cost.

Usually, however, one cannot set a price for each individual sale independent of other sales. To gain an additional sale by charging one customer a lower price normally requires charging other customers, at least others in that same market segment, the lower price as well. Consequently, it is usually misleading to evaluate the profitability of an additional sale by comparing only the price earned from that sale to the cost of that sale. To comprehend the profit implications of a price change, one must compare the change in revenue from all sales with the change in costs.

The need to focus attention on the changes in revenues and costs rather than on their totals requires a different kind of breakeven analysis for pricing decisions. Where traditional breakeven analysis of invest-

ments deals with total revenue and all costs, breakeven analysis of pricing decisions deals with the *change* in revenue in excess of variable cost (the dollar contribution margin) and with the *change* in incremental fixed costs. In the body of this chapter, you learned a number of formulas for breakeven analysis of pricing decisions and saw how to use them in the Westside Manufacturing example. In this appendix, you will learn how to use those equations to develop breakeven graphs and to analyze more complex pricing problems involving multiple sources of fixed costs that become incremental at different quantities.

DEVELOPING A BREAKEVEN CHART

A breakeven chart, such as Exhibit 3-4, is useful in determining the possible effects of a price change. It plots both the change in the dollar contribution margin and the changes in relevant costs, enabling the pricing analyst to see the change in net profit that a change in sales volume would generate. To develop such a chart, it is useful to begin by preparing a table, such as Exhibit 3-5, organizing all relevant data in a concise form.

As an illustration, let us examine the case of PQR Industries. PQR manufactures and markets home video equipment. One of the most popular items in the company's product line is a video tape player with current sales of 4,000 units at $250 each. Sales have been growing rapidly and are expected to reach 4,800 units in the next year if the price remains unchanged. Variable costs are $112.50 per unit, resulting in the following percent contribution margin:

$$\% \, CM = \frac{\$250.00 - \$112.50}{\$250.00}$$

$$= 0.55 = 55\%$$

Despite its projected growth in sales at the current price, PQR is considering a 5 percent price cut to remain competitive and retain its share in this rapidly growing market. Since the cut would be implemented in the next year, the initial sales level, or baseline, is next year's projected sales (4,800 units). Calculation of the breakeven sales change is as follows:

% Breakeven sales change =

$$\frac{-(-5.0)}{55.0 + (-5.0)} = \frac{5}{50}$$

$$= 0.10 = 10\%$$

Unit breakeven sales change = 0.10 × 4,800 units = 480 units

Production capacity is currently limited to 5,000 units but can be increased by purchasing equipment that costs $15,000 for each additional 1,000 units of capacity. The breakeven sales change, considering this change in fixed costs, is:

% Breakeven sales change (with incremental fixed costs)

$$= 10 + \frac{\$15,000}{\$125.00 \times 4,800} = 12.5\%$$

Unit breakeven sales = 0.125 × 4,800 units = 600 units

Note that the price cut brings the price down to $237.50, resulting in a new dollar contribution margin of $125 per unit.

Since the actual sales change that would result from the price cut is unknown, a breakeven table and chart should be prepared to show the profitability of the price change at various possible sales changes.

Exhibit 3B-1 shows a breakeven table for PQR's proposed 5 percent price cut. The first two columns show the potential levels of sales changes. Column 3 shows the change in total contribution margin that would result at each level using the change in profit formula. In the case of a 5 percent change in sales, the result would be:

Change in profit = (240 units − 480 units) × $125/unit = −$30,000

Subtracting the change in fixed costs shown in column 4 from column 3 results in column 5, the change in profit contribution. Alternatively, we could have generated column 5 more directly by calculating the breakeven sales change including the change in fixed costs and substituting that number in the change in profit equation.

When plotted on a graph, the data from this table form a breakeven chart (Exhibit 3B-2). The horizontal axis represents the change in unit sales and the vertical axis represents dollars of change. The line labeled "change in fixed costs" shows the increase in costs due to added capacity, as taken from column 4 of the table. The data in column 3 were used to plot the "change in contribution margin" line. The distance between the two lines represents the change in profit contribution (column 5). At the points where the

		Change in		
(1)	(2)	(3)	(4)	(5)
Sales				
(%)	*(Units)*	*Contribution Margin*	*Fixed Costs*	*Profit Contribution*
0.0	0	−$60,000	0	−$60,000
5.0	240	−$30,000	$15,000	−$45,000
10.0	480	0	$15,000	−$15,000
12.5	600	$15,000	$15,000	0
15.0	720	$30,000	$15,000	$15,000
20.0	960	$60,000	$15,000	$45,000
25.0	1200	$90,000	$15,000	$75,000
30.0	1440	$120,000	$30,000	$90,000
40.0	1920	$180,000	$30,000	$150,000

Note: Proposed change ; nd5% or $12.50/unit; initial price = $250; %*CM* = 45%; semifixed cost = $15,000 per 1,000 units capacity over 5,000 units.

EXHIBIT 3B-1 Breakeven Table for PQR Industries' Proposed 5% Price Cut

EXHIBIT 3B-2 Breakeven Analysis of PQR Industries' 5% Price Cut

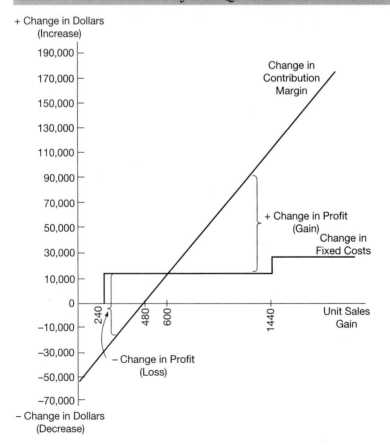

66

"change in contribution margin" line is above the "change in fixed costs" line, the change in profit contribution (and net profit) is positive. The price cut would be profitable if sales changed by those amounts.

BREAKEVEN ANALYSIS WITH MORE THAN ONE INCREMENTAL FIXED COST

To this point, we have always assumed that a company has only one fixed cost that changes with a price change. Frequently, however, a company will have several semifixed costs that change at different levels of volume. This makes analysis of a price change more complicated and the use of breakeven analysis more essential to the management of that complexity.

Let us return to PQR Industries. Because of the cost of adding a machine, management investigated al-ternative methods of increasing pro-duction. It was determined that the addition of one machine operator could delay purchase of a machine until sales exceeded 5,400 units (or 600 units more than the baseline ini-tial sales). Although labor costs are normally variable with production, machine operators are skilled labor-ers who, according to union rules, can only be hired as full-time employees working only at their specialties. The result is that a machine operator's salary is a semifixed cost. It was also discovered that the union contract required one skilled worker to be added for each 1,000 units of in-creased production. Finally, the plant engineer informed management that there was space for only one addi-tional machine. If more equipment were purchased, more space would have to be rented, at a cost of $105,000 per year. The situation is summarized as follows:

Sales	4,800 units
Wholesale price	$250/unit
Variable cost	$112.50/unit
Semifixed costs:	
Machine operators	$7,500 per 1,000 units of added production
Equipment	$15,000 per 1,000 units of added production beyond a 600-unit gain
Space	$105,000 per year for rental if more than one machine is added

Due to the complexity of these costs, there is more than one breakeven sales change and a single calculation is not sufficient. For ex-ample, any increase in sales will re-quire the hiring of a machine operator. The breakeven sales change for a 5 percent price cut becomes:

% Breakeven sales change (with cost of machine operator)

$$= 10\% + \frac{\$7,500}{\$125 \times 4,800}$$

$$= 11.25\%$$

Unit breakeven sales change
$= 0.1125 \times 4,800$ units $= 540$ units

If, however, the total sales exceed 5,400 units and equipment must be purchased, a new calculation is required as follows:

% Breakeven sales change (with cost of equipment)

$$= 11.25\% + \frac{\$15,000}{\$125 \times 4,800}$$

$$= 13.75\%$$

Unit breakeven sales change
$$= 0.1375 \times 4,800 \text{ units} = 660 \text{ units}$$

If more space would have to be rented, still another breakeven calculation would be required.

It seems obvious that when there are multiple sources of incremental fixed costs, analysis via calculation of breakeven sales changes could become both tedious and confusing. A breakeven table and chart are usually essential to the clear sorting out of these problems. Organizing the data into a table (Exhibit 3B-3) and plotting it on a graph (Exhibit 3B-4) make the options much clearer. At changes in sales of between 540 and 600 units, the price change is slightly profitable. Once the change in sales exceeds 600 units, however, fixed costs must rise again due to the need for more equipment, and profits will become negative and will not return to positive again until the change in sales exceeds 660 units, causing the change in contribution to rise above the change in fixed costs.

Note that 12.5 percent, or 600 units, is the maximum sales change possible before additional costs must be incurred. To determine whether the investment in additional equipment is worthwhile, management must decide whether the possibility that sales will grow enough to achieve a profit contribution of more than $7,500 (that is, by more than 15 percent) after the equipment is purchased would be enough to justify forgoing the more certain profit to be gained from reaching only a 12.5 percent increase in sales.

This type of situation arises whenever there is a change in fixed costs, most dramatically when the second machine is bought and space must be rented. It seems unlikely that sales growth due to the price change would be sufficient to justify renting more space. In fact, sales would have to increase by more than 53 percent before such an increase in fixed costs would produce a positive net profit. Moreover, the investment would not be justified if the profit that could be earned by not meeting the entire sales gain were higher.

BREAKEVEN GRAPHS

The calculations for determining breakeven sales changes for a price increase are the same as those for a price cut. For price increases, however, sales volumes decline rather than increase. Consequently, the direction of the horizontal axis measures declines in sales volumes rather than increases.

To illustrate, let us consider again the case of PQR Industries. In addition to VCRs, PQR sells projection televisions for $3,000. Variable costs

Changes in

Sales (%)	(Units)	Contribution Margin ($)	Cost of Operators ($)	Cost of Equipment ($)	Cost of Space ($)	Total Fixed Costs ($)	Profit Contribution ($)
0.00	0	-60,000	0	0	0	0	-60,000
5.00	240	-30,000	7,500	0	0	7,500	-37,500
10.00	480	0	7,500	0	0	7,500	-7,500
11.25	540	7,500	7,500	0	0	7,500	0
12.50	600	15,000	7,500	0	0	7,500	7,500
13.75	660	22,500	7,500	15,000	0	22,500	0
15.00	720	30,000	7,500	15,000	0	22,500	7,500
20.00	960	60,000	7,500	15,000	0	22,500	37,500
25.00	1,200	90,000	15,000	15,000	0	30,000	60,000
30.00	1,440	120,000	15,000	15,000	0	30,000	90,000
35.00	1,680	150,000	15,000	30,000	105,000	150,000	0
40.00	1,920	180,000	15,000	30,000	105,000	150,000	30,000

Note: Proposed change: -5%, or \$12.50/unit; initial price = \$250; %CM = 45%; semifixed costs = \$7,500/1,000 units for machine operators \$15,000/1,000 units over 5,400 units for equipment \$90,000/year for space rental if more than one piece of equipment is added.

EXHIBIT 3B-3   Revised Breakeven Table for PQR Industries' Proposed 5% Price Cut

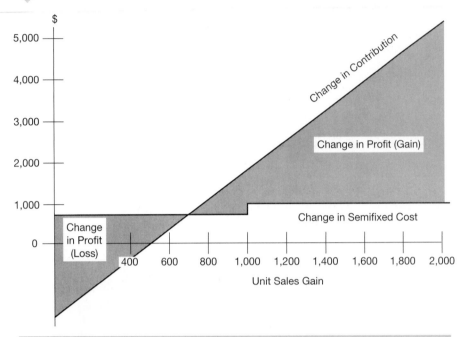

EXHIBIT 3B-4 Revised Breakeven Analysis of PQR Industries' 5% Cut

of $1,650 per unit leave the company with a contribution margin of $1,350 per unit, or 45 percent. The company is considering a price increase next year on this item. The initial sales level for evaluating the increase (next year's projected sales) is 4,000 units, which exceeds the company's current capacity of 3,600 units.

Concern about capacity constraints and the slowing growth of the market for this product have caused management to consider instituting a price increase in order to maximize profits. The breakeven sales change for the proposed 5 percent price increase is:

% Breakeven sales change =

$$\frac{-(5)}{45 + 5} = -10\%$$

Unit breakeven sales change =
$-0.10 \times 4,000$ units $= -400$ units

As long as the price increase causes sales to decline by less than 10 percent or 400 units, the price increase will cause the total dollar contribution from this product to increase.

To increase production beyond the current 3,600 unit capacity, additional equipment must be bought at a cost of $150,000. If, however, as a result of the price increase, sales decrease to the point that current capacity is sufficient, purchase of new equipment would not be necessary. The expenditure avoided is a negative change in fixed costs from the level required to achieve the 4,000 unit baseline sales level. A new breakeven sales change is calculated as follows:

$$\text{\% Breakeven sales change}$$
$$\text{(including change in fixed costs)}$$

$$= -10\% + \frac{-\$150.000}{\$1,500 \times 4,000}$$

$$= -12.5\%$$

On the basis of the data in Exhibit 3B-5, we can produce a breakeven graph for this price change (Exhibit 3B-6). The lines representing changes in contribution margin and fixed costs run opposite to the directions we are accustomed to seeing for price cuts, but the change in profit contribution, as indicated by the relative positions of these lines, is still interpreted as in earlier examples.

To verify this, let us refer to the graph and examine the results of a 5 percent, or 200 unit, sales decrease. At this point, there has been no change in fixed costs. Therefore, the change in profitability should equal a positive $300,000, the distance between the line indicating change in contribution margin and the horizontal axis. Reference to the related table will show that this is indeed true.

EXHIBIT 3B-5 Breakeven Table for PQR Industries' Proposed 5% Price Increase

		Change in		
(1)	*(2)*	*(3)*	*(4)*	*(5)*
Sales				
(%)	*(Units)*	*Contribution Margin ($)*	*Fixed Costs ($)*	*Profit Contribution ($)*
0.0	0	600,000	0	600,000
5.0	200	800,000	0	300,000
10.0	400	0	−150,000	150,000
12.5	500	−150,000	−150,000	0
15.0	600	−300,000	−150,000	−150,000
20.0	800	−600,000	−150,000	−450,000
25.0	1000	−900,000	−150,000	−750,000
30.0	1200	−1,200,000	−150,000	−1,050,000

Note: Proposed change –5% or $150/unit initial price = $3,000; %*CM* = 45%; semifixed cost = $150,000 for capacity over 3,600 units.

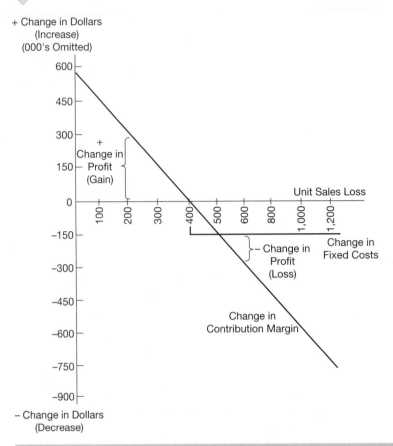

EXHIBIT 3B-6   Breakeven Analysis for PQR Industries' 5% Price Increase

SUMMARY

Predicting the outcome of a price change is not an exact science as later chapters will show. A manager should, therefore, consider all possible outcomes of such a change in order to choose the wisest course of action. Tables and graphs of breakeven analyses are useful, easily produced tools for this purpose.

CHAPTER

Customers

Understanding and Influencing the Purchase Decision

I n Chapter 3, we learned how to prepare an appropriate financial analysis for a pricing decision. In contrast to financial techniques for cost-driven pricing, financial analysis for profit-driven pricing does not by itself determine a price. It specifies only the conditions under which a price change will be profitable. This is not a flaw of the approach, but a virtue, because it forces managers to integrate customer and competitor analysis into pricing decisions.

Pricing is not a decision that can be driven solely by the numbers. Managers who perceive it as such have usually deceived themselves into believing that neither customers nor competitors will react to their pricing decisions. Even managers who realize the importance of market reactions are sometimes taken in by financial analyses that purport to identify *the* right decision based on precise, numerical estimates of customer and competitor responses. Rather than aiding the process of strategic management, however, such analyses often muddle it by obscuring the essential uncertainty of the market.[1]

The goal of strategic planning is to proactively manage market uncertainty, not to obscure it. Financial analysis can set out the necessary conditions for a profitable pricing decision (a minimum gain or maximum loss in sales), but management must understand customers and competitors well enough to evaluate and influence the probabilities that those conditions will be met. Ultimately, good pricing decisions must be based on managerial judgment about uncertain customer and competitor reactions.

To say that pricing is a matter of judgment about market conditions is not to imply that one can successfully make decisions on "hunch" or "intuition." On the contrary, *informed* judgment is arguably what distinguishes good managers from those who wield power blindly. In this chapter we discuss guidelines for understanding how customers use price in their purchase decisions. This understanding enables managers to anticipate and influence customers' reactions to pricing decisions and to segment customers by differences in their probable reactions.

ROLE OF VALUE IN PRICING

Marketers have long admonished companies to set prices that reflect value. Unfortunately, because *value* is often poorly defined, value-based pricing is sometimes rejected as impractical. Consequently, let's begin by explaining what we mean by *value*.

In common usage, the term *value* refers to the total savings or satisfaction that the customer receives from the product. Economists refer to this as *use value*, or the *utility* gained from the product. On a hot summer day at the beach, the "use value" of something cold to drink is extremely high for most people—perhaps as high as $10 for 12 ounces of cold cola or a favorite brand of beer. That information is of little help, however, to a vendor trying to price cold drinks for thirsty sun worshipers, since few potential customers would be willing to pay such a price.

Why not? Because potential customers know that, except in rare situations, they don't have to pay a seller all that a product is really worth to them. They know that competing sellers will give them a better deal, leaving them with "consumer surplus." Perhaps they believe from prior experience that, if they wait a while, another vendor will come along selling cold beverages at prices closer to what they have come to expect from their past experience, say $1.50. Or they may know that about a half mile up the beach is a snack shop where beverages cost just $1. As a last resort, they could drive to a convenience store where they could buy an entire six-pack for only $3.49. Consequently, thirsty sun worshipers will usually reject an unusually high price as "outrageous," even when the product is worth much more to them.

So what do marketers mean when they propose pricing to reflect value? The value that is key to developing effective pricing strategy is not use value, but rather what economists call *exchange value* and what marketers call *economic value to the customer*. This value is determined first and foremost by what customers' alternatives are. Few people will pay even $2 for a cola, even if they value it at $10, if they think the market offers alternatives at substantially lower prices.

Still, only a small segment of customers insists on buying the lowest-priced alternative. It is quite likely that many people would buy a cola at the beach for $1.50, despite the availability of the same product for less at a snack shop or convenience store. By offering the product *at the beach* the vendor is pricing a "differentiated product offering" worth more than the available alternatives to some segments of the market. How much more depends on the value customers place on not having to walk up the beach to the snack shop or not having to drive to the convenience store. For some, that value is very high. They are willing to pay a lot for the convenience of not having to exert themselves. For more athletic types who wouldn't mind a jog along the beach, the premium for convenience may be much less. To ensure the patronage of that segment, the beach vendor would be wise to differentiate his or her offering in some other way that this segment values highly.

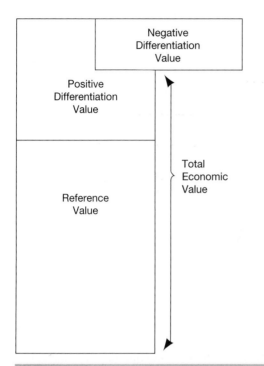

Differentiation Value is the value to the customer (both positive and negative) of any differences between your offering and the reference product.

Reference Value is the cost (adjusted for differences in units) of the competing product that the customer views as the best alternative for this one.

EXHIBIT 4-1 Economic Value Analysis

A product's "economic value," then, is *the price of the customer's best alternative* (called the *reference value*) *plus the value of whatever differentiates the offering from the alternative* (called the *differentiation value*). Differentiation value may have both positive and negative elements. Exhibit 4-1 illustrates these relationships. *Economic value* is the maximum price that a "smart shopper," fully informed about the market and seeking the best value, would pay. In fact, sophisticated business buyers often demand an *economic value estimation*™ that quantifies the benefits of high-priced brands or that shows how low-priced brands can save more than the value of the benefits given up.[2]

Often an economic value estimation™ can demonstrate value much in excess of what buyers might expect given the features of the product. A magazine publisher consistently encountered price resistance from media buyers who pointed to the lower prices of competitors. Despite the fact that the publisher's magazine had better writers, more interesting subjects for articles, nicer photography, and a more loyal and wealthier readership, advertisers still resisted its pricing. They argued that the value of the magazine's quality to them was reflected in the number of subscribers drawn to it. Since the magazine generated 11 percent more circulation than its nearest competitor, media buyers would pay no more than an 11 percent premium to run an ad. Their objections seemed quite reasonable when presented outside the context of value delivered. The

	Competing Magazine	*Our Magazine*	*Advantage*
Circulation	1,400,00	1,550,000	11%
Readers per copy	1.8	2.1	
Readership	2,520,000	3,255,000	29%
% See ad	9.20%	14.50%	
% Motivated/ad seen	1.60%	2.20%	
% Sold/motivated	20%	20%	
# Readers sold	742	2077	180%
Sales per customer	$180	$200	
Gross margin	30%	30%	
Value of ad	$40,062	$124,601	211%
Cost of ad	$29,000	$67,400	
Return on ad	$11,062	$57,201	

EXHIBIT 4-2 Economic Value Estimation™ for Advertising

picture changed radically, however, when the publisher began to think in terms of the value generated for advertisers.

Advertising's value is related to the number of readers, not just subscribers. If the magazine is interesting, it is likely to be read by the subscriber's family members and coworkers, as well as by the subscriber's customers in a waiting room. Moreover, an ad's effectiveness is related to the number of readers who actually see the ads, which they are more likely to do if they are carefully reading the articles. Once readers see the ad, what is the likelihood that they are motivated to act on it? A higher percentage of readers of this magazine were likely to be in the market for the advertiser's product than readers of the competing magazine. Finally, how much do readers spend in the advertiser's category? Is it more or less than readers of a competing magazine spend?

Answering these questions required learning more about advertisers' businesses than this magazine's publisher ever thought he needed to know. That is usually the case. Companies try to sell only the features of their products. They frequently fail to understand customers well enough to quantify the benefits even hypothetically. When they do, however, the results are often astounding. Exhibit 4-2 illustrates the impact of this magazine's superior product on the effectiveness of an advertiser's ad. Although the magazine offered only 11% more circulation, its ads were more likely to be seen, readers were more likely to be in the market for the product, and they spent more when they bought. As a result, what began as an 11% advantage in circulation ballooned to a 211% advantage in value! That difference easily justified a price per ad page more than twice that of the competition!

ECONOMIC VALUE ESTIMATION™: AN ILLUSTRATION

To determine the economic effect that a product or service can have on a business customer, a company should first determine the product's economic value.[3] The following example illustrates how this is done.[4] Du Pont, a company known for its innovation, has often faced the problem of determining economic value for a new, differentiated product. In 1955, for example, Du Pont introduced Alathon 25®, a polyethylene resin designed to compete with other resins in the manufacture of flexible pipe. Alathon had a differentiating advantage in that the pipe made with it was substantially more durable. Tests indicated that Alathon 25® pipe had failure rates of 1 to 3 percent compared with 7 to 8 percent for the competition. What, then, was the product's economic value?

To answer that question, recall that a product's economic value to a customer is the sum of two parts: its reference value and its differentiation value. The *reference value* is the cost of whatever competing product the customer views as the best substitute for the product being evaluated. The reference value equals the competing product's price, adjusted for any difference in the quantity used.

The *differentiation value* is the value of a product's attributes that are different from those of the best substitute. If the buyer likes the differentiating attributes, the differentiation value is positive. If the buyer dislikes them, the differentiation value is negative.

In the case of Alathon 25®, it is appropriate to do two economic value estimations™: one for pipe extruders who purchase Alathon and one for pipe buyers who purchase pipe made of Alathon. We look at the value estimation for pipe buyers first, since the estimation for pipe extruders depends on it.

The most common substitute for Alathon pipe was a pipe made of an off-grade resin selling for $5 to $7 per hundred feet. That is the reference value from which Du Pont would begin to calculate the total value of Alathon-based pipe. The more difficult part of the estimation involves determining differentiation value. One must study how buyers use the product and the impact of its differentiating attributes to determine their value.

Greater durability means that users have to buy less replacement pipe. That difference alone is worth a 5 to 6 percent price premium. But the differentiation value of Alathon is not simply the savings on expenditures for replacement pipe; it includes also the labor saved from not having to replace ruptured sections and from the cleanups and damages avoided. Those values will vary for different users of flexible pipe. Some buyers of flexible pipe bury it underground; others leave it exposed. The differentiation value to the former buyers will be greater, reflecting the greater cost of pipe replacement. Similarly, some buyers use the pipe to carry water, whereas others use it to carry toxic or offensive wastes. The differentiation value for the latter will be greater, reflecting the higher cost to them of postfailure cleanups. Obviously, then, there is no one economic value for a product unless all buyers use it in the same way. Each buyer segment, defined by its use of the product, has a different economic value, depending upon how the differentiating attributes affect the segment.

Let us, then, for illustration, calculate the differentiation value of Alathon for one market segment: farmers who use it as part of below-ground irrigation systems. Exhibit 4-3 illustrates the economic value of Alathon pipe for them.

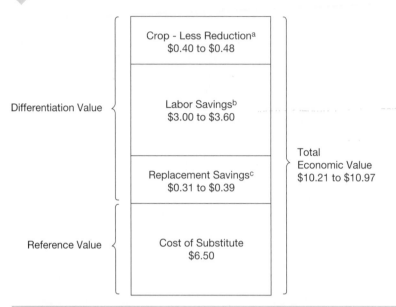

EXHIBIT 4-3 Economic Value of Alathon 25® Pipe for Below-Ground Irrigation (per Hundred Feet)

[a]$40.00 × 0.20 × 5% to 6% = $0.40 to $0.48.
[b]5% to 6% × $60.00 = $3.00 to $3.60.
[c]New value per 100 feet = ($6.50 × 1.08)/1.03 = $6.81.
Differentiation value of failure rate reduction from 8% to 3% = $6.81 − 6.50 − $0.31,
or
New value per 100 feet = ($6.50 × 1.07)/1.01 − $6.89.
Differentiation value of failure rate reduction from 7% to 1% = $6.89 − $6.50 = $0.39.

For that purpose, farmers use a pipe thickness that sells for $6.50 per hundred feet when it is made of off-grade resins. They save $0.31 to $0.39 per hundred feet by not having to purchase as much pipe for replacement. The labor cost of replacing a failed pipe is about $60, so a 5 to 6 percent lower failure rate raises Alathon's differentiation value by $3 to $3.60 per hundred feet. Pipe failures, if not detected quickly, can also damage crops. Crop damage per failure might range from nothing, if the failure occurred after plants were mature and well rooted, to $40 if vulnerable seedlings were washed out. Since young, poorly rooted crops are in place approximately 20 percent of the time that the irrigation system is in use, reduced crop damage would add at least $0.40 to the differentiation value of Alathon pipe ($40 × 0.20 × 0.05). Thus, for this segment, the total economic value of Alathon pipe would be in the range of $10.21 to $10.96 per hundred feet.

Du Pont does not sell flexible pipe; it sells the Alathon from which pipe is made. Thus, the next step is to calculate the economic value of Alathon to extruders who make such pipe for farmers. The calculation is illustrated in Exhibit 4-4.

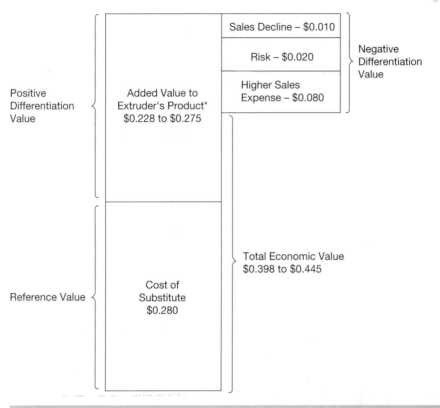

EXHIBIT 4-4 Economic Value of Alathon 25® for Pipe Extruders (per Pound)

*It takes 16.25 pounds of Alathon to make 100 feet of pipe ($4.55/$0.28 = 16.25). Thus, the added value of Alathon pipe per pound of Alathon is (at minimum)($10.21 − $6.50)/16.25 = $0.228 per pound.

The reference value is the cost of the less durable commodity resin, which was $0.28 per pound. That resin enabled an extruder to make a $6.50 pipe for a resin cost of about $4.55. By making the same pipe with Alathon, however, the extruder could produce a product with a value to buyers of $10.21 to $10.96. That adds $0.228 to $0.275 per pound to the differentiation value of Alathon. For extruders, however, there are also some drawbacks to selling Alathon. Because buyers must buy less of it for replacement of failures, an extruder may suffer reduced profits from fewer sales. Given the extruder's contribution of $1.95 per hundred feet of pipe, that corresponds to a negative differentiation value of about $0.01 per pound. Extruders might also expect to be compensated for the risks of having to deal with a single supply source, reducing differentiation value by another $0.02 per pound. Finally, they will encounter higher selling costs for the new pipe, representing about $0.08 per pound.[5] Consequently, the economic value of Alathon for extruders of farm irrigation pipe is $0.384 to $0.480 per pound.

It is important to remember that the economic value derived from this procedure is not necessarily the perceived value that a buyer would actually place on the product. A buyer may be unaware of a product and thus remain influenced by its price (the reference price effect, discussed below). A buyer may be unsure of a product's differentiating attributes and may be unwilling to invest the time and expense to learn about them (the difficult comparison effect). If the product's price is small, the buyer may make an impulse purchase without really thinking about its economic value (the expenditure effect). Similarly, other effects can influence price sensitivity in ways that undermine the influence that economic value has on the purchase decision. A product's market value is determined not only by the product's economic value, but also by the accuracy with which buyers perceive that value and by how much importance they place on getting the most for their money.

This limitation of economic value estimation™ is both a weakness and a strength. It is a weakness in that economic value cannot indicate the appropriate price to charge but only the maximum price that a segment of buyers would pay if they were perfectly cognizant of the product's economic value and motivated by that value in making their purchase decisions. It is also a strength, however, in that it enables a firm to determine whether a product is selling poorly because it is overpriced relative to its true value or because it is underpromoted and thus unappreciated by the market. The only solution to the former problem is to cut price. A better solution to the latter problem is often to maintain or even increase price while aggressively educating the market. That is precisely what Du Pont did with Alathon. After years of cutting Alathon's price to build sales with little success, Du Pont raised its price from $0.355 to $0.380 per pound while at the same time beginning an aggressive marketing campaign. Sales doubled in the following year, as buyers became aware of Alathon's superior economic value to them.

Economic Value Profile

The analysis of economic value shown above was for one segment in Du Pont's total market for Alathon. However, an understanding of only one segment is no basis for formulating a pricing strategy. To determine the role that price should play in a product's marketing, one must determine the economic value of all the segments that comprise the market, as well as the size of each segment. With that information, one can develop an *economic value profile* of the market and determine what market segments can be served most profitably.

Exhibit 4-5 illustrates a hypothetical economic value profile for Alathon. The profile is built from economic value analyses for each of the potential market segments to which the product might be sold. It enables a manager to determine at what price level the product is price competitive for each market segment. The segments are identified by the factors that determine the different ways potential buyers value the product. In this case, the type of buyer (industrial, farming, plumbing), as well as the use for which the buyer purchases the

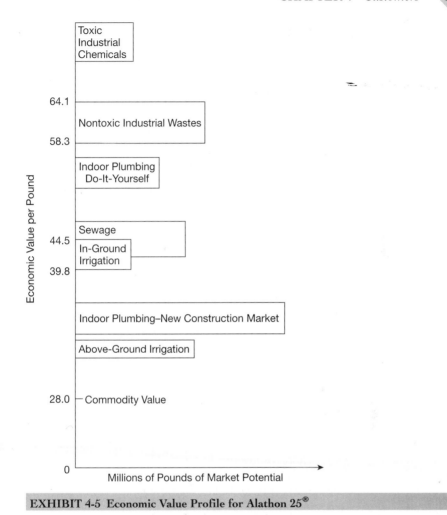

EXHIBIT 4-5 Economic Value Profile for Alathon 25®

product (in-ground versus above-ground irrigation, toxic versus nontoxic chemical transmission), affects the value of the product's differentiating attributes.

The Use of Economic Value Estimation™

Economic value estimation is an especially good sales tool when buyers are facing extreme cost pressures and are, therefore, very price sensitive. Since health-care reimbursement systems were changed to give hospitals and doctors a financial incentive to practice cost-effective medicine, pharmaceutical companies have been forced to go beyond their traditional claims that a product is more clinically effective. Some now offer purchasers elaborate tests to show that differentials in effectiveness are worth the differentials in price. For example, Amgen Inc.'s Neuprogen®, a drug to prevent infections in chemotherapy patients, initially appeared expensive at $1,000 per course of treatment. Amgen successfully countered strong customer resistance by demonstrating that preventing the risk of infection was worth at least $6,000 per treatment in avoided hospital costs.

There are no shortcuts to understanding economic value before setting prices. Many companies shortchange themselves by assuming that if their differentiated product is "x" percent more effective than the competition, then the product will be worth only "x" percent more in price. While this relationship makes sense superficially, more careful examination proves how dangerously wrong it is. If you had cancer and knew of a drug that was 50 percent more effective than the competition's in curing your disease, would you refuse to pay more than a 50 percent higher price? Suppose you were planning to paint your house and discovered a tool that would enable you to finish the job in half the usual time—a doubling of your productivity. Would you pay no more than twice the price of a brush?

As these examples illustrate, the price premium associated with the economic value of a product is often much greater than the percentage increase in technical efficiency. The economic value of a differentiated product is proportional to its technical efficiency only when a buyer can receive the benefits associated with a superior product simply by buying more of the reference product. That would be the case only if using 50 percent more of the competitive cancer drug or painting with two brushes at the same time would produce the same increase in efficiency as using the superior products.[6]

Exhibit 4-6 summarizes the steps necessary to determine economic value. In business markets, where the value of the product translates directly into financial savings or increased revenues for the purchaser, and in some consumer markets, where the value represents cost savings, it is possible to calculate economic value objectively. Where values are less tangible, quantifying value is more difficult. One must frequently rely on inferences made from the pricing of products offering similar differential benefits or on choice-based research techniques—such as trade-off analysis and simulated test markets. When doing so, however, we are substituting willingness to pay as a proxy for economic value—which risks underestimating the true value we deliver.

For uninformed and inexperienced buyers, prices should not be set low enough to meet their depressed willingness to pay. Rather, a value communication strategy—involving advertising, personal sales, programs to induce trial, guarantees and endorsements that minimize perceived risk—should be put in place to raise their willingness to pay to a level comparable to that of better informed and experienced buyers.

FACTORS INFLUENCING PERCEPTIONS OF VALUE

The goal of value-based pricing is to maximize a company's ability to capture the economic value it creates in the profits it earns. If purchasers knew everything about the products offered and their own needs, if they could easily determine

Step 1: Identify the cost of the competitive product or process that the customer views as the best alternative.
Restate the cost of the alternative in terms of units of the product for which you are calculating economic value. This is the product's *reference value*, or value if it were functionally identical to the current product. For example, if one unit of your product replaces two of theirs, then the reference value for your product is the cost of two units of their product.

Step 2: Identify all factors that differentiate your product from the competitive product or process. For example:

- Superior (inferior) performance
- Better (poorer) reliability
- Additional (reduced) features
- Lower (higher) maintenance cost
- Superior (inferior) reliability
- Higher (lower) startup costs
- Faster (slower) service

Step 3: Determine the value to the customer of these differentiating factors. Sources of value may be subjective (for example, greater pleasure in consuming the product) or objective (for example, cost savings, profit gains).
The positive and negative values associated with the product's differentiating attributes comprise the *differentiation value.*

Warnings

- Consider only the value of the *difference* between this product and the alternative. For example, both products may be highly effective, but only the difference in their effectiveness is differentiation value. The economic value of anything that is the same is already captured in reference value.
- Measure the value of the difference either as costs saved to achieve a particular benefit *or* as extra benefits achieved for a given cost. Don't add both; that's double counting.
- Do not assume that the percentage increase in value is simply proportional to the percentage increase in effectiveness of your product. That usually produces a gross underestimation of the actual value to the customer.

Step 4: Sum the reference value and the differentiation value to determine the *total economic value,* the value that someone would pay who was fully informed and economically rational when making the purchase decision.
Determine the selling price, recognizing that new products must usually be priced below economic value as an inducement to purchase. The prices of established products that already have the customer's business can include a "reputation premium," analogous to the inducement that the newcomer must offer. When buyers have little ability or interest to determine economic value, or when the cost of switching suppliers is high, the factors affecting the "inducement" or "premium" may, in fact, be more important for pricing than the economic value.

EXHIBIT 4-6 Steps in Economic Value Estimation™

how the products would help them satisfy their needs, and if they did not believe they could influence the seller's prices through negotiation, then economic value would exactly predict their purchase behavior. In the real world, there are obviously many reasons for gaps between buyers' willingness to pay and the value they receive. Uncertainty, fairness, vanity, and expectations all play roles that mitigate the power of value to drive prices.[7] Value-based pricing strategy involves managing customer perceptions proactively to influence that gap between price paid and value received.

Most companies ignore value in pricing, and set prices in reaction to what customers are willing to pay without understanding what drives it. In doing so, they miss the opportunity to actively influence customer perceptions in ways that can increase their own profitability and their customers' purchase satisfaction. To do so, marketers must first understand what causes the gap between value and willingness to pay. There are nine "effects" that influence willingness to pay and cause buyers to be more or less sensitive to the difference between price and value when making purchase decisions. For each factor, there are tactics that suppliers can use to reduce the gap between the value they offer and the prices they must charge to win business.

Reference Price Effect

Economic value is recognized accurately only by customers who are fully informed about the alternatives. In the real world, customers are rarely so informed; they often flounder in a sea of information.[8] This reality has important implications both for segmenting customers and for influencing their price sensitivity. The *reference price effect* states that buyers are more price sensitive the higher the product's price relative to the prices of the buyers' perceived alternatives.

The key word here is "perceived." Perceptions of the available substitutes and their prices differ widely among customers and across purchase situations. Customers new to a market are usually less aware of the discount brands than people with more experience. Consequently, they usually pay relatively high prices and buy from the most visible suppliers. In a similar vein, restaurateurs in resort areas face far less pressure to compete on price, despite the greater concentration of restaurants in those locations, because their transient clientele is usually unaware of better alternatives. Local residents view restaurants near resort hotels as "tourist traps," precisely because they can charge higher prices than restaurants less visible to tourists but patronized by a more informed clientele.

Effective marketing efforts can position a brand as a good value by targeting customers with a high frame of reference for comparison. Chesebrough-Ponds can price its petroleum jelly 1,400 percent higher per ounce when packaged and sold as Vaseline Lip Therapy® because the perceived substitute for that positioning, Chapstick®, has a similar price. Woolite®, although expensive for a detergent, has successfully positioned itself as an inexpensive alternative to dry cleaning. Loctite Corporation positioned its powerful industrial adhesive as a substitute for nuts and bolts, enabling the company to charge a high price by the standards of its product category and still promise substantial savings for purchasers. Skytel sought to raise the perceived value of a two-way pager, which potential customers had viewed as simply an improved version of a low-cost one-way pager, by positioning it as a substitute for a cell phone (Exhibit 4-7). In this last case, note that Skytel is not even claiming that a pager is a replacement for a cell phone. It is simply, but effectively, using the cost of a cell phone as a favorable basis for comparison.

The method of product distribution can influence the buyers' perception of substitutes. As sales via the Internet replace catalog shopping, some customers are much more informed, and therefore more sensitive about the value of the deal being offered. With a catalog, a consumer who found something she liked usually had little ability to efficiently identify competing offers. Internet "shopping robots," at sites such as DealTime (www.dealtime.com) and R U Sure (www.rusure.com), can easily identify better deals in minutes.

Within stores, sellers can influence buyers' knowledge of substitutes by the method of display. When generic grocery products first became available, some stores placed them beside the corresponding branded products, whereas others placed the generics in a separate section. The sales of low-priced generic products were much greater—and sales of higher-priced branded items correspondingly lower—in stores where the generic and branded products were placed side by side for easy comparison. It is unlikely that Jelly Belly could sustain its premium prices for gourmet, all-natural jelly beans if they were sold in grocery stores next to cheap alternatives. Instead, Jelly Belly relies on sales through specialty and gift stores where the alternatives are gourmet chocolates or fruit baskets.

In personal selling, the reference price effect implies that the salesperson should begin by first showing customers products above their price range, even if the customers will ultimately look at cheaper products as well.[9] This tactic, known as top-down selling, is common in sales of products as diverse as automobiles, luggage, and real estate. Direct-mail catalogs take advantage of this effect by displaying similar products in the order of most to least expensive. Within a retail store, the order effect has implications for product display. It implies, for example, that a grocery store may sell more low-priced (but high-margin) house brands by *not* putting them at eye level where they would be the first to catch the customer's attention. Rather, it may be preferable to have consumers see more expensive brands first and then look to the house brands.

A buyer's reference price is also influenced by recall of prices seen in the past. This has important implications for pricing new products. Many marketing theorists have argued that new products should be priced low to induce trial and thus build a market of repeat purchasers, after which price can be raised. However, if the low initial price lowers buyers' reference prices, it may actually adversely affect some repeat sales. This is precisely the result that some researchers have found. In one well-controlled study,[10] five new brands were introduced to the market in two sets of stores. During an introductory period, one set of stores sold the new brands at a low price without any indication that this

Reason #8 why you need SkyTel even if you have a Cell Phone:

SOMETIMES YOU'D RATHER BE INFORMED FOR 5¢ THAN INTERRUPTED FOR 10¢.

Introducing SkyTel 5: get a message and respond for just 5ᶜ.

The problem with cell phones is that they can ring at the most inconvenient times. And when you answer, you're no longer in control of your time—the caller is. Maybe he'll want to waste time shooting the breeze before he gets to the point. Maybe he's not someone you were ready to talk to just yet. Or maybe you have something or someone more pressing to deal with right now. But with SkyTel interactive messaging, you're in control. A simple text message or e-mail keeps you informed. You can even choose to reply right from your pager. And while cellular companies are bragging about 10¢ a minute, SkyTel is nationwide, toll-free, guaranteed and just 5¢ a message! So get SkyTel. And get informed, not interrupted.

Call 1-800-395-6270 or visit www.skytel.com

5ᶜ messages up to 100 characters. Some restrictions may apply. ©1999 SkyTel.

EXHIBIT 4-7 Establishing a Reference

was a temporary promotional price; other control stores sold the new brands at the regular price. As expected, the brands sold better during the introductory period where they were priced lower. During the weeks following the introduction, however, both sets of stores charged the regular price. In all five cases, sales during the postintroductory period were lower in the experimental stores than in the control stores. Moreover, total sales for the introductory and postintroductory periods combined were greater in the control stores than in the stores where the low price initially stimulated demand. This, and other studies showing similar results, demonstrates the importance of dealing tactics such as coupons, rebates, and special packages that minimize this effect by clearly establishing a product's regular price and offering lower prices only as special discounts. Otherwise, initially low promotional prices can establish low reference prices for judging the value of later purchases.

A customer's perception of the available substitutes is not necessarily based on awareness of specific brands and exact prices. Given the number of product categories and brands from which most people make purchases, maintaining awareness of such a vast amount of information would be impossible, even for the most educated and diligent customer. Consequently, for many product categories, a customer simply maintains a general expectation of a price level that seems reasonable. Psychologists call this expectation the customer's *reference price expectation* for the category.

We know from managerial experience and controlled experiments that these reference price expectations are manageable at the point of sale. For example, a business machine company with three models in its line found the sales of the top-end model disappointing. The company believed that many customers who should have valued the extra features of this high-production machine were instead buying the mid-priced model. Management's initial assumption was that the high-end model must be overpriced. After talking with customers in the appropriate segment, however, they learned that most did not think that the product was overpriced. They simply could not overcome the objections of the financial officer that the company did not need "the most expensive model." The solution: The company added a fourth, even more expensive model to its line. The new model sold very poorly, but sales of what was previously the top-end model increased dramatically.

In some cases, a buyer's reference price depends on his or her expectation about future prices.[11] The effect of future price expectations on a buyer's current reference price will be positively related to that buyer's ability to delay purchase into the future. Products maintained in inventories that can be temporarily drawn down, and durable goods for which there is some discretion regarding when to replace them, will often meet this criterion. Auto companies experienced this when they offered temporary "rebates" on car prices. Initially, the rebates appeared to drive up demand much more than simply reducing prices. The reason for that appearance, however, was that the rebate made the lower prices explicitly temporary. Consequently, they caused people to accelerate purchases they would have eventually made at higher prices. By using rebates repeatedly, auto companies educated auto buyers to wait for the next rebate, even when they otherwise would have purchased sooner at a higher price.

Companies in business markets sometimes create this same downward pressure on prices when they regularly discount prices at the ends of a quarter or year in order to meet sales goals.[12]

Difficult Comparison Effect

The concept of economic value assumes not only that customers are aware of alternatives but that they can cheaply and accurately evaluate what the alternative suppliers have to offer. In fact, it is often quite difficult to determine the true attributes of a product or service prior to purchase. For example, consumers suffering from a headache may be aware of many alternative pain relievers that are cheaper than their usual brand and that claim to be equally effective, but if they are unsure that a cheaper brand is as effective or as free of unwanted side effects as the one they usually buy, they will consider it an inferior substitute even though it could be chemically identical. Most customers will continue paying a higher price for the assurance that their regular brand offers what the substitutes do not: the confidence accumulated from past experience that their brand can do what the others only promise to do.

Even price itself can be difficult to compare across brands, thus reducing price sensitivity. Catalog and Internet retailers often divide their prices into two parts: one part for the items plus a fixed or variable charge for "shipping and handling." Research shows a wide variance among customers in their ability to make accurate comparisons with the single prices offered by traditional stores.[13] Similarly, branded grocery products are often packaged in odd shapes and sizes, making price comparisons with cheaper brands difficult. When, however, stores offer unit pricing (showing the price of all products by the ounce or gallon), grocery shoppers can readily identify the cheaper brands. In one study of unit pricing, the market shares of cheaper brands increased substantially after stores ranked brands by their unit prices.[14]

These examples illustrate the *difficult comparison effect:* Buyers are less sensitive to the price of a known or more reputable product when they have difficulty comparing it to potential alternatives. Rather than attempting to find the best value in the market and risk getting a poor value in the process, many buyers simply settle for what they are confident will be a satisfactory purchase. Their confidence in the brand's reputation may be based either on their own experience with the brand or on the experience of other people whose judgment they trust. Even in business markets, professional buyers will often develop loyal relationships with a list of "approved suppliers" with whom they have had previously satisfactory experience.

The difficult comparison effect is strongest where the product or service is difficult to evaluate and the risk of failure is high. Examples of suppliers whose prices and profitability rest on the trust that consumers associate with their names are AT&T, the *New York Times,* IBM, and John Deere. The trust for which buyers will pay price premiums is not that sellers of these products will necessarily provide the highest quality, but rather that they will consistently provide the good quality that buyers have come to expect from them. Even on the Internet, most people who buy on-line do so from merchants whom they already know, including the traditional "brick and mortar" retailers, despite lower prices from unknown competitors.

Because the difficult comparison effect causes value to be associated with known brand names, market researchers often treat the brand name as a product attribute. Managers of those brands need to realize, however, that there is rarely any inherent value in a name. Its value depends upon the difficulty of making product comparisons and the perceived risk associated with trying an unknown supplier. Consequently, its value may be ephemeral. IBM traditionally enjoyed more than a 20 percent price premium because of its enviable reputation for integrity and service. Customers paid the premium because they feared buying a costly mainframe from a competitor and finding its reliability or performance inadequate. The premium predictably declined, however, as personal and minicomputers replaced mainframes. The risk of trying a new computer supplier is vastly reduced when the trial can be limited to just a small piece of the company's operations and computing capacity. Anything that reduces the buyers' cost of evaluating alternatives (for example, objective quality ratings such as those done by *Consumer Reports*, unit price information, or small trial sizes) will minimize the importance of past experience and increase buyers' willingness to try brands that promise a better value.

There are numerous tactics that a new supplier or a known supplier of a new, untried technology can use to minimize the difficult comparison effect. One is simply to minimize visible differences that could lead consumers to believe that there might be more substantive differences. House brands of over-the-counter medicines and grocery products will copy the shape, size, and color of the packaging of a well-known branded product with the added message "Compare active ingredients with [the branded substitute]." Another effective tactic is to reduce the cost of sampling the product to give customers the experience they need to evaluate it. Coupons, free samples, and money-back guarantees are all ways to minimize the cost of trying new products without cutting the explicit price for making purchases. E-Trade.com offered a $100 deposit in any new brokerage account, and AOL.com offered a month of free usage to induce hesitant buyers to sample.

This effect can particularly undermine willingness to pay when the seller is an untested supplier of an expensive asset. Often a lease option is the way to overcome this, since customers are willing to pay much more for capital equipment and automobiles over the life of a short-term lease than they would for the outright purchase of an untried brand. This is because they are putting less money at risk if the product proves unsatisfactory. If, however, the product proves to be as good as promised, they can extend the lease or purchase the product outright at the end of the lease.

Companies with new products for which they are trying to build cash flow often make the mistake of building the start-up cost of acquiring and servicing a new customer into a large, up-front fee. Because high uncertainty undermines perceived value, such companies lose potential sales and win sales only at lower prices than they otherwise could. By absorbing the up-front cost in higher monthly fees, the seller communicates confidence that customers will be satisfied and enables customers to pay as they enjoy a known value from product usage. Consequently, the seller should close more sales and, assuming that the product or service delivers the promised value so that the customer continues to buy it, the seller can ultimately expect a greater cash flow and a higher net present value (NPV) per customer acquired.

Switching Cost Effect

The greater the added cost (both monetary and nonmonetary) of switching suppliers, the less sensitive buyers are to the price of a product. The reason for this effect is that many products require that the buyer make product-specific investments to use them. If those investments do not need to be repeated when buying from the current supplier, but do when buying from a new supplier, that difference is a switching cost that limits interbrand price sensitivity. For example, airlines are reluctant to change suppliers from, say, Boeing to Airbus planes, because of the added cost to retrain their mechanics and to invest in a stock of new spare parts. Once an airline begins buying from a supplier, it takes a very attractive offer from a competitor to induce them to switch. Similarly, even personal relationships can represent a significant intangible investment that limits the attractiveness of a competing offer. For example, busy executives must invest considerable time in developing a rapport with their accountants, lawyers, and childcare providers. Once these "investments" are made, they are reluctant to repeat them simply because otherwise equally qualified suppliers offer a lower price.

This is the *switching cost effect:* The greater the product-specific investment that a buyer must make to switch suppliers, the less price sensitive that buyer is when choosing between alternatives. Since this effect is often attributed simply to consumer "inertia," it is easy to underestimate its predictability and manageability. In fact, even highly rational, value-seeking consumers are influenced by it. In the 1990s, Digital Equipment's Alpha semiconductor failed to capture much market share, despite being faster and cheaper than competitive chips from Intel. Why? Because designing computers to accommodate a new standard requires learning anew how to solve multiple design problems that engineers had already solved years ago for Intel chips. The switching cost overwhelmed the attractiveness of the Alpha's otherwise better value proposition.

At the time of this writing, Amazon.com commands a stock market capitalization more than ten times its revenue, despite negative earnings. Amazon, and many stock analysts, argue that this is justified by the switching cost effect. Although it costs Amazon a lot to acquire the new customers that drive its rapid revenue growth, Amazon's use of technology to understand customer preferences and help them shop more efficiently may make those customers exceptionally loyal. The more a customer has already shopped with Amazon, the higher the level of service Amazon can provide. Since Amazon's competitors will be unable to provide such a high level of service to new customers, Amazon hopes to retain them even if competitors match or undercut its prices.

We should note, however, that the loyalty associated with switching costs is not necessarily permanent. Whenever complementary investments become obsolete, price sensitivity will increase just as if they had never been made. Much is made of the huge advantage Microsoft enjoys because customers and software developers have already invested in Windows-based architecture. Consequently, there is almost no price that competing operating systems suppliers could charge that would be low enough to get people to switch. However, when technology changes to Web-based computing, to voice-activated computing, or to any other technology that requires relearning and rewriting of software, the Microsoft advantage will disappear.

Aspiring suppliers often absorb part of the switching cost in order to eliminate this effect. They should not do this simply by offering a lower price, however, since then they must give the discount even to previous customers who are not incurring a switching cost. The key is to target the discount selectively to new customers without lowering the price expectation. New suppliers do this by providing free training, by giving generous "trade-in allowances" to customers who replace competitive equipment, or by giving a discount on the first order placed under a long-term contract.

Price-Quality Effect

Generally, price represents nothing more than the money a buyer must give to a seller as part of a purchase agreement. For a few products, however, price means much more. Such products fall into three categories: image products, exclusive products, and products without any other cues to their relative quality. In these cases, price is more than just a burden; it is also a signal of the value a buyer can expect to receive. In such cases, price sensitivity is influenced by the *price-quality effect,* which states that buyers are less sensitive to a product's price to the extent that a higher price signals better quality.

A buyer might use price as a quality signal for a number of reasons. Consider what motivates the purchase of the Rolls-Royce automobile, an obvious image product. One would be hard-pressed to argue that the Rolls offers a value superior to that of luxury cars costing much less. Its parts are less uniform, and the cost of maintenance is very high because a Rolls is handmade. The problems with the Rolls are the ones that mass production was meant to solve: problems of consistency and cost. But Rolls buyers do not purchase the car for cost-effective transportation any more than they buy a Patek Philippe watch to tell time. They buy these items to communicate to others that they can afford them.

People often value such symbols when the product reflects on them personally. Consequently, brands that can offer the consumer *prestige* in addition to the direct benefits of consumption can, and must, command higher prices than similar, less prestigious products. For example, a "gold" credit card costs from 50 to 200 percent more than the less prestigious credit cards issued by the same companies. Purchasers' price sensitivity decreases to the degree that they value the recognition or ego gratification the card gives them. Prestige is more influential for some purchases than for others. For example, a store's prestige image is more important when buying a gift than when buying an item for personal use.

A prestige image is only one reason that buyers might find a more expensive purchase more satisfying. The exclusivity that discourages some people from buying at a high price can, in addition to image, add objectively to the value. Many professionals—doctors, dentists, attorneys, and hairdressers—set high prices to reduce their clientele, enabling them to schedule clients farther apart. This ensures that each client will be served without delay at his or her appointed time, a valuable service for busy people. Some business travelers fly first class, not only because of the legroom or the food, but because the high price reduces the probability of sitting next to a small child or loquacious vacationer who might interfere with the work they must do in flight. Even public restrooms sometimes have pay stalls alongside free ones. The exclusivity resulting from a high price is itself desirable when consuming these products.

Often, the perception of higher quality at higher prices reduces price sensitivity even when consumers seek neither prestige nor exclusivity. This occurs when potential buyers cannot ascertain the objective quality of a product before purchase *and* lack other cues, such as a known brand name, a country of origin, or a trusted endorsement to guide their decision—for example, the name of a restaurant in a strange location, a folk artist at a fair, or a totally new brand with which the buyer has no prior experience. In such cases, consumers will rely somewhat on relative price as a cue to a product's relative quality, apparently assuming that the higher price is probably justified by corresponding higher value.

As an illustration of how strong this effect can be, researchers have reported cases where a new synthetic car wax faced strong consumer resistance until its price was raised. Similarly, sales of new creamy-style cheesecake were poor until the company raised the price to equal that of its heavy (and more costly to produce) regular-style cheesecake. Buyers could not judge the quality of either product before purchase. Consequently, buyers played it safe by avoiding cheap products that they believed were more likely to be inferior.

Extreme cases such as these, where sales respond positively to a higher price, are admittedly rare. They lead one to expect, however, that in other cases sales simply respond less negatively to a higher price than they would if buyers did not associate a higher price with higher expected quality. Numerous studies[15] have shown that, even when the objective quality of a brand is unaffected by its price, consumers use price as a quality cue to the degree that:

1. they believe qualities differ among brands within the product class.
2. they perceive that low quality imposes the risk of a large loss.
3. they lack other information (such as a known brand name) enabling them to evaluate quality before purchase.

	At $1.59 (%)	At $2.29 (%)	Difference (%)
Test 1: Intention to try after concept description			
Definitely would buy	13	13	0
Probably would buy	46	46	0
Might/might not buy	30	30	0
Probably would not buy	9	8	1
Definitely would not buy	2	3	−1
Test 2: Intention to buy after in-home use			
Definitely would buy	34	24	10
Probably would buy	30	24	6
Might/might not buy	10	16	−6
Probably would not buy	14	12	2
Definitely would not buy	12	23	−11

EXHIBIT 4-8 Effect of Price on Purchase Intention for a Product of Unknown Quality

Source: Courtesy of BASES Division, Burke Marketing Services, Inc.

The more consumers must rely on price to judge quality, the less price sensitive they will be. For most purchase decisions, consumers can either examine a product before purchase or infer its quality from past experience with the brand (the difficult comparison effect). Studies indicate that under these conditions, price is not used as a quality cue.[16] Nevertheless, the conditions for using price as a quality cue occur in one very important case: when new products are first offered to a market.

Market researchers frequently observe a low level of buyer price sensitivity for new products. Exhibit 4-8 shows the results of a typical pricing study for a new household product. In the first test, the product was described for buyers who were then asked if they intended to try it when it became available. There was no significant difference in stated purchase intention between those buyers who were told that the product would cost $1.59 and those who were told it would cost $2.29. In a second test, however, buyers who expressed an interest in the product were given a supply to take home. After using the product, they were asked the same questions regarding their purchase intention when the product became available. In this case, a higher price caused purchase intentions to decline significantly. A more recent study on the effect of discounting shows that while large discounts increase sales of familiar brands, they can actually undermine the sales of brands unfamiliar to the consumer.[17]

Expenditure Effect

A buyer's willingness to evaluate alternatives depends also on how large the expenditure is relative to the effort necessary to reduce it. For businesses, this effect is determined by the absolute size of the expenditure; for households, it is determined by the size of the expenditure relative to the available income. The *expenditure effect* states that buyers are more price sensitive when the expenditure is larger, either in dollar terms or as a percentage of household income. The more a buyer spends, the greater the gain from carefully evaluating the expenditure and attempting to find a better deal. This explains why the same person will sometimes shop at an expensive convenience store (for a small purchase) but be very sensitive to price when deciding where to go for the weekly shopping excursion.[18] This partially explains why heating insulation costs much more when sold to maintenance men in lots of twenty-five feet than when sold to building contractors by truckloads of tens of thousands of feet. At the other extreme, small "impulse purchases" are simply not worth any effort to ensure that the price is a good deal. Consequently, percentage price differences across suppliers are often very large.

The effect of the expenditure size on price sensitivity is confounded in consumer markets by the effect of income. A family with five children may spend substantially more on food than a smaller family, yet still be less price sensitive if the cost of food accounts for a smaller portion of the large family's higher income. This relationship between a buyer's price sensitivity and the percentage of income devoted to the product results from the trade-off buyers must make between conserving their limited income and conserving the limited time they have to shop. Higher-income buyers can afford a wider variety of goods but cannot always afford more time to shop for them. Consequently, they cannot afford to shop as carefully as lower-income buyers, and so they accept higher prices as a substitute for time spent shopping.[19]

The expenditure size relative to income is also a constraint on both a business's and a household's primary demand for a product. A young man may long for a sports car, believing that a Porsche clearly has differentiating attributes that justify its premium price relative to similar cars. An economic value estimation™ of sports cars would reveal his decided preference and belief that the Porsche offers a "good value" relative to other sports cars. At his low income, however, he is not making purchase decisions among competing sports cars. Expenditures in other purchase categories (housing, food, and education) are of higher importance than a sports car, and those categories currently consume his income. Until his income rises, or the price of sports cars becomes much less, his brand preference within the category is not relevant.

End-Benefit Effect

An individual purchase is often one of many that a buyer makes to achieve a single benefit. Cream cheese is one of several products that a cook must buy to make a cheesecake. Software is just one component of a computer system, the cost of which may be minor compared to the cost of processor, modem, data storage, etc. The relationship of a purchase to a larger benefit is the basis of the *end benefit effect,* which can be divided into two parts: the derived demand and the price proportion. *Derived demand* is the relationship between a desired end benefit and the buyer's price sensitivity for one of the products that contributes toward achieving that end benefit. The more sensitive buyers are to the cost of the end benefit, the more sensitive they will be to the price of products that contribute to that end benefit. In the examples above, the more price sensitive the buyer is about the decision to make a cheesecake or build a computer system, the more price sensitive she will be to the cost of cream cheese or disk storage devices. *Price proportion cost* refers to the percent of the total cost of the end benefit accounted for by the product's price. The smaller the proportionate share accounted for, the less sensitive the customer will be to price differences. If the price of cream cheese or software accounts for only 10 percent of the cost of a cheesecake or a computer system, even a doubling of price increases the cost of the end benefit by only 5 percent.

Derived demand is most obvious in business markets. The more (less) price sensitive the demand for a company's own product, the more (less) price sensitive that company will be when purchasing supplies. A manufacturer of office furniture purchases sheet steel from which it makes desks. The more desks it can sell, the more steel it will buy. If desk buyers were highly price sensitive, any attempt to pass on steel price increases to the price of desks would cause a large reduction in sales. Consequently, the high price sensitivity of desk buyers would force the desk manufacturer to be highly sensitive to the cost of its desks and, therefore, to the price of steel.

Imagine how the manufacturer's purchase behavior would change, however, if booming demand were to cause an order backlog to lengthen and customers to lose leverage in negotiating desk prices. Since the manufacturer could now more easily pass on added costs to the customer, its goal in purchasing would become less to save money on supplies and more to ensure on-time and defect-free deliveries to keep the manufacturing process running smoothly. It is essential for salespeople in business markets to understand the end benefit that drives a customer's purchase decision (is it cost minimization, maximum output, quality improvement, civic mindedness, or what?) in order to infer the importance of price in the purchase decision.

The relationship between price sensitivity for a product and for the end benefit to which it contributes is not simply an economic phenomenon. There is a strong psychological component that depends on how a buyer perceives the absolute price, or price difference, in proportion to the total cost of the end benefit. Consider how you would respond in each of the following situations if you were a purchasing agent:[20]

- *Scenario A:* You have ordered a new personal computer, which will cost $1,000. You discover that the identical computer is available on the Web from a reliable vendor for only $600. Would you cancel the current order and switch to the other vendor?
- *Scenario B:* You have ordered a computer server, which will cost $20,000. You discover that the identical server is available on the Web from a reliable vendor for only $19,600. Would you cancel the current order and switch to the other vendor?

(In either case, assume that canceling the current order and initiating a new one will take a purchasing clerk one hour and that there are no other costs such as loss of goodwill or delay in delivery.)

Since in both scenarios the amount that could be saved is $400, a purely rational purchaser would compare the benefit to the cost and make the same decision in either case. In fact, most people see these two situations quite differently. When a version of these questions was asked of business executives, who are presumably more rational than the typical purchaser, 89 percent were willing to switch vendors in version A, but only 52 percent were willing to do so in version B. The price difference, $400, seems more important for a $1,000 purchase than for a $20,000 purchase. The results were even more striking when less sophisticated purchasers were asked a similar question regarding the opportunity to save $5 on a calculator. If the calculator cost $15, 68 percent of respondents were willing to drive to another store to save $5; but if it cost $125, only 29 percent of the respondents were willing to do so.[21]

This proportioned price effect states that customers are more price sensitive whenever the purchase price accounts for a larger proportion of the cost of the end benefit and less price sensitive for a small proportion. The total cost of the end benefit may include the cost of purchasing other products as well as the monetary and nonmonetary costs of shopping. This effect points toward opportunities to charge very high prices for products sold to complement much larger expenditures. For example, most people are willing to pay much more for options when added to the purchase price of a new car than if they were to purchase those same options separately. Zymol "vegetarian" car wax, which produces an exceptional shine, is targeted toward owners of BMWs, Rolls-Royces, and classic cars, for whom the total cost of auto ownership is exceptionally high; consequently, they hardly notice the $40 price per eight-ounce jar.[22]

To fully appreciate the marketing implications of the end-benefit effect, managers need to recognize that it is both an economic and a psychological phenomenon. Consider how you would react if, after celebrating a very special occasion at a nice restaurant, your beloved paid for it with a two-for-one discount coupon. Unless you are an economist, this action would probably be seen as rather unromantic. Most people think it tacky to make choices based on price when an end benefit is emotionally important to them. Moreover, one must also recognize that the "total cost" of the end benefit need not be only monetary. Dieters are less sensitive to price than nondieters when treating themselves to chocolates or ice cream because the dollar expenditure is only a small part of the total cost (both monetary and nonmonetary) that they pay for this treat.

The psychological aspects of this effect make it an excellent target for promotional activity. Once a brand is established in customers' minds as somehow "better," advertisers can increase the value of that perceived difference by relating it to end benefits to which the customer already attaches a high value. Michelin ran a very successful advertising campaign for more than a decade that associated purchase of its premium-priced tires with the safety of one's family. The attached message: Buy Michelin (despite the price) because "so much is riding on your tires." Promotional campaigns are frequently designed to portray a purchase as just a small part of a larger end benefit that makes the cost of purchase seem relatively inconsequential. Hammermill ran a series of advertisements portraying the extra cost of its copier paper as trivial when compared with the cost of the copier, or with the cost of the time of those people whose productivity depends on it. Similarly, Mobil Oil positions the cost of its premium-priced Mobil 1® motor oil as well-justified considering the price of the car that the oil is intended to protect.

Shared-cost Effect

Although the portion of the benefit accounted for by the product's price is an important determinant of price sensitivity, so also is the portion of that price actually paid by the buyer. People purchase many products that are actually paid for in whole or in part by someone else. Insurance covers a share of the buyer's cost of a doctor's visit or a prescription drug. Tax deductions cover a share of the cost of publications, educational seminars, and travel related to one's profession. Businesses usually compensate employee travelers for all or part of their travel and entertainment expenses. College-bound students often choose an expensive private school knowing that a scholarship or a generous relative will cover all or part of the tuition. In each case, the smaller the portion of the purchase price buyers must pay themselves, the less price sensitive they are. The effect of partial or complete reimbursement on price sensitivity is called the *shared-cost effect*.

This effect has led to some interesting marketing strategies to reduce price sensitivity. Airlines and hotels offer frequent customer awards which business customers value more highly than a price cut, which would benefit their employers but not them. Tour operators design luxury travel packages to exotic destinations that include training in new dental procedures or lectures on the latest medical research. Dentists and physicians, who are required to take a specified number of hours of training to maintain their licenses and who are in high marginal tax brackets, are inclined to indulge themselves when the trip is deductible. Business schools charge much more per class hour for "Executive MBA" programs, often including luxurious facilities and trips abroad, since employers usually cover the cost of the courses.

Fairness Effect

The concept of a "fair price" has bedeviled marketers for centuries. In the Dark Ages, merchants were put to death for exceeding public norms regarding the "just price." In the more recent dark history of Communism, those who "profiteered" by charging more than the official prices—those very prices at which the state was unable to meet demand—were regarded as criminals. Even in modern market economies, "price gougers" are often criticized in the press, hassled by regulators, and boycotted by the public. Consequently, it is well worth a marketer's time to understand and attempt to manage this phenomenon.

BOX 4-1

Will the Internet Drive Down Prices?

Creating a pricing strategy often requires that managers make qualitative judgments about changes or differences in price sensitivity, often without the benefit of quantitative estimates. The Internet created exactly such a challenge. With more and more commerce moving to the Web, both merchants and manufacturers have struggled with the question "Will customers be more or less price sensitive when buying on the Internet?" Understanding the factors that drive price sensitivity can take one a long way in answering this question for any particular market.

Most obviously, the Internet enables customers to be aware of more alternatives. Making it easier to identify suppliers increases the likelihood of becoming aware of a lower price, even if the distribution of prices on the Internet were exactly the same as the distribution in traditional channels (the reference price effect). Most commentators have focused on just this one factor to argue that the Internet increases price sensitivity and drives down prices, but there are other factors to consider.

The quality of a product sold on the Internet is less certain than in physical space (the difficult comparison effect). A customer can examine the product in a store much more thoroughly than on

the Web. Moreover, if the product proves unsatisfactory after it is purchased, the consumer knows that he or she can return the product to a local merchant. Consequently, consumers should be *less* willing to try a lower-priced but unbranded generic when searching on the Web than if the same alternatives were offered in a store. In fact, when products are unbranded and difficult to compare, as are unbranded products on the Internet, customers may be more likely to avoid the lowest prices to ensure adequate quality (the price-quality effect).

On the service side, when buying from an on-line merchant there is greater uncertainty regarding whether or not the merchant is legitimate, will actually deliver the promised product, and will treat credit card information confidentially. At a store, you do not have to give up your money (or your credit card number) until you have the product in hand. On the Internet, the process is reversed by days or weeks. As customers recognize the higher risk, they will be more willing to pay a premium to deal with a reputable merchant (the difficult comparison effect again). Web shoppers also have higher incomes, which generally makes busy people less price sensitive (the expenditure effect). Consequently, even if Web

BOX 4-1 (*continued*)

shoppers are more price sensitive for the same brand when purchasing on the Web, they are likely to have a preference for higher-quality/higher-priced brands.

Last, but not least, there is the question of value. Research shows that most people shop the Internet not to get a better price but to have a more convenient shopping experience and/or a broader choice of products.

In at least one market—wholesale used cars—car dealers pay higher prices on-line for used car inventory than at auctions, even though they have the choice to buy either way.* The cost of having to attend auctions long enough each week to bid on as many auto choices as one can see each week on-line would be prohibitive. Since the cost to visit a Web site more frequently is much less than the cost to travel to an auction, dealers can also purchase smaller quantities more frequently as the need arises to replace a model in inventory. Thus dealers can visit a Web site to buy cars one at a time, while they must bundle purchases to justify the cost of traveling to an auction. Moreover, the ability to cost-effectively view more cars more frequently enables dealers to acquire cars that more closely meet the demands of their local market. The resulting savings in acquisition and inventory holding costs,

combined with the ability to acquire inventory that more closely meets local needs, are enough to justify higher prices.

So what inferences can we draw from this? There are a few logical scenarios:

1. Branded products sold on the Web are likely to gain share, and/or command more of a price premium, than when sold in physical space, because a brand name is even more important to determine quality in virtual space where one cannot directly observe the product.

2. Internet merchants with well-known reputations for trustworthiness (including those who are also traditional bricks and mortar competitors) are likely to gain share relative to unbranded merchants because of the higher risks of dealing with merchants on the Web.

3. Where a branded Web merchant need compete only against bricks and mortar merchants, Web merchants should be able to charge higher prices due to the convenience of Web-based shopping. However, branded merchants in highly competitive Web markets may still have to charge *lower* prices than in the physical world because branded merchants are better substitutes for each other in virtual than in physical space. Sears, JCPenny, Wal-Mart, and Kmart can all be visited virtually in less time than it takes to visit any one of them physically. There

(continued)

BOX 4-1 (*continued*)

is no differentiation value associated with being the merchant physically located closest to the customer.

4. In cases where it is possible to deliver better service on the Web, the best merchants may be able to create a unique virtual shopping experience, which makes shopping easier or quicker than at competitive sites (the switching cost effect). In that case, those merchants may generate loyalty that is equal in value to the loyalty created in the physical world by location. Amazon.com, for example, uses customers' purchase histories to help them find products they might like and to make their purchase as quick and hassle-free as technically possible.

Although the Web will increase competition at the retail level, that is probably good news for branded manufacturers. We know from research that merchants competing on price are more likely to compete more heavily on the more well-known brands.** Why? Because price cuts on well-known brands will have a greater percentage impact on sales. The reason for this is that brand names enable consumers to compare quality across suppliers more easily. A string of Mikimoto pearls or a pair of Reebok basketball shoes is the same regardless of where you buy it. Consequently, a lower price is certainly a better deal. But the quality of an unbranded string of pearls or pair of shoes may vary greatly between two suppliers, and the Web precludes easy comparison. Consequently, when an unbranded product is offered at a lower price, consumers are more likely to question its relative quality (the price-quality effect) and are, therefore, less likely to be attracted by the offer.

---

*Patrick McKeown, Richard Watson, and George Kingham, "Electronic Commerce and Pricing," University of Georgia, Terry College of Business, working paper, Athens, GA (2000).

**Robert L. Steiner, "Does Advertising Lower Consumer Prices?" *Journal of Marketing,* 37 (October 1973), pp. 19–26; Paul W. Farris, and Mark S. Albion, "The Impact of Advertising on the Price of Consumer Products," *Journal of Marketing,* 44 (Summer 1980), pp. 17–35; Paul W. Farris, "Advertising's Link with Retail Price Competition," *Harvard Business Review,* 59, 1 (January–February 1981), pp. 40, 42, 44; Mark S. Albion, *Advertising's Hidden Effects: Manufacturers' Advertising and Retail Pricing* (Boston: Auburn House, 1983), pp. 185, 199–200.

Buyers are more sensitive to a product's price when it is outside the range that they perceive as "fair" or "reasonable" given the purchase context.[23] But what is fair? Managers should note that the concept of fairness appears to be totally unrelated to issues of supply and demand.[24] It is related to perceptions of the seller's profit, but not entirely. Oil companies have often been accused of gouging, even when their profits are below average. In contrast, popular forms of entertainment (for example, Disney World, state lotteries) are very profitable and expensive, yet their pricing escapes widespread criticism.

Recent research seems to indicate that perceptions of fairness are more subjective, and therefore more manageable, than one might otherwise have thought. Buyers apparently begin by making an inference about the seller's likely margin relative to what they expect the seller earned in the past, or relative to what others earn in similar purchase contexts. The effect of margin on fairness is strongly mitigated, however, by another factor: the inferred motive of the seller. Explaining the action with a "good" motive (e.g., the desire to fund health insurance for one's employees, to fund improvements in service levels) makes the price more acceptable than a "bad" motive (e.g., the exploitation of a shortage in the market to increase stockholders' profits). Finally, the research indicates that companies with good reputations (e.g., Disney) are much more likely to be given the benefit of the doubt that their pricing decisions have good underlying motives, while those with unpopular reputations (e.g., oil companies) are likely to find their motives suspect.[25]

This research is consistent with a phenomenon observed in earlier research: Whether a price is deemed fair or not is contextual. In a now famous experiment, people were asked to imagine that they were lying on a beach, thirsty for a favorite brand of beer. A friend was walking to a nearby location and would bring back beer if the price was not too high. Each person was asked to specify the maximum amount he or she would pay, not knowing that half of them had been told that the friend would patronize a "fancy resort hotel" and the other half that the friend would patronize "a small, rundown grocery store." Although these individuals would not themselves visit (or enjoy the amenities of) the purchase location, the median acceptable price given by those who expected the beer to come from the hotel—$2.65—was dramatically higher than the median acceptable price given by those who expected it to come from the grocery store—$1.50.[26]

Finally, perceptions of fairness seem to be related to whether the price is paid to maintain a previously enjoyed standard of living (the price is paid to avoid a loss) or is paid to get something more out of life (the price is paid to achieve a gain). Products that are necessary to maintain one's current living standards are quickly perceived as "necessities," although humankind has probably survived without them for most of its history. Charging a high price for a "necessity" is generally perceived as unfair. People object to prices for lifesaving drugs since they feel that they shouldn't have to pay to be healthy. After all, they were healthy last year without having to buy prescriptions and medical advice. Why should they have to pay for health now? They have a similar reaction to rent increases. These same people, however, may buy a new car, jewelry, or a vacation without ever objecting to equally high prices or price increases. What distinguishes these expenditures is that a high price simply reduces the amount of the gain (the quality of the car, the size of the diamond, the length of the vacation) that one can obtain, rather than reducing the quality of life that the buyer has come to perceive as "necessary."[27]

Fortunately, perceptions of fairness can be managed. Companies that must frequently adjust prices to reflect supply and demand or to segment buyers with different price sensitivities are careful to set the "regular" price at the highest possible level, rather than at the average or most common price. This enables them to "discount" when necessary to move product at slow times (a "good" motive), rather than have to increase prices when demand is strong (a "bad" motive).[28] Similarly, landlords who raise rents do so along with announcements of improvements they are making, and companies that raise prices do so more successfully when they are launching a new product. Finally, most large companies that value their reputations and their ongoing relationships forgo opportunities to exploit unexpected shortages (e.g., raising prices on a popular Christmas toy in short supply).

The Framing Effect

The preceding discussion about prices and price increases being more objectionable for "necessities" follows from a stream of research called *prospect theory,* which has many important implications for managing price sensitivity.[29] The essential idea of prospect theory is that people "frame" purchase decisions in their minds as a bundle of gains and losses. Moreover, how they frame those decisions affects how attractive they perceive a choice to be. The *framing effect* states that buyers are more price sensitive when they perceive the price as a "loss" rather than as a forgone "gain," and that they are more price sensitive when the price is paid separately rather than as part of a bundle.

To illustrate this effect, ask yourself from which of the two gasoline stations described below you would be more willing to buy gas (assuming that you deem both brands to be equally good and would pay for your purchase the same way at either station):

- *Station A:* Sells gasoline for $1.60 per gallon and gives a $0.10 per gallon discount if the buyer pays with cash.
- *Station B:* Sells gasoline for $1.50 per gallon, and charges a $0.10 surcharge if the buyer pays with a credit card.

Of course, the economic cost of buying gasoline from either station is identical. Yet, most people find the offer from station A more attractive than the one from station B. Why? Because the psychological discomfort associated with purchasing from station A (with a discount) is less than purchasing from station B (with a surcharge).

The reason for the difference, according to prospect theory, is that when evaluating a transaction *people place more weight on "losses" than on equal-size "gains."* This implies, for example, that grocery shoppers who found that products accounting for half of their expenditures were priced 10 percent higher than expected, but the other half were priced 10 percent lower, would not be indifferent to the change. On net, they would find this change objectionable because the satisfaction from the discounts would not be as large as the dissatisfaction with the increases, even though they were monetarily equal. Moreover, *both the gains and losses of an individual transaction are subject, independently, to diminishing returns. This implies, for example, that raising a price by 20 percent is less than twice as objectionable as raising it by 10 percent.*

Exhibit 4-9 illustrates the assumptions of prospect theory graphically. The lines on the graph relating value to gains and losses are similar to the concept of a "utility function" in economic theory except for one thing: They focus only on changes from a baseline level of ownership or consumption. The slope of the line in the lower, left-hand quadrant of "losses" is steeper than the slope in the upper right-hand quadrant of "gains" and illustrates the observation that losses are given more weight in decisions than equal gains. The curving of the lines illustrates the observation of diminishing returns: The same amount of gain or loss has less impact on value when added on top of other gains or losses associated with the decision.

Given these assumptions, the common preference for the offer by station A over that from station B is explainable. The discomfort associated with an extra $0.10 in price at station A is minimized by combining it with the already uncomfortable $1.50: Negative evaluation of the extra price is subject to diminishing returns. The discount for cash, however, stands alone as a gain. In contrast, at station B, the $0.10 saving in price is subject to diminishing returns, while the surcharge for a credit card stands alone as a loss. Since losses are weighted more than gains, the offer by station B is less attractive.

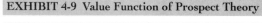

EXHIBIT 4-9 Value Function of Prospect Theory

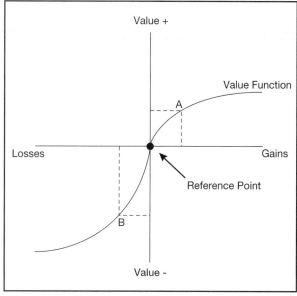

Many marketing implications of prospect theory have been suggested that seem consistent with both common observation and controlled research:[30]

- To make prices less objectionable, make them opportunity costs (gains forgone) rather than out-of-pocket costs. Banks often waive fees for checking accounts in return for maintaining a minimum balance. Even when the interest forgone on the funds in the account exceeds the charge for checking, most people choose the minimum balance option.
- When your product is priced differently to different customers and at different times, set the list price at the highest level and give most people discounts. This type of pricing is so common that we take it for granted. Colleges, for example, charge only a small portion of customers the list price and give everyone else discounts (a.k.a. scholarships). To those who pay at or near the full price, the failure to receive more of a discount (a gain forgone) is much less objectionable than if they were asked to pay a premium because they are not star students, athletes, or good negotiators.
- Unbundle gains, bundle losses. Many companies sell offerings that consist of many individual products and services. For example, a printing company not only prints brochures but helps design the job, matches colors, schedules the job to meet the buyer's time requirements, etc. To maximize the perceived value, the seller should identify each of these as a separate product and identify the value of each one separately (unbundle the gains). However, rather than asking the buyer to make individual expenditure decisions, the seller should identify the customer's needs and offer a package price to meet them (bundle the loss). If the buyer objects to the price, the seller can take away a service, which will then make the service feel like a stand-alone "loss" that will be hard to give up.

Anyone who thinks only in terms of objective economic values will consider these principles far-fetched. One might argue that buyers in these cases could easily think of the same choices as entirely different combinations of "gains" and "losses." That is precisely the point that prospect theorists make. There are many different ways to frame the same transactions, and each way implies somewhat different behavior. Researchers have presented research subjects with many objectively identical choices, changing only the framing of the presentation. They have found that changing how people think about the choice in terms of "gains" and "losses" consistently and predictably changes the choices they make.

MANAGEMENT OF VALUE PERCEPTIONS AND PRICE SENSITIVITY

The formulation of every pricing strategy should begin with a managerial analysis of value perceptions and price sensitivity. There are three reasons why such an analysis should be conducted, even if one ultimately intends to gauge price sensitivity more quantitatively (discussed in Chapter 13). First, a managerial analysis can identify market segments that are likely to have different price sensitivities. This is necessary not only to formulate a segmentation strategy (with different products, channels, and purchase options) that captures the different value to each segment, but also to develop valid quantitative measures of their price sensitivity. Second, a managerial analysis indicates the range of prices within which the firm should ultimately price its product, thus enabling one to design surveys or experiments to focus only on price differences within that range. Thus, a good managerial analysis can both increase the accuracy and reduce the cost of more formal market research.

Third, and most important, managers need to analyze buyer price sensitivity to determine how they can effectively influence it. Pricing strategy has too long suffered from the economist's assumption of a fixed demand curve defining the relationship between price and purchase volume.

Price sensitivity is merely a preference, not a law of nature. If politicians took the same defeatist attitude as many market researchers, they would stop campaigning as soon as they learned that they trailed the leader by more than the margin of error in the poll. Instead, what they do is find out *why* people prefer the leading competitor. They look for both misunderstandings about the candidate's positions and beliefs about what the most important issues are. Then they begin a campaign to change those understandings and beliefs. Marketers should be doing the very same thing whenever they have a credible value proposition that justifies prices customers are not initially willing to pay. (Appendix 4B summarizes the questions that managers should review and attempt to answer before developing a pricing strategy and/or formally estimating volume responses to price changes.)

SEGMENTING FOR VALUE COMMUNICATION AND DELIVERY

An effective managerial analysis of price sensitivity will almost always reveal multiple market segments. Some customers are aware of their alternatives; others are not. Some customers highly value a brand's unique differentiation; others deem it useless at best. Some customers pay all of the cost out of pocket; others can shift some of it to a third-party payer. These differences in perception affect how customers will use information about price and value in making a decision. Understanding these differences is key to developing pricing and value communication strategies that are effective.

A market segmentation based on the price-sensitivity factors described above reveals more differences among customers, and is therefore more useful, than the simple distinction commonly made between "the price-sensitive segment" and "the quality-sensitive segment." To illustrate, divide the factors influencing price sensitivity into those that affect the *perceived value of a product's differences* among suppliers and those that affect the *perceived pain of the price*. The reference price used by the customer, the difficulty of comparison, the importance of the end benefit to which the product contributes, the switching cost, and the effect of price on perceptions of quality all affect the perceived value of differentiation. The size of the expenditure, the proportion of the cost of the end benefit that the product accounts for, the perceived fairness of the price, and the framing of the price as a gain or loss all affect the perceived pain of the price.

Evaluating customers on just those two dimensions reveals the four distinct segments illustrated in Exhibit 4-10.[31] In the upper left-hand corner are buyers who seek to buy at the lowest price consistent with some *minimum* level of acceptable quality that many brands or suppliers could meet. These *price buyers* do not make feature–benefit trade-offs and cannot be convinced to pay more for the unique added value of additional features, service, or supplier reputation. They believe from prior experience that they know what they need and what is worth paying for. Consequently, they announce those needs, often formally in the form of required "specifications," and entertain price offers to meet them. For travel, they are the ones who will use Priceline.com, committing themselves to any airline or hotel that meets their minimum criteria, so long as they get a great price. For groceries, they check the newspaper ads and shop at one or more locations where they can get the best deals that week. For an industrial purchase, they use a reverse auction site like Freemarkets.com. They are not interested in sales calls or promotional information since they have concluded in advance that evaluating the differentiation of higher-priced suppliers is a waste of time; they are never convinced to pay more.

In the lower, right-hand corner are the *relationship buyers* who already have a strong preference for one brand, based on the supplier's unique reputation or on their past experience with the brand. Like the price buyers, they do not believe that a serious evaluation of the alternatives is warranted. If the price of

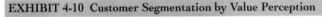

EXHIBIT 4-10 Customer Segmentation by Value Perception

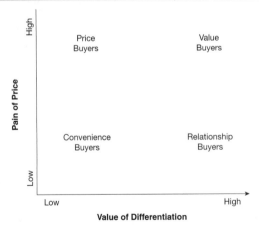

Adapted from a model developed by Richard Harmer in 1988.
©2002 Customer Value Center LLC. Used with permission.

their preferred brand does not exceed what they think is within some reasonable range, they will purchase it without evaluating potential alternatives. Only a loss of trust in the preferred supplier will cause them to seriously consider alternatives. Business buyers may ask for competitive bids, and consumers may check on competitive prices, but only to see if the price differential has grown sufficiently large to justify further evaluation. For travel, these are the people who will specify their preferred airline. For groceries, they go to the same store every time without checking the newspaper ads.

Although these two segments are frequently thought to be two ends of a price–quality continuum, the exhibit clearly reveals two other segments that do not fit with that linear view of markets. Many customers are sufficiently concerned both about paying more than they need to (like the price buyer) and about getting all that they want (like the relationship buyer) that they will invest time and effort to evaluate alternatives on every purchase occasion. Sometimes they may buy a relatively high-priced brand, but will do so only after carefully checking the prices and features of the alternatives and concluding that the added value is worth the added cost. These *value buyers* are represented by the upper right-hand corner of Exhibit 4-10. They probably read *Consumer Reports* before buying a car or an appliance. When traveling, they probably search the Internet for all combinations of fares, airlines, travel dates, and convenient schedule and then agonize over the trade-offs until they are making the best trade-offs between price and other aspects they want. For business purchases, they invest considerable cost to extensively evaluate the features of all alternatives and are solicitous of sellers who will help them define their needs and the trade-offs involved.

Their opposites, represented in the lower left-hand corner, are the *convenience buyers.* These buyers are not particularly concerned about the differences among brands—any brand will do—but they also are not concerned enough about the price to check the prices of multiple vendors before purchase. Consequently, they buy whatever is most readily available, minimizing search and evaluation of prices and features. Such behavior is common when time is of the essence (maybe you need a plumber or a tow truck urgently) or when the expenditure is so small that saving money is not worth the time. Convenience stores cater to those making a small purchase who are willing to pay a premium to minimize time or effort expended.

If a company wishes to serve multiple segments profitably, it must do so with multiple strategies, usually involving multiple products, distribution networks, or service distinctions as well as price differences. The challenge is that in most cases these segments are not necessarily different customers, but rather different purchase occasions. The same person may be a loyal buyer of air travel on business but a value buyer when vacationing with her family. She may usually buy all over-the-counter drugs at a drug discounter but buy aspirin from the nearest convenience store when she gets an unexpected headache. Many businesses buy in truckload quantities from a large wholesaler but still maintain an account at the local distribution center for unplanned purchases.

Price segmentation does not imply that companies must limit their markets and growth to only one segment. They must, however, have multiple products, distribution channels, and messages when serving multiple segments. Pella, a maker of meticulously crafted windows and doors for expensive, customer-designed homes, sells its products exclusively through Pella distributors. Pella also has a lower-priced line, however, designed to appeal to value buyers. That line is also of high quality, but it is more limited in shapes and sizes. This "Proline" series is sold through home stores without the design support of Pella distributors, at prices that are 12 to 20 percent less than the high-priced ones. This strategy serves Pella well since demand for its lower-priced windows is less cyclical than demand for custom windows.

SUMMARY

Although price is often more important to the seller than to the buyer, the buyer can still reject any price offer that is more than he or she is willing to pay. Firms that fail to recognize this fact and base price solely on their internal needs generally fail to attain their full profit potential. An effective pricing strategy requires a good understanding of the value of the product to buyers. This usually requires an analysis estimation of the product's economic value. For most products, however, economic value estimation™ does not fully capture the role of price in individual decision making. Most consumers do not approximate the image of a fully informed "economic buyer" who always seeks the best value in the market regardless of the effort required. The analysis must quickly go beyond economic value to the other factors driving the purchase decision. This understanding is finally integrated to formulate segment markets not only by value, but also by how customers perceive and manage the process of making the price–value trade-offs. Segmented pricing strategy is implemented by designing pricing policies, product policies, value communication, and sales strategies that are tailored to appeal to each segment that the company intends to target. (Chapter 8 on value-based sales and negotiation and Chapter 9 on segmented pricing delve into these issues in more detail.)

Appendix 4A

Economics of Price Sensitivity

Up to this point, we have spoken of price sensitivity without defining it operationally. There are two aspects to price sensitivity: one relating to the decision about *which brand* to buy, the other relating to the buyer's decision about *how much* to buy. We refer to the first as *brand choice elasticity* and the latter as *primary demand elasticity.* To illustrate, if the price of Coke increases, demand for Coke will fall. Individuals who have a strong preference for Coke may continue purchasing only Coke if the price rises, but they may reduce the amount they consume each week. Other people, however, may not change their primary demand for the category at all, but may switch to a cheaper brand. Clearly, the total sales of a brand consist of both of these types of elasticity, and it is important to distinguish them. For example, if competitors will match your price cut, you will probably need to rely on changes in primary demand alone to justify the decision.

The measure of aggregate-level price sensitivity commonly used by price analysts is called *price elasticity.* It is the percentage change in a product's unit sales resulting from a given percentage change in its price.

$$E = \frac{\% \, \text{Change in unit sales}}{\% \, \text{Change in price}}$$

E, the demand elasticity, is usually a negative number, since positive price changes (price increases) generally produce sales declines and negative price changes (price cuts) generally produce sales increases. The greater the absolute value of *E,* the more "elastic" the demand; the smaller its value, the more "inelastic" the demand.

We actually introduced this concept in Chapter 3 when we calculated the percent breakeven sales change required to make a price change profitable. The resulting number divided by the percent price change is actually the minimum elasticity required to justify a price cut or the maximum elasticity that is tolerable to justify a price increase. Thus, if we calculate that the sales change required to justify a 10 percent price increase must be no greater than −25 percent, we are saying that the price change will be unprofitable if the elasticity is less than −2.5. When considering specific price changes, an elasticity can be converted into an expected unit sales change simply by multiplying by the percentage price change under consideration. The percent breakeven calculation enables us to analyze the profitability of a price change without expecting managers to "know" precisely their actual demand curve. Instead, the procedure requires much less information, that is, a judgment about whether the actual elasticity for a specific price change would exceed or fall short of the necessary level.

Exhibit 4A-1 illustrates average price elasticities, disaggregated into brand choice and primary demand elasticities, for price promotions in

Category	Total Mean (Variance)	Brand Choice Mean (Variance)	Primary Demand Mean (Variance)
Bacon	-1.57 (0.078)	-1.25 (0.216)	-0.323 (0.143)
Margarine	-2.34 (0.003)	-2.22 (0.064)	-0.121 (0.051)
Butter	-1.98 (0.004)	-1.24 (0.075)	-0.744 (0.382)
Ice cream	-2.58 (0.004)	-1.89 (0.206)	-0.681 (0.319)
Paper towels	-4.74 (0.061)	-4.00 (0.179)	-0.742 (0.136)
Sugar	-4.60 (0.026)	-4.03 (0.498)	-0.566 (0.243)
Liquid detergents	-5.66 (0.600)	-3.95 (0.704)	-1.707 (0.616)
Coffee	-3.06 (0.049)	-1.65 (0.060)	-1.412 (0.061)
Soft drinks	-3.09 (0.066)	-2.66 (0.108)	-0.423 (0.091)
Bath tissue	-4.66 (0.214)	-3.85 (0.308)	-0.807 (0.228)
Potato chips	-3.38 (0.046)	-2.50 (0.089)	-0.878 (0.071)
Dryer softeners	-5.28 (0.097)	-4.08 (0.128)	-1.193 (0.210)
Yogurt	-1.92 (0.069)	-1.57 (0.084)	-0.348 (0.133)

David Bell, Jeongwen Chiang, and V. Padmanabhan, "The Decomposition of Promotional Response: An Empirical Generalization," *Marketing Science*, 18(4) (Autumn 1999).

EXHIBIT 4A-1 Mean Elasticity Estimates for Promotional Price Changes

multiple grocery categories. The authors' work confirms earlier work indicating that promotional price elasticity is driven much more by brand switching than by changes in quantity purchased.[32] Where quantity purchased did increase, the effect for nonfood products was the result of forward buying, not more consumption. In a few food categories, there was a relatively small, but statistically significant, impact of price promotion on the actual quantity consumed.[33]

There are few simple rules of thumb that one can use to predict relative price elasticities without studying the factors that determine price sensitivity in a particular product category. There is, however, one rule of thumb that is generally reliable across product categories: market-level price elasticities are generally related to market share. Within a product class, and after controlling for differences in relative price, the sales of small market-share brands tend to be more price sensitive than those of brands with larger market shares. Although there is some evidence that large market share brands have a larger share of more loyal consumers,[34] differences in individual customer loyalty are not necessary for this effect. It is rather the result of simple algebra. Imagine a large brand with 80 percent market share and a small brand with a 20 percent market share. For both, nine of ten customers are brand loyal. If the small share company cuts its price to win all the non-brand-loyal customers, it can increase its sales by 40 percent (= 8/20). If the large brand retaliates by cutting its price to win back all the non-brand-loyal customers, it can increase its sales by 14 percent (= 10/72). The difference reflects simply the fact that they are fighting over the same group of non-brand-loyal customers, but those customers represent a smaller share of the large company's base.

Appendix 4B

Preparing a Managerial Price Sensitivity Analysis

The preceding discussion of the factors influencing price sensitivity is aimed at helping managers improve their judgments by indicating what factors to consider and how to evaluate them. A managerial analysis of price sensitivity should be a written document that can be criticized and improved over time. Although the report itself may be compiled by one person, it should reflect the efforts and judgments of all individuals in a firm who are in a position to add useful information or insight. When information from internal resources is inadequate, the evaluation may require market research. Such research, rather than merely measuring price sensitivity directly, should measure the underlying factors that influence it—awareness of alternatives, confidence in making brand comparisons, the price as a portion of the end benefit's total cost, the share of the cost paid by others, and so forth. A managerial analysis of price sensitivity is complete when it answers questions such as the following about each of the factors described in this chapter:

1. The Reference Price Effect

- What alternatives are buyers (or segments of buyers) typically aware of when making a purchase?

- To what extent are buyers aware of the prices of those substitutes?
- To what extent can buyers' price expectations be influenced by the positioning of one brand relative to particular alternatives, or by the alternatives offered them?
- To what extent can buyers speed up or delay purchases based on expectations of future prices?

For a consumer product, finding out what alternatives buyers face usually requires nothing more than a visit or telephone inquiry to a few retailers or distributors. For an industrial product, identifying alternatives may be as easy as simply noting the products displayed at trade shows and asking about their availability in various locations and for various uses. One's sales force, sales agents, or manufacturer representatives are also particularly good sources for identifying buyer awareness of alternatives. For example, a brief form asking the salesperson to note each alternative mentioned by the buyer during a sales presentation can be a cheap, reliable source of information. Finally, survey research that asks a question such as "How many brands of this product can you name?" can be a source of data on awareness of alternatives.

The second part of this effort involves gauging price awareness. Do buyers know the prices of alternatives? Are some segments of buyers much more, or less, informed than others? What do those who cannot recall specific prices believe is a typical price for this product? At what price level would they consider a brand in this market to be expensive or cheap?

2. Difficult Comparison Effect

- How difficult is it for buyers to compare the offers of different suppliers?
- Can the attributes of a product be determined by observation, or must the product be purchased and consumed to learn what it offers?
- What portion of the market has positive past experience with your products? with the brands of the competition?
- Is the product highly complex, requiring costly specialists to evaluate its differentiating attributes?
- Are the prices of different suppliers easily comparable, or are they stated for different sizes and combinations that make comparisons difficult?

Answers to these questions are generally obvious from simple observation of buyers making purchase decisions within the product class. Unfortunately, ascertaining the added value that buyers place on a product due to prior experience with it is particularly difficult. One method is by reference to similar products. In the pharmaceuticals industry, for example, there is much historical evidence for the price premium that known brands of most drugs can sustain over their generic equivalents. As new drugs are developed, the value of a known brand name can be inferred from other categories of drugs with similar levels of risk. In the absence of historical evidence on similar products, the manager must resort to pure judgment based upon his or her understanding of the difficulty of obtaining information and the risks of product trial when assigning value to past experience associated with a brand name.

3. Switching Cost Effect

- To what extent have buyers already made investments (both monetary and psychological) in dealing with one supplier that they would need to incur again if they switched suppliers?
- For how long are buyers locked in by those expenditures?

In most cases, a formal or informal questioning of buyers can produce this information without difficulty.

4. Price–Quality Effect

- Is a prestige image an important attribute of the product?
- Is the product enhanced in value when its price excludes some consumers?
- Is the product of unknown quality, and are there few reliable cues for ascertaining quality before purchase?

These questions are difficult to answer. Survey research by experienced professionals may reveal answers, but these are questions that buyers will not necessarily answer candidly. In many cases, the firm must rely purely upon judgment based on comparison with similar product categories. Occasionally, experimental research is used to measure the value of price as a quality cue.

5. Expenditure Effect

- How significant are buyers' expenditures for the product in absolute dollar terms (for business buyers) and as a portion of income (for end consumers)?

This effect is normally fairly easy to ascertain. One can purchase detailed data on many consumer products from consumer panels showing the consumption rates of brands by numerous demographic classifications, including income. Government agencies, trade associations, and private companies collect data on purchasers of industrial products. When industrial products are used directly in the production of the buying firms' products, total expenditures can often be inferred from publicly available data. A company can conduct its own direct mail or telephone survey at a reasonable cost. As a last resort, an engineering study could estimate buyers' various costs of manufacturing.

6. End-Benefit Effect

- What end benefits do buyers seek from the product?

- How price sensitive are buyers to the cost of the end benefit?
- What portion of the end benefit does the price of the product account for?
- To what extent can the product be repositioned in customers' minds as related to an end benefit for which the buyer is less cost sensitive or which has a larger total cost?

To evaluate a buyer's sensitivity to the cost of the benefit to which a product contributes, one must analyze the benefit with respect to the factors influencing price sensitivity. Determining the share of the benefit's cost for which the product's cost accounts is generally straightforward. For industrial products, the information is often available directly from buyers, but can also be inferred from public data on final sales and a simple engineering study of the buyer's production process. For consumer products, the information generally requires survey research that asks the consumer to identify other product purchases (for example, airfare, hotel and car rental, equipment rental) made in conjunction with the purchase of the product in question (for example, a ski resort lift ticket) to generate a particular end product (a ski vacation).

7. Shared-Cost Effect

- Does the buyer pay the full cost of the product?
- If not, what portion of the cost does the buyer pay?

The answers to these questions are readily available through formal or informal surveys of corporate reimbursement policies, from analyses of insurance coverage available from insurers, and from governmental publications explaining treatment of expenditures for tax deductibility.

8. Fairness Effect

- How does the product's current price compare with prices people have paid in the past for products in this category?
- What do buyers expect to pay for similar products in similar purchase contexts?
- Do customers perceive the product as a "necessity" or as a discretionary purchase?

Answers to these questions are easy to gauge from formal or informal survey research.

9. The Framing Effect

- Do customers see the price as something they pay to avoid a loss, or to achieve a gain?
- Is the price paid as part of a larger cost or does it stand alone?
- Is the price perceived as an out-of-pocket cost or as an opportunity cost?

Answers to these questions can be inferred from the nature of the product, from the extent to which complementary products are purchased at the same time, and from the price metrics.

Notes

1. Decision makers frequently misperceive *concise* estimates of demand elasticity, customer value, or competitive response as precise estimates of stable underlying processes. In fact, concise estimates are often very inaccurate, whereas less concise estimates give the decision maker a more accurate picture of the underlying uncertainty in the data. A method of quantifying decisions without losing sight of the underlying uncertainty in the data is Baysian analysis, definitely the best approach for managers who are comfortable dealing with statistical possibilities.

2. In previous editions, we referred to this concept as *economic value analysis.* Unfortunately that term was subsequently trademarked for an entirely different concept. Our firm, Strategic Pricing Group, Inc., has trademarked *economic value estimation* to preserve its meaning. We hereby grant anyone the right to use the term in this way so long as our trademark registration is acknowledged.

3. For a business customer, economic value can be reduced to revenues gained or costs avoided by purchasing the product. This is also true for some consumer products (e.g., the economic value of purchasing a more energy-efficient appliance). For most consumer products, however, it is difficult if not impossible to quantify value objectively. Consequently, the pricer is forced to work at the level of unquantified benefits (e.g., safety, prestige, satisfaction) and then to measure the subjective value of those benefits. As in business-to-business markets, this

gives an estimate of the value potential for customers who can be educated about and guaranteed those benefits from making a purchase.

4. This illustration is developed from information in E. Raymond Corey, "E. I. Du Pont de Nemours & Co," *Industrial Marketing: Cases and Concepts,* 2nd ed. (Englewood Cliffs, N.J.: Prentice-Hall, Inc., 1976), pp. 179–87; and Benson P. Shapiro and Barbara B. Jackson, "Industrial Pricing to Meet Customer Needs," *Harvard Business Review,* 56 (November–December 1978), pp. 119–27. The numbers are illustrative, not necessarily those actually arrived at by Du Pont.

5. If Alathon were easier or more difficult to extrude, its differentiation value would also be affected. If more or less Alathon were required to replace a pound of commodity resin, then the analysis would have to reflect the cost of whatever amount of the substitute would be required in lieu of one pound of Alathon. Since Alathon is extruded in the same way as commodity-grade resin, and in the same quantities, these factors do not affect the economic value estimation™ in this case.

6. Because of this misunderstanding, many companies committed to value-based pricing have been misled into believing that they cannot price to capture their value if their ratio of *price/use value* would exceed that of their competitors. If, however, more of a product's use value is differentiation, then a higher percentage of that value should be capturable in the price.

7. Gerald E. Smith and Thomas T. Nagle, "Frames of Reference and Buyers' Perception of Price and Value," *California Management Review,* 38(1) (Fall 1995), pp. 98–116.

8. Richard W. Olshavsky and Donald H. Granbois, "Customer Decision Making—Fact or Fiction?" *Journal of Consumer Research,* 6 (September 1979), pp. 93–100.

9. Albert J. Della Bitta and Kent Monroe, "The Influence of Adaptation Levels on Subjective Price Perceptions," in *Advances in Consumer Research, 1973 Proceedings of the Association for Consumer Research,* vol. 1, eds. Peter Wright and Scott Ward (Urbana, Ill.: ACR, 1974), pp. 359–69.

10. Ibid.; and A. Doob and others, "Effect of Initial Selling Price on Subsequent Sales," *Journal of Personality and Social Psychology,* 11 (1969), pp. 345–50.

11. In the second edition, this was referred to as "The Inventory Effect." Subsequently, we can conclude that it is simply a variant of the reference price effect where buyers are using an expected future price as the reference.

12. In Chapter 8, we will show how this effect is triggered when buyers are taught that no price is firm until pushed.

13. Vicki Morwitz, Eric Greenleaf, and Eric Johnson, "Divide and Prosper: Consumers' Reactions to Partitioned Prices," *Journal of Marketing Research,* 35(4) (November 1998).

14. J. Edward Russo, "The Value of Unit Price Information," *Journal of Marketing Research,* 14 (May 1977), pp. 193–201.

15. Harold Leavitt, "A Note on Some Empirical Findings About the Meaning of Price," *Journal of Business,* 27 (July 1954), pp. 205–10; Donald Tull, R. A. Boring, and M. H. Gonsior, "A Note on the Relationship Between Price and Imputed Quality," *Journal of Business,* 37 (April 1964), pp. 186–91; Benson Shapiro, "Price

Reliance: Existence and Sources," *Journal of Marketing Research,* 10 (August 1973), pp. 286–94. For a review of these studies and others on this topic, see Kent Monroe, "Buyers' Subjective Perceptions of Price," *Journal of Marketing Research,* 10 (February 1973), pp. 70–80; Ben Enis and James Stafford, "The Price-Quality Relationship: An Extension," *Journal of Marketing Research,* 6 (November 1969), pp. 256–58; Jacob Jacoby, Jerry Olson, and Rafael Haddock, "Price, Brand Name, and Product Composition Characteristics and Determinants of Perceived Quality," *Journal of Applied Psychology,* 55 (December 1971), pp. 570–78; David Gardner, "An Experimental Investigation of the Price-Quality Relationship," *Journal of Retailing,* 46 (Fall 1970), pp. 25–41; David Gardner, "Is There a Generalized Price Quality Relationship?" *Journal of Marketing Research,* 8 (May 1971), pp. 241–43; Vithala Rao, "Salience of Price in the Perception of Product Quality: A Multidimensional Measurement Approach," *Proceedings: Fall Educators' Conference* (Chicago: American Marketing Association, 1966), pp. 520–31.

16. Ben Enis and James Stafford, "The Price-Quality Relationship: An Extension," *Journal of Marketing Research,* 6 (November 1969), pp. 256–58; Jacob Jacoby, Jerry Olson, and Rafael Haddock, "Price, Brand Name, and Product Composition Characteristics and Determinants of Perceived Quality," *Journal of Applied Psychology,* 55 (December 1971), pp. 570–78; David Gardner, "An Experimental Investigation of the Price-Quality Relationship," *Journal of Retailing,* 46 (Fall 1970), pp. 25–41; David Gardner, "Is There a

Generalized Price Quality Relationship?" *Journal of Marketing Research,* 8(May 1971), pp. 241–43; Vithala Rao, "Salience of Price in the Perception of Product Quality: A Multidimensional Measurement Approach," *Proceedings: Fall Educators' Conference* (Chicago: American Marketing Association, 1966), pp. 520–31.

17. David J. Moore and Richard W. Olshavsky, "Brand Choice and Deep Price Discounts," *Psychology & Marketing,* 6(3) (Fall 1989), pp. 181–96; interestingly, the study indicated that small discounts did not have the same negative effect on sales. Andre Gabor and Clive Granger, "Price as an Index of Quality—Report on an Inquiry," *Economica,* February 1966, pp. 43–70, surveyed 640 housewives and showed that awareness of grocery prices was inversely related to income, except for the poorest and presumably least educated consumers. See also Roger E. Alcaly, "Information and Food Prices," *Bell Journal of Economics,* 7 (Autumn 1976), pp. 658–71.

18. David Bell, Teck-Hua Ho, and Christopher Tang, "Determining Where to Shop: Fixed and Variable Costs of Shopping," *Journal of Marketing Research,* 35(3) (August 1998).

19. Andre Gabor and Clive Granger, "Price as an Index of Quality— Report on an Inquiry," *Economica,* February 1966, pp. 43–70, surveyed 640 housewives and showed that awareness of grocery prices was inversely related to income, except for the poorest and presumably least educated consumers. See also Roger E. Alcaly, "Information and Food Prices," *Bell Journal of Economics,* 7 (Autumn 1976), pp. 658–71.

20. This example is adapted from a study by J. Edward Russo and Paul Schoemaker and is discussed in more detail

in their book *Decision Traps: The Ten Barriers to Brilliant Decision Making & How to Overcome Them* (New York: Doubleday, 1989). See also Richard Thaler, "Toward a Positive Theory of Consumer Choice," *Journal of Economic Behavior and Organization,* 1 (1980), pp. 39–60, for discussion and examples of this pricing phenomenon.

21. Daniel Kahneman and Amos Tversky, "Choices, Values, and Frames," *American Psychologist,* 39(4) (April 1984), pp. 341–50.

22. Jerry Flint, "Fruit Salad Car Wax," *Forbes,* April 27, 1992, pp. 126, 129.

23. Joel Urbany, Thomas Madden, and Peter Dickson, "All's Not Fair in Pricing: An Initial Look at the Dual Entitlement Principle," *Marketing Letters* I(1) (1989), pp. 15–25; Marielza Matins and Kent Monroe, "Perceived Price Fairness: A New Look at an Old Construct," *Advances in Consumer Research,* 21 Provo, UT. Association for Consumer Research, pp. 75–78.

24. Daniel Kahneman, Jack L. Knetsch, and Richard H. Thaler, "Fairness as a Constraint on Profit Seeking: Entitlements in the Market," *American Economic Review,* 76(4) (September 1986), pp. 728–41.

25. Margaret C. Campbell, "Perceptions of Price Unfairness: Antecedents and Consequences," *Journal of Marketing Research,* 36 (May 1999), pp. 187–99.

26. Richard Thaler, "Mental Accounting and Consumer Choice," *Marketing Science,* 4 (Summer 1985), p. 206.

27. Daniel Kahneman, Jack L. Knetsch, and Richard H. Thaler, "The Endowment Effect, Kiss Aversion, and Status Quo Bias," *Journal of Economic Perspectives,* 5(1) (Winter 1991), pp. 203–204.

28. Campbell, op cit.

29. Daniel Kahneman and Amos Tversky, "Prospect Theory: An Analysis of Decision Under Risk," *Econometrica,* 47 (March 1979), pp. 263–91; Daniel Kahneman and Amos Tversky, "The Psychology of Preferences," *Scientific American,* 246 (January 1982), pp. 162–70; Daniel Kahneman and Amos Tversky, "Choices, Values, and Frames," *American Psychologist,* 39, 4 (April 1984), pp. 341–50; Amos Tversky and Daniel Kahneman, "The Framing of Decisions and the Psychology of Choice," in *New Directions for Methodology of Social and Behavioral Science: Question Framing and Response Consistency,* no. 11 (San Francisco: Jossey-Bass, March 1982); Amos Tversky and Daniel Kahneman, "Advances in Prospect Theory: Cumulative Representation of Uncertainty," *Journal of Risk and Uncertainty* (1992).

30. The marketing implications of this theory, including its extension to decision making in nonprobabilistic situations, have been developed primarily by Richard Thaler in "Toward a Positive Theory of Consumer Choice," *Journal of Economic Behavior and Organization,* 1 (1980), pp. 39–60; and in Richard Thaler, "Mental Accounting and Consumer Choice," *Marketing Science,* 4(3) (Summer 1985) pp. 199–214.

31. This model was developed in 1989 by Richard Harmer while at Boston University. He is now a Senior Pricer at the Strategic Pricing Group Inc.

32. These results are based on promotions to consumers, not trade promotions. Other authors have found that trade promotions are very effective in getting the trade to forward buy product for late sale at regular prices.

33. David Bell, Jeongwen Chiang, and V. Padmanabhan, "The Decomposition

of Promotional Response: An Empirical Generalization," *Marketing Science* 18(4) (Autumn 1999).

34. Avijit Ghosh, Scott A. Neslin, and Robert W. Shoemaker, "Are There Associations Between Price Elasticity and Brand Characteristics?" 1983 *AMA Educators' Conference Proceedings* (Chicago, American Marketing Association, 1983) pp. 228–29.

C H A P T E R

Competition

Managing Conflict Thoughtfully

Pricing against competition is more challenging and hazardous than pricing a unique product.[1] In the absence of competition, managers can anticipate the effect of a price change entirely by analyzing buyers' price sensitivity. When a product is just one among many, however, competitors can wreak havoc with such predictions. Price discounting in competitive markets—whether explicit or disguised with rebates, coupons, or generous payment terms—is almost a sure bet to enhance immediate sales and profits. It is easy to become seduced by these quick highs and fail to recognize the longer-term consequences. The price cut that boosts your sales today will invariably change the industry you compete in tomorrow. Frequently, that change is for the worse.

The experience of a large building-products manufacturer illustrates just such a problem. This company had been consistently profitable as a market-share leader. Despite the commodity-like nature of its product, the company enjoyed a small price premium reflecting its perceived technical superiority and exceptional customer service. Still, the company had long been losing market share due to aggressive price competition from smaller competitors. New management, which took control following a leveraged buyout, was determined to reverse this trend.

Although this company offered standard discounts for volume, quick payment, and so forth, the company had historically been reluctant to negotiate prices with any but its largest customers. Consequently, smaller competitors could predictably set their prices just beneath the leader's price umbrella. To thwart the competition, the new management decided to close the umbrella. Whenever an account seemed seriously threatened by a lower-cost bid, sales managers were authorized to negotiate "special deals" that would retain the business at lower, but still profitable, prices. The effect of this policy was immediate and dramatic; the company effectively stopped the loss of established customers, while continuing to gain new business based on quality and service. Over the next few quarters, market share not only stopped declining but actually rose by a few points.

Was this a wise strategic move? The company won more pricing battles and, consequently, gained volume and profits. Management was certainly pleased. But how could we expect the market to change as a result of this new pricing policy? What was the predictable long-run impact of this strategy on the nature of competition in the industry? At first, the market changed very little because the company took pains to limit public knowledge of the new policy. Over time, however, customers talked with one another. The company's traditional customers, who willingly had been paying a price premium for the company's product quality and service, began learning that others got the same quality and service for less. Moreover, they learned that others got lower prices because they were tougher negotiators who threatened to give their business to other suppliers.

It is not difficult to imagine what happened next. Previously loyal buyers resolved no longer "to get taken" simply because they hadn't investigated their alternatives. Purchasing authority was moved from users to purchasing departments; doors opened to competitors that had previously been closed; and, instead of giving this company their business, previously loyal customers began giving it only the last look. With more competitors involved in each sale, the sales cycle grew longer and the number of requests for "special deals" grew exponentially. In fact, within two years, management was looking for a way to automate the process of preparing them and billing customers using many different price schedules.

This company inadvertently created a financial incentive for its buyers to become more difficult, and they responded. Although the policy reversed a decline in market share, both industry prices and the company's price premium declined. Management complained about declining profits and loss of customer loyalty, but it made no connection between those changes and its own policies. Management eventually responded to buyers' reluctance to pay the traditional price premium for quality and service by looking for ways to cut costs in those areas.

Although this company achieved immediate benefits from its policy to thwart the competition, it unwittingly undermined the industry price level and the value of its competitive advantage. The lesson here is not that management should avoid defending market share or should never initiate price cuts. The lesson is that before taking such actions, management must anticipate the long-run strategic consequences and weigh them against the short-term benefits. A pricing decision should never be made simply to make the next sale or to meet some short-term sales objective, but rather to enhance the firm's long-term ability to operate profitably. Pricing is like playing chess: Those who make moves one at a time—seeking to minimize immediate losses or to exploit immediate opportunities—will invariably be beaten by those who envision the game a few moves ahead.

Because price changes affect sales more quickly than other marketing decisions, they are often used as a quick-fix solution to short-term problems. Profitable pricing requires, however, that managers also consider how each decision will affect future competitive behavior and profitability. Procter & Gamble, for example, abandoned a decade-long policy of chronic "price promotion," despite the short-term benefits, after realizing that it caused large retailers to adopt purchasing patterns that substantially raised its costs of manufacturing and distribution.

Pricing decisions should always be made as part of a longer-term marketing strategy to generate and capture more profit contribution. Otherwise, it is possible to win many individual battles for market share and still end up losing the war for profitability. This is not to argue that underpricing the competition is never a successful strategy in the long run, but the conditions necessary to make it successful depend critically upon how customers and competitors react to it. The goal of this chapter is to provide guidelines for anticipating those reactions, influencing them, and integrating them into a long-term strategic plan.

UNDERSTANDING THE PRICING GAME

Pricing is a "game," as defined by game theorists, because success depends not only on a company's own pricing decisions but also on how customers and competitors respond to them. Unfortunately, pricing strategically for sustainable profitability is a type of game requiring skills foreign to many marketing and sales managers. What most of us know about competition we learned from sports, academics, and perhaps from intracompany sales contests. The rules for success in these types of competition are quite different from those for success in pricing. The reason, in technical jargon, is that the former are all examples of "positive-sum" games, whereas pricing is a "negative-sum" game. Understanding the difference is crucial to playing the pricing game successfully.[2]

Positive-sum games are those in which the very process of competition creates benefits. Consequently, the more prolonged and intense the game—in sports, academics, or sales—the greater the rewards to the players. The winner always finds playing such games worthwhile, and even the loser may gain enough from the experience so as not to regret having played. In fact, people with a healthy attitude toward these activities often seek opportunities to challenge themselves simply to benefit from the experience. Such a strong competitive spirit is a criterion commonly used to identify job candidates with potential for success in sales.

Unfortunately, that same gung-ho attraction to competition is quite unhealthy when applied to negative-sum games: those in which the process of competition imposes costs on players. Warfare, labor actions, and dueling are negative-sum games because the loser never benefits from participation. The longer the conflict drags on, the more likely it is that even the winner will find that playing was not worth the cost. Price competition is usually a negative-sum game since the more intense price competition is, the more it undermines the value of the market over which one is competing.[3] Price competitors do well, therefore, to forget what they learned about competing from sports and other positive-sum games, and to try instead to draw lessons from less familiar competitions like warfare or dueling.

Students of actual warfare, who are cognizant of its cost, do not make the mistake of equating success with winning battles. Lidell Hart, author of more than thirty books on military strategy, offers advice to political and military leaders that marketers would do well to note:

> Fighting power is but one of the instruments of grand strategy—
> which should [also] take account of and apply . . . financial pressure,
> diplomatic pressure, commercial pressure, and . . . ethical pressure, to
> weaken the opponent's will. . . . It should not only combine the
> various instruments, but also *regulate their use as to avoid damage to
> the future state of peace.*[4]

In short, winning battles is not an end in itself, and warfare is certainly not the only means to an end.

For marketers, as for diplomats, warfare should be a last resort, and even then the potential benefits of using it must be weighed against the cost. Fortunately, there are many positive-sum ways for marketers to compete. Creating new products, creating new ways to deliver service, communicating more effectively with customers about benefits, and reducing the costs of operation are all positive-sum forms of competition. Precisely because they create profits, rather than dissipate them, building capabilities for positive-sum forms of competition is the basis of a sustainable strategy. Competing on price alone is at best a short-term strategy until competitors find it threatening enough to react.

COMPETITIVE ADVANTAGE: THE ONLY SUSTAINABLE SOURCE OF PROFITABILITY

How can companies become strong competitors? Unfortunately, many managers erroneously believe that the measure of competitive success is market share (see Box 5-1). That may be a successful strategy if only one firm attempts to pursue it. When many competitors pursue this same strategy, they engage in negative-sum competition, which does little more than destroy profitability for everyone. Fortunately, there are strategies that promote positive-sum competition. Rather than attracting customers by taking less in profit, these strategies attract customers by creating more value or more operating efficiency. They involve either adding to the value of what is offered without adding as much to cost or reducing costs without equally reducing the value offered.

We call these sources of profitable growth *competitive advantages* because competitors cannot immediately duplicate them, except at a higher cost. Many managers completely misunderstand the concept of competitive advantage and its importance for long-term profitability. We hear them report that they have a "competitive advantage" in having more stores than the competition, more knowledgeable salespeople, or higher quality. None of these are competitive advantages unless they also enable the firm to deliver value more cost-effectively than one's competitors can. Offering customers a more attractive

BOX 5-1

Market-Share Myth

A common myth among marketers is that market share is the key to profitability. If that were true, of course, recent history would have shown General Motors to be the world's most profitable automobile company; United, the most profitable airline; and Philips, the most profitable manufacturer of electrical products ranging from light bulbs to color televisions. In fact, these companies, while sales leaders, have been financial also-rans. The source of this myth—these examples notwithstanding—is a demonstrable correlation between market share and profitability. As any student of statistics should know, however, correlation does not necessarily imply a causal relationship.

A far more plausible explanation for the correlation is that both profitability and market share are caused by the same underlying source of business success: a sustainable competitive advantage in meeting customer needs more effectively or in doing so more efficiently.* When a company has a competitive advantage, it can earn higher margins due to either a price premium or a lower cost of production. That advantage, if sustainable, also discourages competitors from targeting the company's customers or from effectively resisting its attempts to expand. Consequently, although a less fortunate company would face equally efficient competitors who could take market shares with margin-destroying price competition, a company with a competitive advantage can sustain higher market share even as it earns higher profits. Market share, rather than being the key to profitability, is, like profitability, simply another symptom of a fundamentally well-run company.

Unfortunately, when management misperceives the symptom (insufficient market share) as a cause and seeks it by some inappropriate means, such as price-cutting, the expected profitability doesn't materialize. On the contrary, a grab for market share unjustified by an underlying competitive advantage can often reduce the company's own and its industry's profitability. The ultimate objective of any strategic plan should not be to achieve or even sustain sales volume, but to build and sustain competitive advantage. Profitability and, in many cases, market share will follow. In fact, contrary to the myth that a higher market share causes higher profitability, changes in profitability usually *precede* changes in market share, not the other way around. For example, Wal-Mart's competitive advantages made it the most profitable retailer in the

(*continued*)

BOX 5-1 (*continued*)

United States long before it became the largest, whereas Sears's
poor profitability preceded by
many years its loss of the dominant market share. This pattern of
profitability leading, not following, market share is currently visible in the automobile, steel, and
banking industries.

A strategic plan based on
building volume, rather than on
creating a competitive advantage, is essentially a beggar-thy-
neighbor strategy—a negative-
sum game that ultimately can
only undermine industry profitability. Every point of market
share won by reducing margins
(either by offering a lower price
or by incurring higher costs) in-

variably reduces the value of the
sales gained. Since competitors
can effectively retaliate, they
probably will, at least partially
eliminating any gain in sales
while reducing the value of a sale
even further. The only sustainable way to increase relative
profitability is by achieving a
competitive advantage that will
enable you to increase sales *and*
margins. In short, the goal of a
strategic plan should not be to
become bigger than the competition (although that may happen)
but to become *better*. Such positive-sum competition, rather
than undermining the profitability of an industry, constantly renews it.**

*Robert Jacobson and David Aaker, "Is Market Share All That It's Cracked Up to Be?"
Journal of Marketing, 49 (Fall 1985), pp. 11–22; William W. Alberts, "The Experience Curve
Doctrine Reconsidered," *Journal of Marketing*, 53 (July 1989), pp. 36–49; Cathy Anterasiun,
John L. Graham, and R. Bruce Money, "Are U.S. Managers Superstitious about Market
Share?" *Sloan Management Review* (Summer 1996), pp. 67–77; Linda L. Hellofs and
Robert Jacobson, "Market Share and Customers' Perceptions of Quality: When Can Firms
Grow Their Way to Higher Versus Lower Quality?" *Journal of Marketing*, 63 (January
1999), pp. 16–25.
**For evidence that there are profit leaders in the bottom and middle ranges of market
share almost as frequently as in the top range, see William L. Shanklin, "Market Share Is
Not Destiny," *Journal of Business & Industrial Marketing*, 4 (Winter–Spring 1989), pp. 5–16.

offer by accepting a lower margin than the competition may be a sales advantage, but it is not a sustainable competitive advantage.

How can a firm achieve competitive advantage? Sometimes it's by luck.
Aramco, the Saudi oil company, enjoys oil fields from which oil can be more
cheaply extracted than from those in Alaska, the North Sea, or Kazakhstan. Often, advantage comes from moving first on a new idea. By winning a patent, by
gaining economies of scale, or by preempting the best locations, a firm may
achieve an advantage that would be more costly for a later entrant to match. AOL
established a "virtual community" with its proprietary instant messaging and chat
rooms, the value of which competitors cannot duplicate at a smaller scale.

More often, competitive advantages are carved out of the efficient management of the firm's value chain. Michael Porter, in his path-breaking book, cites three ways that companies can proactively manage operations to achieve competitive advantage.[5]

- "Serving only a particular industry segment" or niche enables the firm to tailor its operations to meet the unique needs of that segment more cost-effectively.
- "Widening or narrowing the geographic markets served" can, depending on the firm's cost structure, create a cost advantage.
- "Competing in related industries with coordinated value chains" or "coalitions that involve coordinating or sharing value chains" can give a company a shared cost or differentiation advantage.

Wausau Paper Mills is one example of a company that follows the "segment" strategy. The company is small by the standards of the industry, but it is more than twice as profitable as the big guys. Its secret is to avoid the high-volume, price-competitive markets and focus on niche markets. One of its focus segments is the market for colored paper. Wausau made the distinctive yellow paper for 3M Post-It notes until other papermakers matched its quality and undercut its price. Rather than compete on price, the company used its experience in making colored papers to create the very bright colors now offered in Kinko's stores. Similarly, the company works closely with food companies to support its innovations. Consequently, it was an early maker of microwave popcorn bags.[6]

The U.S. beer industry offers a classic case of both the "widening" and "narrowing" of geographic reach to achieve competitive advantage. Companies with a national presence, like Anheuser-Busch and Miller, enjoy a huge competitive advantage in purchasing TV advertising space at low national rates. While many regional brewers have been unable to survive with this disadvantage, microbrewers have prospered by staying regionally focused. Beers such as Samuel Adams of Boston, Smooth Talker Pilsner of Novi, Michigan, and Diamondback Wheat Beer of Elk Grove, California, rely on a local cache and word-of-mouth promotion to operate small but profitable businesses.

As traditional public utilities have come under competitive pressure, they have looked for opportunities to gain cost or product advantages by combining value chains. The local electric company has become a consolidator of advertising inserts, which it mails along with the monthly bill. Its incremental mailing costs are lower than for traditional mailers (since a bill has to be sent anyway), and it can promise that a higher percentage of recipients will actually open the envelope rather than file it in the wastebasket. Similarly, AT&T used its database of telephone calling-card holders to identify exceptionally good credit risks. It then offered them a "Universal Card," a combined calling and credit card that gave customers the added value of replacing two cards with one. It quickly became one of the largest and most profitable companies in this new line of business.

America Online (AOL) enjoys a first-mover advantage. By getting ahead of the competition in signing up subscribers, it can now offer access to more fellow subscribers in chat rooms and via its proprietary "instant messaging." It has the most local access lines for travelers. And there is a switching cost to those who decide to change to another service provider: AOL does not allow subscribers to forward their e-mail to a new address.

As these examples illustrate, the key to achieving sustainable profitability is to manage the business for competitive advantage. Unfortunately, most companies in competitive markets are driven by a focus on revenue growth, which they pursue by trying to be all things to all people, rather than by a focus on creating value more cost-effectively. Michael Porter, the Harvard competition guru, calls the failure to achieve either a value or a cost advantage "getting stuck in the middle." When such companies are exposed to competitors, some of whom offer higher quality or service while others offer lower prices, the firm's profitability gets squeezed despite its size.[7]

In the absence of a competitive advantage, it is suicidal to drive growth with price. At the time of this writing, thousands of Internet retailers and willing investors were hoping to prove this statement wrong. They accepted lower, even negative, margins simply to build share in the belief that ultimately the high value of the Internet would make them profitable. They ignored a simple economic principle: Competition drives out profitability except for those with a competitive advantage that prevents competitors from fully matching their costs or their value proposition. As it turns out, the companies with the competitive advantages for competing in Internet space (name recognition, low cost of customer acquisition, economies of scale) are exactly those who have the advantages in bricks and mortar space.

There are a few exceptions, namely those Internet newcomers who could create advantages that competitors could not duplicate. eBay, for example, enjoys margins and profitability that exceed those of both on-line and bricks and mortar competitors, not just because of the high value of trading on-line, but because of the difficulty that price-cutting competitors would face in trying to duplicate its on-line offerings. The value of an auction is directly related to the volume of participants in it (like the value of a telephone network). Once eBay gained a large volume advantage, it became impossible for any competitor to duplicate the value it offers traders. Similarly, Amazon has carefully created profiles of buyer preferences, along with their credit and mailing information, which makes shopping on Amazon a more efficient and pleasant experience than shopping with a new on-line or traditional competitor.

REACTING TO COMPETITION: THINK BEFORE YOU ACT

Many managers are so fully aware of the risks of price wars and the importance of competing from a position of strength that they think coolly and logically before *initiating* price competition. It is much harder for most of us to think logically about whether or how to respond when we are already under attack. Consequently, we will discuss in step-by-step detail how to analyze a competitive situation and formulate responses in price-competitive markets that are not of your making.

When is it financially more prudent to accommodate a competitive threat, at least in the near term until you can improve your capabilities, than to retaliate? Thinking through this question does much more than prepare you, intellectually and psychologically, to make the best competitive response. It also reveals weakness in your competitive position. If you do not like how often you must accommodate a competitor because your company cannot fight the threat successfully, you will begin searching for a competitive strategy that either increases your advantage or moves you further from harm's way.

Exhibit 5-1 illustrates the complex flow of thinking required to make thoughtful decisions about reacting to price competition. The exhibit begins with the assumption that one or more competitors have cut their prices or have introduced new products that offer at least some of your customers more value for their money. How should you respond? Some theorists argue that one should never respond since there are better, positive-sum ways to compete on product or service attributes. While that is often true, the time to have explored and implemented those ways was usually long before a competitive price threat. At the time of the threat, a firm's strategic capabilities are fixed in the short run. The question at hand is whether to respond with price when threatened with a loss of sales by a lower-priced competitor. To determine whether a price response is better than no response, one must answer the following questions and explore the interrelationships illustrated in Exhibit 5-1.

1. Is there a response that would cost less than the preventable sales loss?

Although the need to ask this question might seem obvious, many managers simply stop thinking rationally when threatened. They match any price cut without asking whether the cost is justified by the benefit, or whether the same benefit could be achieved by structuring a more thoughtful response. In Chapter 3, we introduced formulas for financial analysis of a reactive price change. If we conclude that reacting to a price change is cheaper than losing the sales, then it may be a good business decision. On the other hand, if a competitor threatens only a small portion of your expected sales, the sales loss associated with ignoring the threat may be much less than the cost associated with retaliation. Since the threat is small, the cost of cutting the price on all of your sales in order to prevent the small loss is likely to be prohibitively costly. Sometimes the cost of retaliation exceeds the benefits even when the competitor is larger. Regional telecom companies can defend their large market shares from price competition only at the expense of being prohibited by regulators from entering other lucrative telecommunications markets, including long-distance phone service and cable TV.

EXHIBIT 5-1 Thoughtfully Reacting to Price Competition

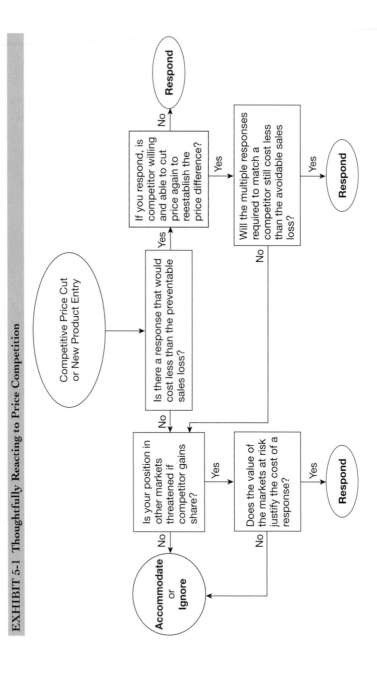

It is also important to be realistic about how much of the projected sales loss is really preventable. When a new grocery chain opens with lower prices, the established competitors can surely reduce the sales loss by matching its prices. Still, even if they match, some people will shift to the new store simply because it is newer or more convenient to where they live. They will not return even if the competitor's price advantage is eliminated. Similarly, companies in business markets sometimes unadvisedly delay lowering prices to their most loyal customers even as market conditions are forcing them to lower prices to others. Once those customers learn, often from a competitor's sales rep, that their loyalty has been taken advantage of, matching price is unlikely to win them back. On the contrary, it may simply confirm that they have been gouged.

By constraining an organization's competitive reactions to only those that are cost-effective, managers also force their organizations to think about how to make their price reactions more cost-effective. Following are some principles that can substantially reduce the cost of reacting to a price threat.

- *Focus your reactive price cut on only those customers likely to be attracted by the competitor's offer.* This requires developing a "flanking" offer that is attractive or available only to the more price-sensitive buyer. Often, such an offer can be developed in a short period of time since it involves merely eliminating some element of the product or service not highly valued by the price-sensitive segments. As the home computer market grew, so too did the demand for cheap semiconductors that could quickly process graphics. Consequently, Intel began losing sales for that segment to lower-priced competitors. Rather than cut the price of its flagship Pentium chip, Intel minimized the cost of responding by creating the Celeron chip. The Celeron involved no additional design or tooling costs, because it was based on the Pentium design, and so could be sold cheaply. To minimize the impact of Celeron pricing on the value of the entire Pentium line, the Celeron chips merely had some Pentium coprocessor capabilities turned off so that they would run poorly on business networks and in data-intensive applications but comparably to a Pentium on home and small-business computers.

- *Focus your reactive price cut on only the incremental volume at risk.* A cheaper competitor will often be unable to entirely replace an incumbent's business, but will be able to gain a share of its competitor's business. For example, if Fox Broadcasting cuts its ad rates, advertisers are not going to abandon ABC, NBC, and CBS; they are, however, going to be more likely to divert some dollars to Fox from the big networks. A big network could neutralize that threat by offering to discount its ad rates to the level of Fox's rates *just for the amount of advertising likely to be diverted.* This could be structured as a discount for all purchases in excess of, say, 80 percent of the prior year's purchases or expected purchases. These types of contracts are common not just for advertising, but also for drugs and medical supplies sold to HMOs. Retaliatory discounts applicable only to the incremental volume at risk are also common when pricing to retailers and distributors.

- *Focus your reactive price cut on a particular geographic area or product line where the competitor has the most to lose,* relative to you, from cutting the price. For example, Kodak may respond to Fuji's retail price promotions in the United States with retail price promotions in Japan, where Fuji has larger market share and margins, and thus more to lose. Remember, the purpose of the retaliation may not be to defend your sales at risk, but to get the competitor to stop the price cutting that puts your sales at risk.

- *Raise the cost to the competitor of its discounting.* If the competitor's price move is limited only to new customers and the competitor has a market of existing customers, it may be possible to retaliate without cutting your own price at all. Retaliate by educating the competitor's existing customers that they are being treated unfairly. A client of ours did this simply by making sales calls to its competitor's most profitable accounts. In the process of the call, the salespeople casually suggested, "You are probably paying about $X for this product now." When the consumer questioned this, the sales-person confessed that he really did not know what they were paying but had surmised the figure based on the prices that his competitor offered re-cently to some other accounts, which he named. In short order, those cus-tomers were on the phone demanding similar discounts, and the competitor quickly backtracked on its aggressive offers. Even in consumer markets, it is sometimes possible to appeal to customers' sense of fairness or civic pride to convince them to reject a discounter. Small, local retailers have successfully done this to prevent Wal-Mart from opening stores in Vermont that would no doubt destroy the less efficient, but traditional, lo-cal retailers.

- *Leverage any competitive advantages to increase the value of your offer as an alternative to matching the price.* The key to doing this without simply replacing a price war with a quality or service war is to make offers that are less costly for you to offer than for your competitor to match. If, for exam-ple, you have much better quality, offer a better warranty. If you have more service centers in more locations, offer faster service. Major airlines bril-liantly responded to price competition from smaller upstarts by offering frequent flyer programs. Because of their large route systems, flyers could accumulate miles faster and had more choices of destinations for which to use them. Moreover, the more sophisticated yield management systems of the large airlines minimized the cost of such programs more effectively than smaller carriers could.

If any of these options is less costly than simply allowing the competitor to take some sales, it is worth continuing to pursue the idea of a response, using the question on the right side of Exhibit 5-1. If, on the other hand, it would cost more to respond than to accept the sales loss, one should continue to examine the option of not responding, using the questions on the left-hand side.

2. If you respond, is your competitor willing and able to cut price again to reestablish the price difference?

Matching a price cut will do you no good if the competitor will simply reestablish the advantage. Ask yourself why the competitor chose to compete on price in the first place. If that competitor currently has little market share relative to the share that could be gained with a price advantage, and has no other way to attract customers, then it has little to lose from bringing price down as low as necessary to gain sales. This is especially the case where large sunk costs create substantial "exit barriers."

At one point, we had a pharmaceuticals company ask us to recommend a pricing strategy to defend against a new entrant. Management was initially surprised when we told them that defending their sales with price was foolhardy. Only after thinking about the problem from the competitor's standpoint did they fully understand the competitive dynamics they faced. Customers had no reason to try the competitor's new drug without a price advantage since it offered no clinical advantages. The new entrant had absolutely nothing to lose by taking the price down, since it had no sales anyway. Given that the huge investment to develop and test the drug was entirely sunk but that the manufacturing cost was small, winning sales even at a low price would be a gain. The conclusion was obvious that the competitor would cut price as often as necessary to establish a price advantage.

3. Will the multiple responses required to match a competitor still cost less than the avoidable sales loss?

Think about the total cost of a price war, not just the cost of the first shot, before concluding that the cost is worth bearing to defend the sales at risk. If our pharmaceuticals client had retaliated and closed the price gap enough to keep the competitor from winning sales, the competitor would simply have to cut its price still further. The process would have continued until one or the other stopped it, which was likely to be our client, who had much more to lose from a downward price spiral. If our client was ultimately going to let the competitor have a price advantage, it was better to let them have it at a high price than at a low one. Once the competitor gained some sales, it too would have something to lose from a downward price spiral. At that time, an effort to stop the discount and redirect competition to more positive-sum activities, such as sales calls, product improvement, and patient education, would be more likely to succeed.

4. Is your position in other (geographic or product) markets threatened if a competitor is successful in gaining share? Does the value of the markets at risk justify the cost of a response?

Some sales have a value that far exceeds the contribution directly associated with them. In 1999, AT&T slashed its lowest long-distance price from $0.10 to $0.07 per minute for residential customers. The purpose was to stop losing customers to cheap, second-tier providers, whom AT&T had previously allowed to maintain a large price differential. AT&T had now, at a huge cost, become less accepting of that differential because its strategy had changed. Rather than competing in the long-distance market alone, AT&T intended to use it to become a "one-stop" supplier of an integrated bundle of telecommunications services (long-distance, local, TV, Internet access, and others being developed). AT&T had assembled a nationwide network of cable and cellular providers that would be the core of a new strategy that it hoped would be more profitable. The key to that strategy was first to win a customer's long-distance business, even at prices that did not maximize AT&T's profits in long-distance alone.[8]

Still, retaliatory price cuts are all too often justified by vague "strategic" reasons unrelated to profitability. Before approving any retaliatory price cut for strategic reasons, two things should be required. The first is a clear statement of what the long-term strategic benefit and risks are. The benefit can be additional sales in this market in the future. It can be additional immediate sales of complementary products, such as sales of software and peripherals if one wins the sale of a computer. It can be a lower cost of future sales because of a competitive cost advantage resulting from the added volume. The risks are that a targeted price cut will spread to other customers and other markets, and that competitors will react, again creating a downward price spiral that undermines profits and any possibility of long-term gain.

The second requirement to justify a strategic price cut is a quantitative estimate of the value of the strategic benefit. This need to quantify often encounters resistance because managers feel that the task is too onerous and will require unnecessary delay. Usually, however, rough estimates are all that is necessary to achieve enough precision to make a decision. A company told us that they always defended price in the institutional segment of their market because sales in that segment drove retail sales. While the relationship was no doubt true, the magnitude of the effect was important given that pricing to the institutional segment had fallen to less than manufacturing cost. A simple survey of retail customers about how they began using the product revealed that only about 16 percent of retail sales were driven by institutional sales. We then estimated the cost of maintaining those sales by retaining all of the client's current institutional sales and compared that with the cost of replacing those sales through expenditures on alternative forms of promotion. That simple analysis drove a complete change in the institutional pricing strategy. Moreover, as institutional prices rose, "leakage" of cheap institutional product into the retail chain market declined, producing an additional return that had not been anticipated.

HOW SHOULD YOU REACT?

Competitive pricing strategy involves more than just deciding whether or not to react with price. It also involves deciding how to adapt your company's competitive strategy to the new situation. Exhibit 5-2 summarizes the strategic op-

Competitor Is Strategically

	Weaker	Neutral or Stronger
Too Costly	IGNORE	ACCOMMODATE
Cost-Justified	ATTACK	DEFEND

(Price Reaction Is)

EXHIBIT 5-2 Options for Reacting to Price Competition

tions and when to use them. In addition to the costs and benefits of retaliation that are weighed using the process described in Exhibit 5-1, this exhibit introduces the concept of strategic "weakness" and "strength." These concepts refer to a competitor's relative competitive advantage. Competitive "weakness" and "strength" have little to do with market share, despite the common tendency to equate them. The high cost structure of General Motors makes the company a relatively weak competitor in the automobile market, despite a high market share, because (at least in the North American automobile market) it has higher incremental costs per dollar revenue than its major rivals do. In contrast, the low cost structure of Southwest Airlines makes it a stronger competitor, even when competing against larger airlines, because its low cost per seat mile generates higher profits despite its somewhat lower prices.

When you decide that retaliation is not cost-effective, one option is simply to *ignore* the threat. This is the appropriate response when facing a "weak" competitor, with no competitive product or cost advantages. In that case, the amount of your sales at risk is small and is likely to remain so. In these same circumstances, some authors and consultants recommend a more aggressive option—commonly known as the "deep pockets" strategy—and pursue it to their own detriment. Their logic is that even if retaliation is too costly relative to the immediate sales gained, a large company can win a price war because it can afford to subsidize losses in a market longer than its weak competitor can. Two misconceptions lead people down this dead-end path. One is the meaning of "winning." This is no doubt a strategy to successfully defend market share, but the goal, at least for a publicly owned company, is not market share but profit. The second misconception is that by destroying a weak competitor one can actually destroy competition. In fact, often the assets of the bankrupt competitor are bought cheaply by a new competitor now able to compete from a lower cost base. Even if the assets are not bought, elimination of a weak competitor serving the price-sensitive segment of the market creates the opportunity for a stronger competitor to enter and use that as a basis from which to grow. Consequently, a costly strategy to kill weak competitors makes sense only in an unprofitable industry where a new entrant is unlikely to replace the one eliminated.[9]

When a price-cutting competitor is relatively "strong" and the cost of retaliation is greater than the value of the sales loss prevented, one cannot afford simply to ignore the threat and proceed as if nothing had changed. A strong competitor gaining share is a threat to survival. To maintain a profitable future, one must actively accommodate the threat with changes in strategy. This is what Sears faced as Wal-Mart's network of stores grew to include Sears's traditional suburban markets. There was simply no way that Sears could match Wal-Mart's prices, given Wal-Mart's famously efficient distribution system and Sears's more costly locations.

Sears's only logical response was to *accommodate* Wal-Mart as a competitor in its markets. Accommodating a threat is not the same as ignoring or confronting it. Accommodating means actively adjusting your own competitive strategy to minimize the adverse impact of the threat while reconciling yourself to live with it. Sears opted to eliminate its lower-margin product lines, remaking its image as a high-fashion retailer that competed less with Wal-Mart and more with traditional department stores.

A European industrial manufacturer took this same tack when it learned that an American company that previously exported product to Europe was about to build production capacity in the United Kingdom, with a generous government subsidy. Realizing that defending its market directly would produce nothing but a bloody price battle, the company refocused its marketing strategy away from the more price-sensitive segments, while creating incentives for less price-sensitive segments to sign longer-term contracts. As a result, the American firm's sales were focused in the least desirable segment where price-sensitive customers made it more vulnerable to a price war than were the traditional European competitors. Accommodating the competitor's entry was costly, but much less so than a futile attempt to prevent the entry with price competition.

The only situation in which it makes sense to use an *attack* response is when the competitor is weaker and the attack is cost justified. One reason this is rare is that it usually requires a misjudgment on the part of the competitor, who attempts to use price as a weapon from a position of weakness. Still, such misjudgments do occur. The largest U.S. grocery chain effectively destroyed itself in the 1970s after initiating a discount pricing strategy to regain market share. Its major competitors initially followed an accommodation strategy, believing that the A&P chain's huge buying power and well-known house brands gave it a cost advantage. When A&P began reporting huge losses, however, its competitors figured out that its high labor costs made the company much more vulnerable than they had thought. They switched to an attack strategy that ultimately forced the company to close half of its stores and sell the others to a more efficient suitor.

More common is the case where the price-cutting competitor is strong, or at least as strong as the defending companies whose sales are under attack. Often because of the attacker's strategic strength, the amount of sales at risk is so great that a vigorous defense is cost justified. The purpose of a "defend" response is not to eliminate the competitor, but rather simply to convince the competitor to back off. The goal is to get the competitor to recognize that aggressive pricing is really in its financial interest and to refrain from it in the future. This is often the position taken by American Airlines in its competition with other carriers, many of which have lower cost structures. American is careful to limit the time period and the depth of its price responses, signaling a willingness to return prices to prior levels as soon as the competitor withdraws the threat. Sometimes these battles last no more than days, or even hours, as competitors watch to see if American can fashion a cost-effective defense.

Partisans of pricing for market share would no doubt disagree with the restrained approach that we have prescribed. Large market-share companies, they would argue, are often better capitalized and thus better able to finance a price war than are smaller competitors. Although price-cutting might be more costly for the larger firm in the short run, it can bankrupt smaller competitors and, in the long run, reestablish the leader's market share and its freedom to control market prices. Although such a "predatory" response to competition sounds good in theory, there are two reasons why it rarely works in practice. First, predatory pricing is a violation of U.S. and European antitrust laws if the predatory price is below the predator's variable cost. Such a pricing tactic may in some cases be a violation when the price is below the average of all costs.[10] Consequently, even if a large competitor can afford to price low enough to bankrupt its smaller competitors, it often cannot do so legally. Second, and more important, predation is cost effective only if the predator gains some competitive advantage as a result of winning the war. This occurs in only two cases: when eliminating a competitor destroys an important differentiating asset (for example, its accumulated goodwill with customers) or when it enables the predator to gain such a cost advantage (for example, economies of experience or scale) that it can profitably keep its prices low enough to discourage new entrants. In the absence of this, new entrants can purchase the assets of the bankrupt competitor, operating at a lower cost base and competing against a large firm now itself financially weakened by the cost of the price war.

Still, for many managers the idea of choosing some confrontations while avoiding others seems weak. Adhering to the John Wayne model of competition, they instinctively stand their ground to defend market share, despite the adverse impact of that move on profitability. They forget that, while John Wayne could die valiantly at the Alamo and still go on to make more movies, those who fight real-world negative-sum games are not so fortunate. The real-world competitor who insists on fighting every battle will soon become so exhausted that the company will be unable to compete successfully when the odds are most favorable. The key to surviving a negative-sum pricing game is to fight only those battles for which the likely benefit exceeds the likely cost.

A far better model than John Wayne for dealing with negative-sum competition is Indiana Jones. Unlike John, Indiana acknowledges his vulnerability and doesn't pretend to be bigger or tougher than all competitors—just smarter. He thoughtfully manages the process of competition, choosing his battles carefully. If dominated by superior skill, strength, or numbers, he changes the nature of the confrontation to leverage his advantages. (Remember how Indiana dealt with being confronted by a larger, superior swordsman in a North African bazaar? He did not fight honorably on his competitor's terms. Instead, he shot him.) If Indiana cannot dominate the competition, he runs away to fight another day when the odds are more favorable.

These guidelines are useful for businesses in hostile competitive environments. Managers must choose their confrontations carefully and structure them to leverage their strengths. That is what AT&T did adroitly when facing intense competition in the mobile telephony market. With the proliferation of small mobile carriers in most major markets, price competition initiated by new entrants fighting to gain share was increasingly intense. AT&T's response was to compete from its strength. Being a long-distance carrier with plenty of capacity, and having coverage in most major markets, AT&T bundled airtime, long-distance charges, and roaming fees to create its One Rate™ plan. Smaller competitors, who would have to buy long distance and pay other companies roaming charges, were at a severe cost disadvantage in matching the package.

The key to surviving a negative-sum pricing game is to avoid confrontation unless you can structure it in a way that you can win and the likely benefit from winning exceeds the likely cost. Do not initiate price discounts unless the short-term gain is worth it *after taking account of competitors' long-term reactions.* Do not react to a competitor's price discounts except with price and nonprice tactics that cost *less than accommodating the competitor's behavior would cost.* If managers in general were to follow these two simple rules, far fewer industries would be ravaged by destructive price competition.

MANAGING COMPETITIVE INFORMATION

The key to managing competition profitably is diplomacy, not generalship. This does not necessarily mean being "Mr. Nice Guy." Diplomats are not always nice, but they manage information and expectations to achieve their goals without unnecessary confrontation. If they find it necessary to use force, they seek to limit its use to the amount necessary to make their point. In the diplomacy of price competition, the meaning that competitors ascribe to a move is often far more important than the move itself.

The decision to cut price to gain a customer may have radically different long-term effects, depending upon how the competitor interprets the move. Without any other information, the competitor would probably interpret the move as an opportunistic grab for market share and respond with defensive cuts of its own. If, however, the discount is structured to mimic exactly an offer that the same competitor made recently to one of your loyal customers, the competitor may interpret the cut as reflecting your resolve to defend that segment of the market. As such, the cut may actually reduce future opportunism and help stabilize industry prices.

Consider how the competitor might interpret one more alternative: Your price cut is totally unprovoked but is exceptionally large, more than you have ever offered before and probably more than is necessary to take the business. Moreover, it is preceded by an announcement that your company's new, patented manufacturing process not only added to capacity but also substantially reduced incremental manufacturing costs. In this case, an intelligent competitor might well interpret the price cut as fair warning that resistance against your grab for market share will be futile.

Managing information to influence a competitor's expectations, and to accurately form your own expectations, is the key to achieving goals without unnecessary negative-sum confrontation. Managing information requires collecting and evaluating information about the competition, as well as communicating information to the market that may influence competitors' moves in ways desirable to your own objectives.

Collect and Evaluate Information

Many companies operate while ignorant of their competitors' prices and pricing strategies. Consequently, they cannot respond quickly to changes. In highly competitive markets, such ignorance creates conditions that invite price warfare. Why would an opportunist ever cut price if it believed that other companies were willing to retaliate? The answer is that the opportunist's management believes that, by quietly negotiating or concealing its price cuts, it can gain sufficient sales volume to justify the move before the competitors find out. This is especially likely in industries with high fixed costs (high $\%CMs$) and during peak seasons when disproportionate amounts of business are at stake.

To minimize such opportunistic behavior, competitors must identify and react to it as quickly as possible.[11] If competitors can react in one week rather than three, the opportunist's potential benefit from price-cutting is reduced by two-thirds. At the extreme, if competitors could somehow react instantly, nearly all benefit from being the first to cut price could be eliminated. In highly competitive markets, managers "shop" the competitors' stores and monitor their advertising on a daily basis to adjust their pricing,[12] and the large chains maintain communication systems enabling them to make price changes quickly in response to a competitive threat.[13] As a consequence, by the time most customers even learn what the competition is promoting in a given week, the major competitors have already matched the price.

Knowledge of competitors' prices also helps minimize a purchasing agent's ability to promulgate misinformation. Frequently in business-to-business markets, price wars begin without the intention of any competitor involved. They are caused by a purchasing agent's manipulation of information. A purchasing agent, frustrated by the inability to get a better price from a favored supplier, may falsely claim that he or she has been offered a better deal from a competitor. If the salesperson doesn't respond, a smart purchasing agent may give the threat more credibility by giving the next order to a competitor even without a price concession. Now the first company believes that its competitor is out "buying business" and will, perhaps, match the claimed "lower price" on future orders to this customer, rewarding this customer's duplicitous behavior. If the first company is more skilled in price competition, it will not match the "lower price," but rather will retaliate by offering the same discount to other good customers of the competitor. The competitor will now see this company as a threat and begin its own cuts to defend its share. Without either competitor intending to undermine the industry price level, each has unwittingly been led to do so. The only way to minimize such manipulation is to monitor competitors' prices closely enough so that you can confidently predict when a customer is lying.[14]

Even when purchasers do not lie openly, their selective communication of information often leaves salespeople with a biased perspective. Most salespeople at most companies think that their companies' prices are too high for market conditions. Think about how a salesperson is informed about price. Whenever he or she loses a piece of business, the purchaser informs the salesperson that the price was "too high." When he or she wins the business, however, the purchaser never tells the salesperson that the price was unnecessarily low. The purchaser says the job was won with "the right price." Salespeople get little or no information about how much margin they may have left on the table.

There are many potential sources of data about competitors' prices, but collecting that data and converting it into useful information usually require a formalized process. Many companies require that the salesforce regularly include information on competitors' pricing in their call reports. Having such current information can substantially reduce the time necessary to respond to opportunism since someone collecting information from multiple salespeople and regions can spot a trend much more quickly than can an individual salesperson or sales manager. Favored customers can also be a good source of information. Those who are loyal to the company, perhaps because of its quality or good service, do not want their competitors to get lower prices from another source. Consequently, they will warn the favored company when competitors issue new price sheets or when they hear that someone is discounting to someone else. A partnership with such a customer is very valuable and should be treated as such by the seller.

In highly competitive markets, the information collected should not be limited to prices. Understanding plans and intentions is equally important. We recently worked with a client frustrated by the low profitability in its service industry, despite record revenue growth. In the process, we learned that the industry had suffered from overcapacity but recently had experienced multiple mergers. What was the purpose of those mergers? Was it to gain cost efficiencies in manufacturing or sales that would enable the new company to offer low prices more profitably? Or was it to eliminate some inefficient capacity, enabling the merged company to consolidate its most profitable customers in fewer plants, eliminating the need to win "incremental business." We found answers to those questions in the competitor's briefings to securities analysts, causing our client to rethink its own strategy.

Trade associations, independent industry monitoring organizations, securities analysts, distributors, and technical consultants who advise customers on large purchases are all good sources of information about competitors' current pricing moves and future intentions. Sometimes trade associations will collect information on prices charged in the prior week and disseminate it to members who have submitted their own prices. The airlines' computerized reservations systems give the owners of those systems an advance look at all price changes, enabling them to respond even before travel agents see changes. Monitoring price discussions at trade shows can also be another early tip-off. In retail businesses, one can simply "shop" the competitive retailers on a regular basis. In the hotel industry, nearby competitors regularly check their competitors' prices and room availability on particular nights by calling to make an unguaranteed reservation. If price competition is important enough as a determinant of profit in an industry, managers can easily justify the cost to monitor it.[15]

Selectively Communicate Information

It is usually much easier for managers to see the value of collecting competitive information than it is for them to see the value in knowingly revealing similar information to the competition. After all, information is power. Why should anyone want to reveal a competitive advantage? The answer: So that you can avoid having to use your advantage in a negative-sum confrontation.

The value of sharing information was obvious, after the fact, to a company supplying the construction industry. Unlike most of its competitors as well as most economists, the company accurately predicted the recession and construction slowdown in the early 1990s. To prepare, the company wisely pared back its inventories and shelved expansion plans just as its competitors were continuing to expand. The company's only mistake was to keep its insight a secret. Management correctly felt that by retrenching more quickly than its competitors, it could weather the hard times more successfully, but when competitors desperately cut prices to clear bloated inventories, the entire industry suffered. Had the company shared its insight and discouraged everyone from overexpansion, its own financial performance, while perhaps *relatively* less outstanding, would have been *absolutely* more profitable. It is usually better to earn just an average return in a profitable industry than to earn an exceptional return in an unprofitable one.

Even company-specific information—about intentions, capabilities, and future plans—can be useful to reveal unless doing so would preclude achieving a first-mover advantage into a new market. Such information, and the information contained in competitors' responses, enables a company to establish plans "on paper" that are consistent with competitors' intentions, rather than having to reach consistency through the painful process of confrontation.

Preannounce Price Increases

One of the most important times to communicate intentions is when planning a price increase. Even when a price increase is in the independent interest of all suppliers, an attempt to raise prices will often fail. All may not immediately recognize that an increase is in their interest, and some may hope to gain sales at the expense of the price leaders by lagging in meeting the increase. Other times, an increase may not be in the competitor's interest (perhaps because its costs are lower), meaning that any attempt to raise prices will ultimately fail. Consequently, before initiating a price increase that it expects competitors to follow, a firm's management should publicly explain the industry's need for higher prices and, if possible, announce its own increase far in advance of the effective date.

This move to "test the waters before diving in" has two purposes: First, it gives competitors time to analyze whether a price increase is in their interest, and second, it gives the firm an opportunity to back off from the increase if some competitors fail to join in. Even when a price increase is in the interest of all firms, it may be necessary to announce and then withdraw it a number of times until potentially opportunistic competitors get the message that no price increase will go through without them. It may also be necessary to scale back a price increase if some competitors remain unconvinced that an increase as large as the one proposed is in their interest.

Of all the types of competitive communication, this is the most risky from a legal perspective. There is a murky distinction between "collusion," which is illegal, and "conscious parallelism," which the courts have usually upheld as lawful and intelligent planning. Still, the cost of fighting antitrust litigation is so high that companies often find it better to settle for a modest sum than to fight the issue. For example, the courts and law journals expressed sympathy for the airlines' use of reservations systems to post prices and watch for the competitive response. Despite that, U.S. airlines agreed to various restrictions on their ability to post fares in advance of sale and collectively contributed to a settlement amounting to nearly $500 million in cash and free tickets.[16]

Show Willingness and Ability to Defend

When threatened by the potential opportunism of others, a firm may deter the threat by clearly signaling its commitment and ability to defend its market. For example, Chrysler had the largest U.S. market share for minivans in the early 1990s. Because of the popularity and profitability of this line of automobiles, an onslaught of rivals planned to launch new models. Chrysler was worried about how the new models might be priced, since it depended heavily on profits from its minivans. In a speech to its dealers covered by the business press, Chrysler sent a clear message to its competitors. Chrysler's president announced that the company had a plan to build a very low-priced version of its minivan. He explained, however, "It's something we have in the desk drawer if we need it," and he added, lest anyone should miss the point, "If it ever comes to a price war in minivans, I'm convinced we can win it."[17] Chrysler was speaking to its competitors: "Don't destabilize the market by undercutting our prices, because if you do, we have the capability to meet your challenge and beat it!"

Such communications can also be useful even after competitors have started an attack. Such posturing is common in the airline industry. When America West undercut the fare for Northwest Airlines's busy Minneapolis–Los Angeles route by $50, Northwest declined to match the cut. Instead, Northwest struck at America West's Phoenix hub by cutting fares a similar amount on the competitor's profitable Phoenix–New York route. Northwest's response fare was initially available for only a limited time, signaling that this was not a price that Northwest wished to sustain any longer than necessary. It could, however, be extended as long as necessary—if America West failed to back off in Minneapolis.[18]

Sometimes, simply publicizing a competitor's opportunism is sufficient to stop it. A client of ours in a nationwide service business dominated the most profitable regions of the country, the Northeast and Midwest. These regions had most of the largest customers. The major competitor had its profitable accounts in the South and West, where its reputation was stronger. In its drive to expand, the competitor began targeting some of our client's best customers with very low pricing. At first, our client attempted to meet these threats selectively, but was gradually losing control of its pricing as a result. Other customers were learning about these deals and demanding them, too. Moreover, since low offers cost the competition very little, matching them did not diminish the competitor's enthusiasm to offer them.

What to do? At first one might suggest going to the best customers and offering the same kinds of deals. We, however, felt in this case that was not the best idea because it undermined the integrity of the company's pricing. In fact, we encouraged the firm to develop a fixed-price policy across customers and to promote it as a fairer way to deal with everyone. We felt that, at least initially, our client should neither match the competitor's prices nor attack the competitor. Instead, we suggested a better alternative.

We proposed asking for an opportunity to make presentations to the competitor's best customers. During those presentations, the company's reps explained their "fair price" policy and why they felt that those prices were well justified by the value offered. During the presentation, they made a low estimate of what the customer was probably paying for the service from the competitor, based on the low-ball offers that the competitor had been making selectively. When quizzed by the customers, they explained how they based their estimates on other bids that the competitor had recently made. Needless to say, within minutes of the completion of the presentation, the customers were on the phone to the competitor, demanding the discounts that were their due as the company's best customers. As we predicted, once the competitor learned that its low-price forays would become the basis of negotiations with its profitable current customers, it stopped selective discounting.

Back Up Opportunism with Information

While an opportunistic price cut to buy market share is usually shortsighted, it is sometimes an element of a thoughtful strategy. This is most often the case when a company uses pricing to leverage or to enhance a durable cost advantage. Even companies with competitive advantages, however, often win only pyric victories in battles for market share. Although they ultimately can force competitors to cede market share, the costs of battle frequently exceed the ultimate value of the reward. This is especially true when the war reduces customer price expectations and undermines loyal buyer–seller relationships.

The key to profitably using price as a weapon is to convince competitors to capitulate. Not long ago, a Japanese company invited the two top operations managers of its American competitor to the opening of its new plant. After attending the opening ceremony, the company took all guests through the highly automated facility. The American managers were surprised to see the process so highly automated, all the way to final packing, since quality control usually required human intervention at many points in the process. When asked about this, the Japanese hosts informed the guests that this plant was the first to use a new, proprietary process that essentially eliminated the major source of defects. They also indicated that development of the process had taken them more than a decade.

On the way home, realizing now what could be done, the American engineers were eagerly speculating about how this improvement might be achieved and how much they should ask for in a budget to pursue research. They also wondered why their Japanese counterparts would reveal the existence of such an important trade secret. Within a few months they got their answer. The Japanese competitor announced a 20 percent price cut for exports of this product to the American market. If you were the American competitor with a large market share, how would knowledge of this trade secret change your likely response? In this case, the American company wisely chose to "adapt" rather than "defend."

Although the information disclosures discussed here are the most common, they are hardly comprehensive. Almost every public decision a company makes will be gleaned for information by astute competitors.[19] Consequently, companies in price-competitive industries should take steps to manage how their moves are seen by competitors, just as they manage the perceptions of stockholders and securities analysts. For example, will competitors in a highly price-competitive industry interpret closure of a plant as a sign of financial weakness or as a sign that the company is taking steps to end an industrywide overcapacity problem? How they interpret such a move will probably affect how they react to it. Consequently, it is in the company's interest to supply information that helps them make a favorable interpretation. Think twice, however, before disseminating misleading information that competitors will ultimately discover is incorrect. You may gain in the short run; however, you will undermine your ability to influence competitors' decisions and, therefore, to manage price competition in the long run.

WHEN SHOULD YOU COMPETE ON PRICE?

We have been discussing the benefits of avoiding negative-sum competitive confrontation, but some companies clearly benefit from underpricing their competitors. Did not the Japanese auto makers in the 1970s, Wal-Mart in the 1980s, and Dell Computer in the 1990s build their strategies around gaining share with lower prices? Yes, and understanding the special circumstances that enabled them to grow using price is necessary for anyone trying to replicate such success. For each of those companies at the times and places they used price to grow, price competition was not a negative-sum game. Every one of these successful price competitors first created business models that enabled them to cut incremental costs below those of their competitors. So long as each could attract customers with a price difference smaller than its cost advantage, it could win customers without reducing industry profitability. In fact, by serving customers more cost-effectively, these companies actually earned profits from each customer in excess of those earned by the competition—making their competitive efforts a positive-sum game.

However, a competitive cost advantage was not by itself enough to succeed. All of these companies also orchestrated a campaign of information to convince their competitors that their cost advantages were decisive. Consequently, their competitors wisely allowed them to maintain attractive price differentials, at least temporarily, until the competitors could figure out how to replicate those costs. Eventually, even these companies recognize that unless they can continue to cut costs faster than competitors, price-cutting cannot be a profitable growth strategy indefinitely. Consequently, they ultimately shift their strategies toward adding more value in ways that enable them to sustain their large market shares without having to sustain a price advantage indefinitely.

Under what conditions are the rewards of aggressive pricing large enough to justify such a move? There are only four:

1. If a company enjoys a substantial incremental cost advantage or can achieve one with a low-price strategy, its competitors may be unable to match its price cuts. Wal-Mart, Dell, and Southwest Airlines created low-cost business models that enabled them to grow profitably using price. In some markets, there may be an "experience effect" that justifies aggressive pricing based on the promise of lower costs. By pricing low and accumulating volume faster than competitors, a firm reduces its costs below those of competitors, thus creating a competitive advantage through low pricing. The conditions necessary for an experience strategy to succeed are described in Chapter 12.

2. If a company's product offering is attractive to only a small share of the market served by competitors, it may rightly assume that competitors will be unwilling to respond to the threat. The key to such a strategy, however, is to remain focused. Soon after airlines were deregulated, a few carriers began serving the "backpacker" market previously served only by buses. For a while they succeeded, until they grew large enough and their service grew good enough to threaten larger carriers. At that point, they were quickly crushed by the competition. Similarly, small computer manufacturers such as Packard Bell succeeded serving just the home computer segment until larger players decided that this low end of the market was attractive to them as well. Obviously, this is in almost all cases a temporary strategy to gain the time to build a durable cost or product advantage.

3. If a company can effectively subsidize losses in one market because of the profits it can generate selling complementary products, it may be able to establish a price differential that competitors will be unable to close. Microsoft, for example, priced its Windows software very low relative to value in order to increase sales of other Microsoft software that runs on it. Amazon.com's rationale for its low pricing on books was to build up a body of loyal customers to which it could sell a broad range of other products.

4. Sometimes price competition expands a market sufficiently that, despite lower margins and competitors' refusals to allow another company to undercut them, industry profitability can still increase. Managers who take this course are assuming that they have insight that their competitors lack and are, in effect, leading the industry toward pricing that is, in fact, in everyone's best interest. Before embarking on a price-based strategy, ask which of these is your rationale and recognize that the strategy can rarely be built on price alone or sustained indefinitely.

SUMMARY

No other weapon in a marketer's arsenal can boost sales more quickly or effectively than price. Price discounting—whether explicit or disguised with rebates, coupons, or generous terms—is usually a sure way to enhance immediate profitability. However, gaining sales with price is consistent with long-term profitability only when managed as part of a marketing strategy for achieving, exploiting, or sustaining a longer-term competitive advantage. No price cut should ever be initiated simply to make the next sale or to meet some short-term sales objective without being balanced against the likely reactions of competitors and customers. The key to profitable pricing is building and sustaining competitive advantage. There are times when price-cutting is consistent with building advantage, but it is never an appropriate substitute for it.

Notes

1. Sections of this chapter were first published as an article entitled "Managing Price Competition," *Marketing Management,* 2(1)(Spring 1993), pp. 36–45.

2. For more on the practical applications of game theory, see Adam Brandenburger and Barry Nalebuff, *Competition* (New York: Doubleday, 1996); Rita Koselka, "Evolutionary Economics: Nice Guys Don't Finish Last," *Fortune,* October 11, 1993, pp. 110–14; and Kenichi Ohmae, "Getting Back to Strategy," *Harvard Business Review* (November/December 1988), pp. 149–56.

3. Price competition is a positive-sum game only when total industry contribution rises as a result. This can happen when market demand is sufficiently stimulated by the price cuts, when a low-cost competitor can win share with a price advantage less than its cost advantage, or when a firm's costs are sufficiently reduced by a gain in market share that total industry profits can increase even as prices fall.

4. B. H. Liddell Hart, *Strategy* (New York: Meridian, 1967), p. 322.

5. Michael E. Porter, *Competitive Strategy* (New York: The Free Press, 1980), p. 34.

6. Marcia Berss, "Take It or Leave It," *Forbes,* January 1, 1996, pp. 46–47.

7. Porter, *Competitive Strategy,* pp. 41–43. A firm can become large without getting "stuck in the middle" simply by taking on multiple segments. The segments must be managed, however, as a conglomerate of focused businesses rather than as a one-size-fits-all marketing organization. Procter & Gamble is an excellent example of a large company that nevertheless carefully targets each product to meet the needs of a particular focused segment.

8. "Why Talk Is So Cheap," *Business Week,* September 13, 1999, pp. 34–36.

9. See Pricing in Decline in Chapter 7.

10. See the discussion on predatory pricing in Chapter 14.

11. Note that this principle applies in the other direction as well. If competitors quickly follow price increases, the cost of leading such increases is vastly reduced. Consequently, companies that wish to encourage responsible leadership by other firms would do well to follow their moves quickly, whether up or down.

12. See Francine Schwadel, "Ferocious Competition Tests the Pricing Skills of a Retail Manager," *Wall Street Journal,* December 11, 1989, p. 1.

13. Even before modern telecommunications, retailers used systems for quick reaction to control opportunistic price-cutting. J. Sainsbury, the leading British grocery retailer, is renowned in the industry for its "cascade" telephone alert system in which each store calls five others to alert them to price changes. Within one hour, systemwide price changes can be implemented in response to competitive moves.

14. Another useful tactic that can control such duplicitous behavior in U.S. markets is to require the customer, in order to get the lower price, to initial a clause on the order form that states the customer understands this is "a discriminatorily low price offered solely to meet the price offered by a competitor." Since falsely soliciting a discriminatorily low price is a Robinson-Patman Act violation, the purchasing agent is discouraged from using leverage unless he or she actually has it.

15. For more guidance on collecting competitive information, see "These Guys Aren't Spooks, They're Competitive Analysts," *Business Week,* October 14, 1991, p. 97; and Leonard M. Fuld, *Competitor Intelligence: How to Get It—How to Use It* (New York: Wiley & Sons, 1985).

16. Oliver P. Heil and Arlen W. Langvardt, "The Interface Between Competitive Market Signaling and Antitrust Law," *Journal of Marketing,* 58(3) (July 1994), pp. 81–96.

17. "Chrysler Mulls Cut-Rate Minivan," *USA Today,* April 26, 1990, p. 6B.

18. "Fair Game: Airlines May Be Using a Price-Data Network to Lessen Competition," *Wall Street Journal,* June 28, 1990, p. 1.

19. For a comprehensive and insightful survey of the research on communicating competitive information, see Oliver P. Heil and Arlen W. Langvardt, "The Interface Between Competitive Market Signaling and Antitrust Law,." *Journal of Marketing,* 58(3) (July 1994), pp. 81–96.

CHAPTER 6

Pricing Strategy

Managing Your Market Proactively

This need to manage a market proactively is not obvious. Both business practitioners and academics labor under the economic assumption of a "demand curve" to which the effective pricer must optimally adapt. Demand curves are useful concepts for understanding how markets work, but they can be very misleading as a guide to pricing. Why? Because they are based on the assumption that prices are set, and by implication should be set, while holding "all other things equal." The essence of effective pricing strategy, however, is the coordinated management of those "other things."

The importance to profitability of managing more than just the price became clear to one of this book's authors when he was a young business school professor. As companies learned about his seminars on pricing, they began inquiring as to whether he might present the course at their companies. If so, what would he charge? After some agonizing, the professor set upon $9,000, which, although more than the university paid him for public programs, was about half what a company would pay to send a group of twenty people to a university-sponsored continuing education seminar. As a result, he was sure that the price would be well received. Experience proved him wrong. Although he got frequent requests for proposals, no one called back to schedule a program.

Fortunately, one day he learned why. Someone who had asked for a quote called again to inform him that her boss was quite upset by the proposed price. Did he not see the value? "On the contrary," she replied, "he thought your public seminar was great and he wants everyone in marketing and sales to go through it." Why then did her boss not feel that the price was justified? "Because we don't pay $3,000 a day even to consultants who are well-known and experienced. Your price is simply out of line."

The young assistant professor thought about what he heard, thought about his unpaid student loans, and asked, "What would he be willing to pay?" The potential client offered $6,000, the professor accepted, and a deal was done. Soon after, however, the professor began feeling remorse and embarrassment,

147

particularly as he stood in front of this group lecturing them on value-based pricing. If pricing should be value-based, and if the value were there, why had he been able to capture so little of it in the price? Fortunately, this was not a one-time pricing opportunity. By the time of the next inquiry, the professor had a new strategy to try out.

His response when next asked for the price was the following: "The cost of the university-sponsored program that you have heard about is $780 per participant. However, since the participants in your program would all be from one company, I can focus the discussion more on the issues that are of greatest importance to you and can illustrate the principles by applying them to your specific pricing challenges. Still, without the middleman, I can actually do the program for less. The cost of your in-house program would be only $480 per participant, for a minimum of twenty participants."

The training manager requesting the quote responded with these questions: "Do we get all the same course materials like at the university?" "Is it as long?" "Are you the same instructor who does the course at the university?" Until the price was raised quite a few hundred dollars, no one objected to it. In fact, there were concerns that the "low" price signaled that some element of quality might be missing. (If you don't yet see why this is paradoxical, multiply $480 times 20 and note that this is now the *minimum* charge for what previously was priced at an objectionable $9,000!)

What changed? First, by changing the pricing metric from days of a trainer's time to numbers of people trained, the buyer's attention was shifted from units of cost to units of value. Second, by citing the price of a comparable product, the buyer was given a credible benchmark against which to compare the price. Third, by explaining how the product was actually better than the alternative (a public seminar), the buyer's expectation regarding what value he might receive, and what price might be justified, was enhanced even further. Consequently, even a higher price seemed reasonable within this new frame of reference.

PRICE SETTING VERSUS STRATEGIC PRICING

Many companies approach pricing like the initially naive professor. They set pricing goals based on their own needs and adjust those prices based on what customers say they are willing to pay. Only a few exceptional companies question *why* someone is willing to pay no more than a particular amount. They never think about *how* that willingness can be changed by changing customers' product perceptions, their price expectations, or their perceived alternatives. Moreover, few companies make conscious choices about the markets they should serve. Consequently, few companies proactively manage their businesses to create the conditions that foster more profitable pricing.

This should not be surprising since even the leading minds on marketing strategy often miss this point. They speak of product strategy, communication strategy, distribution strategy, and pricing strategy as independent activities, with pricing the last to be considered. Unfortunately, pricing problems are often rooted in faulty interfaces between pricing and the other elements of marketing and operations. These faulty interfaces occur because product, promotion, distribution, and operations strategies often have developed without the benefit of a clearly defined pricing strategy. Consequently, those decisions do not look faulty when made, but only later when someone tries to establish prices that reflect value without the appropriate organizational support to do so.

The difference between price setting and pricing strategically is the difference between reacting to market conditions and proactively managing them.[1] Price setting is one tactical decision in a sales effort. Pricing strategy is the coordination of interrelated marketing, competitive, and financial decisions to maximize the ability to set prices profitability. Only after reasonable pricing objectives are developed and made an objective of business strategy is it possible to select target markets, create product and service bundles, develop promotional messages that communicate value, and design price structures that will maximize customers' willingness to pay.

For example, while most segments of a market might see value-added differentiation as desirable, the value that it represents for them will vary. Will the company deliver the differentiation only to customers willing to pay the most (high-end watches, leading management consulting firms), or will it try to deliver the differentiation to multiple segments at different price points (automobiles, pharmaceuticals)? If the latter, will the different prices be maintained by creating different product bundles (different car lines) or by relying on different channels of distribution (clothing) or by making the product available at the lower prices only in certain locations (neighborhood and off-brand gasoline stations) or at certain times (discount airline tickets) when high-value buyers are less likely to purchase? How will the value message be framed for each segment?

Of course, every company must ultimately set prices that reflect what customers are willing to pay. Too many companies, however, ensure their own failure by treating customers' willingness to pay as a constraint on their pricing, rather than as a variable that needs to be managed. The drivers of a value-based pricing strategy are the firm's potential to create economic value for customers, its costs to create that value, and its competitive advantages in creating value that competitors cannot immediately duplicate at the same cost. The key to greater profitability is to let economic value drive pricing goals and objectives, and then manage willingness to pay with marketing and competitive activities that support those goals and objectives.

CREATING A PRICING STRATEGY

Strategy is the coordination of multiple activities to achieve a common objective: in this case, profitable price. If managers think about pricing only when they must set a price, there is little that they can control but the price level. When, however, they think about capturing value as an objective, they can expand their ability to set prices profitably by controlling much more than the price level. For example, when facing price resistance, they can change the product/service options they offer (how many option packages and price points?), the price justification they communicate (what is the relevant alternative and the value proposition associated with the product's differentiation?), and the price metrics they select (is the price "quantity-based" like gasoline, "access-based" like health clubs, Internet access, and all-you-can-eat salad bars, or "performance-based" like investment banking and some legal services?).

When pricing is inadequately profitable, the problem is often that price structure, marketing, and competitive decisions have been made without profitable pricing as a goal. Rather, different functional areas in the firm have different, often conflicting, subsidiary goals—such as increasing awareness, building market share, achieving "top line" growth, improving margins—that they pursue independently. A pricing strategy involves establishing cross-functional objectives and synergistic goals to create an organization that can profitably produce and capture value.

To optimize long-term profitability, price setting must occur within the context of a pricing process and structure that is *proactive*. Proactive pricing must in turn be part of a marketing strategy that is *value-based*. A longer-term competitive positioning that is *profit-driven,* rather than driven by sales or market share, must guide the value-based marketing strategy. Exhibit 6-1 illustrates these multiple levels of a pricing strategy, where success within each circle is limited by the successful execution of the ones surrounding it.

The remainder of this chapter will describe the interfaces between successful price setting and each of the other activities upon which its success depends.

PROACTIVE PRICING: STRUCTURE AND PROCESS

Before entering an entirely new market, it is logical to build a pricing strategy from the outside in—beginning first with competitive strategy, then value-based marketing, and finally price structure and process. When reevaluating pricing strategy in a market where the firm is already doing business, it is better to begin from the inside out. Fixing problems closer to the center involves fewer steps and, therefore, the fix can be implemented more quickly. Even if a company's competitive strategy is flawed, it might as well capture as much profitability as possible from whatever economic value it is creating. Moreover, while improving marketing or competitive strategy can impact sales volume, it cannot improve margins unless there is a price structure and process in place for capturing value. Fortunately, in companies already delivering good value that at least some customers recognize, making the pricing process and structure more proactive and value-based can quickly increase profits, thus building organizational support for addressing the more difficult issues in the outer circles.

A company we worked with in the printing industry illustrates the importance of process and structure. The company built its reputation on quality work with high levels of customer service. Despite this commitment, both the

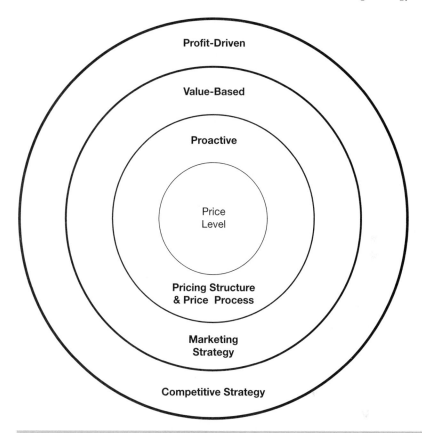

EXHIBIT 6-1 The Domain of Pricing Strategy

company and its customers thought of the product in terms of units of printing rather than in terms of value delivered. They priced "pre-press design," "impressions," and "binding," while giving away the service that differentiated them. Consequently, they were often on the defensive when a potential customer compared the company's printing bid with that of a less service-oriented competitor. Moreover, they were berated and embarrassed when a customer found that another was getting a lower price to do a similar print job, even though the same job for different customers might involve vastly different amounts of service. As a result of not having a price structure that reflected the value of service, the company's prices were beaten down in price negotiations. Despite a strong market share, its costs were high and its profitability was disappointing.

The solution to this company's problem was to determine what about its service added value for customers and to charge for it. Once people at the company started thinking in terms of value, tens of services that were taken for granted became sources of revenue. Charges for correcting copy, adapting to late delivery of copy, redesigning jobs to save on mailing costs, reducing color variability within a job, and scheduling jobs at peak times all became either sources of revenue or incentives for customers to change their behavior to eliminate costs. The ability to offer customers objective trade-offs between price and service levels gave salespeople alternatives to simple price concessions and forced customers to acknowledge what they valued. By unbundling service elements and charging for them, the company became more price competitive with less differentiated suppliers, while recovering the costs and capturing the value of differentiation from customers that required some or all of its services.

The Price Structure

To capture value with pricing, the price structure must reflect differences in the economic value delivered by the product or service. Structure consists of two elements: *segmentation fences* and *value metrics*. Segmentation fences are criteria that customers must meet to qualify for discounts. At movie theaters, segmentation fences are usually based on age (with discounts for children under twelve and for seniors) but are sometimes also based on educational status (full-time students get discounts). Value metrics are the units to which the price is applied. A health club could set its prices per hour, per visit, for unlimited access (an annual membership), or for performance (per inch lost at the waist or gained at the chest). It could also vary prices by time of day (peak/off-peak) or by season of the year.[2]

Segmentation fences are the least complicated way to charge different prices to reflect different levels of value. Airlines are masters at identifying customer segments and establishing value-based segmentation fences. To reflect differences in value delivered to business and leisure travelers, they offer large discounts to passengers whose trips involve a Saturday night stay or are planned far in advance. They also give substantial discounts to senior citizens. Unfortunately, segmentation fences are ineffective at keeping buyers paying different prices unless the product is not easily resold and the fence is based on objective criteria. Thus segmentation fences work well for pricing services and low-value items that are not worth the effort to resell, and where the segmentation criteria are something verifiable, such as the buyer's age (e.g., seniors) or legal status (e.g., consumer vs. business, nonprofit vs. for-profit).

Unfortunately, while simple to administer, segmentation fences are frequently too easy for customers to get over whenever there is an economic incentive to do so. In Europe, where there are large differences in incomes and the economic values within the European Economic Union, companies have long tried to sell the same products at different prices within different countries. So long as there were costly border controls on the movement of goods, this worked acceptably well. Now, however, distributors and even consumers travel to the countries with the lowest prices to buy their products. For example, in some categories where shipping costs are low relative to product value, more than half of the products sold into Spain, Greece, and Italy are reshipped to countries in northern Europe with higher list prices.

The measure of a good price structure is its ability to vary price with variation in the potential contribution margin, which is defined as the difference between the value delivered to a customer with a purchase and the incremental cost incurred to deliver it. Some pharmaceuticals companies do a good job setting pricing metrics that track value alone (which is appropriate since incremental costs are usually very low). For the latest generation of gastrointestinal products, prices are proportionately higher the larger the dose. This pricing reflects value because more seriously ill people require larger doses, and there are no good substitutes for treating the most seriously ill patients other than with the latest drugs. In contrast, the price per dose of the most popular antidepressants is the same regardless of whether the patient requires a 10-, 20-, or 40-milligram dose. This reflects the fact that the amount of the drug required for effective treatment is unrelated to the severity of the symptoms and, therefore, the value obtained from using it.

To see the importance of value-based metrics, consider the alternative. When on-line databases were launched, they charged by minutes of access time. This initially seemed logical because it tracked a major element of cost. Unfortunately, it poorly tracked value. Inexperienced users spent a lot of time searching, producing a high cost of search, while experienced users, who knew what they needed and where to get it, could substantially cut the time, and therefore the cost, of a search. That created an incentive for companies and institutions to limit searches to experienced users, precluding trial by new users. One data supplier revealed to us that, as a result of this metric, it required an ever-growing body of novice users. Profits from high-volume, loyal users were slim to none.

By finding metrics that more closely track with differences in value, companies can often gain both by driving more sales and more margins. Exhibit 6-2 illustrates the challenge in designing price metrics. The trick is to find metrics that allow prices to vary automatically with value delivered, keeping all customers in the "Price $\approx$ Value" range. Newspapers and magazines, for example, are high–fixed-cost businesses that have traditionally undermined their profitability with poor price structures. The price metric for ad space is usually pages and column inches, and the pricing process involves individual customer negotiation with the largest advertisers. Thus, many small advertisers ended up in the "Missed Opportunities" range, unable to afford newspaper advertising but lacking the clout to negotiate better rates. Large advertisers used their leverage to get the best locations in the paper, producing the highest response to their advertising, but still negotiating the lowest rates. They populate the "Unharvested Value" category.

During the past decade, some newspapers have added price metrics to profitably correct these imbalances. Single-location suburban advertisers often fit into the "Missed Opportunities" section because they can benefit from advertising to only a portion of a paper's metro-area circulation. To become more attractive to such advertisers, many papers have created a few "zoned" pages where they can print different ads for editions being delivered to different geographic

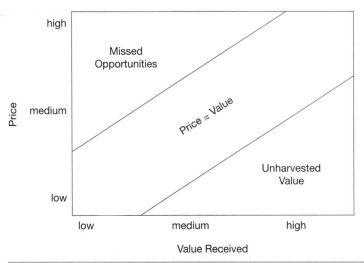

EXHIBIT 6-2 Aligning Price with Value

zones. In that way, an advertiser who values reaching only 50 percent of the paper's readers can get a price that is, say, only 65 percent of the "full run" price. The value to that advertiser does not change, but the price comes down in a way that prevents advertisers who value all of the paper's circulation from opting for the same deal.

To capture more of the value provided advertisers in the "Unharvested Value" sector, newspapers have added additional metrics. Rather than give away the best locations or times to their highest-volume advertisers (who get the lowest prices anyway), they have established premiums for the best ad locations (e.g., behind main news and on back pages), for peak advertising days, and for services such as accommodating delivery of late copy. The ability to offer a variety of pricing options empowered salespeople to respond to price pressure with feature–price trade-offs rather than with simple price concessions. Moreover, putting prices on these scarce features, rather than giving them to the largest advertisers, created more demand for them. In some cases, new advertisers have come to the papers because they could buy locations that were previously available only to the largest customers.

Another way to reach such customers in the "Missed Opportunity" segments, instead of discounting, is to selectively add value that justifies the higher price. Northwest Airlines developed a program for winning more "Missed Opportunities" without having to discount prices to passengers for whom it delivered high value. Northwest had a nearly complete monopoly, and therefore the ability to charge high prices, on nonstop service from many of its hub cities (Minneapolis–St.Paul, Detroit, and Seattle). The missed opportunities were passengers who could connect through its hubs, or the hubs of any competing airline, making them relatively price sensitive. Northwest's solution was to selectively add value. With its "Connect First" program, Northwest automatically upgraded to first class any customer with a business-class ticket if that customer's travel connected through a Northwest hub. The value added by first class made the Northwest offer competitive for travelers who might otherwise have connected at lower cost through another airline's hub.

A value-based price metric may involve measuring some attribute of the customer, rather than of the product delivered. Software suppliers will send one disk to load on the company server, but will charge for it based on the number of workstations that will have access to it. Film distributors charge for first-run movies based on the number of seats in the theater. Real estate agents charge a percentage of the selling price of the house, which is only partly related to the level of service they deliver.

When customers' behavior influences the incremental cost to serve them and those costs are significant, profit-maximizing price metrics need to reflect that as well. A service cost is significant if the cost of measuring, monitoring, and charging for differences in its usage exceeds the cost to deliver it. Software suppliers eventually had to add a price metric for on-line support rather than bundling it with the software price. A relatively small number of people were using a lot of telephone support disproportionate to the revenue earned from them. Similarly, banks have added charges for small account holders to use a teller, or even a teller machine.

In one case where a company provided free equipment to use with its consumables, customers were discarding equipment whenever it needed to be cleaned since it was, for them, free. They also requested multiple pieces of equipment so that it would be conveniently available in multiple locations. Our recommendation that customers be charged a monthly fee for equipment, with a correspondingly lower charge for consumables, vastly reduced requests for new equipment and improved equipment utilization. Savings in equipment cost far exceeded the cost of tracking and billing.

There are cases, however, where it is more profitable to base the price totally on units of value despite potential cost variability. This is a good strategy where costs may vary in ways over which customers have little ability to predict or control. It is a great strategy where the seller believes that the risk associated with unexpected costs is less than what customers believe. It is also useful when both sellers and customers have comparable risk perceptions but the seller is in a better position to pool and manage the risk.

General Electric used bundling to reduce risk when it launched a new series of highly efficient aircraft engines, its GE90 series. These engines promised greater fuel efficiency and power that could make them much more profitable to operate. The catch was a high degree of uncertainty about the cost of maintenance. Some airlines feared that these high-powered engines might need to be overhauled more frequently, thus easily wiping out the financial benefits from operating them. This undermined GE's ability to win buyers at the price premium that power and fuel efficiency would otherwise justify.

Rather than accept a lower price to account for a buyer's perceived risk, GE absorbed the risk by changing the price metric. Instead of selling or leasing an engine alone, GE offered to sell "power by the hour." For the first time, customers could lease a GE aircraft engine for a fee per hour flown that included all costs of scheduled and unscheduled maintenance. Without the uncertainty of maintenance cost, GE90 engines quickly became popular despite a price premium. In fact, the program was so popular that GE extended it by offering a "Maintenance Cost per Hour" program on its older engines with established maintenance track records.

The key to finding good fences and metrics is to study how segments differ in what drives (or undermines) value for them and what drives the cost to serve them. The challenge is to search for fences and metrics that can be creatively combined to automatically charge more (or less) when and where a sale creates more (or less) value for the buyer or predictably higher (or lower) incremental costs for the seller.

The Pricing Process

A value-based price structure is not, by itself, sufficient for good pricing. The process for setting price levels within that structure must be proactive. Many companies have no formal process for making price changes or granting price exceptions. No one can identify who in the organization is ultimately responsible for the overall profitability of prices. In some cases, literally no one is. Consequently, pricing is temporarily adopted by one functional area or another to solve a near-term problem for one customer, product line, or even salesperson. Without any analysis to determine the best decision for the organization as a whole, evaluated considering the implication of the decision for the longer term, pricing decisions often create more problems than they solve.

At a large consumer packaged-goods company, we were told that the criterion for establishing list prices was what the product needed, given its full manufacturing cost, to achieve a targeted profit margin. The actual price, however, depended on how much the marketing department decided to "price promote" the product—either to the consumer or to the trade. The criterion driving that decision was whether or not the product was meeting its sales goal. Since sales goals were evaluated quarterly, price promotions were regular occurrences for many products at the end of every quarter. The tragedy of this process was that no one estimated the effect that discounting one brand was having on sales of the same company's other brands. Perhaps the reason one brand was not meeting its sales goal was that another from the same company, selling at full price, was already winning the sales. Moreover, no one estimated how much of the sales gain was actually sustainable sales growth or simply a shift forward from the next quarter.

Companies in business-to-business markets commonly have even less well-defined pricing processes simply because, by selling directly, they can more easily get away without consistent rules. Many have eschewed fixed-price policies and strict criteria for discounting, relying instead on nonpolicies that make any price negotiable so long as the sale meets some minimum profit criteria. Salespeople initiate "customer specific" pricing decisions, which management reviews without any consistent criteria other then whether they "need" the sale to achieve the current quarter's sales goal.[3]

By adopting these reactive, ad hoc policies, managers often think that their companies will respond more quickly to market conditions while limiting discounting to only situations where competitive pressure and customer resistance make it necessary. Experience usually proves them wrong. In markets where customers purchase a product regularly or communicate with others who do, they learn from experience. Before long, they notice that discounts are larger and more forthcoming to buyers who negotiate aggressively. The smart ones adapt to take advantage of this situation. They institute policies to limit the seller's exposure to satisfied users, requiring salespeople to work through purchasing agents. They begin courting competitors, offering them a piece of the business to gain negotiating leverage against their preferred supplier. They form buying cooperatives to increase the pressure on sellers to make concessions. They also hold their orders to ends of fiscal quarters when they know that desperate sales managers are more likely to grant concessions. In short, when sellers replace price policies with freely negotiated pricing, they create economic incentives for "good customers" to become "difficult customers."

To reestablish value-based price integrity, companies must rebuild pricing processes to eliminate these perverse incentives. They must set their prices and discount levels proactively, by policy, not in reaction to individual customer misinformation and manipulation. Since customers are different in their needs, and therefore in what they will pay for, pricing policies must accommodate those differences, but must do so while maintaining price integrity. To achieve that, a value-based pricing process usually requires replacing flexible pricing for a fixed product offering with fixed prices for a variety of flexible, offerings.

Exhibit 6-3 illustrates a simple price "menu" of flexible product/service offerings. Salespeople negotiating from such a menu have no authority to change any of the prices. They can, however, offer customers various combinations of prices and product or service features, enabling them to reach a price point. They can also offer discounts for meeting preestablished and transparent criteria, such as being a nonprofit organization, giving the seller an exclusive contract to meet the buyer's needs, or purchasing larger quantities. Negotiating within such constraints forces customers who claim not to value the company's differentiating features to forgo them in order to obtain a better price. It prevents buyers from separating the process of needs identification from the process of price determination. It also eliminates the incentive to supply the salesperson with misinformation about needs, or to maintain multiple supplier relationships simply to gain negotiating leverage. With a fixed-price constraint, customers have the incentive to be open and honest about their needs so as to help their sales reps find the price and offer that gives them the best value.

A pricing process based on a fixed-price menu can be highly decentralized in implementation, facilitating quicker response to customer requests for

	Turn-Around	Special Processing	Long-Term Contract	On-Site Customer Support
Low price package	3–7 days, when available	Not available	Not available	Not available
Regular package	3 days (+15% for 24 hour)	Service A +3% Service B +7% Service C +5%	-10%	+15%
Full service package	24 hour	A,B,C included with added performance guarantee Service D +9%	1 year minimum	Included

EXHIBIT 6-3 A Nonnegotiable Price Menu

BOX 6-1

A Revolution in Pricing? Not Quite

With the Internet, alternative systems are doable—just not desirable most of the time.

Priceline.com flipped pricing on its head when it launched in 1998. Usually, businesses post prices, then lower them if no one's willing to buy. At Priceline.com Inc. (PCLN), it was buyers who posted the prices they would pay—then raised them if no one was willing to sell.

Economists were gleeful. It was like detecting a new subatomic particle—a pricing model that had been theorized to exist but was never before observed. The early successes of Priceline, as well as on-line auctioneers such as eBay Inc. (EBAY) and other dotcoms with alternative pricing systems, convinced many experts that conventional seller-posted prices were relics of the Industrial Age. "We've suddenly made the interaction cost so cheap, there's no pragmatic reason not to have competitive bidding on everything," Stuart I. Feldman, director of IBM Corporation's Institute for Advanced Commerce in Hawthorne, New York, said in a 1998 *Business Week* story.

However, although technology and venture capital have produced dozens of alternatives to seller-posted prices, most have flopped and none has moved beyond a narrow niche. For most products, and most consumers, a system of prices posted by sellers is still perceived as more convenient and fair. Says Robert L. Phillips, chief technology officer of Atlanta-based Talus Solutions Inc., which makes pricing soft-

BOX 6-1 (*continued*)

ware, "It's going to be very difficult to build a business plan around a pricing model alone."

Why did so many entrepreneurs and investors overestimate the popularity of alternative pricing schemes? Partly because they confused what's technologically possible with what buyers and sellers actually want. Auctions, for example, are suited for one-of-a-kind items whose value is uncertain, such as a painting that's worth nothing to most people but a lot to some idiosyncratic collector. The brilliance of eBay is that it opened auctions to a much broader public and lowered transaction costs so it became feasible to auction even low-priced items. But economists say that auctions have no advantage for mass merchandise because there's nothing idiosyncratic about the demand for it—it's just easier to slap on a price tag.

What's more, companies don't want to sell all their stuff to bargain hunters. That's why customers who buy via Priceline can't choose their airline or what time of day they'll fly. The airlines fill seats by appealing to price-sensitive customers who otherwise would not fly at all—without having to lower prices for their regular customers. To get airlines or other companies to participate, Priceline must keep its system deliberately inconvenient—which naturally limits its potential market. "I see Priceline as a variation on coupons," says Hal R. Varian, an economist at the University of California at Berkeley.

There's still innovation in pricing, but it's focused on how to set posted prices. Companies are getting better at using instant feedback from the marketplace. Deborah Vollmer Dahlke, CEO of Zilliant Inc. of Austin, Texas, an Internet pricing management company, says the number of price changes in desktop computers is going up 20 percent a year. Plus, companies are figuring out how to segment their customers by willingness to pay, as the airlines have long done. One trick: Publish a high list price, but send out coupons to price-sensitive customers who otherwise wouldn't buy. IBM's Feldman says maneuvers like that fit his loose definition of auctioning.

If this stuff doesn't sound revolutionary, that's the point. The revolution—alternative pricing—didn't live up to its press. Last spring, Priceline founder Jay S. Walker said, "There have only been five pricing systems in the history of the world. This is the sixth pricing system. This one will become the preferred pricing system."[6] Of course, Priceline's stock is down 98 percent from its peak. Maybe our ancestors weren't clueless about business after all.

quotes than a variable price system. The development of such a policy, including the details of the price metrics, the fixed-price levels, and the discount policies, must be centralized to cover all customers who might cross-ship products or exchange information about prices. A pricing committee or department, usually containing representatives from finance, marketing, and sales, regularly reviews the prices and price policies and is responsible for coordinating initiatives to support profitable pricing.

When sales seem inadequate, the committee does not make pricing policy exceptions; it reengineers the pricing strategy. That may involve a simple tactical change, such as lowering a price or developing a segmentation scheme for discounting to a target customer group. Even simple schemes usually have operation implications, requiring that the pricing group have direct access to a high level of authority. For example, a new loyalty discount criterion could require a tracking system to monitor customers (e.g., is this customer really giving the seller at least 80 percent of its purchases?).

When simple changes in price structure are inadequate, the pricing committee must be able to lead the company to make more fundamental changes. This may involve instructing others to design and manufacture different versions of the product (such as a flanking brand to protect the company from a lower-cost competitor, or a performance-priced product and service package for the customer segment that is willing to pay to eliminate risk). If the pricing committee concludes that the company's pricing is justified by objective value that customers do not recognize, it might commission a new advertising or sales support program that better communicates the misunderstood aspects of the value proposition. Whatever the pricing problem, a strategic solution usually requires an organizational response involving cross-functional coordination and a high degree of consistency across customers.

As with every rule, there are exceptions to the rule that pricing by policy is preferable to ad hoc price negotiations. Where each purchase is a unique product or service, it is difficult to have an entirely standard formula. Freely negotiated pricing may also prove more profitable whenever customers purchase infrequently. Lacking information about their alternatives and the experience to evaluate them, they are more likely to seek a satisfactory purchase than to find the best value in the market. Traditionally, this has been true for retail auto sales. Lastly, when there is an industry leader against whose pricing all other companies are compared and that leader's pricing is inconsistent and unpredictable, it may be necessary for competitors to negotiate prices in order to remain competitive.

Still, although price-only negotiation may be justified in these circumstances, they still introduce the risk that smart buyers will use any flexibility in pricing to disconnect prices from the value they receive, creating a market in which everything is priced as a commodity. As customers have learned that auto dealers exploit the uneducated buyer, they have flocked to auto buying groups, such as those offered by Sam's Club or the American Automobile Association, which negotiate better deals. A. T. Kearny has a very successful, and rapidly growing, supply-chain management group that monitors industrial pricing practices and trains customers to manipulate sellers to get better deals. Freemarkets.com enables customers to create "reverse auctions" where the buyer has all the information about the offers but the sellers see only the prices. While all of these buying tactics are arguably "unfair" to sellers, they were created to protect customers from the equally unfair and inconsistent pricing policies of the sellers.[4]

To manage these risks, negotiated pricing must be centralized not only at the level of policy but also in its application. That slows response time and raises the cost of administration relative to a fixed-price/flexible-offer pricing policy. Given the frequency of individual pricing decisions in the absence of nonnegotiable policies, the decision makers will almost certainly become a pricing department rather than just a committee. As negotiated pricing became the rule in the pharmaceuticals industry in the 1980s and 1990s, companies first established pricing groups to coordinate pricing globally. These groups can make strategic trade-offs, such as not launching a drug in a country that will demand lower prices (e.g., Greece, Italy) until they can negotiate prices for countries where they can command higher prices (e.g., Germany, Japan, and the United States). They also evaluate the impact of a deal with one buyer on the prices that other buyers will demand, and simply walk from those deals that do not promise enough additional volume to justify the adverse impact they will have on pricing to other customers.

Whatever the pricing process, evaluate it by the following criteria: Does the system encourage proactive pricing decisions to exploit opportunities, or only decisions necessary to solve problems? Does it integrate all the relevant information, including the impact that the deal being considered would have on the prices those other customers will demand? Do salespeople have the incentives to justify prices to the customer, or is it easier and more profitable for them to advocate within their company to meet the customers' demands? Does it force customers to acknowledge the differential value that your company offers, or does it reward them for discounting that value? Unless the answer to all of these questions is "yes," there is room for a process improvement.

VALUE-BASED MARKETING STRATEGY

Strategic pricing is not only about setting price structures, processes, and levels that capture value. The amount of value that can be profitably captured is limited by the amount that is created and communicated. Consequently, strategic pricing is also about establishing value-based marketing goals for the creation and communication of value. Value-based marketing strategy involves (1) using services to convert technical capabilities into customer benefits, (2) developing the value message associated with those benefits, and (3) managing a sales, advertising, and distribution effort to deliver that message. By creating and establishing a clear value proposition, value-based marketing undermines the tendency of customers to make easy comparisons between competing prices and instead make comparisons between price and value.

Creating Customer Benefits

Marketing adds value by creating an internal understanding of the benefits that customers seek and organizing the company to supply those benefits. Frequently, the reason that companies cannot get the prices they seek is not that they lack the capabilities and technologies to deliver high value, but that the company has not understood customers' needs well enough to make that potential a reality. A few years ago, a large "home center" was built near our office. This vendor, HQ, sold every imaginable hardware and home improvement product and was always crowded with customers. About a year after it opened, a Home Depot opened about a mile away. The Home Depot looked almost exactly like the HQ and had a slightly less desirable location. Still, within a year, the Home Depot had caused the HQ to close its doors.

The Home Depot's secret was its understanding of what customers need. HQ offered everything, but finding it was difficult and finding someone to explain how to use it was impossible. Home Depot, on the other hand, understood that do-it-yourselfers require a lot of help finding the right item and may need an explanation of how to use it. Consequently, Home Depot stores are full of knowledgeable, patient sales associates. The customer, who left the HQ feeling frustrated and bewildered, could now leave the Home Depot feeling supported and empowered with exactly the same items.

Few people realize that Intel's strong profitability was also built not on superior technology but on superior ancillary service. When Intel launched the second in its now dominant series of microprocessors, it faced much customer resistance and low internal morale. David Davidow, vice president of marketing, described the situation as follows:

"Everyone on the task force accepted the harsh truth that Motorola and Zilog had better devices. If Intel tried to fight the battle only by claiming our microprocessor was better than theirs, we were going to lose. But we also knew that a designer needed more than just the processor, and we had our competitors beaten hands down when it came to the extras. We had been playing to our competitor's strengths, and it was time we started selling our own."[5]

Davidow's task force at Intel set out to do the first task in marketing: taking the basic product or service and adding to it whatever is necessary to create an offering that represents a complete benefit for the buyer. In this case, buyers struggled to design products that used microprocessors. Since Motorola and Zilog technologies were more innovative, designing products around them was even more difficult. Consequently, Intel focused on the customer support and peripherals that they would supply, thus enabling a customer to design their new product around the Intel chip faster and cheaper. To show customers that the technology would not remain stagnant, Intel also developed and published a "futures" catalog of all the products in the pipeline. With a product service package that better met the customers' needs without price concessions, Intel achieved 85 percent market share for its microprocessor.[6]

This is not to say that the only way to offer a superior value proposition is to add services. Warehouse stores and direct-to-consumer computer manufacturers were initially so successful because they cut out services for which some segment of customers was unwilling to pay. The message is that value is determined by more than the core product or service for sale; it is determined by a package of information, access, and complementary services necessary to realize value potential. A marketer should never ask whether or not she offers a good product relative to the competition, but rather whether or not the product she offers is a good value. When a product or service with high value potential is not selling profitably, the problem may not be the price. It may be that the company is not adequately empowering the customer to achieve that value. Or it may be that some buyers do not need and are unwilling to pay for more information, access, or service than they need.

Communicating the Value Proposition

Value-based pricing will fail unless customers actually perceive the value for which the pricing process and price structure are designed to make them pay. Even when a company offers value that justifies its prices, sales growth or margins will still be stunted unless the company's marketing program effectively communicates that value. While most marketers recognize the truth of this statement for new, innovative products, it is often disregarded for established products. One of the great misconceptions of marketing research is that customers who have been using a product know, without being told, what it is worth to them.

We have proven that belief wrong many times in our work as pricing consultants. We have seen long-time, high-volume buyers of newspaper ad space, trucks, dedicated telephone lines, medical capital equipment, OEM parts, and financial services (to name a few) spends millions each year on items whose value they did not understand. While they often had a preference for a particular supplier's reliability, service, or differentiation, they had neither a quantitative nor a qualitative understanding of the economic value associated with that preference. Consequently, the highest-quality suppliers in those markets were consistently vulnerable to suppliers who could offer a precisely quantified price advantage in return for forgoing "qualitative" advantages that seemed simply "nice to have."

Buyers who are ignorant of the monetary value of a firm's product and service differentiation generally tend to underestimate it. The purpose of value communication—involving advertising, personal sales, programs to induce trial, endorsements, and guarantees that communicate confidence in the promises made—is to raise uninformed buyers' willingness to pay to a level comparable to that of better-informed and experienced buyers. Caterpillar Corporation has enviable loyalty among heavy-equipment users who carefully track downtime and the lifetime costs of ownership. There are, however, many

- **Comprehend** what drives sustainable value for customers
- **Create** value for customers
- **Communicate** the value that you create
  — Tangible features
  — Intangible features
- **Convince** customers that they must pay for value received
- **Capture** value with appropriate price metrics and fences

EXHIBIT 6-4 The Five Cs of Value-Based Marketing

other users of equipment who are not so diligent. Convincing them to pay a large premium for a CAT is not so easy. Caterpillar understands, however, that knowledgeable buyers are better buyers, and so it uses value-based communication to support pricing for nearly all of its products. Its Web site and sales materials compare the economics of ownership for Caterpillar to competitive products by quantifying the value for a product's differentiating features.

The exact nature of the value communication effort differs between products and services that are sold direct, as in most business-to-business markets, and those that are sold through distribution channels. In direct sales, the message can be much more complex and customer-specific since it will be delivered in a lengthy one-to-one contact with a sales rep or a Web site. When relying on distribution channels, the seller's only direct contact with the buyer may be via a short, generic advertisement or the external information on the packaging. In all cases, however, the goal is to influence the buyer's evaluation of the product relative to its price.

Exhibit 6-4 summarizes the responsibility of marketing management to the success of a pricing strategy. The "Five Cs" of this framework are arranged chronologically from top to bottom in the order that they are executed. When diagnosing pricing problems and recommendations for solving them, one should think of this as a system rather than as a set of discrete steps.

PROFIT-DRIVEN COMPETITIVE POSITIONING

Before developing a product/service offering, a value communication plan, a distribution strategy, and a price structure, a firm must identify segments of the market that it can serve profitably and position itself to do so. To quote Philip Kotler, the leading marketing educator of the past forty years, "If the targeting and positioning decisions are made correctly, the other things will follow. If they're made incorrectly, nothing good will follow."[7] This competitive positioning is arguably the most important decision that a business strategist makes. Unless a company has positioned itself to create and sustain economic value, the best possible effort at value communication and capture can produce at best mediocre results.

Companies that position themselves well (Sears when it targeted first the rural farmer, then the suburban homeowner; Apple when it targeted the education and graphics design markets) enjoy margins that enable them to survive even with less than stellar operational excellence. Companies that position themselves poorly (like Amazon, Peapod, and other Internet start-ups) have margins that are always under competitive pressure, leaving little room for operational error if they are to survive, let alone prosper. Companies that both target markets well and serve them efficiently (Wal-Mart, Southwest Airlines, Siebel Systems) have the basis for both exceptional profit and growth.

Many companies fail to find profitable segments upon which to focus because they do not use appropriate selection criteria. They target the largest or the fastest-growing segments, rather than the segments that they could serve with any competitive advantage. As a result, many companies grow without profit. In contrast, Wal-Mart originally targeted a declining segment (rural America), and Southwest targeted a small segment (low-volume cities), which competitors either ignored or served poorly. Intel had the courage to abandon the high-volume memory-chip segment, accepting criticism from the business press, to focus on what were smaller and slower growth segments that had the potential for greater profitability.

Essential to the selection of market segments based on potential profitability is some idea of how you would price to those segments. Could you profit by capturing exceptionally high margins from a segment of willing buyers unattracted by the prices of less differentiated alternatives (as does Nordstrom in retailing, Johnnie Walker Black Label for scotch whiskey, Patek Philippe for watches, and Peterbilt for trucks)? Could you profit by winning from competitors' market share that they would be unwilling or unable to defend (as Wal-Mart did in retailing, Bic in pens, razors, and lighters, and Supercuts did in haircutting)? Or could you profit by developing operational advantages enabling you to win customers without either a strong price or product advantage (as McDonald's did by picking the best locations and establishing systems for more efficient operation, as Anheuser-Busch has done with superior brand marketing and management of its distributor network)? These three pricing strategies are commonly labeled "skim," "penetration," and "neutral" pricing.[8] Understanding which is viable for any market segment is necessary to determine its potential profitability, and therefore the desirability of focusing resources on it.

These three strategies are *not* defined by the product's price relative to the competition, but rather by the use of price to drive sales. *Skim pricing* involves setting price high relative to the distribution of economic values that it could deliver to potential customers. The strategy makes sense when the profit from serving the upper end of the distribution exceeds the profit from pricing competitively for the bulk of customers in the middle. *Penetration pricing* involves setting price low relative to economic value in order to gain from high market share or from the low cost of marketing to a price-sensitive segment—using price as the draw. *Neutral pricing* involves setting prices at levels that eliminate price as a decision criterion for the largest segment of buyers.

A skim price is not necessarily higher, nor is a penetration price necessarily lower, than other prices in the market. A high price can still be a penetration price if perceived value is even higher, while a low price can be a skim price if the value is low to all but a minority of the market. For example, Saab, a luxury car brand, has deliberately penetration-priced its cars in recent years to build market share. To preserve the premium image, the penetration prices were disguised as very low-cost financing for up to five years. At the other extreme, bottled water is the cheapest drink that one can buy in a bar. Price, however is not the selling point, since anyone really looking for a good value in water would not buy it in a bar. Bottled water is skim priced in bars because it meets the need for those who want something nonalcoholic but do not want to appear cheap or uncool.

Hartmann® and Louis Vuitton® both charge similar prices for competitive products, but position them to appeal to different market segments. Louis Vuitton uses a typical skim strategy, positioning its luggage as "art" for the discriminating traveler, who is happy to pay for the prestige and exclusivity that the Vuitton price, name, and distinctive styling evoke. Vuitton's position is not that it offers a generally good value, but rather that it offers something special for those who can afford it. Hartmann, in contrast, positions similarly priced luggage as an "investment" that justifies its price by extra durability. Although Hartmann charges prices comparable to Louis Vuitton, its *neutral strategy* appeals to the buyer looking for a good value that will cost no more in the long run, rather than to those for whom getting the most for their money is not the issue.

Although different competitive price positions often coexist in the same market, selection of a strategy is not arbitrary. A firm's cost structure, its targeted customers' motivations, and its relative competitive capabilities will favor one strategy over others in each case. The following sections describe the conditions under which each strategy is appropriate. In some industries, particularly those with high fixed costs, profitable growth may require simultaneously pursuing multiple segments that require multiple strategies.

Skim Pricing

Skim pricing (or skimming) is designed to capture high margins at the expense of high sales volume. By definition, skim prices are high in relation to what most buyers are willing to pay under most circumstances. Consequently, this strategy is viable only when the profit from selling to a price-insensitive segment exceeds that from selling to a larger market at a lower price.

Customers

Buyers are often price insensitive because they belong to a market segment that places exceptionally high value on a product's differentiating attributes. The *New York Times* successfully pursues a skim-pricing strategy because an educated elite of newspaper readers strongly prefers its in-depth reporting on international affairs, politics, travel, and the arts. A segment of sports enthusiasts will often pay comparatively astronomical prices for the bike, or club, or racquet that will give them an edge. For example, you can buy a plain aluminum canoe paddle for $35. You can buy a Bending Birches Journey paddle (wood laminate, 44 oz.) for $129. Or you can buy the Werner Camano (graphite, 26 oz.) for $349. The Werner Camano not only makes canoeing long distances easier but also signals that one belongs to a select group that has a very serious commitment to the sport.

Although unique product attributes can support skim pricing, other factors (discussed in Chapter 4) can support a skimming strategy as well. When the expenditure is small, some buyers purchase on "impulse" without even considering the alternatives. Another good target for skim pricing are buyers who travel on business and bill others. Restaurants, rental car companies, and hotels often skim price their products when they focus on that market segment. Similarly, the importance attached to the end benefit blinds proud parents when planning weddings for their children. Photographers, caterers, and florists all profit handsomely from skim pricing to this segment. Buyers who value prestige and exclusivity will pay more simply because they know that others can't buy the product. Steuben Glass increased its cachet and prices when it reduced the number of retail outlets to one per region and increased its prices.

Costs

In addition to a price-insensitive customer segment, a particular cost environment also favors successful skim pricing. When variable costs represent a large share of a product's price (say 80 percent), even a small price premium (5 percent) will drive up the contribution margin by a substantial amount (25 percent). Moreover, since expenditures on variable costs vary proportionately with sales volume, there is no need to maintain volume to remain cost competitive. If variable costs are 90 percent of a product's price (yielding a 10 percent contribution margin), a skimming strategy to increase prices by 15 percent would make a product more profitable so long as the firm lost no more than 60 percent of its sales volume.

Marketers often assume that skim pricing is impractical when production economies are large. While that is potentially true, it is not necessarily the case. If only 15 percent of a market is price insensitive, but many other firms are competing to serve the other 85 percent, the only firm that targets a niche market could become as large, and probably much more profitable, than the largest competitor focusing on the mass market. Skim pricing is also practical when the firm has a product line of lower-priced products that potential customers will purchase if deterred by the price of the skim product. Branded gasoline retailers set a skim price for their super premium, high octane grade, knowing that anyone deterred by the price is more likely to purchase a lower grade than to drive to a competitive station. Therefore, when evaluating the possibility of successful skim (or penetration) pricing of a product within a product line, it is important to use the *adjusted contribution margin* described in the discussion of product line pricing in Chapter 10.

Competition

The competitive environment must be right for skimming. A firm must have some source of competitive protection to ensure long-term profitability by precluding competitors from providing lower-priced alternatives. Patents or copyrights are one source of protection against competitive threats. Pharmaceuticals companies can justify their huge expenditures on research because of the skim prices they command until a superior drug's patent expires. Even then, they enjoy some premium because of the name recognition. Other forms of protection include a brand's reputation for quality, access to a scarce resource, preemption of the best distribution channel, and even image.

A skim price should not necessarily be avoided even when a firm lacks the ability to prevent competition in the future. If a firm introduces a new product with a high price relative to its manufacturing cost, competitors will be attracted even if the product is priced low relative to its economic value. Pricing low in the face of competition makes sense only when it serves either to establish a competitive advantage or to sustain one that already exists. If it cannot do either, the best rule for pricing is to earn what you can while you can. When competitors enter by duplicating the product's differentiating attributes and thus undermining its economic value, the firm can then choose to reevaluate its strategy.

Sequential Skimming

With some type of competitive protection, a firm selling a repeat-purchase product can maintain a skim price indefinitely. If, however, the product is either (1) a long-lived durable good such as a camera or (2) a product that most buyers would purchase only once, such as a ticket to a stage play, the market can be skimmed for only a limited time at each price. Skimming, in such cases, cannot be maintained indefinitely, but its dynamic variant, *sequential skimming,* may remain profitable for some time. Sequential skimming, like the more sustainable variety of skimming, begins with a price that attracts the least price-sensitive buyers first. After the firm has "skimmed the cream" of buyers, however, that market is gone. Consequently, to maintain its sales, the firm lowers its price enough to sell to the next most lucrative segment. The firm continues this process until it has exhausted all opportunities for skimming, either because it has cut price low enough to attract even the most price-sensitive buyers or because it could not profitably lower the price further.

In theory, a firm could sequentially skim the market for a durable good or a one-time purchase by lowering its price in hundreds of small steps, thus charging every segment the maximum it would pay for the product. In practice, however, potential buyers catch on rather quickly and begin delaying their purchases, anticipating further price reductions. To minimize this problem, the firm can cut price less frequently, thus forcing potential buyers to bear a significant cost of waiting. It can also launch less attractive models as it cuts the price. This is the strategy Polaroid followed, introducing ever-cheaper models of its automatic-developing camera, to bring ever-larger segments into the market (see Exhibit 6-5). The makers of digital cameras are now duplicating that same strategy. It is the strategy that theater companies follow when they perform first in each major city at a high price and return later to perform again at a lower price. Auto dealers can also sequentially cut price on end-of-season models because buyers know that if they wait to purchase at a lower price, the choice of colors and options will be diminished.

Sequential skimming is not always appropriate for durable goods. Often the profit from selling exclusively to price-insensitive buyers is greater than the profit from selling to everyone. Such is the case for products that have added value for some segment *because* of their limited availability (see the discussion in Chapter 4 concerning the price–quality effect). Much of the value that buyers place on collectors' items (commemorative coins, lithographs, porcelain figurines) stems from the expectation that they will remain rare. To maintain price premiums, sellers often number their products and pledge to produce no more than a certain quantity.

Price Dates of Sales	Lowest-Priced Model	In Current Dollars	In 1975 Dollars*
Black and White Cameras			
1948–1953	Model 95	$89.75	$200
1954–1957	Model 95A	89.75	181
1957–1959	Model 80A	72.75	139
1959–1961	Model SOB	72.75	133
1961–1963	Model J33	74.95	134
1965–1970	Model 20	19.95	35
1974–1977	Zip Land	13.95	15
Color Cameras			
1963–1966	Model 100	$164.95	$290
1964–1967	Model 101	134.95	234
1965–1967	Model 104	59.95	103
1969–1972	Color Pack II	29.95	44
1971–1973	Big Shot Portrait**	19.95	26
1975–1977	Super Shooter 25.00	25	

*Current dollars converted to 1975 dollars using Consumer Price Index.

**Fixed-focus portrait camera that took only flash pictures at a fixed distance (approximately 39 inches from subject).

Source: The First Thirty Years, 1948–78: A Chronology of Polaroid Photographic Products (Cambridge. MA: Polaroid Corporation, 1979).

EXHIBIT 6-5 Sequential Skim Pricing a Patented Product (Polaroid Amateur Cameras)

Sometimes, sequential skimming is a good strategy for introducing even nondurable, repeat-purchased products. A firm gains in two ways by only gradually lowering price to expand into new markets. First, if the product has a variety of potential uses, all of which require substantial effort in technical research and marketing from the seller, the company may more efficiently introduce the product by focusing all of its efforts on one use at a time. In fact, it may actually capture the most lucrative markets more quickly than if it spread its resources more thinly. Even if the product's initial growth is slowed, the firm may still benefit in the long run.

Second, sequential skimming enables the firm to build production capacity more gradually. As it expands capacity, it can build new production facilities to incorporate the learning that resulted from production of earlier built facilities and can finance new facilities with the cash flow that the product is already generating. Moreover, because the firm initially built less capacity, it bears less risk that demand will not be as great as expected. Having begun with a skim price, the firm can easily minimize the effect of overly optimistic forecasts by scaling back its intended expansion and increasing the rate of its price reductions.

Penetration Pricing

Penetration pricing involves setting a price low enough to attract and hold a large base of customers, or to attract a base of customers who can be served at a cost that is less than the price differential to attract them. Penetration prices are not necessarily cheap, but they are low relative to perceived economic value. Lexus, for example, quickly penetrated the luxury car market, and induced many near-luxury buyers to trade up, because buyers perceived it as representing an exceptionally good value despite being a high-priced car. Similarly, Wal-Mart, Priceline.com, and Nortel Networks (Exhibit 6-6) position themselves as offering the same or better value as their competitors at lower prices.

Customers

First and foremost, penetration pricing will work only if a large share of the market is willing to try a product or change suppliers in response to a price differential. A common misconception is that every market will respond to a price differential, which is one reason why unsuccessful penetration pricing schemes are so common. Low prices will attract few buyers of prestige or exclusive products and can, in fact, undermine the prestige value of their brand names. When Lacoste allowed its "alligator" shirts to be discounted by lower-priced mass merchants, high-image retailers refused to carry the product and consumers migrated to more exclusive brands. Penetration pricing will attract few buyers to products for which the price is a trivial expenditure (chewing gum) or to products for which value is difficult to compare across suppliers (medical care). Finally, penetration pricing will not work where quality is difficult to evaluate (the price–quality effect). Potential customers will simply assume that lower-priced products are of lower value.

A router is a router is a router.

Until you write the check.

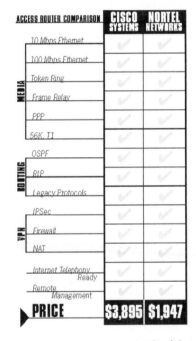

ACCESS ROUTER COMPARISON	CISCO SYSTEMS	NORTEL NETWORKS
MEDIA		
10 Mbps Ethernet	✓	✓
100 Mbps Ethernet	✓	✓
Token Ring	✓	✓
Frame Relay	✓	✓
PPP	✓	✓
56K, T1	✓	✓
ROUTING		
OSPF	✓	✓
RIP	✓	✓
Legacy Protocols	✓	✓
VPN		
IPSec	✓	✓
Firewall	✓	✓
NAT	✓	✓
Internet Telephony Ready	✓	✓
Remote Management	✓	✓
▶ PRICE	**$3,895**	**$1,947**

With the escalating cost of routing, why would you pay twice as much for one router over another when they both do virtually the same thing for your network? You wouldn't.

Introducing Nortel Networks™ Open IP Environment, a new world routing software that embeds routing and other IP functions directly into a variety of hardware platforms and operating systems, making stand-alone, data-access routers an old-world commodity. In other words, we're changing the economics of network-routing technology by driving down the cost. Which is why we're cutting the price of our data-access routers by up to 50 percent below the leading competitor.

You see, our leading, new Open IP Environment software makes routing universally available. Soon, everything from personal appliances to processors and servers will be Internet-routing enabled with more than 75 companies already leveraging Nortel Networks' Open IP technology.

So the next time you're ready to write a check for data-access routers, you might want to ask yourself this simple question: Why pay more? Come together, right now with Nortel Networks. nortelnetworks.com

NØRTEL NETWORKS™
How the world shares ideas.

EXHIBIT 6-6 Positioning for Penetration Pricing

Of course, not all buyers need to be price sensitive for penetration pricing to succeed, but enough of the market must be adequately price sensitive to justify pricing low to capture its patronage. Warehouse clubs (Sam's, Costco, B.J.'s) have used penetration pricing to target only buyers willing to purchase in large quantities. Charter vacation operators sell heavily discounted travel to people who do not mind the inflexibility of scheduling. Discount retail stores (T.J.Maxx, Trader Joe's, Buck-a-Book) target those price-sensitive customers willing to shop frequently through limited and rapidly changing stocks to find a bargain. Some wholesalers of sheet steel use penetration prices to attract the high-volume buyers, who require no selling or service and who buy truckload quantities.

Costs

To determine how much volume one must gain to justify penetration pricing, a manager must also consider the cost environment. Costs are more favorable for penetration pricing when incremental costs (variable and incremental semifixed) represent a small share of the price, so that each additional sale provides a large contribution to profit. Moreover, because the contribution per sale is already high, a lower price does not represent a large cut in the contribution from each sale. For example, even if a company had to cut its prices 10 percent to attract a large segment of buyers, penetration pricing could still be profitable if the product had a high contribution margin. In order for the strategy to pay with a 90 percent contribution margin, the sales gain would need to exceed only 12.5 percent. The lower the contribution per sale, the larger the sales gain required before penetration pricing is profitable.

Penetration pricing can succeed without a high contribution margin if the strategy creates sufficient variable cost economies, enabling the seller to offer penetration prices without suffering lower margins. The price sensitivity of target customers enables warehouse clubs to vary the brands they offer depending upon who gives them the best deal, thus increasing their leverage with suppliers. The penetration prices of warehouse clubs enable them to maintain such high turnover, high sales per square foot, and high sales per employee that they can in many markets undercut full-service retailers while still earning equal or better profits per sale.

Penetration pricing is often a viable strategy for manufacturers as well. As personal computer users became more knowledgeable buyers, manufacturers such as Dell and Gateway leveraged the economies of mail-order distribution to sell high-quality products using penetration pricing. Competitors who distributed through retail stores could not match their prices, so knowledgeable buyers flocked to them.

Competition

For penetration pricing to succeed, competitors must allow a company to set a price that is attractive to a large segment of the market. Competitors always have the option of undercutting a penetration strategy by cutting their own prices, thus preventing the penetration pricer from offering a better value.

Only when competitors lack the ability or incentive to do so is penetration pricing a practical strategy for gaining and holding market share. There are three common situations in which this is likely to occur:

1. When the firm has a significant cost advantage and/or a resource advantage so that its competitors believe they would lose if they began a price war.
2. When the firm has a broader line of complementary products, enabling it to use one as a penetration-priced "loss leader" in order to drive sales of others.
3. When the firm is currently so small that it can significantly increase its sales without affecting the sales of its competitors enough to prompt a response.

As telecom markets have opened to competition in most developed countries, new suppliers have successfully used penetration pricing to capture market share. The low variable costs of carrying a call or message make such a strategy desirable. Regulatory constraints and the inability of the large, established competitors to match the lower prices of new entrants on their large installed base of customers has made the strategy successful in many markets.

Occasionally, penetration pricing can be structured to attract new volume to a market without even threatening the current customers of competitors. For this strategy to work, the penetration pricer must somehow minimize interbrand price sensitivity at the same time that it attempts to encourage and exploit primary price sensitivity. Charter airline carriers can substantially undercut the prices of scheduled airlines without retaliation because their low service and inflexible schedules make them unattractive to most passengers of scheduled airlines. Warehouse clubs can undercut traditional groceries because their limited selection, large sizes, and spartan shopping environments will not attract most people from traditional grocery chains.

Penetration pricing also can prove useful when there is not yet significant competition in a market but when potential entrants are on the horizon. If a firm can rapidly achieve significant cost economies by using penetration pricing, it can in some cases increase its long-run profits while discouraging entry by new competitors that lack such economies. If the product is an infrequently purchased durable good, penetration pricing in the face of new competition may be the most profitable strategy even in the absence of such economies. A penetration price can enable a firm to capture more of the potential market before it must compete for those sales with other firms. If the product is frequently purchased, penetration pricing can enable a firm to attract trial use before buyers have had the opportunity to try a competing brand. If quality is difficult to compare, it will then enjoy the lower price sensitivity of a known brand competing against the promises of later entrants (the difficult comparison effect).[9]

Neutral Pricing

Neutral pricing involves a strategic decision not to use price to gain market share, while not allowing price alone to restrict it. Neutral pricing minimizes the role of price as a marketing tool in favor of other tools that management believes are more powerful or cost-effective for a product's market. This does not mean that neutral pricing is easier. On the contrary; it is less difficult to choose a price that is sufficiently high to skim or sufficiently low to penetrate than to choose one that strikes a near perfect balance.

A firm generally adopts a neutral pricing strategy by default, because the conditions are not sufficient to support either a skim or penetration strategy. For example, a marketer may be unable to adopt skim pricing because the products in a particular market are so generally viewed as substitutable that no significant segment will pay a premium. That same firm may be unable to adopt a penetration pricing strategy because, as it is a newcomer to the market, customers would be unable to judge its quality before purchase and would infer low quality from low prices (the price–quality effect) or because competitors would respond vigorously to any price that undercut the established price structure. Neutral pricing is especially common in industries where customers are quite value-sensitive, precluding skimming, but competitors are quite volume-sensitive, precluding successful penetration.

Another reason to adopt a neutral pricing strategy is to promote a product line. Auto companies have traditionally priced popular cars (Mazda Miata, Chrysler PT Cruiser) at a neutral level, even when they could not meet the demand for them. Auto companies want people across a broad range of potential car buyers to see their "hot" cars and associate the brand with them. Their experience has shown them that one very popular style draws people into showrooms who buy more of other models of cars as well. Similarly, performers often price their concert tickets at levels that leave many willing buyers unable to get a ticket because they know that people who attend concerts buy recordings and influence their friends to buy them. These effects would be seriously stifled if prices were set high enough that only high-income buyers, or people who were already the most passionate fans of performers, were willing to buy.

Although neutral pricing is less proactive than skimming or penetration pricing, its proper execution is no less difficult or important to profitability. Neutral prices are not necessarily equal to those of competitors or near the middle of the range. A neutral price can, in principle, be the highest or lowest price in the market and still be neutral. Toshiba laptop computers and Sony TVs are consistently priced above competitors, yet they capture large market shares because of the high perceived value associated with their clear screens and reliable performance. Like a skim or penetration price, a neutral price is defined relative to the perceived economic value of the product.

SUMMARY

What appear to be pricing problems, and only pricing problems, are often not problems with price.

- If price metrics do not track value, a significant share of customers will object and refuse to pay the price. It would be wrong, however, to lower the price across the board since it may be totally justified by value for an even larger share of the customer base. The challenge is to find a metric that tracks value or a fence that enables price discounts to stay targeted.
- If customers appear always to be looking for discounts and withholding purchases until they get them, the problem may once again not be with the price level. It may be that customers have learned that price resistance is rewarded. The pricer's challenge, then, is not to figure out how much to discount; it is to reestablish price integrity so that customers who do not object are no longer treated unfairly.
- If customers are unwilling to pay the price because they do not see the value, the problem may not be that the price is unjustified by the value potential. The pricer's challenge may be to estimate the value, relative to competitive alternatives, and challenge the company's advertising, sales, and distribution network to communicate that value.
- If customers lacks the complementary resources, such as training on how most effectively to use the seller's product, or even the knowledge of how to market effectively their own products with the added features that the seller's product makes possible, then the pricer's job is to establish a marketing strategy to deliver the necessary "product augmentation."
- If customers—currently, after expected competitive entry, or even after a seller's anticipated product launch—will not receive economic value that justifies exceptionally profitable pricing to the company's target market, the pricer's job is to reestablish the targets and the generic pricing goals for them.

In short, pricing strategy must be more than a tactical afterthought to marketing and competitive strategy; it must establish the goals and objectives of those strategies. While pricing is the last of the four marketing activities to be implemented, it must be the first of the four to be planned. As Raymond Corey of the Harvard Business School wrote in 1960, "All of marketing comes to focus in the pricing decision."[10] It is never too early in a business plan for marketing and competitive strategy to get a profit focus.

Notes

1. The bias toward a reactive concept of "market orientation" has been described by Bernard Jaworski, Ajay Kohli, and Arvind Sahay in "Market-Driven Versus Driving Markets," *Journal of the Academy of Marketing Science,* 28(1) (Winter 2000), pp. 45–54.

2. The concept of "fences" was first introduced by Richard Harmer, in a speech at PRICEX 93, March 23–24, 1993.

3. Discount "policies" that give wider bands of authority to higher levels of managers are not in fact pricing policies. Pricing policies would be the

criteria that each level of management uses to decide how much of a discount to approve. Our experience from interviews is that different managers at the same level, or even the same manager on different days, often have no consistent criteria. Consequently, the companies have no real "policies."

4. Chapter 4 describes further the negotiation tactics necessary to reestablish a process with integrity that reduces buyers' incentives and ability to disconnect pricing from value received.

5. David Davidow, *Marketing High Technology: An Insider's View* (New York: The Free Press, 1986), p. 6.

6. Ibid., p. 10.

7. As quoted in Kevin J. Clancy and Peter C. Krieg, *Counterintuitive Marketing* (New York: The Free Press, 2000), pp. 283-84.

8. The following discussion builds on seminal work by Joel Dean in *Managerial Economics* (Englewood Cliffs, NJ: Prentice-Hall, Inc., 1951), pp. 419–26; and in "Pricing Policies for New Products," *Harvard Business Review*, 18 (November 1950), pp. 45–56, reprinted in vol. 54 (November–December 1976), pp. 141–53.

9. See Richard Schmalensee, "Product Differentiation Advantages of Pioneering Brands," *American Economic Review*, 72 (June 1982), pp. 349–65.

10. E. Raymond Corey, *Industrial Marketing: Cases and Concepts* (Englewood Cliffs, NJ: Prentice Hall, 1962).

CHAPTER

Life Cycle Pricing

Adapting Strategy in a Changing Environment

roduct concepts, like people, typically pass through predictable phases. There are, of course, exceptions. Death sometimes comes prematurely, dashing expectations before they even begin to materialize; and youth sometimes extends inordinately, deceiving the unwary into thinking it can last forever. Still, the exceptions notwithstanding, the typical life pattern affords one a chance to understand the present, anticipate the future, and prepare to make the most of both. Such understanding, anticipation, and preparation comprise a firm's long-run strategic plan. Profitable pricing is the bottom line measure of that plan's success.

Although different authors have applied the life-cycle idea to individual brands (for example, Ford, Chevrolet) and styles (convertibles, minivans, sports cars), the idea has proven most useful when applied to the general product concept that defines a market (that is, the automobile).[1] A market evolves despite changes in brands and styles. A product concept is born, gradually gains in buyer acceptance, eventually attains full buyer acceptance, and is ultimately discarded for something better. The market defined by that product concept evolves correspondingly through four phases: development, growth, maturity, and decline, as Exhibit 7-1 illustrates.[2]

In each of its phases, the market has a unique personality. In preceding chapters, we analyzed the three factors that determine the success or failure of a pricing strategy: the product's relevant costs (Chapter 2), the buyer's price sensitivity (Chapter 4), and the behavior of competitors (Chapter 5). These factors vary predictably as the market for a product moves through the phases of its life cycle. Accordingly, one's pricing strategy must vary if it is to remain appropriate, and one's tactics must vary if they are to remain effective. The following sections explain the rationale for these changes in strategy.[3]

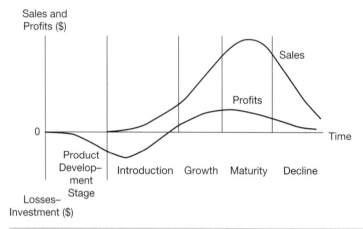

EXHIBIT 7-1   Sales and Profits over the Product's Life From Inception to Demise

PRICING THE INNOVATION FOR MARKET INTRODUCTION

An *innovation* is a product so new and unique that buyers find the concept somewhat foreign. It does not yet have a place in buyers' lifestyles or business practices. Consequently, the market requires substantial education before buyers recognize a product's benefits and accept it as a legitimate way to satisfy their needs. The first automobiles, vacuum cleaners, and prepackaged convenience foods initially had to overcome considerable buyer apathy. The first business computers had to overcome skepticism bordering on hostility. Today, innovations from home banking to video conferencing have encountered similar consumer reluctance, despite their legitimate promise of substantial value. An innovation requires buyers to alter the way they evaluate satisfying their needs. Consequently, before a product can become a success, its market must be developed through the difficult process of buyer education.

Not all new products are innovations, at least from a marketing perspective. Sometimes a new product results from a technological breakthrough that simply lowers the cost of a product concept already well accepted among buyers. In 1909 Ford's Model T was a new product born in the technology of mass production, but its forerunners had already paved the way for its acceptance by consumers. Sometimes a new product simply improves on an already well-established concept, as was the case with the 3.5-inch computer diskette, the plain paper fax, and the digital watch, all of which required little or no market development.[4] Even when a product provides a completely new benefit, it may not be an innovation from the standpoint of buyers. For example, drugs are so readily accepted as cures in our culture that new ones are generally adopted with little hesitation by both doctors and patients.

A new product that embodies a new concept for fulfilling buyers' needs is an innovation whose success requires buyer education. An important aspect of that educational process is called *information diffusion.* Most of what individuals learn about innovative products comes from seeing and hearing about the experiences of others.[5] The diffusion of that information from person to person has proved especially influential for large-expenditure items, such as consumer durables, where buyers take a significant risk the first time they buy an innovative product. For example, an early study on the diffusion of innovations found that the most important factor influencing a family's first purchase of a window air conditioner was neither an economic factor such as income nor a need factor such as exposure of bedrooms to the sun. The most important factor was social interaction with another family that already had a window air conditioner.[6]

Recognition of the diffusion process is extremely important in formulating a marketing plan for two reasons: First, when information must diffuse through a population of potential buyers, the long-run demand for an innovative product at any time in the future depends on the number of initial buyers. Empirical studies indicate that demand does not begin to accelerate until the first 2 to 5 percent of potential buyers adopt the product.[7] The attainment of those initial sales is often the hardest part of marketing an innovation. Obviously, the sooner the seller can close those first sales, the sooner he or she will secure long-run sales and profit potential.

Second, the "innovators," people who try the new product early, are not generally a random sample of buyers. They are people particularly suited to evaluate the product before purchase. They are also people to whom the later adopters, or "imitators," look for guidance and advice. However, even innovators know little about how attributes or major attribute combinations should be valued. Marketing effects can, therefore, readily influence which attributes drive purchase decisions and how those attributes are valued. Identifying the innovators and making every effort to ensure that their experience is positive is an essential part of marketing an innovation.[8]

What is the appropriate strategy for pricing an innovative new product? To answer that question, it is important to recognize that consumers' price sensitivity when they first encounter an innovation bears little or no relationship to their long-run price sensitivity. Most buyers are relatively price insensitive when facing a new innovation because they tend to use price as a proxy for quality and because there are usually no alternative brands with which to compare. Moreover, until they learn about the product's benefits, they may not even recognize a need for it. They lack a reference for determining value and to evaluate what would constitute a fair or bargain price. Consequently, most potential buyers are understandably unimpressed by a low price relative to the product's value, while the innovators are often undeterred by a high one.

It is ironic, therefore, that the greatest innovation of the past decade, the Internet, was promoted as a channel for discounting. In fact, researchers discovered that, as in other cases, most users did not switch to Internet shopping to save money, but to save time and to get access to a broader array of goods and services. Not suprisingly, then, most Internet ventures failed. The few that have succeeded offer unique products or a business model that vastly enhances the value or convenience of the shopping experience. Although grocery delivery companies in the United States took the discount road and failed, Tesco in Great Britain has succeeded with a high-service, full-price model. Similarly, Indulge.com and Dressmart.com cater profitably to customers looking for unique clothing for which they are willing to pay top dollar. Consequently, although those sites have remained small, they became profitable quickly.

Given the problem of buyer ignorance, the firm's primary goal in the market development stage is to educate potential buyers concerning the product's worth. Consequently, the regular or list price for a new innovation should be set to communicate the product's value to the marketplace. It is the price that a seller believes satisfied buyers would pay for a repeat purchase. It gives buyers a reference from which to estimate the product's worth and assess the value of price discounts and future price reductions. If the seller plans a skim-pricing strategy, the list price should be near the relative value that price-insensitive buyers will place on the product. If the seller plans a neutral strategy, the list price should be near the relative value for the more typical potential user. The seller of an innovation should not set a list price for market penetration, however, since the low price sensitivity of uninformed buyers will make that strategy ineffective and may, due to the price–quality effect, damage the product's reputation.

Marketing Innovations Through Price-Induced Sampling

Whether the list price is the actual price first-time buyers are asked to pay is another question entirely. The answer should depend on the relative cost of different methods for educating buyers about the product's benefits. If the product is frequently purchased, has a low incremental production cost, and its benefits are obvious after just one use, the cheapest and most effective way to educate buyers may be to let them sample the product. For example, America Online built its commanding market share by sending every family in America a mailing, including a diskette, for a thirty-day, free, trial membership.

Not all innovative products can be economically promoted by price-induced sampling, however. Many innovations are durable goods for which price cutting to induce trial is rarely cost-effective. A seller can hardly afford to give the product away and then wait years for a repeat purchase. Moreover, many innovative products, both durables and nondurables, will not immediately reveal their value when sampled once. Few people who sampled smoke alarms, for example, would find them so satisfying that they would yearn to buy more and encourage their friends to do the same. And many innovations (for example, personal computers) require that buyers learn skills before they can realize the product's benefits. Without a marketing program to convince buyers that learning those skills is worth the effort and strong support to ensure that they learn properly, few buyers will sample at any price, and fewer still will find the product worthwhile when they do. In such cases, price-induced sampling does not effectively establish the product's worth in buyers' minds. Instead, market development requires more direct education of buyers before they make their first purchases.

Marketing Innovations Through Direct Sales

For innovations that involve a large dollar expenditure per purchase, education usually involves a direct sales force trained to evaluate buyers' needs and to explain how the product will satisfy them. The first refrigerators, for example, were sold door to door to reluctant buyers. The salesperson's job was to help buyers imagine the benefits that a refrigerator offered, beyond those that an ice chest was already capable of providing. Only then would those first buyers abandon tradition to make a large capital expenditure on new, risky technology. Business buyers are equally skeptical of the value of new innovations. In the 1950s, most potential users of air freight service thought they had no need for such rapid delivery. American Airlines built the market for this new innovation by offering free logistics consultation. American's sales consultants showed potential buyers how this high-priced innovation in transportation could replace local warehouses, thereby actually saving money.[9] They taught the shippers how to see their distribution problems differently, from a perspective that revealed the previously unrecognized value of rapid delivery by American's planes.

When the innovation is more complicated than refrigeration or air freight, even a convincing evaluation of buyers' needs may leave them too uncertain about the product's benefits to adopt it. For example, a business computer in the 1950s was quite a risky purchase. Even if a buyer was certain about the quality of the computer hardware, he or she had no assurance that a computer system could actually do the billing, payroll, and production scheduling that the salesperson claimed it could do. IBM increased the business adoption rate of computers, quickly overcoming Sperry Rand's three-year lead as a mainframe manufacturer, by mitigating this source of uncertainty. IBM did so by marketing as a single package the hardware, software, systems analysis, and employee training required to guarantee the benefits its salespeople promised.

Neither American nor IBM priced their products cheaply despite their desire for rapid sales growth. Instead, they educated their markets, showing why their products were worth the price, and they aided buyers' adoption to minimize the risk of failure. They funded these high levels of education and service with the high prices buyers paid for the perceived value of the products. Du Pont has employed this same high-price, high-promotion strategy in introducing numerous synthetic fabrics and specialty plastics. Apple employed it in developing the market for personal computers. And the most successful marketers of industrial robots are using it today.[10]

Marketing Innovations Through Distribution Channels

Not all products have sufficiently large sales per customer to make direct selling practical. This is particularly true of innovative products that are sold indirectly through channels of distribution. However, the problem of educating buyers and minimizing their risk does not go away when the product is handed over to a distributor. It simply makes the need to rely on an independent distribution network problematic. The innovator must somehow convince the distributors who carry the product to promote it vigorously. One way to do this is with low wholesale pricing to distributors. The purpose of the low wholesale prices is not for distributors to pass the discounts on to consumers. The purpose is to leave distributors and retailers with high margins, giving them an incentive to promote the product with buyer education and service. While that works whenever distribution is relatively exclusive, there is the risk whenever distribution is less restricted that competition will simply cause the extra margin to be passed on in price discounts, thus losing the promotional incentive. To overcome that challenge, innovators may keep the margins at normal levels but pay incentive fees for stocking new products, for co-op advertising, for in-store displays, for premium shelf space, and for on-site service and demonstration. They may also offer incentives directly to the middleman's salespeople for taking the time to understand and promote the product. For example, Cuisinart, Inc., successfully introduced its food processors to the United States by giving retailers substantial incentives for promotion. Department and cookware stores responded enthusiastically, spurring sales with in-store demonstrations and classes in Cuisinart cooking. Millions of consumers then willingly paid the Cuisinart's high retail price once they learned it was justified by the product's benefits.

PRICING THE NEW PRODUCT FOR GROWTH

Once a product concept gains a foothold in the marketplace, the pricing problem begins to change. Repeat purchasers are no longer uncertain of the product's value since they can judge it from their previous experience. First-time buyers can rely on reports from innovators as the process of information diffusion begins. In growth, therefore, the buyer's concern about the product's utility begins to give way to a more calculating concern about the costs and benefits of alternative brands. Unless a successful innovation is unusually well protected from imitation, the market is ripe for the growth of competition.

As competition begins to break out in the innovative industry, both the original innovator and the later entrants begin to assume competitive positions and prepare to defend them. In doing so, each must decide where it will place its marketing strategy on the continuum between a pure differentiated product strategy and a pure cost leadership strategy.[11]

With a *differentiated product strategy,* the firm directs its marketing efforts toward developing unique attributes (or images) for its product. In growth, the firm must quickly establish a position in research, in production, and in buyer perception as the dominant supplier of those attributes. Then, as competition becomes more intense, the uniqueness of its product creates a value effect that attenuates buyers' price sensitivity, enabling the firm to price profitably despite increasing numbers of competitors. Xerox created such a reputation during the growth stage of photocopiers, first for its quick on-site service and then for the reliability of its copiers. As a result, the Xerox name carries a premium. Intel did this for its chips, creating a customer perception that a computer was more reliable with "Intel inside." Paccar's heavy-duty trucks carry a premium from the reputation the company built for exceptional reliability and style. With a *cost leadership strategy*, the firm directs its marketing efforts toward becoming a low-cost producer. In growth, the firm must focus on developing a product that it can produce at minimum cost, usually but not necessarily by making the product less differentiated. The firm expects that its lower costs will enable it to profit despite competitive pricing. EMC established this position in data storage by getting ahead of competitors in cost-cutting technology. Thus when price warfare broke out during a slowdown in demand, EMC was able to cut its prices by more than 50 percent over twelve months, yet still report growth in earnings per share.

Pricing the Differentiated Product

A differentiated product strategy may be focused on a particular buyer segment or directed industrywide. In either case, the role of pricing is to collect the rewards from producing attributes that buyers find uniquely valuable. If the differentiated product strategy is focused, the firm earns its rewards by skim pricing to the segment that values the product most highly. For example, Godiva (chocolate), BMW (automobiles), and Gucci (apparel) use skim pricing to focus their differentiated product strategies. In contrast, when the differentiated product strategy is industrywide, the firm sets neutral or penetration prices and earns its rewards from the sales volume that its product can then attract. Kodak (photographic film and paper), Toyota (automobiles), and Caterpillar (construction equipment) use neutral pricing to sell their differentiated products to a large share of the market.

Penetration pricing is also possible for a differentiated product, although the penetration price is often at least equal to the dollar prices of less differentiated substitutes. This is common in industrial products where a company may develop a superior piece of equipment, computer software, or service, but price it no more than the competition. The price is used to lock in a large market share before competitors imitate, and therefore eliminate, the product's differential advantage. Although the Windows operating system is clearly a unique product, Microsoft used penetration pricing to ensure that its product became the dominant architecture and default standard for software application programmers. Penetration pricing is less commonly successful for differentiated consumer products, since buyers who can afford to cater to their desire for the attributes of differentiated products can often also afford to buy them without shopping for bargains.

Pricing the Low-Cost Product

Like the differentiated product strategy, a cost leadership strategy can also be either focused or directed industrywide. If a firm is seeking industrywide cost leadership, penetration pricing often plays an active role in the strategy's implementation. For example, when the source of the firm's anticipated cost advantage depends on selling a large volume, it may set low penetration prices during growth to gain a dominant market share. Later, it maintains those penetration prices as a competitive deterrent, while still earning profits due to its superior cost position. Wal-Mart uses this strategy successfully to achieve substantial cost economies in distribution and high sales per square foot. Even when the source of the cost advantage is not a large volume but a more cost-efficient product design, the firm may set low penetration prices to exploit that advantage. Japanese manufacturers used penetration pricing to exploit their cost advantages and dominate world markets for television sets after extensively redesigning the manufacturing production process with automated insertion equipment, modular assembly, and standardized designs.

At this point a definite word of warning is in order. Much of the business literature implies that penetration pricing is the only proper strategy for establishing and exploiting industrywide cost leadership. That literature is dangerously misleading. If a market is not particularly price sensitive, penetration pricing will not enable a firm to gain enough share to achieve or exploit a cost advantage. In that case, neutral pricing is the most appropriate pricing strategy and can still be quite consistent with the successful pursuit of cost leadership. The marketing histories of many cost leaders (for example, Honda in electric generators and R. J. Reynolds in cigarettes) confirm that industrywide cost leadership is attainable without penetration pricing. The battle for the dominant share and cost leadership in those markets and many others is fought and won with weapons such as cost-efficient technological leadership, advertising, and extensive distribution. In many cases, the battle is won against competitors with lower prices.

Penetration pricing is not always appropriate when cost leadership is based on a narrow customer focus. If the focused firm's cost advantage depends directly on selling to only one or a few large buyers, penetration pricing may be necessary to hold their patronage. For example, suppliers that sell exclusively to Wal-Mart or to the auto industry enjoy lower costs of selling and distribution but usually have to charge penetration prices to retain that business. When, however, the firm's cost advantage is derived simply from remaining small and flexible, neutral pricing is compatible with focused cost leadership. For example, specialized component assembly is often done by small contract manufacturers that are cost leaders because their small size enables them to maintain nonunion labor, low overhead, and flexibility in accepting and scheduling orders. Since those cost advantages do not depend on maintaining a large volume of orders, and since the buyers that those companies serve are more concerned about quality and reliability than about price, their pricing strategy is usually neutral. When an order requires an especially fast turnaround and the buyer has little time to look for alternatives, those same manufacturers will occasionally even skim price their services.

Choosing a Growth Strategy

In some growth markets, both the differentiated product and cost leadership strategies are viable concurrently. This is possible when a segment demanding a specialized product for which it will pay a premium coexists with a market segment that will accept a relatively undifferentiated product for a low price. Hewlett-Packard, for example, successfully implemented a differentiated product strategy when the calculator market was in the growth stage, whereas Texas Instruments successfully followed a cost leadership strategy. Unfortunately, not all markets reward and not all firms can implement either strategy. Before selecting a product strategy, with its corresponding pricing strategy, a firm should consider the following questions about its market and its capabilities:

Is there a market segment that desires unique product benefits and is willing to pay premium prices for them? An obvious prerequisite for a focused, differentiated product strategy is to find a market segment that highly values unique product attributes. Contrary to popular misconception, even small firms can be profitable in most industries when they identify such a segment.[12] Two small companies, Harley-Davidson (motorcycles) and Premier (industrial distribution), have found niches in an industry dominated by low-cost competitors by serving buyers who desire unique designs and high performance. Jeep (now part of Chrysler) has done well in competing with its lower-cost competitors by serving buyers who want a vehicle that can go where the roads do not.

Does the firm have the requisite distinctive competence to produce and market a differentiated product? The appropriateness of a differentiated product strategy depends not only on the desires of the market, but also on the seller's strengths and weaknesses in production and marketing. Hewlett-Packard was uniquely suited to pursue a differentiated product strategy in laser printers because of its technical knowledge and its reputation in the engineering and scientific markets for producing other high-quality products. Lexus was uniquely suited to pursue a differentiated product strategy in the luxury/performance segment of the automobile market given its parent company's (Toyota) reputation as a manufacturer of superior quality.

Is the market sufficiently price sensitive to produce significant cost economies? Successful penetration pricing to establish industrywide cost leadership requires that a large segment of the market be price sensitive. Dell, and later Compaq, recognized that the increased price sensitivity associated with the migration from growth into maturity created a huge opportunity for penetration pricing of high-powered desktop computers. Their high volume enabled them to succeed despite low pricing. If the price-sensitive segment is not substantially larger than the segment willing to pay premium prices for superior quality, a cost leadership strategy based on achieving superior production economies through low prices will not succeed. AGFA, for example, has failed repeatedly to capture a significant share of the U.S. photocopy and x-ray films market using penetration pricing. Apparently, the company still does not realize that the difficult comparison, end-benefit, and price-quality effects mitigate against purchasing film based purely on price, even in maturity.

Is the firm willing to commit the resources and bear the risk necessary to see through a cost leadership strategy until it pays off? Attempting to establish a cost advantage, either by penetration pricing or by redesigning the product and manufacturing process, is not for the poor and fainthearted. The firm must forgo immediate cash flow and commit itself to substantial investment. It does so with only a promise that future profits will be forthcoming. General Electric and RCA both lost fortunes trying to become low-cost computer manufacturers, only to find belatedly that their goal required a much greater commitment of resources than they were willing or able to make.[13] At the same time, Amdahl, Inc. made a fortune producing skim-priced differentiated computers and risked comparatively little capital to do so.

Are there cost advantages that firms with small market share can exploit? Small firms can occasionally be more effective cost leaders than their larger competitors. The closer contact between management and labor in a small firm can often enable it to remain nonunion in an otherwise unionized industry, avoiding costly work rules and strikes, as well as higher wages. Moreover, there is considerable evidence that when small firms focus on a narrow, standardized product line, gaining a reputation as a quality producer of that line, they sometimes gain substantial cost advantages in marketing expenditures.[14] In such cases, even a small firm can be profitable as a low price, mass marketer. Intuit, the manufacturer of Quicken® financial-management software, leads its market niche without a sales force. Word of mouth and great press save this company millions in marketing expenses.

Having chosen a strategy, a firm must also decide just how far to pursue it.

How much product specialization will the market pay for? Firms that pursue differentiated product strategies cannot survive if they completely ignore cost economies to achieve maximum product specialization. Although hundreds of auto manufacturers in the early twentieth century pursued narrowly focused, differentiated product strategies with some success, they ultimately failed as the cost economies of large-scale production overwhelmed the price premium they could charge. The differentiated product marketers who prosper today in the auto industry (for example, Mercedes and Jeep) do so by supplying only those aspects of product specialization that can command a price premium sufficient to cover the extra cost.

How much specialization will the market sacrifice to attain the lowest price? Even if a large segment of the market is primarily price sensitive, these buyers may still be willing to pay for some product specialization. The success of Hunt

Club, JCPenney's high-quality brand of men's casual clothing, has effectively shown that traditionally price-sensitive target segments will pay some premium for limited product specialization. Similarly, Presidents Choice, a premium house brand of grocery products, offers value-conscious customers quality higher than store brands at prices still below that of nationally advertised brands.

Rarely is a pure differentiated product strategy or a pure cost leadership strategy viable. What distinguishes the strategies of firms within a given industry is not their purity but their emphasis on price or product differentiation relative to the strategies of competitors. A successful strategy involves a mix of price and product features that corresponds to the demands of some segment of the market. "Our buyers aren't concerned about price" are the famous last words of a differentiated product marketer. At some point, the price premium can always become too large for even the least price-sensitive segment to accept. "We have to compete on price" are the famous last words of a cost leader. Almost any product can be slightly differentiated in some way that will make otherwise price-sensitive buyers willing to pay at least a small price premium.

No doubt some observers will cite evidence that all this strategic positioning is superfluous. They will point to successful firms in growth industries that neither produce distinctive products nor have costs among the industry's lowest. There are such firms in growth industries, but few survive the inevitable transition to maturity when price competition chills the profits of all who have not insulated themselves by developing a distinctive and defensible competitive position.[15] The time to begin developing such a position is in the peak of growth, when high prices and cash flow can support the necessary investment, and before the best positions are preempted by one's competitors.

Examples from Internet-based businesses illustrate how some of these companies are developing defensible positions during the growth stage by strengthening the loyalty of their customers through personalization of their offerings. Seven Cycles, the number-one custom–bike-frame maker in the United States, uses its Web site to personalize service and speed up production. A customer goes to the Web site to pick a frame and components such as hubs, spokes, and handlebars. The customer then can check—as frequently as wanted—on the status of the order on Seven Cycles's "Where's My Frame?" Web page, and may correspond via E-mail on the bike's progress. Customers can track the status of their bikes as they go through production, find out what's being done in each phase, and even identify who's working on the bikes. Allowing customers to be intimately involved throughout the process is the kind of customization that the Internet can enable. The Internet's ability to process information about individuals is allowing companies to differentiate themselves by offering to the customer a meaningful, personalized buying experience. Amazon similarly built competitive advantage by using information on customers' past purchases to personalize and enhance the on-line service that it provides.

At the growth stage, in addition to establishing differentiation, companies should also prepare for the maturity phase by identifying more cost-effective ways to do business. E-tailers, for instance, now realize that even though they do not have physical stores, they still have to build warehouses and infrastructures, and hire people to deal with returned merchandise. Amazon.com, for example, is deferring profits, and investing significantly in building distribution facilities.

Seven Cycles uses customer information not only to customize bike orders but also to standardize some elements of its production. Consequently, it can now build more than 1,000 custom cycles annually with a total staff of only nineteen people.

Price Reductions in Growth

The best price for the growth stage, regardless of one's product strategy, is normally less than the price set during the market development stage. In most cases, new competition in the growth stage gives buyers more alternatives from which to choose, while their growing familiarity with the product enables them to better evaluate those alternatives. Both factors will increase price sensitivity over what it was in the development stage. Moreover, even if the firm enjoys a patented monopoly, reducing price after the innovation stage speeds the product adoption process and enables the firm to profit from faster market growth.[16] Such price reductions are usually possible without sacrificing profits because of cost economies from an increasing scale of output and accumulating experience.

Pricing in the growth stage is not generally cutthroat. The growth stage is characterized by a rapidly expanding sales base. New firms can generally enter and existing ones expand without forcing their competitors' sales to (correspondingly) contract. For example, sales of the first personal computer manufacturer, Apple, continued to grow rapidly following the 1981 introduction of IBM's PC, despite losses of market share. Because new entrants can grow without forcing established firms to contract, the growth stage normally will not precipitate aggressive price competition. The exceptions occur in the following situations:

1. The production economies resulting from producing greater volumes are large and the market is price-sensitive. Consequently, each firm sees the battle for volume as a battle for long-run survival (as often occurs in the electronics industry).
2. Sales volume determines which of competing technologies becomes the industry standard (as occurred in the market for video cassette recorders).
3. The growth of production capacity jumps ahead of the growth in sales (as occurred in the 1970s in the snowmobile market).

In these cases, price competition can become bitter as firms sacrifice short-term profit during growth to ensure their profitability in maturity.

Whether or not pricing competition becomes intense, the most profitable pricing strategies in growth are usually segmented. The logic for this is simple.

In the introduction phase, all customers are new to the market and technology is simple. In growth, customers naturally segment themselves between those who are coming new to the market and those who are knowledgeable and experienced purchasers. That by itself may call for a segmented strategy. IBM and Compaq faced this challenge when a growing segment of knowledgeable buyers began purchasing exactly what they wanted at lower cost from Dell, Gateway, and local generic assemblers. IBM and Compaq's bundled packages purchased through computer stores at higher prices remained the preferred channel for new and less knowledgeable buyers. With some difficulty (see Chapter 11), these companies were forced to develop dual pricing and distribution systems to accommodate those different segments.

PRICING THE ESTABLISHED PRODUCT IN MATURITY

A typical product spends most of its life in maturity, the phase in which effective pricing is essential for survival, although latitude in decision making is far more limited. Without the rapid sales growth and increasing cost economies that characterize the growth phase, earning a profit in maturity hinges on exploiting whatever latitude one has. Many firms fail to make the transition to market maturity because they failed in growth to achieve strong competitive positions with differentiated products or a cost advantage.[17] Firms that have successfully executed their growth strategies are usually able to price profitably in maturity, although rarely as profitably as at the height of industry growth.

In growth, the source of profit was sales to an expanding market. In maturity that source has been nearly depleted. A maturity strategy predicated on continued expansion of one's customer base will likely be dashed by one's competitors' determination to defend their market shares. In contrast to the growth stage, when competitors could lose share in an expanding market and suffer only a slower rate of sales increase, competitors who lose share in a mature market suffer an absolute sales decline. Having made capacity investments to produce a certain level of output, they will usually defend their market shares to avoid being overwhelmed by sunk costs.[18] Pricing latitude is further reduced by the following factors increasing price competition as the market moves from growth to maturity:

1. The accumulated purchase experience of repeat buyers improves their ability to evaluate and compare competing products, reducing brand loyalty and the value of a brand's reputation.
2. The imitation of the most successful product designs, technologies, and marketing strategies reduces product differentiation, making the various brands of different firms more directly competitive with one another. This homogenizing process is sometimes speeded up when product standards are set by government agencies or by respected independent testing agencies like Underwriters Laboratories.

3. Buyers' increased price sensitivity and the lower risk that accompanies production of a proven standardized product attract new competitors whose distinctive competence is efficient production and distribution of commodity products. These are often foreign competitors but may also be large domestic firms with years of experience producing or marketing similar products.

All three of these factors worked to reduce prices and margins for photocopiers during the early 1980s and for personal computers and peripherals during the 1990s, as those markets entered maturity.

Unless a firm can discover a marketing strategy that renews industry growth or a technological breakthrough that enables it to introduce a more differentiated product, it must simply learn to live with these new competitive pressures.[19] Effective pricing in maturity focuses not on valiant efforts to buy market share but on making the most of whatever competitive advantages the firm has. Even before industry growth is exhausted and maturity sets in, a firm does well to seek out opportunities to improve its pricing effectiveness to maintain its profits in maturity, despite increased competition among firms and increased sophistication among buyers. Fertile ground for such opportunities lies in the following areas:

Unbundling related products and services. The goal in the market development stage is to make it easy for potential buyers to try the product and to see its benefits. Consequently, it makes sense to sell everything needed to achieve the benefit for a single price. During the early years of office automation, IBM sold the total office solution, bundling hardware, software, training, and ongoing maintenance contracts. In growth, it makes sense for the leading firms to continue bundling products for a different reason: The bundle makes it more difficult for competitors to enter. When all products required for a benefit are priced as a bundle, no new competitor can break in by offering a better version of just one part of that bundle.

As a market moves toward maturity, bundling normally becomes less a competitive defense and more a competitive invitation. As their number increases, competitors more closely imitate the differentiating aspects of products in the leading company's bundle. This makes it easier for someone to develop just one superior part, allowing buyers to purchase other parts from the leading company's other competitors. If buyers are forced to purchase from the leading company only as a bundle, the more knowledgeable ones will often abandon it altogether to purchase individual pieces from innovative competitors. Unless the leading company can maintain overall superiority in all products, it is generally better to accommodate competitors in maturity. This is accomplished by selling many buyers most of the products they need for a benefit rather than selling the entire bundle to ever fewer of them. An example of this tactic can be seen in the desktop computer industry, when experienced buyers seeking increased performance and customized configurations chose to satisfy their unique performance needs by purchasing options provided by innovative specialized suppliers. To avoid losing part of their sales, the dominant manufacturers were forced to unbundle the packages they had offered successfully during growth.

Improved estimation of price sensitivity. In the instability of growth when new buyers and sellers are constantly entering the market, formal estimation of buyers' price sensitivity is often a futile exercise. In maturity, when the source of demand is repeat buyers and competition remains more stable, one may better gauge the incremental revenue from a price change and discover that a little fine tuning can significantly improve profits. (The techniques for making such estimates of price sensitivity are outlined in Chapter 13.)

Improved control and utilization of costs. As the number of customers and product variations increases during the growth stage, a firm may justifiably allocate costs among them arbitrarily. New customers and new products initially require technical, sales, and managerial support that is reasonably allocated to overhead during growth, since it is as much a cost of future sales as of the initial ones. In the transition to maturity, a more accurate allocation of incremental costs to sales may reveal opportunities to significantly increase profit. For example, one may find that sales at certain times of the year, the week, or even the day require capacity that is underutilized during other times. Sales at these times should be priced higher to reflect the cost of capacity.

More important, a careful cost analysis will identify those products and customers that are simply not carrying their own weight. If some products in the line require a disproportionate sales effort, that should be reflected in the incremental cost of their sales and in their prices. If demand cannot support higher prices for them, they are prime candidates for pruning from the line.[20] The same holds true for customers. If some require technical support disproportionate to their contribution, one might well implement a pricing policy of charging separately for such services. While the growth stage provides fertile ground to make long-term investments in product variations and in developing new customer accounts, maturity is the time to cut one's losses on those that have not begun to pay dividends and that cannot be expected to do so.[21]

Expansion of the product line. Although increased competition and buyer sophistication in the maturity phase erode one's pricing latitude for the primary product, the firm may be able to leverage its position (as a differentiated or as a low-cost producer) to sell peripheral goods or services that it can price more profitably. Watterau, Inc., a grocery wholesaler that targets small, independent supermarkets, has remained profitable in maturity by using its established trade relationships to sell its services in store designing, shelf space utilization, employee training, and financing.[22] The benefits are not only higher profits for Watterau in the short run, but also a customer base more likely to survive and grow in the long run.

Reevaluation of distribution channels. Finally, in the transition to maturity, most manufacturers begin to reevaluate their wholesale prices with an eye to reducing dealer margins. There is no need in maturity to pay dealers to promote the product to new buyers. Repeat purchasers know what they want and are more likely to consider cost rather than the advice and promotion of the distributor or retailer as a guide to purchase. There is also no longer any need to restrict the kind of retailers with whom one deals. The exclusive distribution networks for Apple, Compaq, and even IBM have given way to low-service, low-margin distributors such as discount computer chains, off-price office supply houses, and even warehouse clubs. The discounters who earlier could destroy one's market development effort can in maturity ensure one's competitiveness among price-sensitive buyers.

PRICING A PRODUCT IN MARKET DECLINE

A downward trend in demand characterizes the market in decline. The trend may be localized, as in the housing markets of shrinking Northeastern cities, or general, as in the market for mechanical watches. The decline may be limited, as in the automobile tire market of the late 1970s, or nearly complete, as in the displacement of vinyl records by cassettes and compact discs. The effect of such trends on price depends on the difficulty the industry has in eliminating excess capacity.

When production costs are largely variable, industry capacity tends to adjust quickly to declining demand with little or no effect on prices. Although the demand for haircuts declined precipitously in the late 1960s and early 1970s, prices declined little if at all. Barbers simply left the industry for alternate employment.

When production costs are fixed but easily redirected, the value of the fixed capital in other markets places a lower bound on prices. When political violence reduced the demand for air travel to Beirut, it did not cause a price war between carriers. Airlines simply reallocated their planes to more promising markets.

When an industry's production costs are largely fixed and sunk because capital is specialized to the particular market, the effects of market decline are more onerous. Firms in such industries face the prospect of a fatal cash hemorrhage if they cannot maintain a reasonable rate of capacity utilization. Consequently, each firm scrambles for business at the expense of its competitors by cutting prices. Unfortunately, since the price cuts rarely stimulate enough additional market demand to reverse the decline, the inevitable result is reduced profitability industrywide. The goal of strategy in decline is not to win anything; for some it is to exit with minimum losses. For others the goal is simply to survive the decline with their competitive positions intact and perhaps strengthened by the experience.

Alternative Strategies in Decline

There are three general strategic approaches that one might take toward a market in decline: retrenchment, harvesting, or consolidation. The tire industry in the 1970s illustrates a market where each of these three alternative competitive strategies was employed.

The tire industry has been a major force in the U.S. economy, with sales in the tens of billions of dollars. In the 1970s, however, the industry was hit with a demand-depressing shock. The increase in oil prices reduced driving and attracted buyers to lighter cars, which cut tire wear and drove up the cost of tire production. Moreover, the steel-belted radial tire, which lasts as long as two or more bias-ply tires, became a more cost-effective purchase because of its positive effect on gas mileage. The result of all this was a decline in the tire market to about two-thirds its previous size. At least one company in the industry followed each of the alternative strategies for dealing with the redefined market environment.

Firestone chose retrenchment. A *retrenchment strategy* involves either partial or complete capitulation of some market segments to refocus resources on others where the firm has a stronger position. The firm deliberately forgoes market share but positions itself to be more profitable with the share it retains. Not all firms that forgo market share in a declining market do so as a deliberate strategic decision. Some are forced to sell out to satisfy creditors. Retrenchment, in contrast, is a carefully planned and executed strategy to put the firm in a more viable competitive position, not an immediate necessity to stave off collapse.

By 1979, Firestone realized the error of its earlier belief that it could cheaply adapt old bias-ply tire plants to produce high-quality radials. Before coming to that realization, it lost $400 million and faced the prospect of comparable losses in the future.[23] In that year, Firestone hired a new CEO, John Nevin, whose retrenchment strategy turned the company's fortune around.

Nevin quickly closed seven of Firestone's outmoded plants, slashed inventory, divested the company's plastics subsidiary, and even sold the Firestone Country Club, freeing a total of more than $600 million in working capital. Although plant closings forced a severe trimming of the company's product line, it raised capacity utilization at the remaining plants from 60 to 90 percent, quickly turning Firestone into a low-cost, efficient, and profitable producer. As a result, it could price low to defend its share of these lines without suffering losses. Moreover, the retrenchment freed enough cash for Firestone to strengthen its position as a tire retailer and as a provider of reliable, brand-name auto maintenance. Despite intense price competition from rivals, increased efficiency in production and distribution to its remaining markets enabled Firestone to return to profitability within two years. Firestone's retrenchment strategy continued during the 1980s with closure or sale of five more tire plants and divestiture of additional business units in its diversified products group and all or most of its equity positions in tire manufacturing facilities worldwide. Ultimately, Firestone was acquired by Bridgestone in 1988.[24]

The essence of a retrenchment strategy is liquidation of those assets and withdrawal from those markets that represent the weakest links in the firm's competitive position, leaving it leaner but more defensible. It involves an explicit strategic decision, not a reaction to crisis. Uniroyal, for example, also sold some assets and abandoned some markets, but only belatedly when forced by the demands of creditors.[25] Such crisis retrenchment is not a strategy designed to strengthen the company in the future but simply to buy it time in the present.

In contrast to Firestone, BF Goodrich chose to harvest its tire business. A *harvesting strategy* is a phased withdrawal from an industry. It begins like a retrenchment strategy with abandonment of the weakest links. However, the goal of harvesting is not a smaller, more defensible competitive position but a withdrawal from the industry. The harvesting firm does not price to defend its remaining market share but rather to maximize its income. The harvesting firm may make short-term investments in the industry to keep its position from deteriorating too rapidly, but it avoids fundamental long-term investments, preferring instead to treat its competitive position in the declining market as a "cash cow" for funding more promising ventures in other markets.

Goodrich had the foresight to begin its withdrawal in the mid-1970s, while many of its competitors were still vainly hoping for an industry recovery. By 1980, Goodrich had eliminated all unprofitable tire lines, had sold off its European plants, and had divested most of its warehouses and retail outlets.[26] With the resulting $150 million in freed capital as leverage to borrow more, Goodrich sought to move its business to greener pastures, investing most heavily in its profitable polyvinyl chloride operations. In 1981, with more than half of its earnings already coming from nontire sales, the company announced that it would withdraw from the original equipment tire market, effectively completing its harvest. Ultimately Goodrich was acquired by the Michelin Tire Corporation in May of 1990.[27]

Goodyear, the largest and most profitable producer in the industry, decided to take advantage of the decline to consolidate its position. A *consolidation strategy* is an attempt to gain a stronger position in a declining industry. Such a strategy is viable only for a firm that begins the decline in a strong financial position, enabling it to weather the storm that forces its competitors to flee. A successful consolidation leaves a firm poised to profit after a shakeout, with a larger market share in a restructured, less-competitive industry.

With its competitors retrenching and harvesting, Goodyear pursued a consolidation strategy, investing $2 billion on new plant and equipment by the end of the 1970s and expecting to invest close to an additional $400 million per year into the 1980s. The goal was not to increase capacity but to position the firm as the lowest-cost producer of high-quality radials. The company closed its inefficient plants in the Northeast and replaced them with automated plants in the South. In each market where its competitors cut back, Goodyear sought to improve its products and lower its costs to capture the sales its competitors abandoned. Throughout the consolidation process, Goodyear (along with Michelin) kept pressure on its weaker rivals by shaving prices, especially in the original equipment market.[28]

Because of its initial position of strength, Goodyear could pursue such a strategy while its competitors could not. It began the decline as a profitable company and stayed in the black during the shakeout. As a result, it could finance the consolidation by borrowing heavily against its earnings. Goodyear already had the largest sales volume, which enabled it to spread more thinly the research and development cost (close to $200 million per year) necessary to take the lead in quality and production efficiency. Although Goodyear's profitability declined during the late 1980s, its adherence to a consolidation strategy lead by nontire asset sales, cost cutting, and expanded product and distribution enabled the company to achieve record profits in 1992.

The lesson from this is that there are strategic choices that can improve even the worst phases of life cycles, but the choice is not arbitrary. It depends on a firm's relative ability to pursue a strategy to successful completion, and it requires forethought and planning.

For any of the strategic choices during the decline phase, timing, foresight, and creativity are crucial for successful implementation.

Act decisively. Companies in a declining industry first need to face reality as soon as possible, and not be in denial that they are, in fact, operating in an industry where unit shipments are in a long-term and irreversible decline. The sooner managers face this reality, the more time they have to craft strategies appropriate for their firms. Timing is particularly critical during the decline stage. A firm following a harvesting strategy has to cash in early before other firms reach the same conclusion. A consolidating company has to identify early on the segments where demand will endure and know when to buy competitors' assets and when to send preemptive, competitive signals. The retrenching business has to determine when to prune product lines.

Act strategically and creatively. Consolidating firms, in particular, have to apply creative insight to their strategies. They will have opportunities to buy competitors and retire obsolete assets while revitalizing existing capacity. However, they have to be careful so their retired assets do not fall into the hands of competitors. In the 1970s, Westinghouse Electric exited from the electronic receiving tubes industry and sold its equipment to a Taiwanese firm. In 1975, Sylvania bought the old Westinghouse Electric equipment, loaded it on a barge, and sank it to eliminate foreign competition. By contrast, rayon manufacturer Beaunit Corporation sold its equipment for scrap to a dealer who then resold it to a Spanish competitor, who, in turn, reassembled and used it to compete against Beaunit itself.[29]

BRAND STAGE VERSUS PRODUCT LIFE CYCLE

As mentioned at the beginning of this chapter, the product life cycle applies predictably to product classes or technologies, but it has not proved particularly useful as a guide to managing over the life of a brand. Managers, however, control their brands, not the market. Are we meant to conclude that management of a brand across the product life cycle is independent of the life stage of the brand? Recently we encountered a thoughtful resolution to this canundrum. E. M. Kolassa argues that while brands do not go through predictable life cycles,

Product Category Life Cycle

Brand Stage	Introduction	Growth	Maturity	Decline
Launch	Price to establish, communicate, and promote the value of the product.	Identify appropriate segment before commercialization. Choose segments based on long-term strategy, not short-term tactics.	Target unique, underserved niches at premium prices with a product advantage, or use aggressive pricing to dominate the low price segment if you have a large cost advantage.	Not recommended
Maintenance	N/A	Segment and target for long-term advantage. Lower price as necessary to maintain market growth. Do not price compete except to establish a market standard or to gain a cost advantage.	Unbundle. Price products and services separately. Rationalize product line and distribution strategy. Stop pricing for sales growth! Manage competition diplomatically to maximize profitability, not market share. Use profitable maturity to fund growth of related product lines.	Recommended only for companies with strong competitive advantage. Consolidate through aggressive pricing or acquisition to gain cost or service leadership. Invest to survive over the long term if there is a sustainable demand.
Retirement	N/A	Price to clear inventory quickly while launching new models at old prices.	Slowly price yourself out of business.	Withdraw cash with incrementally higher prices.

EXHIBIT 7-2 The Interaction Between the Product Life Cycle and Brand Stages

one must consider a brand's stage when considering how to manage it within that cycle.[30] Unlike stages in the life cycle, brand stages are not defined by changes in the market; they are about changes in strategic objectives. Kolassa defines three chronological brand stages: launch, maintenance, and retirement. Multiple competing brands may be in different brand stages in the same life cycle stage. Exhibit 7-2 integrates the product life cycles and brand stages, with recommendations for pricing strategy.

SUMMARY

The factors that influence pricing strategy change over the life of a product concept. The market defined by a product concept passes through four phases: development, growth, maturity, and decline. Briefly, the changes in the strategic environment over those phases are as follows:

Market development. Buyers are price insensitive because they lack knowledge of the product's benefits. Both production and promotional costs are high. Competitors are either nonexistent or few and not a threat since the potential gains from market development exceed those from competitive rivalry. Pricing strategy signals the product's value to potential buyers, but buyer education remains the key to sales growth.

Market growth. Buyers are increasingly informed about product attributes either from personal experience or from communication with innovators. Consequently, they are increasingly responsive to lower prices. If diffusion strongly affects later sales, price reductions can substantially increase the rate of market growth and the product's long-run profitability. Moreover, cost economies accompanying growth usually enable one to cut price while still maintaining profit margins. Although competition increases during this phase, high rates of market growth enable industrywide expansion, generally precluding the advent of price competition. Price-cutting to drive out competitors may occur, however. Cost advantages associated with sales volume are substantial if current market share is expected to determine which competing technology becomes the industry standard, or if capacity outstrips sales growth.

Market maturity. Most buyers are repeat purchasers who are familiar with the product. Increasing homogeneity enables them to better compare competing brands. Consequently, price sensitivity reaches its maximum in this phase. Competition begins to put downward pressure on prices since any firm can grow only by taking sales from its competitors. Despite such competition, profitability depends on having achieved a defensible competitive position through cost leadership or differentiation and on exploiting it effectively. Common opportunities to maintain margins by increasing pricing effectiveness include unbundling related products, improved demand estimation, improved control and utilization of costs, expansion of the product line, and reevaluation of distribution channels.

Market decline. Reduced buyer demand and excess capacity characterize this phase. If costs are largely variable or if capital can be easily reallocated to more promising markets, prices need fall only slightly to induce some firms to cut capacity. If costs are largely fixed and sunk, average costs soar due to reduced capacity utilization, while price competition increases as firms attempt to increase their capacity utilization by capturing a larger share of a declining market. Three options are available: retrench to one's strongest product lines and price to defend one's share in them, harvest one's entire business by pricing for maximum cash flow, or consolidate one's position by price-cutting to drive out weak competitors and capture their markets.

Notes

1. Polli, Rolando, and Victor Cook, "Validity of the Product Life Cycle," *Journal of Business*, 42 (October 9, 1969), pp. 385–400; Nariman K. Dhalla, and Sonia Yuspeh, "Forget the Product Life Cycle Concept," *Harvard Business Review*, 54(1) (January–February 1976), pp. 102–112.

2. See Theodore Levitt, "Exploit the Product Life Cycle," *Harvard Business Review*, 43 (November–December 1965), pp. 81–94; John E. Smallwood, "The Product Life Cycle: A Key to Strategic Market Planning," *MSU Business Topics*, Winter 1973, pp. 29–35; and George Day, "The Product Life Cycle: Analysis and Applications," *Journal of Marketing*, 45(4) (Fall 1981), pp. 60–67. For a criticism of the life-cycle concept, especially when applied to individual brands, see Nariman K. Dhalla and Sonia Yosper, "Forget the Product Life Cycle Concept," *Harvard Business Review*, 54 (January–February 1976), pp. 102–12.

3. For a general overview of marketing strategy over the life cycle, see Michael E. Porter, *Competitive Strategy: Techniques for Analyzing Industries and Competitors* (New York: The Free Press, 1980), Chapter 8.

4. William Qualls, Richard W. Olshavsky, and Ronald E. Michaels, "Shorting of the PLC—An Empirical Test," *Journal of Marketing*, 45(4) (Fall 1981), pp. 76–80.

5. See Everett M. Rogers and F. Floyd Shoemaker, *Communication of Innovations*, 2nd ed. (New York: The Free Press, 1971); Frank M. Bass, "A New Product Growth Model for Consumer Durables," *Management Science*, 15 (January 1969), pp. 215–27.

6. William H. Whyte, "The Web of Word of Mouth," *Fortune*, 50 (November 1954), pp. 140–43, 204–12.

7. Rogers and Shoemaker, *Communication of Innovations*, pp. 180–82.

8. See Everett M. Rogers, *Diffusion of Innovations* (New York: The Free Press, 1962), Chapters 7 and 8; Rogers and Shoemaker, *Communication of Innovations*, Chapter 6; Gregory S. Carpenter and Kent Nakamoto, "Consumer Preference Formation and Pioneering Advantage," *Journal of Marketing Research*, 26 (August 1989), pp. 285–98.

9. Theodore Levitt, *The Marketing Mode* (New York: McGraw-Hill, 1969), pp. 7–8.

10. See Philip Maher, "Coming to Grips with the Robot Market," *Industrial Marketing* (January 1982), pp. 93–98.

11. Porter, *Competitive Strategy*, pp. 34–41.

12. See R. G. Hamermesh, M. J. Anderson, Jr., and J. T. Harris, "Strategies for Low Market Shoe Businesses," *Harvard Business Review*, 56 (May–June 1978), pp. 95–102.

13. William E. Fruhan, Jr., "Pyrrhic Victories in Fights for Market Share," *Harvard Business Review*, 50, no.5

(September–October 1972), pp. 101–102.

14. See Carolyn Y. Woo and Arnold C. Cooper, "The Surprising Case for Low Market Share," *Harvard Business Review*, 60 (November–December 1982), pp. 106–13; and Porter, *Competitive Strategy*, pp. 38–40.

15. See William Hall, "Survival Strategies in a Hostile Environment," *Harvard Business Review*, 58 (September–October 1980), pp. 75–83.

16. See Abel P. Jeuland, "Parsimonious Models of Diffusion of Innovation, Part B: Incorporating the Variable of Price," University of Chicago working paper (July 1981).

17. See Hall, "Survival Strategies," pp. 75–85.

18. This problem can even result in a period of intensely competitive, unprofitably low pricing in the maturity phase if, as sometimes happens, the industry fails to anticipate the leveling off of sales growth and thus enters maturity having built excess capacity.

19. See Porter, *Competitive Strategy*, pp. 247–49, for a discussion of the problems faced by firms that do not acknowledge the transition to maturity.

20. See Philip Kotler, "Phasing Out Weak Products," *Harvard Business Review*, 43 (March–April 1965), pp. 107–18.

21. Theodore Levitt, "Marketing When Things Change," *Harvard Business Review*, 55 (November–December 1977), pp. 107–13; Porter, *Competitive Strategy*, pp. 159, 241–49.

22. "A Food Supplier's Bigger Bite," *Business Week*, February 22, 1982, p. 136.

23. "I'm Paid to Be an S.O.B.," *Forbes*, September 15, 1980, pp. 161–62.

24. "Firestone: It Worked," *Forbes*, August 17, 1981, pp. 56–57; John J. Nevin, "The Bridgestone Firestone Story," *California Management Review*, Summer 1990, pp. 114–32.

25. "Uniroyal Consolidates to Get into the Black," *Business Week*, February 1, 1980, pp. 40–42.

26. "The Industry Pessimist," *Forbes*, September 15, 1980, pp. 168–69.

27. "Goodrich: Speeding the Switch from Tires to Industrial Chemicals," *Business Week*, March 9, 1981, pp. 48–50.

28. "No Retreat, No Surrender," *Forbes*, September 15, 1980, pp. 160–61.

29. Kathryn Rudie Harrigan, *Managing Maturing Businesses: Restructuring Declining Industries and Revitalizing Troubled Operations* (Lexington, MA: Lexington Books, 1988).

30. E. M. Kolassa, "Life Cycle Pricing: Correcting the Misconceptions," Presentation at *Pricex99*, a conference sponsored by the Institute for International Research, 1999.

CHAPTER

Value-Based Sales and Negotiation

Influencing Customer Behavior

P rice negotiation is usually a David-versus-Goliath confrontation. David, the salesperson, has much less influence over what his company sells than the purchasing agent has over what his company buys. Purchasing agents are better informed since it is legal for them to compare prices and terms with other buyers, while it is illegal for sellers to do so. Finally, salespeople are usually paid for making sales, while purchasing agents are paid for saving money. Not surprisingly, Goliath, the purchasing agent, usually wins, in part because David, the salesperson, expects to lose.

Unfortunately, an ever larger share of prices has become negotiable. Companies that for decades enjoyed leading market shares in office equipment, pharmaceuticals, and telecommunications are today negotiating discounts to retain sales. Hospitals are negotiating with HMOs, law firms with corporate clients, large travel agencies with airlines. Even in consumer markets, savvy buyers negotiate discounts on hotel rooms, credit-card fees, and the services of real-estate agents. While this trend slowed in the booming 1990s, price negotiation continued even in some industries where capacity was constrained and supply had become scarce. When managers and salespeople in those industries were asked why they were not raising prices to ration demand, they typically responded with the sputtered response "Our customers would never stand for that!" That ominous admission is indicative of the extent to which companies, particularly in business-to-business markets, have lost the ability to manage pricing proactively.

It wasn't always so. In fact, it used to be that market-leading companies never negotiated prices. As markets became more competitive and inflation all but disappeared, managers found that their old pricing strategies were no longer working. Rather than design new proactive pricing strategies appropriate for very new market conditions, many companies, particularly those in business-to-business markets, took the easy way out. They gave up trying to create and manage a consistent pricing strategy, instead "empowering" sales to set prices tactically one deal at a time. By doing so, they thought their companies could respond more quickly to market conditions while limiting discounting only to situations where competitive pressure and customer resistance made it necessary. They were wrong.

When companies replace price policies with price negotiation, they create economic incentives for "good customers" to become "bad customers" who never willingly acknowledge value and act as if all suppliers are interchangeable. Negotiable price policies also teach salespeople to close sales the easy way—with price—rather than to raise the customers' willingness to pay by selling value. Companies often further encourage discounting by rewarding salespeople for achieving top-line sales rather than profit contribution.

To regain the power to set prices based on value, managers must rebuild strategies that correct these perverse incentives. Faced with customers in the new century who, due to cross-company partnerships and the Internet, are much more informed about prices in the market, companies are trying to recreate proactive pricing strategies. They must relearn to develop price structures that reflect differences in value rather than differences in a customer's negotiating skill. Salespeople must relearn how to communicate value rather than negotiate discounts. And managers must relearn the art of managing nonnegotiable price policies while still responding to changing market conditions. That is the idea behind the "price menu" described in Chapter 6. Companies that hope to get paid for providing exceptional value while maintaining win-win relationships with their customers have little choice but to establish and maintain nonnegotiable price policies that realistically reflect market conditions.

VALUE: THE BASIS FOR POLICY-DRIVEN PRICING

The key to breaking the downward spiral of negotiated pricing is to anchor your pricing to value. This requires an investment on the seller's part, an investment that shortsighted managers are often reluctant to make. In the long view, however, the investment actually saves time and money. Price negotiation takes time—usually involving people at multiple levels in the seller's organization. Moreover, ad hoc price negotiation undermines prices. Pricing by policy enables management to make decisions once that cover multiple customers, and management's commitment to hold those prices eliminates the incentive for customers to prolong the sales process in order to extract a better deal. In some cases, policies also smooth out distribution peaks and valleys caused by customers waiting for the most opportune times to cut deals.

Before you conclude that a nonnegotiable price policy cannot work in some particular industry, recognize that such a policy need not be a one-price policy. You can and should provide fixed discounts for volume, long-term contracts and for bundled purchases. You can also maintain different margins for different products in your line (for example, higher margins for Cadillacs than for Chevrolets) and for objective customer segments (for example, senior citizens). A fixed price policy means simply that the price for any particular offer (product, quantity, terms, and so forth) sold to someone in a particular customer segment is nonnegotiable. If a customer needs a lower price, he or she must be prepared to give up something to qualify for a better discount.

Creating a nonnegotiable price policy is not as simple as just getting tough about discounting. Not all customers can or will pay the same prices. To make it work, your prices must realistically reflect value. Your price metrics must track either value delivered to the customer (so that customers who receive lower value pay less automatically) or the variable cost to serve (so that customers who are priced out are ones you can easily afford to lose). To maintain price differences across segments, you must have logical fences and not rely on customers' ignorance of what others are paying, and you have to communicate the value you deliver to justify your pricing to decision makers.

It is important to note that there are situations where pure price negotiations are both desirable and necessary. When customers purchase unique products (for example, new construction, a telecommunications satellite, or a new home), negotiable prices permit the seller to price based on the buyer's ability and willingness to pay. When customers purchase very infrequently, they may lack the incentive to develop the knowledge and expertise to determine the prices that other customers pay. Still, even in cases where companies can get away with a lack of price integrity, managing negotiation according to value-based principles will minimize the ability of customers to exploit the situation.

Undoing the Damage

For companies that have already lost price integrity in the eyes of buyers, the problem becomes how to work their way back toward a value-based pricing policy. You may be unable to impose fixed prices until you begin to change expectations. The following guidelines will help you begin the process.

1. *Force low-priced customers to make trade-offs. Never accept the request for a lower price without demanding something in return.* In the absence of a quid pro quo, even the most naive negotiator will learn to resist whatever price you offer. You might, however, accept a lower price in return for the customer accepting lower quality or less service, or purchasing in ways that reduce your costs (electronic ordering, larger but less frequent shipments). If you already have some of these customers under contract, begin to strip out services that you are not absolutely contractually committed to offer. If they object, use that as an opportunity to reopen the contract. If they are willing to forgo those things, they are beginning to help you design justifiable criteria for discounting in a price menu.

2. *When negotiating with customers who are already paying above the average, commit to giving them your best and educating them as to what they are getting.* In doing so, you are preparing a justification for the day when they learn that they are paying more and want to know why. While we were helping one client to move toward nonnegotiable pricing, a premium-priced customer unexpectedly demanded a 5 percent price cut on its next contract. The buyer had learned

that others were paying much less. Rather than cut the price, our client explained that this customer's work was given priority, which gave the customer a lot of flexibility in scheduling. The customer quickly acknowledged that it valued priority, but pointedly noted a recent case where failure to receive priority service cost it dearly. Based on that information, a deal was put together that guaranteed (with a financial penalty for noncompliance) that the customer would receive expedited service for which the customer agreed to a price increase! Again, value-based negotiation helped define a service-based pricing criteria, this time justifying a premium.

3. *If some low-priced customers won't accept a lesser product–service bundle commensurate with the lower prices they receive, walk away from the business to protect the integrity of the price structure.* One company where strategy was historically driven by market share walked away from 16 percent of its sales in the first two years of adopting value-based pricing. It also, however, increased profits by a factor of four and cash flow by even more. That newfound cash flow is funding development of new business opportunities in more promising markets. You can only take money, not market share, to the bank!

4. *Introduce fixed prices first on new products and services, retaining negotiable pricing only for the more "commodity" products.* This strategy works fantastically well in markets where technology is constantly improving the product. As products with fixed prices become "commoditized," do not make their prices negotiable. Reduce them. Over time, more of the market moves to the new strategy. The message is "We won't allow the jewels to be degraded but will stay competitive on the commodities."

5. *Change the sales force compensation to reward salespeople for making profitable sales, not just sales revenue.* (A formula for doing this is in Appendix 8A.) The principle is that the commission should reflect the contribution of the sale. If the firm's contribution is 30 percent at the target price, a 10 percent price cut should reduce the commission by at least one-third, while a 6 percent price increase should increase the commission by at least 20 percent.

6. *Make price concessions temporary and up front in return for getting low-price customers to the mean.* If you tell a customer that you require a 15 percent price increase to continue doing business, do not compromise on 9 percent. Instead, it would be better to offer a three-year contract with 3 percent of the increase in the first year, 9 percent the second year, and 15 percent the third year. Although the present value of this is less, at the end of the three years you will be negotiating your next contract from a higher base.

Use nonprice "closers" as an alternative to price cuts. Added value, in the form of free supplies, extra training, or even a signing bonus, can hide a price discount that can more easily be eliminated when you are able to eliminate ad hoc negotiation entirely. Make sure you account for the costs of these on a per account basis, just as you would a lower price, for sales compensation.

Perhaps the greatest problem with negotiated pricing is that price negotiation is usually only a small portion of a salesperson's job. For buyers, however, it is often a full-time job. Thus buyers are more skilled in using tricks to get more value without paying for it. Following are a few maneuvers that salespeople need to look out for, even when constrained by the process described above:

- Separating the price negotiation from needs identification.
  This is one of the oldest and most successful purchasing techniques to get value from suppliers without paying for it. In its most successful form, the buyer asks the seller to compete for sales of a simple product, sometimes through a bidding process. Upon awarding the deal at a price, the purchasing department then invites the selling company in to discuss the "details" of the contract. Those details include the customer's requirements for special packaging, reporting, billing terms, training, service, etc., that drive up the benefits for the customer and the cost for the seller. A wary salesperson supported by a profit-driven company would, at that point, begin specifying the additional charges for those items. Unfortunately, many companies just book the business and roll the costs into overhead.
- Discounting in return for "incremental volume".
  Sometimes buyers will offer a seller incremental volume in return for a price concession. This is not in principle a bad idea, even under a fixed price policy. In practice, however, sellers often get taken. For example, assume that the buyer is spending $1,000. He offers to purchase 10 percent more volume, which means he would be buying $100 worth of additional product at the prediscounted price. If the buyer receives a 2 percent discount on that $1,100 worth of product, he gets $22 off. Thus the buyer who offers to purchase 10 percent more volume in return for a 2 percent price discount is actually getting a 22 percent price cut on the incremental volume.

  If sellers actually calculated that incremental discount, many would never be willing to make such a large concession. Actually, the cost of the concession is usually much more than what the seller gives up in that year, since most sellers fail to segregate the extra discount from the base price, perhaps in the form of a year-end rebate. Consequently, the 2 percent price concession becomes incorporated into the basis for all future negotiations.

  If you are going to give a discount for incremental business, focus the entire amount of the concession on the increment, or give it as a rebate. This not only maximizes the incentive for the customer to give the incremental business; it also prevents duplicitous buyers from getting a reward simply for promising more purchase volume than they can really deliver. With the discount focused entirely on the increment, they do not get the savings until they deliver the volume, and the discount does not get incorporated into the buyers' expected price level.
- Contracts with one-sided obligations.
  Among the most costly mistakes that we encounter are those made by companies that sign contracts committing them to accept business at fixed prices

but not committing customers to deliver volume at any particular time. If prices go down in the market, the customer can buy elsewhere; if they go up, the customer has a supply at a guaranteed price. A variant of this is fixed prices for annual purchase volumes in industries with seasonal demand for capacity. Without any constraint on when they must purchase, smart buyers usually find that they can get "spot" deals for off-peak purchases when everyone has capacity and is eager for incremental volume. Then they purchase their entire contract obligation during the peak season when supplies are tight.

Not surprisingly in these cases, the high-service suppliers, with whom everyone signs contracts at slight "premium" prices, often end up using their capacity less effectively and therefore remaining less profitable than many of their lower-service rivals who take whatever prices they can get. The solution to this problem is to write contracts that commit customers to separate prices for peak and off-peak business.

- Freezing the price-performance ratio.
  The idea that price should be proportionate to performance is so commonly accepted that challenging it usually requires extensive buyer education. Still, it should be challenged since the logic is flawed and the results are unfair to differentiated suppliers. The problem lies in allowing your product or service to be positioned strictly on relative performance, rather than on relative value. Recall the example (Exhibit 4-2 in Chapter 4) of the magazine whose 11 percent greater circulation and 29 percent greater readership was worth 211 percent more to an advertiser. Similarly, some technology buyers argue that a chip or a switch that operates twice as fast should cost no more than twice as much. In both cases, however, negotiators are focusing on performance rather than on value. The only time that relative value is proportional to relative performance is when simply purchasing more of the lower-performing product or service can produce the same result as the higher-performing one.

Understanding Buying Centers

One common excuse for why companies in business markets cannot set prices that reflect value is that the people doing the purchasing refuse to acknowledge the value. This problem is solved in part by the requirement that buyers make trade-offs to get discounts, which requires getting users involved to specify the acceptable trade-offs. Even that fails, however, if those who would benefit from the product or service do not yet know about it. Value-based pricing requires value-based communication to those who benefit from the value.

A particularly extreme example of this was observed by a company that created a product for sales-force management. The product took various pieces of raw data and processed them into information quickly, e-mailing them directly to salespeople. The result was that salespeople got much more timely information about opportunities and the performance of their territories. Although the company was excited about the product, it bombed when presented to customers, who in this case were data processing departments. The DP customers argued that data required their careful review and manipulation into company-specific reports to maintain consistency, even though that process delayed its use for weeks. Without the DP department's support, purchasing was unwilling to even consider budgeting for a trial of the new service.

Fortunately, the company had a breakthrough when someone was meeting a group of executives at one large customer. The customer's vice president of sales mentioned the need for timely information to support a new product launch, giving the seller the chance to describe the new service that addressed exactly that need. Before the meeting ended, he had agreement that the customer would try the new service for three months. At the end of that period, a delighted sales management was demanding the same timely information for all products. Pressure from sales management caused a budget allocation for creating such information, forcing the DP department to evaluate the service. The company not only won the deal; it also learned that the target for selling this product was not the DP department but sales management.

Before you can formulate an effective value communication and pricing strategy, you must first understand who in the buying organization benefits from what you have to sell and understand their roles in the purchasing process. The combination of people and roles that they play in determining an organization's purchases is called the *buying center* (Exhibit 8-1). Sales to organizations are far more complex than sales to individuals because each member of the buying center evaluates products and suppliers based on their own unique criteria. Buying centers generally consist of individuals who fulfill the following roles:[1]

1. *Initiators* start the purchasing process. Front-line production workers or supply personnel may initiate routine product purchases. In complex purchases, initiators might come from engineering, research and development, the sales force, the customers of the buying organization, or even consultants to the buying organization.
2. *Users* use the product or service. Although easy to identify, users may not have a great deal of power in the purchasing process. Consumers of most prescription drugs do not know enough to state a brand preference and may be constrained by managed-care guidelines in what their doctor can prescribe. In contrast, surgeons who specialize in procedures that are either highly profitable or prestigious for a hospital can usually get the surgical equipment that they want, despite budgets.
3. *Buyers* have the formal responsibility for purchasing products and services. Although purchasing agents often fulfill this traditional role, it is not unusual to have other members of the organization perform this task, especially in small organizations or when purchasing capital equipment.
4. *Gatekeepers* control the flow of information and external contact with supply firms and are often considered experts in a particular product area. Of-

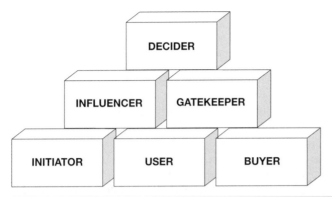

EXHIBIT 8-1 The Buying Center: Where Is the Product Valued?

Source: Thomas Bonoma "Major Sales, Who Really Does the Buying?" *Harvard Business Review* (May–June 1982), pp. 111–19.

ten, this role is fulfilled by a non–decision maker, who can only influence the decision process. A common mistake is to assume that the gatekeeper is the decision maker.

5. *Deciders* possess the final authority to select the vendor(s) that will supply the product. The real decision maker is often shielded by a host of individuals filling other roles.

6. *Influencers* may have no authority but a lot of influence over those who do. A well-regarded journalist, an outside consultant, or a colleague from another company or department may strongly influence the decisions of people more directly involved in the decision.

A common mistake is concentrating all communication and sales effort on the gatekeeper or the user, thus underestimating the impact that other members have on the final decision. A request from engineering might initiate evaluation of new equipment based on a review of it by an influential journalist. That evaluation focuses on performance and quality. The decision may then move to purchasing, where product attributes are secondary to price and past experience with the supplier. The ultimate decider, however, may be someone in finance who needs to balance cash flows. Failure to identify that last person in the process could result in a missed opportunity to close the sale simply by restructuring the payment terms. It is imperative that the seller recognizes these influences and their differing purchase criteria. Selling differentiating attributes to a purchasing agent who does not value them is a useless exercise. By the time you negotiate a deal with the purchasing agent, you must have created support for your product elsewhere in the organization or be prepared to deal on price.

TYPES OF BUYERS AND THEIR NEGOTIATION STRATEGIES

In addition to understanding who in the buying organization will recognize and advocate for the value you offer, it is also necessary to understand how the buying organization will make the purchase decision. We introduced four buyer types in Chapter 4: price, relationship, value, and convenience. Effective negotiators must understand the various buying behaviors associated with different types of buyers and their different purchase agendas.

Although all buyers attempt to maximize the difference between the price they pay and the value they receive, they approach the purchase with different strategies for doing that. There are good reasons why not everyone is a logical and methodical value buyer. Value buying is very time and resource intensive. Why should someone repeatedly reevaluate suppliers when the best deal is always the one with the lowest price that meets minimum purchase criteria (price buyers) or is always the one offered by a particular supplier (value buyers)? We label these price buyers and loyal buyers not because value is unimportant to them but because they believe they have already determined a more efficient strategy for getting the most for their money. Understanding what kind of buyer you are dealing with and presenting the appropriate offer for that type is key to winning and retaining profitable business.

Negotiating with Price Buyers

Price buyers begin the purchase process knowing precisely what they want to buy and selecting among suppliers based on price. In business markets, they begin by publishing required specs and soliciting bids. The specs are not necessarily for a low-quality product. Auto companies are notorious price buyers who often require very stringent specs. Price buyers, however, will not consider making trade-offs between price and anything that a supplier might offer that exceeds the spec. Consequently, purchasing departments are careful to control sellers' access to others in the organization who could be convinced to make the decision more complex by considering criteria other than price. Most U.S. federal and state government contracting is managed this way, as is the purchase of "commodities" by many large organizations. The price buyers' narrow focus on price greatly inhibits the ability of sellers to negotiate based on the value of the product.

The clearest symptom of a genuine price buyer is a "sealed bid" purchasing process. In this case, the price buyer commits in writing to the specifications of an acceptable offer. Potential suppliers then submit bids at a specified time. There is no opportunity to negotiate. This type of purchasing has become much more popular as Web-based companies, such as Freemarkets.com, have simplified the solicitation and bidding process. The Web has enabled buyers to create bids with multiple rounds of bidding in quick succession. Such a process has one clear benefit for sellers: It is now easier to find a genuine price buyer to whom you can unload excess inventory when you need to. For most companies, however, their lack of sophistication in preparing and analyzing bids makes the risks much greater than the benefits. Managing the competitive bidding process profitably is a science in itself. (For an introduction to that process, see Appendix 8A.)

More commonly, selling to price buyers involves some explicit negotiation. There are several strategies for negotiating with price buyers. The first and certainly most difficult option is to refocus attention on product value and to raise their willingness to pay by proving that added value is cost justified. This is usually not possible at the time of purchase or through communicating with the purchasing department. It requires a major investment at higher levels in the organization to convince decision makers that your innovative differentiation promises such large potential benefits that it is worth shifting the purchase process from price buying to value buying. For example, American Hospital Supply Company successfully converted hospitals that were traditionally price buyers to value buyers by convincing hospital CFOs that they could cut out costs by eliminating multiple suppliers (and the purchasing agents who dealt with them). They did so by introducing computerized ordering linked to sophisticated information systems that eliminated the need to manage large inventories. The net result was a more efficient system enabling the customer to save more money from better inventory management than by focusing strictly on supply prices.

Examples to the contrary notwithstanding, most price buyers will never change. Companies often invest resources to serve price buyers in the vain belief that someday their efforts will prove profitable. Resist the temptation to negotiate to unprofitable levels for a price buyer's business in anticipation of future profits—they rarely materialize. Companies that successfully serve price buyers adopt a strategy of *selective participation,* carefully evaluating the short-term profitability of these transactions and accepting them only when they (a) provide incremental contribution and (b) do not undermine more profitable business with other customers. Airlines and auto rental companies, for example, will sell some excess capacity cheaply to vacation tour operators. However, regular full-service companies serve the tour market, at its low prices, only at times when they have excess capacity. They will not add capacity to serve that market on a consistent basis.

If you can't participate in a price buyer's business profitably, walk away. The marketer of an electronic commodity had an excellent relationship with Ford and considered the company a loyal customer. Although it also sold to General Motors for many years, GM was strictly a price buyer. Due to its volume and negotiating power, GM received a 15 percent discount on most purchases. The supplier was careful, however, to sell GM only its undifferentiated, older technologies. When the supplier developed a new technology that saved customers money in the production process, Ford was first to receive it. The supplier did not offer the technology to GM, fearing that its adversarial negotiators would force the company to supply the new technology at a lower price or face losing all business with GM. Despite the long-term and persuasive evidence that

GM's major competitors' value-driven purchasing policies are successful, GM remains a price buyer to most suppliers, much to its detriment.

Fortunately, the long-term consequences of walking away from a price buyer's business are minimal. Since, by definition, price buyers react to low prices, you can always go back and participate in their business later by offering a low price when it is strategically prudent and profitable to do so. More important, selective participation sends a significant signal to your other customers that your loyalty when supplies are tighter is to those customers whose business is still there when supplies are more available. Sales, service, and support personnel should focus on servicing value buyers and loyal buyers, since profits there are more certain.

The prospect of walking away from price buyers is terrifying to many marketers since price buyers are often very large customers. By focusing on large customers, many firms are investing resources in negotiations with the toughest price buyers and are losing the opportunity to capture additional profits from more profitable segments. The "80/20 rule" states that 80 percent of the volume in a particular industry will come from 20 percent of the largest customers. The net result for suppliers unfortunate enough to become dependent on this segment is increased sales volume but little or no profit. Hundreds of unprofitable suppliers to the auto industry are in this situation. One company that stopped playing the price game with U.S. auto companies is Cooper Tire.

The result has been more limited volume but profits among the highest in the industry. Still, it may be difficult to totally walk away from all price buyers' business. Fortunately, because large customers often negotiate with multiple suppliers, marketers can look for favorable opportunities for selective participation. When a bidding war occurs, it is best to get in at the end of the process, when sellers are less likely to be emotionally committed to winning the battle. When it becomes necessary to bid a lower price, it is just as easy to say to the buyer "When you're ready to place the purchase order, I'll give you my best price." This limits the damage that a buyer can do by "shopping" the price with competitors and allows the salesperson to take the order "off the street."

The greatest danger in dealing with price buyers is that value buyers will disguise themselves as price buyers to get a better deal. Soon it will appear that ever more buyers are buying on price. Moreover, with the volume from value buyers shrinking correspondingly, the seller needs ever more "incremental" business. Soon he becomes locked into an unprofitable market where it no longer pays to offer high service, support, etc. In one case, a chemical company suffered eroding margins on a product every year until it could no longer afford to replace outdated equipment. In consideration of its customers, it gave them three months, notice that it was withdrawing from the market. Within days, purchasing people who had beaten down prices for years were calling to ask the company to reconsider. Apparently, the time and cost to transport product from other suppliers would substantially raise the cost. Unfortunately for the company, it had never before understood its value. Purchasing people had shared with them only competitive prices, not the added costs of purchasing from competitors.

Negotiating with Relationship Buyers

Relationship buyers are the polar opposite of price buyers. They strongly prefer brands with reputations and suppliers with whom they have had prior positive experience. They value consistent product quality and performance, and they rely on trusted suppliers to continue providing it. Their ongoing loyalty is driven fundamentally by the risk and uncertainty associated with untested suppliers. The critical implications of inadequate performance outweigh for the loyal buyer the benefit of lower price in the short term. Here, confidence in "tried and true" existing solutions from proven vendors sustains ongoing relationships.

For these buyers, one must fortify existing relationships by focusing attention on past performance. Stress the impact of inferior product performance on the buyer's firm, the sunk cost of previous investments, and compatibility with future requirements. Utilize unique price and quality metrics to make comparisons between and among vendors more difficult. Above all, make clear your commitment to meeting customers' current and future needs and to eliminating their incentive to look for alternative solutions. Invest sales and management time to thoroughly understand loyal buyers' sources of value. Over time you will be better positioned to react to their needs and reinforce your position as a trusted vendor.

In contrast to adversarial negotiations with price buyers, negotiations with relationship buyers are more amiable and focus on solutions that satisfy the business goals of both buyer and supplier. Less tangible, more augmented features, such as technical expertise, reliability of service, and dedication to customer satisfaction, have measurable value in the evaluation process. Although satisfactory past performance is fundamental, a clear indication of future commitment is also critical.

During the early years of the development of mainframe computers, IBM was competing with another vendor for a large manufacturing firm's accounting business. The customer, aware that it was making an extremely long-term commitment for a mission-critical application, decided to divide its business between the two vendors and let each one run half the payroll and accounting systems for one year. At the end of the year, the results would be evaluated and a long-term contract signed with the premier vendor. Halfway through the trial period, a power surge crashed the systems of both vendors, requiring a three-week restart. The competitor assembled a team of forty engineers and technicians to attack the problem and restart the system. IBM also assigned technicians to restart the system, but in addition IBM recognized that the customer still had a problem. To solve it, IBM assembled a team of 300 clerical workers to process the customer's payroll until the system was restored. IBM won an exclusive contract. Implementing such creative solutions shows commitment to total customer satisfaction and helps retain loyal customers for the long run.

Although the relationship segment may be large during the growth stage, it invariably shrinks in maturity as more competitors develop good reputations and buyers become more knowledgeable repeat purchasers. The relationship segment also contracts during recessions, when even otherwise loyal buyers may be scrambling to cut costs. Thus, a classic dilemma arises: Should the company cut its prices and service levels to focus on relationship customers who are migrating to the value segment, or should it maintain its prices and services to focus on the customers who remain loyal? The answer is both. By unbundling the costs of service (for example, training, installation) and by designing equally reliable but cheaper products, companies can leverage the reputation they developed while buyers were loyal and continue capturing the business of those buyers as they become more value conscious. This segmentation pricing strategy is the key to growth in difficult times for such market leaders as General Electric.[2]

Although obtaining business from relationship buyers justifies the investment of a firm's resources, the theory of selective participation is once again applicable when negotiating with customers already loyal to your competitors. By definition, these are customers, and the likelihood of them changing suppliers could be extremely low. Intelligent marketers must evaluate their accounts carefully, selecting only those customers who are likely to switch and yield profitable opportunities. They should never attempt to buy their way into a relationship account. Such accounts are won on service and security, not price.

Negotiating with Value Buyers

Value buyers represent the largest group of buyers in most markets. They strive to maximize economic value delivered for the price they pay. They seek neither the highest quality nor the cheapest price. Instead, they make their purchase decisions by carefully weighing attributes and analyzing trade-offs, ultimately purchasing the product offering the greatest difference between satisfaction with purchase and dissatisfaction with the price.

Unlike price buyers who focus on differences in price alone, value buyers both recognize and cost justify the added utility available from more expensive options. They are more willing to try new products and services, if the selling proposition can credibly demonstrate real incremental economic value to the buyer. They also are sophisticated buyers, who have the ability to recognize and appreciate the true economic value they receive from the seller. This segment, therefore, represents an exceptional opportunity for profits to the firm that can effectively communicate superior value. The difficult challenge with these customers is to retain their business over time since, unlike Relationship buyers, they are constantly reevaluating their alternatives.

The decision to invest resources and develop long-term relationships with value buyers is a difficult one to make. Unlike relationship buyers, who clearly justify investment, value buyers have no predetermined alliances. Although they may indeed repeatedly purchase your competitively priced and well-performing product for a while, apparent loyalty quickly erodes when competitors' products imitate your product's features. Given the potential of a short-term relationship, marketers must once again ask whether doing business by investing in this segment represents the most effective allocation of the firm's resources. When negotiating with value buyers, one's objective is to capture the value of the differentiation on each individual sale. However, educating the customer as to the value of that differentiation may well be worthwhile, even at a cost that is not justified by the contribution of the first sale, if the educated customer is likely to be a repeat purchaser.

Successful implementation of a value-based pricing strategy depends upon a salesperson's ability to distinguish among situations in which a lower price is required, situations in which the customer simply wants a commitment that the seller will meet its needs, and situations in which the customer must be educated as to the quantitative value of the benefits that the seller can deliver. Salespeople must be trained to understand how customers value their products, to use economic value estimation methods, and to use value-based selling techniques and negotiating skills to communicate that value to customers. Finally, salespeople must master techniques used to reduce the damage done when price negotiations do occur.

MANAGING THE SALES FORCE TOWARD VALUE-BASED PRICING

If actions suggested in this chapter improve profitably, and they do, why are they not more widely used? The answer given by many managers is that their sales force cannot or would not implement a fixed-price, value-based strategy. In truth, salespeople will resist such a strategy if management's support is limited to explaining the principles and admonishing the sales force to apply them. Value-based pricing is not primarily a sales strategy; it is a marketing strategy whose implementation requires a different sales approach. When the process is clearly articulated, the value-based messages are provided, and the sales force is rewarded for generating profitability, salespeople not only do not resist such an approach, but they generally embrace it.

Account Planning

Given the years of sales force "empowerment," salespeople at most companies need to learn or relearn how to think about value. Never should a salesperson meet with a client to discuss price without knowing what creates value for that customer. If that information can only be learned by talking with the company, then initial visits should focus on data collection. Leading up to the negotiation, the buying center participants need to be identified, the benefits they are seeking need to be determined, and the information required to influence them needs to be collected and communicated. When the issue of price is raised, the salesperson should be ready to present an offer rather than react to the customer's offer. When he or she encounters price resistance, the salesperson should have a plan for what to ask for in return for a price reduction. Exhibit 8-2 summarizes these questions in detail.

THE VALUE: WHAT DO THEY NEED AND WHAT IS IT WORTH TO THEM?

- What needs motivate the customer to purchase?
- What else could the customer make or buy to meet those needs? At what cost?
- How do product, service, and support differ from anything else the customer could make or buy to satisfy that need?
- What benefits/problems could result for the customer from that difference?
- Is the buyer currently our customer for this product? If not, why not? If so, what has been the customer's experience with our product and the promised benefits? If not, what has been the experience with the competitor?
- Who (if anyone) cares about those benefits/problems within the customer organization? Why do they care? What is most important to them?
- How could we estimate and communicate the value of our benefits (either quantitatively or qualitatively)?
- To what is that value related (e.g., size of the customer's sales, competitiveness of customer's market, sophistication of customer's data department)?
- What product/service options would materially affect the value provided to this customer? What options would be of little value to them?

THE BUYING CENTER: WHO INFLUENCES THE PURCHASE DECISION?

- What kind of buyer are we *really* dealing with (price, loyal, value, convenience)?
- Who does the purchasing? Is that person aware of the benefits and the value? Does the value impact them personally?
- What are the key purchase criteria? Who establishes or influences those criteria? Do they understand our value?
- Who in the buying center is a supporter, neutral, or against us as a supplier?
- Do these people expect to pay for value? If not, how can we influence their expectations before beginning the negotiation?

THE DEAL: WHAT SHOULD WE OFFER?

- What package or product/service combination meets this customer's needs?
- What package of product/service should we offer this customer?
- At what discount?
    How does that discount relate to those offered other customers?
    How will you convince this customer that the discount is "fair"?
    How would you justify this discount to other customers if they demanded an explanation?

EXHIBIT 8-2 Preparing for a Value-Based Sale

THE NEGOTIATION: HOW WILL WE MAKE THIS PROFITABLE?

- How might this customer use manipulation and misinformation to avoid paying for value? How can we head off or thwart such attempts?
- What product/service options could we eliminate to reduce the cost to the customer?
- What other trade-offs (not concessions) would we be prepared to offer?
- What would constitute a good deal for this company, given the realistic constraints that we face on what we can offer? What would constitute a good deal for us given the realistic constraints on what the customer can accept? Can these interests be made to converge before we begin negotiation?
- At what price/service level is it in our company's interest to walk? Will our company support us for doing so at least as well as if we accepted a bad deal? How do we ensure that support?

EXHIBIT 8-2 (*continued*)

Profit-Focused Sales Incentives

One of the main reasons that business-to-business strategies fail is that the sales force does not execute them. As a result, the planners of strategy become hostile toward the sales organization, which becomes even less willing to cooperate. The source of this problem is rarely the salespeople themselves; it is the way their performance is measured and compensated. There is no aspect of business strategy where this disconnect is more common than in pricing strategy.

Most companies reward salespeople for making larger and more frequent sales, not for making more profitable sales. Consequently, the easiest way to make the goal is to "cut deals" for large buyers, regardless of the contribution those deals may generate. Consider the dilemma facing sales representatives (or independent deals or manufacturers' representatives) who are compensated as a percentage of sales. They have a fixed number of hours available for selling. They must choose between selling to high-volume customers who demand a 15 percent price concession or to customers who buy only half the volume but will pay full price. If the time required to deliver a sales presentation is equal for both, clearly they will target the larger customers. They earn 35 percent more sales in the same amount of time. Also consider the case when they can quickly close a sale by meeting their competitors' 15 percent lower price or invest twice the time to sell the value and avoid the price cut. If their objective is to maximize sales volume, they will sell on price, moving on quickly to the next sale.

Is this volume-maximizing behavior good for the firm? Often not. If the firm has only a 20 percent contribution margin at full price, a 15 percent discount slashes the profitability of a sale by 75 percent! To break even on that 15 percent price cut, the company needs to sell at least four times as much volume to make the same contribution. Consequently, price-cutting may benefit sales-people while undermining the profitability of the firm.

The key to inducing the sales force to sell value is to measure their per-formance and compensate them not just for sales volume, but for *profit contri-bution*. Although some companies have achieved this by adding Rube Goldberg–like complexity to their compensation scheme, there is a fairly sim-ple, intuitive way to accomplish the same objective. Give salespeople sales goals as before, but tell them that the sales goals are set at "target" prices. If they sell at prices below or above the "target," the sales credit they earn will be adjusted by the profitability of the sale.

The key to determine the sales credit that someone would earn for making a sale is calculating the *profitability factor* for each class of product. To induce salespeople to maximize their contribution to the firm, actual sales revenue should be multiplied by that profitability factor (called the sales "kicker") to determine the sales credit. Here is the formula:

Sales Credit = [Target Price − k (Target Price − Actual Price)] Units Sold

where k is the profitability factor (or "kicker")

The profitability factor should be at least equal to 1 divided by the per-centage contribution margin at the target price. When equal, the salesperson's sales credit varies directly and in the same proportion as the firm's profitabil-ity. In the above case, where the contribution margin was 20 percent, the prof-itability factor would equal 5. When the 15 percent price discount is multiplied by the profitability factor of 5, it reduces the sales credit by 75 percent, rather than by 15 percent if there were no profitability adjustment. Consequently, when $1,000 worth of product is sold for $850, it produces only $250 of sales credit, but when $500 worth of product is sold for $550 (a 10 percent price pre-mium), the salesperson earns $750 of sales credit ($500 + [5 × $50]). In fact, because salespeople are more likely to take a short-term view of profitability (they can always move on to another firm), the optimal profitability factor for the firm is usually *higher* than the minimum based solely on the contribution margin. Obviously, the importance of this adjustment is directly related to the variable contribution margin. The lower it is, the greater the divergence when rewarding top-line revenue between what is good for the salesperson and what is good for the company.

This is not merely a theory. As companies have moved toward more nego-tiated pricing, many have adopted this scheme in markets as diverse as office equipment, market research services, and door-to-door sales. Although a small percentage of salespeople cannot make the transition to value selling and profit-based compensation, most embrace it with enthusiasm. Managers should be prepared for the consequences, however, since salespeople's complaints about the company's competitiveness do not subside. Instead, salespeople who previously complained about the company's high prices begin complaining about slow deliveries, quality defects, lack of innovative product features, and the need for better sales support to demonstrate value. In short, since sales-people cannot sell value that does not exist, they become strong advocates for steps to enhance the value the organization provides.

Once sales incentives are aligned, salespeople will begin clamoring for the other things they need to succeed. Successful value-based pricing and sales require an upfront investment to understand the value delivered to customers. It is unreasonable to expect each individual salesperson to make that investment; the effort should be centralized and the cost shared. The results then need to be transformed into value-based sales tools that reflect the economics of the purchase decision. Salespeople have the right to expect product-specific sales training that focuses not only on the principles of value-based selling, but on how to apply segment-specific tools to measure and demonstrate value to customers.

Measuring the "Pocket Price"

One common reason why companies fail to reward salespeople on profitability is that they do not have accounting systems that accurately track the costs of sales. In a classic and often-quoted article, two McKinsey consultants showed how simply managing the plethora of discounts can vastly improve company profitability.[3] Exhibit 8-3 illustrates the issue. Although the company may estimate account profitability by the list or the invoice price, there are often many other sources of profit "leakage" along the way. The "pocket price," or revenue that is actually earned after all the discounts are netted out, is often much less. More importantly, the amount of that "leakage" may range from very small to the absurd. In one case, a company that analyzed its pocket prices discovered that sales to a small share of its customers actually resulted in more "leakages" than the list price. In addition to the salesperson's commission, there was a volume incentive for the retailer, a commission for the buying group to which the retailer belonged, a co-op advertising incentive, an incentive discount for the distributor to hold inventories, an early payment discount for the distributor, a coupon for the end customer, and various fees for processing the coupons.

In many business markets the salesperson is instrumental in negotiating these "leakages." Agreements to let the customer pay later, to let the customer place smaller orders, to give the customer extra service at no cost all add up. The result can become a much wider variance in the pocket prices than in the invoice prices. Moreover, since such concessions are often monitored less closely than explicit price discounts, they have a tendency to grow. This does not mean that such discounts should be stopped. They often provide valuable incentives and can be effective in hiding discounts while still maintaining the important appearance of price integrity. The danger is simply in letting them go unmanaged. If sales representatives' and managers' compensation is tied to the profitability of "pocket prices" rather than to list or invoice prices, they can make thoughtful judgments about when such discounts may be worth the cost.

(dollars per square yard)

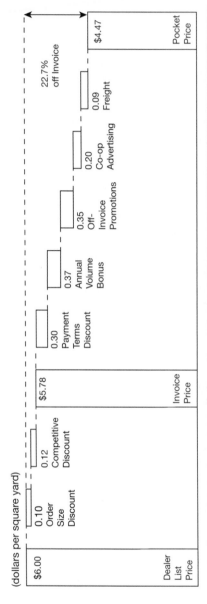

EXHIBIT 8-5 The Pocket Price Waterfall

Reprinted by permission of *Harvard Business Review.* [Exhibit 2] from "Managing Price, Gaining Profit" by Michael Marn and Robert Rosiello, issue Sept-Oct, 1992. Copyright © 1992 by the Harvard Business School Publishing Corporation; all rights reserved.

SUMMARY

Capturing the rewards justified by superior products, service, and availability is not automatic. It requires active management of a process for comprehending, communicating, and capturing value. The seller's disadvantage in price negotiation may be a devious purchasing agent or simply a buyer who understands no better than the seller the true value of the product being purchased. In either case, when you understand your product's value and you communicate that value to buyers, you create buyers who know the value of what you are offering them, and who know that you know. The net result is a lot more leverage in price negotiation, and a lot more profitability.

This chapter focused on three issues that arise when implementing pricing strategy via direct negotiation with customers. First, we described the long-term problems that companies create when they permit customers to negotiate prices, and we explained how fixed price policies can limit the damage. Managers often believe that fixed price policies will not work in their markets. However, once they understand that fixed price policies need not be one-price policies, most companies can develop segmented pricing policies to charge different prices without undermining the relationship between price and value. Second, we developed strategies for selling to price buyers, loyal buyers, and value buyers. Finally, we described sales incentive and account tracking mechanisms to motivate and support salespeople whom the firm wants to motivate to sell value.

Appendix 8A

Preparing Competitive Bids

PREPARING COMPETITIVE BIDS

Competitive bidding is an alternative to negotiation for price buyers. The buyer develops the specifications and asks for prices. In some cases, such as sales to government, there is no opportunity to sell "value" and the business goes to the lowest bidder. In other cases, you may be able to talk with the buyers and determine what added features might make your bid more attractive despite a higher price. Pricing an order or project for a competitive bid is the ultimate price-buyer situation.[4] It often involves a huge investment on the part of the supplier hoping that its bid will win a *job*. Because competitive bidding is used most often for very large projects, winning or losing can have an exceptional impact on a company's financial health and ultimate survival.

In complex bid situations, every aspect of pricing—costs, price sensitivity, and competition—is uncertain to some degree. No firm is ever entirely certain what each input will be and how it should impact the final pricing strategy. In some cases, the degree of uncertainty is low enough to allow informal judgments to be made. Many companies in industries such as construction, telecommunications, computer and systems integration are involved in complex, long-term bid situations. Informal judgments do not provide these companies with adequate solutions for developing pricing strategy, which makes pricing in competitive bidding situations particularly risky. Thus companies placing competitive bids are especially willing to use more quantitative techniques to ensure that they make the best possible decisions.

Quantitative Analysis

Quantitative analysis brings no new data to the bidding problem. Instead, it helps managers examine the implications of the data. Attempts to make unassisted pricing judgments when facing multiple sources of uncertainty are likely to prove frustrating if not impossible since they require managers to think of more factors simultaneously than is humanly possible. Consequently, managers often disregard data that could improve their decisions. Quantitative bidding analysis enables managers to think about the problem in more tractable pieces, which can then be combined and reviewed. It helps to pinpoint sources of disagreement and to focus on them in discussion. Further, it forces the manager to go to other sources of judgment, and it facilitates evaluating risk-return trade-offs. Finally, since quantitative analysis requires documenting the decision, it helps managers learn from past experiences.

Dollar Amount*	Profit Contribution*	Probability of Success	Expected Value*
$40	$12	.24	$2.9
39	11	.32	3.5
38	10	.44	4.4
37	9	.47	4.2

Note: Expected value of bid (column 4) represents the profit contribution (column 2) multiplied by the probability of success (column 3).

*Figures are in millions of dollars.

EXHIBIT 8A-1 Expected Value of Alternative Competitive Bids

Exhibit 8A-1 illustrates a quantitative analysis for a competitive bid. After listing possible bids that it might make, the company calculates the profit contribution associated with each bid.[5] The company then lists the subjective probability of winning, given each possible bid, and multiplies that probability times the profit contribution if it wins the contract with that bid. The last column shows the resulting expected value of each bid.

The bid with the highest expected value (in this case, the bid of $38 million) is the best choice for companies with many bidding opportunities. Others may wish to consider trade-offs between earning the highest expected profit and the assurance of earning at least enough profit contribution to avoid severe financial difficulty. The role of the analysis in the latter case is to identify the trade-off. How much expected profit must be sacrificed for an increase in the probability of winning?

Although simple in theory, competitive bidding is quite challenging in practice, since neither the profit contribution nor the probability of success is ever obvious. The incremental cost of winning a job varies significantly, depending on the amount of other business that a company has already won. If a company has excess capacity, the contribution from winning a bid may be quite large since many costs will be sunk. However, if completing a job requires added capacity or costly delays in other jobs, incremental costs will be high and the profit contribution relatively low. Similarly, a bidder should consider the opportunity cost of committing capacity too early. Bidding low enough to win many early bids may preclude bidding on more lucrative jobs later on.

Even more difficult is assigning the probability that a given bid will be successful. Typically, assigning probabilities is a blend of research and judgment. The more a company knows about past bidding behavior in the industry and the current bidding situation, the better are its chances of producing a profitable winning bid. There are two methods for estimating a bid's probability of success: the average opponent approach and the specific opponent approach.[6] The choice between them depends on the amount of information available.

Probability of Success

Average Opponent Approach

The average opponent approach is used to establish probability of success when a company has little knowledge about or past experience bidding against any specific competitors. The approach treats all competitors as essentially the same in the aggressiveness of their bidding. The company using this approach begins with an analysis of past bidding behavior. First, it collects as much information as possible about bids on past jobs that were similar to the current job. Then, to facilitate comparison of bids from different jobs, it expresses each bid as a ratio: the bid price divided by the firm's own estimated cost of the job. If the company estimates the cost of a job as $5 million, a bid of $6 million is expressed as 1.2 ($6/$5) and a loss-leader bid of $4.5 million as 0.95 ($4.5/$5). After doing this for as many jobs as possible, the company calculates the percentage of times that competitors' bids exceeded any particular value of the ratio, as follows:

Bids Ratio	Competitive Bids Exceeding Bid Ratio (%)
0.95	100
1.00	98
1.05	92
1.10	80
1.15	67
1.20	55
1.25	42
1.30	20
1.35	8

If management has no other information, the company could use these historical bid frequencies as the probabilities that it would underbid any single competitor on a single bid. For any particular bid ratio, R, we will label the probability (P) of underbidding any single competitor as $P(R)$, that is, $P \times R$. In practice, management usually has additional information about differences between the current bid and previous bids, which it uses to make subjective adjustments to the historical bid frequencies before adopting them as current bid probabilities. For example, if the industry is operating at higher capacity levels now than in the past, management assigns subjective probabilities somewhat higher than the historical bid frequencies. On the other hand, if this job is particularly attractive because of the additional business that winning it might produce in the future, management might expect competitors to bid lower than usual. In the latter case, management assigns subjective probabilities somewhat lower than the historical bid frequencies.

To calculate the probability of winning a particular job, management must next consider the number of bidding competitors. The more bidding competitors, the lower the probability that any one bid will win the job. Since the average opponent approach assumes that management cannot distinguish among its competitors, the probability of underbidding each of them is the same. Consequently, if the number of bidders is N, the probability of winning the job with any particular bid ratio is $P_{win}(R)$; then

$$P_{win}R = P(R)^N$$

If the historical bid frequencies shown above equal the subjective probabilities of underbidding a competitor, the probability of winning against two average competitors with a bid ratio of 1.1 is:

$$P_{win}(1.1) = .80^2 = .64 \ or \ 64\%$$

Exhibit 8A-2 illustrates the probability of winning for each bid ratio, given two, four, or six opponents.

Bidders often do not know how many competitors they will be bidding against, which adds further uncertainty to the problem. Management must formulate subjective probabilities for the number of expected opponents. It then uses those subjective probabilities to weight different calculations of P_{win} that assume different numbers of competitors. For example, if management's subjective probabilities for the number of other bidders are:

2 other bidders .5
3 other bidders .4
4 other bidders .1

the probability of winning with a bid ratio of 1.1 in the example given above is as follows:[7]

$$P_{win}(1.1) = (.5 \times .80^2) + (.4 \times .80^3) \\ + (.1 \times .80^4) = .565 \ or \ 56.5\%$$

Specific Opponent Approach

The average opponent approach to establishing probability of success is appropriate only when a company knows little about its individual competitors. Usually, however, a company does know who its competitive bidders are and their different motivations. When bidding for government contracts, for example, potential bidders must state an intention to bid some months before the bids are actually due; the list of those firms is available to all competitors. When bidding for specialized construction projects, such as large hydroelectric power plants, the number of qualified

Bid Ratio	Competitive Bids Exceeding Bid Ratio(%)	Probability of Winning Job		
		2 Opponents	4 Opponents	6 Opponents
0.95	100%	1.000	1.000	1.000
1.00	98	.964	.922	.866
1.05	92	.846	.716	.606
1.10	80	.640	.410	.262
1.15	67	.449	.202	.090
1.20	55	.302	.092	.028
1.25	42	.176	.031	.005
1.30	20	.040	.002	*
1.35	8	.006	*	*

*Asterisk denotes a probability of less than .001.

EXHIBIT 8A-2 Calculating P_{WIN} Using the Average Opponent Approach

bidders is so small that bidding is always against the same three or four competitors. When a company knows who the competitors will be and their prior bidding behavior, the *specific opponent approach* can help them make more successful bids.

The specific opponent approach begins much like the average opponent approach, with an analysis of historical bidding behavior of the competitors. The bidding behavior of each competitor, however, is separately analyzed. For example, if both opponent A and opponent B are frequent bidders, a company using this approach would separate them from other competitors when attempting to estimate the probabilities of underbidding them. For each value of the bid ratio, R, it would calculate the number of times each specific competitor's bid exceeded R. If other bidders, called *peripheral opponents*, are also bidding, they are treated as a separate group using the average opponent approach. An analysis of historical bidding behavior might look like Exhibit 8A-3.

As with the average opponent approach, the company uses any information about differences between this bid and previous bids to adjust the historical frequencies before using them as the probabilities of underbidding competitors on the current job. In addition, it would adjust the historical frequencies for each specific opponent based on whatever information it has about that company. For example, if opponent B recently installed a new president, who announced corporate goals including a substantial increase in market share, one might expect that the probability of B's bid exceeding any given bid ratio would now be lower. Similarly, if opponent A recently won a large contract committing much of its capacity, one might expect the probability that A's bid would exceed any given bid ratio to now be higher.

The probability of winning the job, P_{win}, is the probability of underbidding the specific opponents and the peripheral opponents. Let $P_A(R)$ and $P_B(R)$ be the probability of underbidding specific opponents A and B, re-

---

EXHIBIT 8A-3 Analysis of Historical Bid Frequencies: Specific Opponent Approach

	Opponents' Competitive Bids Exceeding Bid Ratio (%)		
Bid Ratio	*Opponent A*	*Opponent B*	*Peripheral Opponents*
0.95	100%	100%	98%
1.00	98	100	95
1.05	90	95	85
1.10	80	78	70
1.15	70	65	58
1.20	55	60	40
1.25	47	55	33
1.30	30	46	20
1.35	24	33	11

spectively, and let $P_O(R)$ be the probability of underbidding one of the peripheral opponents for any particular bid ratio R. If the current job involves bidding against opponents A and B in addition to N peripheral opponents, the probability of winning with any given bid ratio R is as follows:

$$P_{win}(R) = P_A(R) \times P_B(R) \times P_O(R)^N$$

If the historical bid frequencies in Exhibit 8A-3 are used without adjustment as the probabilities of underbidding the opponents, the probability of winning a job with a bid ratio of 1.2 when bidding against opponents A and B and two peripheral opponents is as follows:

$$P_{win}(1.2) = .55 \times .60 \times .40^2 = .053$$
$$or\ 5.3\%$$

If management is uncertain whether opponents A or B will bid, it weights the bids of the specific opponents by the subjective probability that each one would bid. If the company is uncertain about the number of peripheral opponents who would bid, it weights the calculation of underbidding exactly as shown for the average opponent approach.

The Winner's Curse

Competitive bidding is notorious for causing the winning bidders to lose money.[8] In fact, research shows that even bidders who use sophisticated models and formalized techniques often lose money.[9] The reason is the winner's curse. To understand the curse, imagine first that you are one of two bidders and you win a bid with the lower price. You will probably be quite happy. Now imagine that you are one of ten bidders and you believe that your competitors are sophisticated businesspeople who know how to bid a job. Again you win. Are you still as happy? What does it mean that you bid below nine other knowledgeable bidders? Perhaps it means that you were willing to take less profit on the job. On the other hand, it could also mean that you underestimated the cost to complete the work.

The more bidders there are, the more likely you will lose money on every job you win, *even if on average you estimate costs correctly and both you and your competitors set bids that include a reasonable margin of profit.* The reason: The bids you win are not a random sample of the bids you make. You are much more likely to win jobs for which you have underestimated your costs and are unlikely to win those for which you have overestimated your cost. Consequently, the expected profitability of a job, *conditional on the fact that you have won it,* is much less than the expected profitability before winning. The difference between the conditional and unconditional probabilities increases with the number of competitors against whom you must bid.

The only solution to this is, in effect, to formalize the principle of "selective participation" described above. You do that by adding a "fudge factor" to each bid to reflect an estimate of how much you are likely to have underestimated your costs if you actually win a bid. Needless to say, adding this factor will reduce the number of bids you win, but it will ensure that you won't ultimately regret having won them.

Notes

1. Thomas V. Bonoma, "Major Sales: Who Really Does the Buying?" *Harvard Business Review* (May–June 1982), pp. 111–19.

2. Stratford Sherman, "How to Prosper in the Value Decade," *Fortune*, November 30, 1992, pp. 91–103.

3. Michael Marn and Robert Rosiello, "Managing Price, Gaining Profit," *Harvard Business Review* (September–October 1992), pp. 84–93.

4. See *In re Minolta Camera Products Litigation*, 668 F.Supp. 456 (D.Md. 1987). Other prominent cases have involved Panasonic: *In re Panasonic Consumer Electronics Antitrust Litigation*, No. 89–CV 0368 (SWK) (S.D.N.Y. filed January 18, 1989) (charging Panasonic with establishing and enforcing a minimum price for its goods; settlement provided for refunds of up to $16 million to 600,000 purchasers); Mitsubishi Electronics, *Maryland ex rel Curran* v. *Mitsubishi Electronics of America*, Civ. No. S–91–815 (D.Md. filed March 27, 1991) (alleging that Mitsubishi attempted to set resale prices on all its products; the dealers were told that failure to maintain those prices could result in termination; the settlement required Mitsubishi to refund $7.95 million to consumers who purchased specific TVs during 1988); and Nintendo, *Nebraska* v. *Nintendo of Am., Inc.*, No.

91–CV 2498 (RWS) (S.D.N.Y. filed April 10, 1991) (charging Nintendo with conspiring to maintain prices; settlement provided that consumers were eligible for a $5 coupon). The discussion above is based on *ABA Antitrust Section, Antitrust Law Developments*, 3rd ed. (1992), pp. 610–11.

5. Although this review focuses on the legal constraints on pricing, the antitrust laws proscribe other business practices (for example, anticompetitive mergers) as well.

6. Quoted in A. D. Neale and D. G. Goyder, *Antitrust Laws of the United States*, 3rd ed. (Cambridge: University of Cambridge, 1980), p. 15.

7. The Webb-Pomerene Act of 1918 and the Export Trading Company Act of 1982 provide substantial protection for agreements among direct rivals concerning export trade.

8. As the Supreme Court later noted, "Congress did not intend the text of the Sherman Act to delineate the full meaning of the statute or its application in concrete situations. The legislative history makes it perfectly clear that it expected the courts to give shape to the statute's broad mandate. . . ." *National Society of Professional Engineers* v. *United States*, 98 S.Ct. 1355 (1978).

9. *United States* v. *Northern Securities* [A *Railway* case], 193 U.S. 197 (1904).

CHAPTER

9

Segmented Pricing

Tactics for Separating Markets

Market segmentation is the division of buyers into distinct subsets, or segments, enabling a company to tailor marketing programs more appropriate for the buyers in each segment. Segmentation is important for every aspect of marketing, but especially for pricing. We have seen that an appropriate pricing strategy depends on costs, price sensitivity, and competition. Usually one or more of these factors vary significantly across market segments. When this happens, a pricing strategy based on a single price for all sales is an imperfect compromise. With segmented pricing, management minimizes the need to compromise. Customers who are relatively price insensitive, costly to serve, or poorly served by competitors can be charged more than those who are relatively price sensitive, less costly to serve, or well-served by competitors. Both sales and profitability improve.

To illustrate the advantages of segmented pricing, suppose that a supplier identified five different segments, all willing to pay a different price to get the benefits they sought from purchase of the product or service (see Exhibit 9-1). Segment 1 with sales potential of 50,000 units is willing to pay $20 for the firm's product. Segment 2 with sales potential of 150,000 units is willing to pay $15, and so on. What price should the firm set? The right answer in principle is whatever price maximizes profit contribution. If you calculate the profit contribution at each of the five prices assuming a variable cost of $5 per unit, the single price that produces the maximum contribution: ($2,750) is $10.

There are two obvious shortcomings to this single price strategy, however. First, the firm clearly is leaving excess money on the table for many buyers who are willing to pay more: those willing to pay $20 and $15. These high-end buyers may perceive significantly greater value from purchasing this product, relative to other buyers. This excess value that consumers receive by paying a lower price, when in fact they are willing to pay a higher price, is referred to by economists as "consumer surplus." The firm would be better off if it could capture some of this surplus by charging higher prices to these buyers.

The second problem with a single price strategy is that the firm leaves nearly half of the market unsatisfied, even though it could serve it at prices

	A	B	C	D	E	Total
Viable prices	$20	$15	$10	$ 8	$ 6	
Segment's sales potential (000)	50	150	350	250	200	1,000
Percent of market	5	15	35	25	20	100
Contribution (,000) with:						
1 Price $10	$250	$750	$1,750	0	0	**$2,750**
2 Prices $15, $8	$500	$1,500	$1,050	$750	0	**$3,800**
5 Prices $20,$15, $10,$8,$6	$750	$1,000	$1,750	$750	$200	**$4,950**

EXHIBIT 9-1 The Benefits of Price Segmentation

Source: Richard Harmer. "Strategies for Segmented Pricing," The Pricing Institute 6th Annual Conference (Chicago, March 22–25, 1993).

above the $5 per unit variable cost. In industries with high fixed costs, serving those additional customers is very tempting, and possibly very profitable. Moreover, by ignoring these buyers, the firm leaves wide open an opportunity for low-cost competitors to enter the market and establish a competitive presence. Xerox's dominance of the photocopier market was undermined when Japanese competitors entered with low-end copiers to serve markets that Xerox considered too marginal to be bothered pursuing. When those competitors won a large enough installed base at the low end to establish a reliable service network, they were then able to attack Xerox's higher-margin markets.

The rule then of segmented pricing is this: It is better to serve different market segments with separate price points, rather than serve the entire market with one price point. How many segments with associated price points should the firm serve? To return to our illustration, Exhibit 9-1 shows that if the firm were to set two price points serving two general price segments—high-end buyers willing to pay $15 or more, and mid-level buyers willing to pay $8 or more—it could increase profit contribution by 40 percent. But if the firm could charge separate prices to each of the five market segments it could increase profit contribution by 80 percent more than the single price strategy.

If charging different customers prices that reflect different value were easy, everyone would do it. In fact, customers who received higher prices, have every incentive to undermine segmented pricing—and often do. Customers whom management would like to charge a higher price will not identify themselves as members of a relatively price-insensitive segment simply to help the seller charge them a higher price. Rather, they will learn how to disguise themselves as customers who qualify for a lower price. Distributors can undermine a segmented-pricing strategy as well. If they can figure out how to buy the product cheaply and resell it to segments that will pay more, they can capture the profit from segmented pricing for themselves. Finally, some segmented pricing tactics violate federal antitrust laws.[1]

How can the firm charge different prices for essentially the same product or service? The answer is the very essence of segmented pricing: The firm does not vary prices for the same product offer, but creatively varies the offer or the criteria to qualify for it. Different segments are willing to pay more or less depending on their ability to pay, or on the economic value they receive. As described in Chapter 6, the ideal way to get different customers to pay what something is worth to them is to establish a price metric that tracks with differences in value. Unfortunately, in almost all industries, even the most viable metrics are a distant approximation of the ideal. Consequently, firms also resort to establishing pricing policy "fences" that separate customers into segments with different price sensitivities.[2]

Many service companies with highly perishable inventories, such as airlines, hotels, and auto rental companies, have learned to master the art and science of segmentation pricing. They establish fences based on time of purchase (advance reservation rates), location of purchase (direct, travel agent, or online), buyer identification (AARP discounts), and bundling (discounts for vacation packages). We will describe nine generic approaches to segmented pricing and the criteria necessary for their success. We will also illustrate the creative ways that each has been used. Your success with segmented pricing will depend on picking a generic approach consistent with your own industry circumstances and creating metrics and fences that reflect an accurate understanding of the value you can deliver to different customer segments.

SEGMENTING BY BUYER IDENTIFICATION

Occasionally pricing differently among segments is easy because buyers in the different segments have obvious characteristics that distinguish them. Barbers charge different prices for short and long hair because long hair is usually more difficult to cut. At times when they have excess capacity, barbers cut children's hair at a substantial discount because many parents view home haircuts as acceptable alternatives to costly barber cuts for their children. For barbers, simple observation of the customers is the key to segmented pricing.

Although observation is the most common method of segmentation, it is often ineffective or counterproductive. Too often sellers naively think they can segment simply by being responsive to those customers who complain about the price. For example, during the 1980s when overcapacity plagued the lodging industry, some mid- and even upper-level hotel chains instructed their reservations agents to offer customers the "regular" room rate first. If the customer indicated that the price was too high, they were to query the customer about possible ways they might qualify for a small discount (for example, AAA membership). If the customer still resisted and the hotel projected excess capacity for that night, the reservation agent used some excuse to offer a still better rate from a special block of discounted rooms.

Although some hotels still do this, most have learned their lesson. The customers who complain are rarely the most price sensitive. On the contrary, they are the frequent, seasoned business travelers who learn quickly about a hotel's segmentation scheme and love to negotiate. They also love to brag to the other business travelers they meet at the bar about how they paid a lower rate. In contrast, the people who don't complain are more likely to be pleasure travelers who are more price sensitive but don't know the game. Finding the need to economize embarrassing, many will not complain about the price. They will simply hang up or make some excuse about why they cannot book the reservation immediately, and then they will call Motel 6.

Even less effective is the tactic of some business-to-business salespeople of discounting when customers complain about prices. Large business customers can afford professional actors—better known as purchasing agents—who have mastered the art of acting price sensitive even when they are not. When constrained by engineering or manufacturing to purchase from a particular supplier, they may still use other bids to extract discounts. Salespeople who don't understand this game end up giving away value unnecessarily to these largest customers. Effective price segmentation requires basing discounts on more objective indicators of price sensitivity than mere complaining.

Obtaining Information

Rarely is identification of customers in different segments straightforward. Yet, management can sometimes structure a pricing policy that induces the most price-sensitive buyers to volunteer objective information necessary to segment them based on known demographic data that clearly identifies a price sensitive segment. For example, teachers and educators in the public sector are more price sensitive than similar professionals within companies (due to shared cost and end-benefit effects), yet they are highly desirable customers because of their influence on other potential buyers. Consequently, software companies will offer substantial discounts to teachers and educators provided they present documentation verifying their current status as educators. Theaters give discounts to college students who are more price sensitive because of their low incomes and their alternative sources of campus entertainment. Students readily volunteer their college identification cards to prove that they are members of the price-sensitive segment. Members of the less price-sensitive segment identify themselves by not producing such identification. Business-to-business companies frequently offer greater discounts to nonprofit and charitable organizations that provide documentation on their status as nonprofits.

Even schools and colleges charge variable tuitions for the same education based on their estimates of their students' price sensitivities. Although the official school catalogs list just one tuition, it is not the one most students pay. Many students receive substantial discounts called "tuition remission scholarships" obtained by revealing personal information on financial-aid applications. By evaluating family income and assets, colleges can set a tuition for each student that makes attendance attractive while still maximizing the school's income.

Another form of self-induced buyer identification is the use of coupons, a frequent tool of consumer marketers. Coupons provided by the seller give deal-prone shoppers a way to identify themselves.[3] Supermarkets put coupons in their newspaper ads because people who read those ads are part of the segment that compares prices before deciding where to shop. Packaged-goods manufacturers print coupons directly on the packages, expecting that only price-sensitive shoppers will make the effort to clip them out and use them for future purchases. Small-appliance manufacturers use rebates for the same purpose, expecting that only the most price-sensitive shoppers will take the time to fill out a rebate form and mail it in.[4]

Adept consumer marketers use coupons with differing discount levels to attract different price segments. For example, deep discount coupons are used to attract brand switchers or first-time users. More modest discount coupons are often included inside the product's package to encourage buyers to repurchase the brand; these repeat buyers are less price sensitive than brand switchers because they have experienced the benefits of the product. People who use the coupons are, however, assumed to be more price sensitive than people who cannot be bothered to use coupons at all.

The key to inducing buyers of any product to reveal their price sensitivities is simply to set prices high and give discounts for information or behavior that reveals a higher price sensitivity. Those buyers whom the seller wishes to charge the full price need not cooperate; they are identified simply by the process of elimination. Discounts from high prices have the added advantage of making the seller appear charitable to the price-sensitive buyer. Physicians use this argument to justify the higher prices they charge people with comprehensive health insurance.[5] They are not charging more to people with insurance, but rather charging less to people without it. Of course, how you see it depends on your perspective.

Often a buyer's relative price sensitivity does not depend on anything immediately observable or on factors a customer freely reveals. It depends instead on how well informed about alternatives a customer is and on the personal values the customer places on the differentiating attributes of the seller's offer.[6] In such cases, the classification of buyers by segment usually requires an expert salesperson trained in soliciting and evaluating the information necessary for segmented pricing.

The retail price of an automobile is typically set by the salesperson, who evaluates the buyer's willingness to pay. Notice how the salesperson takes a personal interest in the customer, asking what the customer does for a living (ability to pay), how long he has lived in the area (knowledge of the market), what kinds of cars he has bought before (loyalty to a particular brand), where he lives (value placed on the dealer's location), and whether he has looked at, or is planning to look at, other cars (awareness of alternatives). By the time a deal has been put together, the experienced salesperson has a fairly good idea how sensitive the buyer's purchase decision will be to the product's price.

Since expert salespeople are costly, segmented pricing by a sales force is limited to items that involve large expenditures and is far more prevalent in business than in consumer markets.[7] First-time industrial buyers frequently pay higher prices because of their unfamiliarity with alternative suppliers. To become informed they need to seek out alternative suppliers. Their inexperience with the product makes evaluating various suppliers difficult. However, in time new buyers learn what is important in the evaluation of different suppliers. Competing suppliers learn that the new buyers now use the product, and their salespeople are sent to increase awareness of alternatives. Buyers' feelings of obligation to the initial seller wane after repeated purchases. Industrial salespeople must detect these changes, adjusting price to compensate for buyers' increasing price sensitivity.

SEGMENTING BY PURCHASE LOCATION

If customers in one market segment purchase at a different location, they can be segmented by purchase location. This is common practice for a wide range of products. Dentists, opticians, and other professionals sometimes have multiple offices in different parts of a city, each with a different price schedule reflecting differences in their clients' price sensitivity. Many grocery chains classify their stores by intensity of competition and apply lower markups in those localities where competition is most intense. Ski resorts near Denver use purchase location to segment sales of lift tickets. Tickets purchased slopeside cost $37 to $39 and are bought by the most affluent skiers who stay in the slopeside hotels and condos. Tickets are cheaper (approximately 10 percent less) at hotels in the nearby town of Dillon, where less affluent skiers stay in cheaper, off-slope accommodations. In Denver, tickets can be bought at grocery stores and self-serve gas stations for larger discounts (approximately 20 percent less). These discounts attract locals, who know the market well, including the less advertised tourist spots, and who are generally more price sensitive (due to share of cost accounted for by the lift ticket in the end benefit).

Segmentation by location occurs quite often in international marketing. Deutsche Grammophon historically has sold its records for up to 50 percent more in the European market than in the highly competitive U.S. market. Japanese steel mills are often accused of "dumping" when they charge U.S. buyers less than they charge buyers in Japan. Many industrial manufacturers must charge less to the bargain-conscious Chinese than to the wealthy sheiks of the Mideast. This tactic works when high shipping costs and the need for after-sale service ensure that buyers in low-price countries will not order goods for resale in countries where prices are higher.

Price segmentation based on distance is very common for many products, usually in the form of an added shipping or handling charge. Customers who are willing to have the product shipped are often less price sensitive because they prefer to avoid the cost of searching local alternatives, or because they have few local alternatives available to them. In addition to its regular shipping charges that already reflect different prices for different distances, UPS also charges a "remote delivery charge" and "extended area charges" for parcels delivered to remote or difficult-to-access areas, and customers readily pay the charges since they have no alternatives available to have the product delivered. Customers also perceive the greater cost involved in shipping the product long distances, or to remote areas, and therefore consider it fair to pay more.

A related tactic often used to segment markets for pricing bulky industrial products such as steel and wood is *freight absorption*. Freight absorption is the agreement by the seller to bear all or part of the shipping costs of the product. This tactic gives buyers who are farther from the seller a larger effective discount. The purpose is to segment buyers to reflect the attractiveness of their alternatives. A steel mill in Pittsburgh, for example, might agree to charge buyers in the Midwest for shipping only from Chicago, even though the product is actually shipped from Pittsburgh. A buyer in Milwaukee would then pay shipping only from Chicago. The seller in Pittsburgh receives only the price the buyer pays, less the absorbed portion of the shipping costs. Thus, the seller accepts less for the same product from the more distant buyers than from the buyer next door.

Why should a seller agree to absorb freight charges rather than to employ the more common practice of selling FOB, requiring buyers to bear all freight charges?[8] Competition. Buyers who can purchase from a local supplier and incur less shipping cost will have less value for product of a more distant supplier. The supplier in Pittsburgh who wants to overcome the negative differentiation value associated with its more distant location absorbs the freight cost up to the location of the Chicago competitor. This enables the Pittsburgh supplier to cut price to customers nearer the competitor without having to cut price for more local sales. The Chicago competitor probably uses the same tactic to become more competitive for buyers near Pittsburgh.

With trade barriers coming down, particularly in Europe but also in North America, segmenting by location will become increasingly more difficult for goods easily shipped from one location to another. It will no longer be possible simply to charge less for goods shipped to Athens or Mexico City than for those shipped to Paris or New York. Wholesalers will simply buy where the product is cheap and "cross-ship" it to where it is dear. Moreover, large multinational companies can quickly detect differences in prices across borders and buy from the cheapest location.

Fortunately, the alternatives to segmenting by location may actually improve profitability. Many companies have used segmenting by location simply because the average buyer in Italy is more price sensitive than the average buyer in Germany. Still, being right "on average" leaves a lot of room for costly error. Some Italians are quite wealthy, even by international standards, whereas some Germans are quite poor and price sensitive. Thus, the low average price in Italy is too low for some customers, resulting in lost profits from people who would have paid more, whereas the high price in Germany is too high, resulting in lost profit from people who don't buy. The international companies that will benefit from the integration of previously divided economies will be those that quickly adopt more sophisticated segmentation strategies, enabling them to offer common prices across borders while segmenting buyers by other criteria.

SEGMENTING BY TIME OF PURCHASE

When customers in different market segments purchase at different times, one can segment them for pricing by time of purchase. Theaters segment their markets by offering midday matinees at substantially reduced prices, attracting the price-sensitive retirees, students, and unemployed workers who can most easily attend at such times. Less price-sensitive evening patrons cannot so easily arrange dates or work schedules to take advantage of the cheaper midday ticket prices. Similarly, restaurants usually charge more to their evening patrons, even if they cater primarily to a lunch crowd. There are more numerous inexpensive substitutes for lunches than there are for dinners. A Big Mac or a brown bag, acceptable for lunch, is generally viewed as a poor substitute for a formal dinner as part of an evening's entertainment.

Priority pricing is another example of segmenting by time of purchase. New products are offered at full price, or sometimes premium surcharges over full price in the case of extreme excess demand. Over time, as product appeal fades in comparison to other newer and better competitive alternatives, buyers discount the product's value until they are willing to pay only a fraction of its original price for leftover models. This is a frequent tactic in the fashion and automobile industries, where customers with high incomes and low price sensitivity pay premium prices for the latest lines and models and can choose from a full inventory of sizes and colors. Over time, as inventories age and the availability of sizes and colors declines, prices are reduced in successive rounds of promotions to appeal to more price-sensitive buyers who are willing to wait for the opportunity to buy high-quality, but less trendy, inventory and with less certainty of obtaining their preferred size or color.

Priority pricing also applies in business-to-business purchases. A favorite strategy of Intel is to introduce a leading-edge semiconductor at a premium price, and then discount its existing semiconductor product lines. Leading edge OEM computer manufacturers who produce and sell the fastest and latest computers to innovative professional buyers with low price sensitivity pay the price premium for the latest chip technology. More price-sensitive buyers who are willing to accept slightly outdated technology are then offered older-model computers equipped with Intel's now older semiconductors at lower prices.

Similarly, most television and radio stations charge premium prices for their highly perishable inventory of advertising time by charging "preemptible" premiums. Price-sensitive buyers of advertising inventory pay low prices for high levels of preemptibility. When other less price-sensitive buyers come along wanting a highly desirable prime-time advertising slot that has already been sold to a customer paying a lower preemptible rate, the original price-sensitive customer's ad can be displaced. A tactic of smart election candidates is to purchase the best prime-time advertising inventory at a non-preemptible rate for the eve of the final election to ensure they have the last and best opportunity to communicate to voters.

Periodic sales, offering the same merchandise at discounted prices, can also segment markets. This tactic is most successful in markets with a combination of occasional buyers who are relatively unfamiliar with the market, and with more regular buyers who know when the sales are and plan their purchases accordingly. Furniture manufacturers employ this tactic with sales every February and August, months when most people usually would not think about buying furniture. However, people who regularly buy home furnishings, and who are more price sensitive because of the reference price and total expenditure effects, know to plan their purchases to coincide with these sales.

Peak-Load Pricing

Segmenting by time is also useful when the cost of serving a buyer varies significantly with the time of purchase. This time sensitivity occurs when demand varies at different times but the product is not storable. Airlines, for example, face greater demand for seats on Mondays, Thursdays, and Fridays than on other days. Early morning and late afternoon departures are also more in demand than departures during the midday and evening. Similar variations in demand are common in practically all industries (autos, clothing), but they are usually solved by simply storing excess production when demand is low and selling it when demand exceeds production capacity. An airline, however, cannot store the excess seats it has on Tuesdays in order to meet exceptional demand on Fridays. Seats left unused on Tuesday flights are lost, whereas the ability to serve customers on Friday afternoon is limited by capacity at that time. The same general problem plagues hotels and restaurants, electric utilities, long-distance telephone companies, theaters, computer time-sharing companies, beauty salons, toll bridges, and parking garages. Unable to move supplies of their products from one time to another, their only option is to manage demand. One way of doing so is with *peak-load pricing*.[9]

The principle of peak-load pricing follows from our discussion in Chapter 2 on the distinction between avoidable and sunk costs. Industries with peak-load problems have two different kinds of costs: operating costs and capacity costs. Operating costs are incremental and avoidable regardless of whether demand is at peak or nonpeak levels. The cost of fuel is an operating cost for an electric utility because it is a cost incurred only as needed to meet demand. *Capacity costs*, on the other hand, are the costs of simultaneously purchasing resources for both peak and nonpeak sales. The cost of building generating capacity is a capacity cost because the utility cannot purchase it only for those days or hours when demand is greatest. To have capacity available for hot summer days, the utility must pay for it year-round.

Setting Peak-Load Prices

Setting peak-load prices is often straightforward. Capacity is incremental only for changes in sales during peak periods. Consequently, capacity costs are relevant only for the pricing of peak-period sales when lowering price to serve more customers would require adding more capacity, whereas raising price to serve fewer customers could enable the company to avoid building new capacity. Capacity costs should be ignored when pricing sales in nonpeak periods, since the cost of capacity up to the amount used at peak times is not avoidable. The percent contribution margin for nonpeak sales will, therefore, be greater than for sales at peak times. This will normally result in lower prices being set for nonpeak time periods than for peak time periods.[10]

Peak-load pricing is not always that simple. Consider what happened when the Bell telephone system first decided to set different prices for calls placed at different times of the day. Bell originally noted that when it charged the same price for all calls, the number of calls was greatest during the business day and dropped off substantially in the evenings and on weekends. Concluding that the cost of capacity was relevant only for calls made during the business day, management proceeded to set prices for daytime calls that reflected the entire cost of capacity while setting prices for evenings and weekends that reflected none of the capacity cost. The result was a substantial increase in calls in the evenings and on weekends, an increase so great that more calls were made during less expensive, nonpeak times than during the peak period of the business day.

Bell had encountered a classic problem called *peak reversal*. Clearly, when the quantity of calls placed in the low-priced nonpeak time period is straining capacity, the cost of building new capacity is relevant for the pricing of those calls. If nonpeak calls were forced to bear all, or even an equal share, of the cost of capacity, the peak calling time would reverse again, reestablishing excess capacity during evenings and weekends. The solution to its peak-reversal problem, as Bell soon discovered, was first to raise the low nonpeak price just enough so that the number of calls people wanted to make at that time was no greater than the capacity available. In evaluating future decisions to change prices or to add to capacity, Bell needed to consider the contribution generated by both peak and nonpeak calls. Since peak prices were higher, they contributed more to the cost of capacity than did nonpeak calls. Since nonpeak calls still fully used capacity, they also contributed in part.

Peak-load prices are set properly by allocating the cost of capacity to the time period that requires it. Allocating the entire cost of capacity to the peak demand period and pricing accordingly is correct if peak period sales continue to exceed nonpeak sales. If lower pricing in the nonpeak period causes sales to equal or exceed those in the peak period, one must logically conclude that nonpeak sales also partly account for the need to increase capacity. In that case, nonpeak sales should be made to share part of the cost of capacity.[11]

Yield Management

A more sophisticated version of peak-load pricing, now widely used in the air-line, cruise ship, and lodging industries, is *yield management.* Unlike peak-load pricing, or segmentation based on different costs of serving customers, yield management simultaneously integrates differences both in the cost and in price sensitivity. It is not difficult to see how yield management represents a huge opportunity for increased profitability. Airlines enjoy peak demand from business travelers on Monday mornings and Friday afternoons on many routes, enabling airlines to fill the planes at full coach fares. However, smaller demand at full coach fares would leave many seats unfilled at less popular times. Rather than discounting all seats at those times, as simple peak-load pricing would suggest, the airlines discount only the seats that they cannot sell at full coach fare.

This "selective discounting" is a much superior strategy. After all, business travelers flying midweek do not value getting to the destinations any less than those flying on Mondays or Fridays. The airline's problem is simply that there are not enough midweek business travelers to fill the planes. It makes no sense, therefore, to discount tickets to business travelers since the airline would generate few added sales and would leave a lot of potential revenue "on the table." The goal is to attract new segments when capacity is available without undermining income from segments that would still fly at higher prices. They do this by offering "super saver" fares that are attractive only to price-sensitive segments of customers. Most business travelers don't like the weekend stay requirement and the no-cancellation restrictions that "super saver" fares include.

The purpose of yield-management systems is to help sellers determine how much of their capacity they can afford to sell at discount prices without undermining their ability to serve those customers willing to pay full price. This task presents a problem, because it is usually not possible to sell first to all those customers willing to pay full price and only then to sell the remaining capacity to customers who require a discount. In the airline industry, for example, the normal purchase pattern is exactly the opposite. Business travelers usually do not want to book their seats until near the time of travel, often even the same day, whereas pleasure travelers want to book their vacations at discount fares far in advance. How can an airline decide how many discount seats it can sell weeks before a flight and still have enough seats left to serve its best customers at full fare?

Clearly, one way is to average past sales for a particular flight to estimate how many seats business travelers will buy and then to sell discount tickets to fill the remaining seats. Unfortunately, the average of past sales is only a very rough indicator of the future. It would result in substantial under- and overestimates of seats available for discount sales. A better way is to use past experience to create an "historical booking path" for seat sales beginning thirty days before departure. (See Exhibit 9-2.) If business sales are above the number normally booked thirty days before a flight, then the airline allocates that many fewer seats for discount sales. If business sales fall below the projected booking path, the airline allocates more seats for discount sales. Each day the

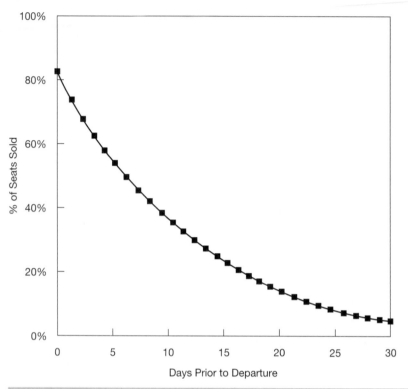

EXHIBIT 9-2 Historical Booking Path for One Airline Route

estimate of actual business sales, and the number of seats available for discount sales, is revised. This practice explains why a pleasure traveler may be told that all discount seats are currently sold, but discover a week later that some have become available. By constantly adjusting the number of seats available at discount, airlines can optimize the total "yield" earned on their investment in their planes, minimizing both the number of full-fare passengers turned away and the number of seats flown empty.[12]

Pricing on the Channel Tunnel that runs under the English Channel is an interesting application of segmented pricing for a product with fixed capacity. The Channel Tunnel allows transport of an automobile and its occupants by rail for a flat price (see fares schedule in Exhibit 9-3) between London, England, and Calais, France. This segmentation pricing has the same economic logic as airline pricing—yield management and pricing to value—but the application is somewhat different. Note the standard versus discount rates. Standard rates apply during peak time periods of the day and season. If you are willing to drive through the tunnel at 2:00 A.M., you can get a substantial discount that reflects the availability of unused capacity. The discount price is not so low (£97 versus

	Same Day	Monday–Thursday	Monday–Friday	Thursday–Monday	Friday–Monday	Monday–Monday	Month Trip
Standard	£127	£127	£137	£137	£137	£227	£227
Discount	67	67	97	97	97	177	177

EXHIBIT 9-3 The Channel Tunnel

£67) for weekend trips when the return trip would be late Sunday night or early Monday morning. The reason is that this is a high demand period.

Pricing for the different lengths of travel time reflects differences in value to different types of buyers. Note that prices are higher for longer stays of a week to a month, although for an airline a longer stay is usually associated with a discount. Can you explain this? Think of what differentiates a Channel trip from travel between England and continental Europe by car or train.

Taking the Channel enables the traveler to have access to her auto during the trip. The value of that access is directly related to how long the trip will be. If going to France for a day or two, it is relatively cheap to take local transportation or rent a car. If going for a week or more, the cost saving associated with having one's own car becomes substantial.

SEGMENTING BY PURCHASE QUANTITY

When customers in different segments buy different quantities, one can sometimes segment them for pricing with quantity discounts. Quantity discount tactics are of four types: volume discounts, order discounts, step discounts, and two-part prices. All are common when dealing with differences in price sensitivity, costs, and competition.[13]

Volume Discounts

Customers who buy in large volume are usually more price sensitive. They have a larger financial incentive to learn about all alternatives and to negotiate the best possible deal. Moreover, the attractiveness of selling to them generally increases competition for their business. Large buyers are often less costly to serve. Costs of selling and servicing an account generally do not increase proportionately with the volume of purchases. In such cases, volume discounting is a useful tactic for segmented pricing.

Volume discounts are most common when selling products to business customers. Steel manufacturers grant auto companies substantially lower prices than they offer other industrial buyers. They do so because auto manufacturers use such large volumes they could easily operate their own mills or send negotiators around the world to secure better prices.

Volume discounts are based on the customer's total purchases over a month or year rather than on the amount purchased at any one time. At some companies, the discount is calculated on the volume of all purchases; at others, it is calculated by product or product class. For example, Xerox gives volume discounts based on a buyer's total purchases of copiers, typewriters, and printers. A large health products company, for example, offers its institutional coustomers separate volume discounts structures for purchases of pharmaceuticals, diagnostics, medical devices, and commodity products like syringes and bandage.

Although less common, some consumer products are volume discounted as well. Larger packages of most food, health, and cleaning products usually cost less per ounce, and canned beverages cost less in twelve-packs than in six-packs. These differences reflect both cost economies for suppliers and the greater price sensitivity for these products by large families. Warehouse food stores, such as Wal-Mart, Costco, Sam's, and BJ's, often require consumers to buy in large-quantity packages to qualify for discounted prices. When offering volume discounts on products sold to business buyers, one must be very careful that quantity discounts do not result in higher costs for small firms than for large ones in the same industry. Volume discounts that make it more difficult for small buyers to compete with larger ones clearly violate the legal prohibition against "discrimination in price . . . where the effect may be substantially to lessen competition," unless the discounts are fully justified by cost differences. (Services are exempt from this restriction.) Morton Salt lost a landmark case in which it gave grocery chains a 12.5 percent discount if they bought 5,000 cases a year and a 15 percent discount if they bought 50,000. This policy was found to give larger chains an unfair competitive advantage over smaller grocery retailers and was thus declared illegal.[14]

Order Discounts

Often the cost of processing and shipping increases very little with the size of a customer's order. Consequently, the per-unit cost of processing and shipping declines significantly with the quantity ordered. For this reason, sellers generally prefer that buyers place large infrequent orders, rather than small frequent ones. To encourage them to do so, sellers often give discounts based on the quantity purchased in a given order. Such discounts may be offered in addition to volume discounts for total purchases in a year, because volume discounts and order discounts serve separate purposes. The volume discount is given to retain the business of large customers. The order discount is given to encourage customers to place large orders.

Order discounts are the most common of all quantity discounts. Almost all office supplies are sold with order discounts. Copier paper, for example, can be purchased as a case of 10 reams for about $21.50, but purchased individually, it costs several dollars per ream.

Step Discounts

Step discounts, or *block discounts*, differ from order discounts in that they do not apply to the total quantity purchased, but only to the purchase beyond a specified amount. The rationale is to encourage individual buyers to purchase more of a product without having to cut the price on smaller quantities for which they would pay a higher price. Thus, in contrast to other segmentation tactics, step discounting may segment not only different customers but also different purchases by the same customers. Such pricing is common for public utilities from which customers buy water and electricity for multiple uses and place a different value on it for each use.

Consider, for example, the dilemma that local electric companies face when pricing their product. Most people place a very high value on having some electricity for general use, such as lighting and running appliances. The substitutes (gaslights, oil lamps, and hand-cranked appliances) are not very acceptable. For heating, however, most people use alternative fuels (gas, oil, coal, and kerosene) because of their lower cost. Utilities would like to sell more power for heating and could do so at a price above the cost of generating it. They do not want to cut the price of electricity across the board, however, since that would involve unnecessary discounts on power for higher-valued uses.

One solution to this dilemma is a step-price schedule. Assume that the electric company could charge a typical consumer $0.06 per KWH for general electricity usage but that it must cut its price to $0.04 per KWH to make electricity competitive for heating. If the company charged the lower price to encourage electricity usage for heating, it would forgo a third of the revenue it could earn from supplying power for other uses. By replacing a single price with a block-price schedule, $0.06 per KWH for the first block of 100 KWH and $0.04 for usage thereafter, the company could encourage people to install electric heating without forgoing the higher income it can earn on power for other purposes. To encourage people to use electricity for still more uses, utilities often add still another step discount for quantities in excess of those for general use and heating. Exhibit 9-4 illustrates a step-price schedule for an electric utility.

Two-Part Pricing

Two-part prices involve two separate charges to consume a single product. For example, amusement parks sometimes have an entry fee plus a ticket charge for each ride, car rental companies have a daily rate plus a mileage charge, and health clubs charge an annual membership fee plus additional fees for racquetball and tennis court time. In each of these cases, heavy users pay less than do light users for the same product, since the fixed fee is spread over more units. Sometimes the rationale for two-part pricing is obvious: There are two distinguishable benefits. Nightclubs, for example, offer patrons both entertainment and drinks. They could include the entertainment in the price of the drinks, but then heavy drinkers would pay disproportionately for it and light drinkers would pay little. The heavy drinkers might therefore go elsewhere, while entertainment revenue that could be earned from light drinkers would be lost. To overcome this problem, nightclubs have both a cover charge for the entertainment and a charge for drinks.[15]

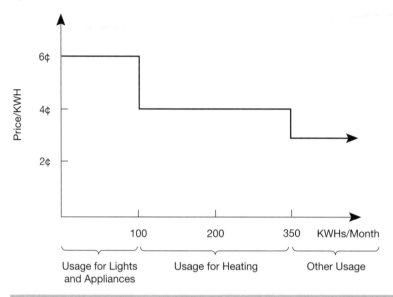

EXHIBIT 9-4 Step-Price Schedule for Electricity

The presence of two products is not, however, the reason for most two-part pricing. Car renters, for example, do not obtain value from merely having the car; they also want to go somewhere in it. The rationale for two-part pricing in this case is simply that there are significant differences in the incremental cost of serving different types of car renters. Since cars depreciate the more they are driven, it costs more to rent a car to someone who puts more mileage on it. Car rental companies sometimes charge a daily fee based on the average number of miles driven. But, as might be recalled from Chapter 2, there is a danger in averaging costs for different types of buyers: Competitors undercut prices for the most profitable customers. When costs are incurred in two parts, segmentation by two-part pricing enables a company to remain competitive in serving low-cost customers while still profitably serving the high-cost segment.

Given the clear increase in profit using either step discounts or two-part pricing to segment the purchases of each individual customer, why do most companies still charge each individual customer a single price? The answer is that segmenting different purchases by each customer is possible only under limited conditions. It is profitable only when all of the following are true:

1. *Purchase volume by individual buyers is significantly price sensitive.* For many products, an individual buyer's demand is an all-or-nothing proposition. Think of some common products (toilet paper, soap, salt, refrigerators, breakfast cereals, umbrellas), and ask yourself whether the quantity bought is really sensitive to even large price variations. Either individual customers buy the product or they do not, but price has very little effect on how much they buy. In this situation, step discounting and two-part pricing are futile.

2. *The product cannot be easily resold or stored for later use.* If resale is easy, one buyer could purchase large quantities at a low price (bearing the high prices of initial steps or the fixed fee of a two-part price only once) and resell it to others who want only small amounts and would otherwise have to pay a higher price or a fixed fee to get them. If storage is easy, buyers could obtain discounts by purchasing large quantities at a time without significantly increasing their total use of the product.

3. *Buyers' demands are similar, or it is possible to segment buyers for pricing into groups with similar demands.* The more diversity there is among buyers in the quantities that they are willing to purchase at various prices, the less possible it is to effectively segment purchases. The right step-price schedule or fixed fee for one buyer would be wrong for another.

SEGMENTING BY PRODUCT DESIGN

Of the preceding segmentation tactics, only segmenting by buyer identification actually prohibits some buyers from purchasing at the lowest price. Segmenting by location, time, and purchase quantity gives all buyers the option to pay the lowest price if they want it. Marketers use such strategies effectively because they realize that people do not make purchases by evaluating the products alone but by evaluating the entire purchase opportunity. The same narrowly defined product or service may be seen by buyers in different contexts as a substantially different purchase opportunity. A loaf of bread available at a convenience store is not the same purchase opportunity as one available in a crowded supermarket. A movie shown at 1:00 P.M. is not the same purchase opportunity as the same film shown in the evening. Segmentation by location, time, and purchase quantity all involve creating different purchase opportunities designed to induce the price-insensitive or higher-cost buyers to purchase willingly at a higher price.

Although varying such aspects of the purchase opportunity often works, some of the most efficient segmentations involve offering different versions of the product or service itself. The important factor in such a strategy is not differences in production costs: There is frequently little or no cost difference in the different versions. A leading manufacturer of pocket calculators, for example, sold a card-programmable version of one calculator for much more than the nonprogrammable version. The only practical difference between the two was a slot in the plastic case of the programmable version where the cards could be inserted. Similarly, oil companies sell premium gasoline for $0.10 to $0.15 more than regular grade, although the added cost of refining it is only $0.04. To make this tactic work, one must offer a lower-priced version that is in some way inadequate to meet the needs of price-insensitive buyers (such as engineers and owners of high-performance cars in the examples above) but still acceptable to price-sensitive buyers.

Airlines have used this tactic quite successfully. Their market consists of both a price-insensitive business traveler and a very price-sensitive vacation traveler. Analysis of these segments revealed that businesspeople place a high value on flexible scheduling. They often do not know in advance exactly when they want to leave or how long they will have to stay. In contrast, vacationers generally plan their trips far in advance. Capitalizing on this difference, airlines set regular ticket prices high and offer discounts only to buyers who purchase their tickets well before departure, or to those who stay at their destination over a weekend, when businesspeople want to be home. By offering lower fares only with inflexible scheduling, airlines have been able to price low enough to attract price-sensitive buyers without making unnecessary concessions to those who are less price sensitive.

Segmenting by product design is easy when selling a service such as air travel because the seller can limit resale of the product. If airline tickets were not issued to specific passengers, firms would soon spring up to buy discounted tickets in advance for resale to businesspeople closer to flight times. When the product is not a service, controlling such arbitrage between the low- and high-priced markets becomes more difficult.

Rohm and Haas Chemical faced this problem with its plastic molding powder, methyl methacrylate. The firm enjoyed a large industrial demand for its product at a price of $0.85 per pound. With only slightly more processing, the firm also sold the product for dental applications at $22 per pound. With such a large price difference, distributors soon began buying the industrial-grade plastic, doing the additional processing themselves, and selling it to the dental market at prices undercutting Rohm and Haas.

To solve this problem, Rohm and Haas needed to change the low-priced product in some way that made adapting it for sale in the high-priced market impractical. Cooking wines, for example, can sell in grocery stores for less than do drinking wines in liquor stores because the addition of salt to the cooking wine precludes arbitrage. Rohm and Haas considered adding a toxic substance to its industrial-grade plastic to make it unusable in the dental market, which the company would serve with a higher-priced, nontoxic version. Had it initially sold the pure and the adulterated products under different brand names, this would have been a viable strategy. Unfortunately, the firm's belated recognition of this opportunity precluded such a solution since dental users who had successfully used the industrial grade might fail to heed the warning to stop using it for oral applications. Rohm and Haas was forced instead to adopt the less effective tactic of simply planting a rumor that it had adulterated the industrial-grade plastic.[16]

SEGMENTING BY PRODUCT BUNDLING

Product bundling is a widely used tactic for segmented pricing, although its rationale often goes unnoticed. Retailers bundle free parking with a purchase in their stores. Grocery stores and fast-food outlets bundle chances in games with purchase of their products. Newspapers with morning and evening editions bundle advertising space in both of them. Restaurants bundle foods into fixed-price

Advertiser	Morning Edition	Evening Edition
Segment A (grocers, retailers)	$1,000	$400
Segment B (theaters, restaurants)	700	600

EXHIBIT 9-5 Value of Advertising Space by Two Different Segments

dinners, generally a cheaper alternative to the same items served à la carte. Symphony orchestras bundle diverse concerts into season subscription tickets. These are but a small fraction of the goods sold in bundles, but they illustrate the breadth of the practice—from commodities to services, from necessities to entertainment. What makes bundling a successful segmented-pricing tactic? In each case the products bundled together have a particular relationship to one another in their value to different buyer segments.[17]

Consider how that relationship applies when bundling advertising space for the morning and evening editions in a newspaper. Advertising space in the morning edition is valued more by one segment of advertisers (for example, grocers, retailers) than by another segment (for example, theaters, restaurants), whereas the reverse is true for the evening edition. Exhibit 9-5 shows hypothetical valuations of advertising space by these two types of buyers. Both value advertising space in the morning edition more than in the evening edition. What is important for a bundling strategy, however, is that segment A values space in the morning edition more than does segment B ($1,000 versus $700), whereas the reverse is true for the evening edition ($400 versus $600).

Why would the newspaper want to bundle morning and evening advertising together, requiring buyers to purchase both in order to get either? Without bundling, the paper would have to charge no more than $700 for a morning ad and $400 for an evening ad to attract both segments for both editions. Thus it would collect $1,100 ($700 + $400) from each advertiser. But how much does each segment value the bundle? Segment A values it at $1,400 ($1,000 + $400), whereas segment B values it at $1,300 ($700 + $600). Thus the newspaper can sell a bundle of morning and evening advertising space to both segments for up to $1,300. That is $200 more per buyer than it could earn if it sold the same space separately.

Why is this segmented pricing? Because each segment pays the difference between the separate price of the advertising ($1,100) and the bundled price ($1,300) for a different product. Segment A pays the extra money because of the value it places on morning advertising; segment B pays because of the value it places on the evening edition.[18]

Optional Bundling

Generally products are not sold only in indivisible bundles. Most firms follow the tactic of optional bundling where products can be bought separately, but the option is available to buy them in a bundle at prices below their cost if bought separately. Optional bundling is more profitable than indivisible bundling whenever some buyers value one of the items in the bundle very highly but value the other less than it costs to offer it. For such a customer, the extra revenue the firm earns from selling the bundle is less than the extra cost of producing it.

Supermarkets often use optional bundling in the form of special promotions. For example, a supermarket might offer anyone who buys $5 worth of groceries the opportunity to buy one stoneware dish at a very low price. The purpose of this optional bundle is to segment the market. Some customers are loyal shoppers at whatever store is most convenient. They are willing to pay a lot to shop at a particular store but do not value stoneware dishes. In contrast, lower-income customers and those with large families will shop around for the best prices. They are not willing to pay as much for the convenience of shopping at any particular store. Many of those shoppers, however, may value the opportunity to buy a nice set of dishes inexpensively. Thus the necessary condition for bundling (a reversal in the relative valuation of the products) is met. Supermarkets make the bundle optional because some shoppers may not want the stoneware dish even at the low price. To force them to purchase it would create unnecessary resentment that could drive them away.

Similarly, giving buyers the option to buy parts separately is common in most cases where bundles are offered. Although tickets to sporting and cultural events are available at a discount in a season ticket bundle, they can be purchased individually as well. Restaurants offer their customers dinner specials (appetizer, entrée, dessert, and beverage bundles), but customers can buy just some of the individual parts at higher à la carte prices. For purposes of segmentation, there is never any reason not to give buyers the option of purchasing separately at higher prices. There are, however, psychological reasons for bundling that may justify making the bundles indivisible. (We discuss these reasons in Chapter 4 in the section called Framing.)

Value-Added Bundling

A subtle variation on mixed bundling is value-added bundling. Rather than cutting prices to price-sensitive customers, the value-added bundler instead offers them an additional value of a kind that less price-sensitive buyers do not want. With that strategy, a company can attract price-sensitive buyers without reducing prices to those who are relatively price insensitive. For only $1 extra, Qantas airlines of Australia offered travelers a choice of "land packages" for tourist-class hotels and sightseeing packages in Australia or for a camper–van for five days in New Zealand. These options would be unattractive to the typical business traveler but make traveling on Qantas attractive to pleasure travelers whose alternatives would be a charter flight to Australia or a less expensive vacation elsewhere. Alcoa used value-added strategy to encourage the use of aluminum-core electrical cable. For most buyers, aluminum's light weight gives it unique and highly valued advantages over competing materials, and Alcoa's prices reflected that value. At those high prices, however, aluminum could not compete with copper in making electrical cable. To overcome this problem, Alcoa began manufacturing aluminum-core electrical cable itself. It did not, however, pass on the full cost of converting aluminum into cable when pricing cable. In effect, it sold the aluminum in cable for less than it sold virgin aluminum. [19]The combination of the raw aluminum and the processing into cable created an effective bundle since buyers who valued the processing more valued the raw aluminum less.

SEGMENTING BY TIE-INS AND METERING

Segmentation by tie-ins or metering is often extremely important for pricing assets. The reason is that buyers generally place greater value on an asset the more intensely they use it. The buyer of a photocopying machine who makes 20,000 copies a month will value it more than the buyer who makes 5,000 copies. Food processors canning fruit year-round in California value canning machines more than fish packers do in Alaska, who can salmon only a few months each year. In such cases, tactics that segment buyers by use intensity can substantially improve the effectiveness of a pricing strategy.

Tie-In Sales

Before the Clayton Antitrust Act of 1914, a common method of monitoring usage intensity was the tie-in sale. Along with the purchase or lease of a machine, a buyer contractually agreed to purchase a commodity used with the machine exclusively from the seller. Thus the Heaton Peninsular Company sold its shoe-making machines with the provision that buyers buy only Heaton Peninsular buttons.[20] The A. B. Dick Company sold its mimeograph equipment with the provision that buyers buy paper, stencils, and ink only from the A. B. Dick Company.[21] American Can leased its canning machines with the provision that they be used to close only American's cans.[22]

In each of these cases, the asset itself sold for a very low explicit price, close to the incremental cost of production. The tied commodity, however, was priced at a premium. Thus the true cost of the asset was its low explicit price, plus the sum of the price premiums paid for the tied-in commodity. Since buyers who used the asset more intensely bought more of the tied commodity, they effectively paid more for the asset.

Tie-in contracts are frequently used by telecommunications companies to reduce the cost for new buyers to try their services. Wireless phone providers offer a digital telephone for a nominal fee if the buyer agrees to purchase a long-term service contract to use the company's wireless network for twelve or twenty-four months. Satellite entertainment companies offer households a satellite dish and receiver unit for a much reduced price or for free, if the buyer agrees to subscribe to a higher-priced entertainment package of channels and outlets, for a minimum of twelve or twenty-four months. Buyers more than pay for the initial price of the dish and receiver by agreeing to purchase high-margin entertainment packages instead of lower-margin packages. These packages can be particularly effective for low-knowledge buyers, who perceive significant risk in investing in a new and little-known technology—and then developing them into loyal buyers who become accustomed to the firm's technology and programming.

Since passage of the Clayton Act, the courts have refused to enforce tying contracts that tie other purchases to the sale of a patented or unique product, except for service contracts where service is essential to maintain the performance and the reputation of the product.[23] Thus if one company had a patent on the technology for the digital PCS phone, it could not require customers to buy phone service from a particular supplier in order to buy a phone.

Although tying by exclusive sales contracts is generally illegal when used for segmented pricing,[24] opportunities to use this tactic without contracts still exist. No court has ever considered prohibiting theaters from requiring that food consumed on the premises be purchased only from the premium-priced, in-house concession; nor has any court considered prohibiting razor manufacturers from creating unique shaving technologies that tie blades to razors. Maintenance and repair services are natural tie-ins to the sale of equipment. Recently, the U.S. Supreme Court explicitly confirmed that such noncontractual tie-ins are an acceptable pricing tactic.[25]

Metering

The courts have, nevertheless, severely limited tie-in arrangements in precisely the cases where they are most dramatically effective. Rulings challenge sellers to monitor use without restricting competition. In modern times, that challenge has frequently been met by monitoring with simple metering devices.

Xerox Corporation developed a metered price policy for its copiers, measuring not only intensity but also type of use. Until the late 1970s, the company leased its machines rather than selling them. Exhibit 9-6 shows the fee schedule for leasing what was a popular Xerox copier. The lessee paid a usage fee for the number of copies made in addition to a monthly minimum charge of $185. Thus, lessees who copied more paid more. Note also, however, that the usage charge fluctuated substantially with the number of copies made per original.

Why would Xerox make the usage charge lower for copying many copies per original? The rationale did not depend on the technology of photocopying. The technology for making ten copies from the same original was the same as that for making ten copies from ten originals. The machine scanned the original each time in either case. The rationale for this policy was, rather, differences in price sensitivity caused by differences in the available alternatives.

Price sensitivity (recall the discussion in Chapter 4) depends critically on the value buyers place on the attributes that differentiate a product from its substitutes. For users who made many copies of each original, photocopiers offered little advantage over offset presses or duplicators. Both these alternative technologies produced clear, high-quality copies at a per-copy cost of labor and materials that declined rapidly with the number of copies made per original. In

Basic Monthly	Monthly Meter	Total Monthly	Meter Rate per Copy from Same Original		
Use Charge	*Minimum*	*Minumum*	*1–3*	*4–10*	*11+*
$50	$135	$185	$0.046	$0.03	$0.02

EXHIBIT 9-6 Metered Pricing (Xerox Copier)

Total cost per month for 10,000 copies, 3 copies per original = $510; total cost per month for 10,000 copies, 50 copies per original = $279.60.

contrast, for users who made few copies per original, these alternative technologies were poor substitutes for a Xerox machine. The preparation of a master plate or stencil for offsetting or duplicating was prohibitively costly for only a few copies.

Photocopying represented a substantial improvement for making a few copies per original. The other alternatives—retyping or using carbon paper—were either very costly or dismally inferior. Consequently, users who made few copies per original were willing to pay much more per copy than were users who made many copies. The usage charge reflected that difference in value.[26] The monthly cost of the copier in Exhibit 9-6 for users who made eleven or more copies per original was $279.60 for 10,000 copies. For users who made three or fewer copies per original, it was $510 for 10,000 copies. The monthly cost for both types of users also varied with use intensity. Xerox used metering to distinguish segments along two different dimensions with obvious success.

The tactic of monitoring use intensity is not limited to machines and may not involve an actual physical counting device. Nationally syndicated newspaper columns are sold to local papers at prices based on use intensity. The monitoring device is simply the papers' circulation figures. Film distributors rent movies at prices based on the number of seats in the theater. Franchisers lease their brand names and reputations to franchisees not for a fixed fee but for a percentage of sales. No matter how intangible the asset, monitoring use can be an important part of its pricing.

IMPORTANCE OF SEGMENTED PRICING

For industries with high fixed costs, segmented pricing is often essential. The U.S. rail system, for example, could never have been built and could not currently be maintained were it not for a strategy of extensively segmented prices. Railroad tariffs are based on the value of the goods hauled. Coal and unprocessed grains, for example, are carried at much lower cost per carload than are manufactured goods. If railroads had to charge all shippers the same tariff charged for unprocessed grain, they would lack sufficient income per shipment to cover their fixed costs. Were they required to charge all shippers the tariff for manufactured goods, they would lose many shippers and would again lack sufficient revenue. Without segmented pricing, many rail lines could never cover their costs, whereas others would be forced either to raise tariffs above the highest currently charged or suffer the same fate. The railroads survive to serve all their customers at reasonable rates only because the customers can be effectively segmented for pricing.

Segmented pricing also spurs competitive innovation. Companies improve their products because improvement enables them to charge more profitable prices, but such improvements are often valued differently by different buyers. When only a subsegment of a firm's buyers value a potential improvement, the ability to segment them for pricing—to recover costs of development and to earn a profit—provides the sole incentive for such advances. Without segmented pricing, the unique demands of small market segments would more often go unsatisfied.

Segmented pricing is clearly among the most difficult of strategies to implement. While the types of segmentation tactics discussed can serve as a guide to separating markets, finding a basis for a segmentation (that is, a particular buyer characteristic or a particular bundling combination) ultimately requires creative insight. Since each example of segmented pricing is unique in its method of implementation, there can be no simple formula. Finding a basis for segmentation is the key to maintaining a strong competitive position; in some cases, it is essential to remaining viable.

Xerox lost much of its strong competitive position in the copier market precisely because of its reluctance to serve the more price-sensitive segments of the market. The company recognized that the big profits were in serving users who demanded high-quality copies in high volume. Although it served those users well and carefully segmented them for pricing by volume and number of copies per original, it ignored the less profitable market of small offices. It left that market to the Japanese, who could not effectively compete with Xerox because they lacked a comparable distribution and service network. Unfortunately for Xerox, the Japanese used small office copiers to gain enough volume that they ultimately could afford the fixed cost of better distribution and service. Then they could challenge Xerox for a share of more profitable copier segments. The lesson is clear: Ignoring a more price-sensitive segment can leave a dangerous opening for competitors, who eventually can threaten one's competitiveness in the less price-sensitive segment as well.

SUMMARY

Segmented pricing enables a company to develop pricing strategies that are more appropriate for the buyers in each market segment. Buyers who are less price sensitive, more costly to serve, or less well served by competitors can be charged more without the loss of buyers whom the firm can serve more profitably at a lower price. Separating segments for pricing is not easy. It requires creative tactics that keep markets separated while avoiding illegalities. This chapter has explained and illustrated seven general types of segmentation tactics that have proved effective and legal in practice:

- Segmentation by buyer identification
- Segmentation by purchase location
- Segmentation by time of purchase
- Segmentation by purchase quantity
- Segmentation by product design
- Segmentation by product bundling
- Segmentation by tie-ins and metering

Creating a segmented pricing strategy requires a flash of insight. Managers must recognize different segments and separate them with pricing policies that are unique for each product. Managers are most likely to find such insight when they know where to look. The purpose of this chapter is to guide that search.

Notes

1. See discussion in Chapter 13 of the Robinson–Patman Act.
2. We have adopted the terms "metrics" and "fences" from Richard Harmer, "Strategies for Segmented Pricing," The Pricing Institute 6th Annual Conference (Chicago, March 22–25, 1993).
3. See Narasimhan Chakravarthi, "Coupons as Price Discrimination Devices—A Theoretical Perspective and Empirical Analysis," *Marketing Science,* 3 (Spring 1984), pp. 128–47; Naufel J. Vilcassim and Dick R. Wittink, "Supporting a Higher Shelf Price Through Coupon Distributions," *Journal of Consumer Marketing,* 4, no. 2 (Spring 1987), pp. 29–39.
4. See discussion in Chapter 4 of the framing effect to understand why rebates may influence purchases by customers who do not ultimately redeem them.
5. For a study on segmented pricing of physicians' services by buyer identification, see Reuben Kessel, "Price Discrimination in Medicine," *Journal of Law and Economics,* 2 (October 1958), pp. 20–53.
6. See Walter J. Primeaux Jr., "The Effect of Consumer Knowledge and Bargaining Strength on Final Selling Price: A Case Study," *Journal of Business,* 43 (October 1970), pp. 419–26.
7. In less developed countries where the services of salespeople are less costly, segmented pricing by salespeople is widely practiced for even small purchases.
8. FOB (free on board) means that the buyer takes possession and thus bears shipping costs from the time the seller loads the goods onboard the shipper's vehicle.
9. See Romarao Desiraju and Steven Shugan, "Strategic Service Pricing and Yield Management," *Journal of Marketing* 63(1) (January 1999) pp. 44–56.
10. Exceptions occur when nonpeak demanders are so much less price sensitive than peak demanders that the difference overwhelms the effect of the cost difference. For example, on transatlantic flights between New York and London, the peak-season demand period is during the summer tourist season, which is also the time when the airlines offer their lowest discount fares. Demand is less price sensitive during the off-peak season when most passengers are traveling on business.

11. For more on the technical details of peak-load pricing, see Peter O. Steiner, "Peak Loads and Efficient Pricing," *Quarterly Journal of Economics,* 71 (November 1957), 585–610; Jack Hirshleifer, "Peak Loads and Efficient Pricing: Comment," *Quarterly Journal of Economics,* 72 (August 1958), pp. 451–62; and "Symposium on Peak-Load Pricing," *Bell Journal of Economics,* 7 (Spring 1976), pp. 197–250.

12. Fred Glover, Randy Glover, Joe Lorenzo, et al., "The Passenger-Mix Problem in the Scheduled Airlines," *Interfaces,* 12(3) (June 1982), pp. 73–79; Eric B. Orkin, "Boosting Your Bottom Line with Yield Management," *Cornell Hotel and Restaurant Administration Quarterly,* February 1988, pp. 52–56.

13. For an in-depth discussion of the motivations for quantity discounting, see Robert J. Dolan, "Pricing Structures with Quantity Discounts: Managerial Issues and Research Opportunities," Harvard Business School working paper, 1985.

14. *Federal Trade Commission v. Morton Salt,* 334 U.S. 37 (1948).

15. Sometimes charging a single price for a bundle of two separate products is necessary for segmented pricing. It is an effective strategy, however, only when preferences for the two products meet certain conditions. See Segmenting by Product Bundling later in this chapter.

16. G. W. Stocking and M. W. Watkins, *Cartels in Action* (New York: Twentieth Century Fund, 1946), pp. 402–404.

17. This principle was first identified in George Stigler, "United States v. Loew's Inc.: A Note on Block Booking," *The Supreme Court Law Review* (1965), pp. 152–57; see also Gary D. Eppen, Ward A. Hanson, and R. Kipp Martin, "Bundling—New Products, New Markets, Low Risk," *Sloan Management Review,* 32, no. 4 (Summer 1991), pp. 7–14. The section entitled Framing Multiple Gains or Losses in Chapter 12 gives another rationale for bundling.

18. This is only one of the ways newspapers practice segmented pricing. They also charge higher prices for the same advertising space if the ad is from a national rather than a local advertiser. They charge different prices for different types of advertising, and they give volume discounts. Radio and television stations use similar tactics.

19. Ralph Cassady Jr., "Techniques and Purposes of Price Discrimination," *Journal of Marketing,* 11, no. 1 (July 1946), pp. 141.

20. *Heaton Peninsular v. Eureka Specialty Co.,* 77F288 (6th Circuit Court, 1896).

21. *Henry v. A. B. Dick,* 224 U.S. 1 (1912).

22. *United States v. American Can Company* (Northern District Court of California, 1949).

23. *United States v. Jerrold Electronics Co.,* 187 F.Supp. 545 (E.D. Pa., 1960), affirmed 365 U.S. 567 (1961). *Motion Picture Patents Co. v. Universal Film Mfg. Co.* 243 U.S. 502 (1917). *United Shoe Machinery Corporation v. United States* (Supreme Court, 1922). *International Business Machines Corporation v. United States* (Supreme Court, 1936).

24. See Chapter 14, Tie-In Sales and Requirements Contracts, for situations when contractual tie-ins are legal for purposes other than pricing.

25. *Berkey Photo v. Eastman Kodak Company* (Second Circuit Court of Appeals, 1979).

26. An example of how product design must often accommodate a pricing tactic is how Xerox was forced to add to its machines covers that had to be closed in order for the user to get the low-usage rate. Before the covers, some nimble users would set the machine to make many copies per original and then quickly change originals between cycles, thus foiling Xerox's strategy.

CHAPTER

10

Pricing in the Marketing Mix

Developing an Integrated Strategy

P ricing can never be entirely separated from the other elements in a firm's marketing strategy. A product's price affects the market's perception of its attributes and the attributes of other products with which it is sold, the effectiveness of its advertising, and the attention it receives in channels of distribution. Moreover, the interactions go both ways: The product, its advertising, and its distribution affect the success of a particular pricing strategy. Although the process of pricing is a unique and specialized marketing activity, the resulting pricing strategy is an integral part of a larger effort. The success of that effort requires coordination among pricing and the product, promotion, and distribution decisions that together comprise a firm's marketing mix.

To get the most from its various marketing efforts, a firm must coordinate them into a cohesive strategy. In this chapter, we identify the interactions among pricing and other elements of the marketing mix—the product, the promotion, and the distribution—that a firm must manage effectively if its marketing program is to be successful.

PRICING AND THE PRODUCT LINE

The product is management's most powerful tool to influence the pricing environment. It can be designed to appeal to a price-insensitive segment of buyers, thus facilitating a skimming strategy. It can be designed for maximum cost economies, thus facilitating a penetration strategy. In Chapter 4, we discussed how the product line can affect customers' perceptions of value. In Chapter 9, we saw how the product can be designed to facilitate segmented pricing by product design, tying, or bundling. Product-line strategy, using flanking brands or brands that attract more price-sensitive segments to the market, may be the key to effective competitive and segmentation strategies. Clearly, much of what we discuss elsewhere in this book involves the relationship between a product and its pricing since an effective product strategy is often the key to capturing value. In this section, we expand our discussion of breakeven sales analysis to account for the cross-product interactions among prices and sales.

Most firms sell multiple products. Auto companies sell different models of cars as well as accessories. Hotels not only rent rooms but also offer meals and cater parties. Supermarkets sell products as diverse as meats, produce, and packaged goods and sometimes offer a limited selection of dinnerware, lawn furniture, toys, and clothing. If one product's sales do not affect the sales of the firm's other products, it can be priced in isolation. Often, however, the sales of different products in a firm's line are interdependent. To maximize profit, prices must reflect that interaction.

The effect of one product's sales on another's can be either adverse or favorable. If adverse, the products are *substitutes*. Most substitutes are different brands in the same product class. For example, generic and branded paper towels are substitutes because increased sales of one reduce sales of the other. Sometimes, however, substitutes appear in completely different product classes. The sales of macaroni products noticeably rise whenever price increases reduce the sales of beef.

If one product's sales favorably affect sales of another, the products are *complements*. Complementarity can arise for either of two reasons: (1) *The products are used together in producing satisfaction.* Popcorn and tickets to a movie are complements because, for many people, each enhances the pleasure they get from the other. Jet engines and spare parts are complements since the higher the sales of engines, the greater the follow-on sales of parts. Consequently, manufacturers compete fiercely for initial sales. (2) *The products are most efficiently purchased together.* Buyers often seek to conserve time by purchasing a set of products from a single seller. For example, consumers who patronize a particular supermarket in order to buy advertised specials are more likely to buy other items at that store, as well as other products of the same manufacturer.[1] An industrial purchasing agent may patronize a vendor for a particular grinding wheel and then simplify his or her purchasing by ordering other abrasives from the same vendor.

Substitutes and complements call for adjustments in pricing when the products are sold by the same company as part of a product line. To correctly evaluate the effect of a price change, management must examine the changes in revenues and costs not only for the product being priced, but also for the other products affected by the price change. To see how this is done, consider the examples in the following section.

Pricing Substitute Products

A gasoline station offers both a regular and a premium grade of unleaded gasoline. These two products are substitutes; the higher the price of the premium grade, the more people are likely to switch to regular grade. Assume for now that the current prices and costs of the two grades of gasoline are as follows:

	Price/Gal.	Variable Cost/Gal.	Dollar Contribution Margin/Gal.
Regular unleaded	$1.30	$1.10	$0.20
Premium unleaded	1.50	1.20	0.30

How should the station owner evaluate the effect of a 5 percent price increase for premium grade?

If sales of regular and premium are *entirely* independent, the owner simply calculates the percent contribution margin for premium (20 percent) and proceeds to calculate the breakeven sales change as follows:

$$\frac{-5.0}{20.0 + 5.0} = -20.0\%$$

But in this case, −20% is misleading. A decline greater than 20 percent could still leave the 5 percent price increase profitable. The reason is that some customers who refused to pay 5 percent more for premium would will not go to another station but instead will fill up with regular. Consequently, each gallon of lost premium sales would does not represent a loss of $0.30 contribution, since some of the loss would will be recovered in contribution from increased sales of regular gasoline.

To properly account for this shifting of profit from one product to another, we need to calculate an adjusted contribution margin for the change in sales of premium. The amount of the adjustment is uncertain because it depends on the share of additional sales of regular that come from reduced sales of premium. From past experience, the manager of this station estimates that approximately half the customers who would decline to buy premium at the higher price would not leave the station but would purchase the regular grade instead. Consequently, the dollar contribution lost from a decline in the sales of premium is really $0.30 per gallon minus the gain in contribution from additional sales of regular.

Adjusted $CM = $0.30 − (0.5 × $0.20) = $0.20

which represents an adjusted percent contribution margin of

$$\frac{\$0.20}{\$1.50} = 13.3\%$$

As a result, the breakeven sales quantity for a 5 percent price increase on premium is actually

$$\frac{-5.0}{13.3 + 5.0} = -27.3\%$$

This station can actually profit from a price increase on premium despite a decrease in sales greater than 20 percent.

Pricing Complementary Products

Pricing complementary products is like pricing substitutes except that one must add to, rather than subtract from, the contribution margin to adjust it appropriately. The College Computer Store sells personal computers, software, and printers. These products are complements since the typical computer buyer also purchases three software programs from the same retailer at the time of the computer purchase, and half of all purchasers buy a printer, and 20 percent buy a game upgrade package of joysticks, an enhanced graphics card, and speakers. College Computer's current price on a leading personal computer and the complementary software is as follows:

	Unit Price	Unit Variable Cost	$ Contribution Margin
Personal computer	$1,500	$1,000	$500
Software program	175	100	75
Printer	400	250	150
Game package	325	200	125

College Computer is considering dropping the price of the computer by 10 percent to spur sales. If management treats computer sales as independent, it would calculate that the company earns a 33.3 percent contribution margin on sales of its computers. Consequently, the breakeven sales quantity for a 10 percent price cut would be 42.9 percent.

In fact, since additional computer sales will cause an increase in sales of software and printers, the relevant contribution margin for a computer sale is much higher than 33.3 percent. If each computer buyer also buys two software packages, half buy a printer, and 80 percent buy a game package, the relevant contribution from selling a computer is

$$\text{Adjusted } \$CM = \$500 + (2 \times \$75) + 0.5(150) + 0.8(\$125) = \$825$$

which represents an adjusted percent contribution margin of

$$\$825/\$1500 = 55.0\%$$

Recognizing this interaction, College Computer can profitably cut its price even if it expects a percentage increase in sales much less than 42.9 percent. In fact, the breakeven sales change, considering the effect of a sale on the store's total profits from the computer, the software, the printer, and games is only

$$-(-10\%)/(55\% - 10\%) = +22.2\%$$

When pricing substitutes or complements, managers should evaluate the decision using the adjusted contribution margin, which reflects the effect of a sale on the profitability of a company's total product line. The general equation for the *adjustment for a substitute* is

$$\text{Adjusted } \$CM = \text{Unadjusted } \$CM - \text{Change in sales of substitute} \\ \times \$CM \text{ of substitute}$$

where the change in sales of a substitute equals the change per unit of sales of the product being priced. For complements, the adjustment is the same, except that the adjustment is an addition to rather than a subtraction from the unadjusted contribution margin. The equation for the *adjustment for a complement* is:

$$\text{Adjusted } \$CM = \text{Unadjusted } \$CM + \text{Change in sales of complement} \times \$CM \text{ of complement}$$

where the change in sales of complement equals the expected additional complementary sales for each additional sale of the product being priced.

Complementary sales interactions need not occur at the same point in time. In fact, some of the most important sales follow much later. Pharmaceuticals companies price aggressively for sales in teaching hospitals since physicians trained there are much more likely to prescribe those brands when they enter private practice. Rock stars require that concert promoters keep ticket prices low, even though they could fill the stadium at a higher price, in order to ensure that teenagers are not priced out of the market. They do so because teenage attendance has an especially large effect on subsequent record sales. Complementary products are not necessarily sold even to the same buyers. Singles bars often suspend or reduce their cover charges for women in the belief that when more women patronize their establishments, more men will do so as well.

When there is more than one substitute or complement in a line, it is necessary to make multiple adjustments to the contribution margin to reflect them. Thus, in a grocery store, a low promotional price on strawberries may cause increased sales of both shortcakes and whipped cream, while reducing sales of other fruits. Consequently, the adjusted contribution margin involves both positive and negative adjustments. It is impractical to adjust a contribution margin for every individual interaction with every other product in a broad product line. To overcome this problem, managers can rely on some aggregation. For example, in cutting the price of strawberries, they might calculate the effect on the dollar sales of all other fruits combined and multiply it times the average dollar contribution margin per dollar sales of fruit.

Selecting Loss Leaders

In some cases, it can even pay to price a complementary product as a *loss leader,* that is, below its variable cost in order to attract customers to the remaining product line. The pricing of some products has a very strong effect on a customer's choice of which store to patronize. If customers purchase many other products once they are in the store, sales of those products increase the adjusted contribution margin of the product that attracts buyers to the store. Consequently, it may be quite sensible to price that product so low that it has a negative unadjusted contribution margin because the adjusted contribution margin for its sales is still quite high.

Loss leaders are common in grocery pricing. Supermarkets regularly take losses on a few advertised items in order to attract buyers to their stores because those buyers will then purchase the remainder of their needs at profitable prices.[2] White bread, eggs, flour, and at least one brand of peanut butter are common candidates for pricing as loss leaders. There are two reasons why some products make good loss leaders.[3]

- First, it is impossible for a typical shopper to remember more than a small portion of the prices at various stores. Comparison shopping on an item-by-item basis is impossible. Most buyers remember the prices of only a few of the items they buy and use those prices to infer the general levels of prices at different stores. The prices that consumers are most likely to remember are those of the products they purchase most frequently. Consequently, frequently purchased products often make good loss leaders.
- Second, different segments of shoppers not only have different price sensitivities but also purchase different combinations of products. For example, because families with children buy more food, they are generally more price sensitive in deciding where to shop. Moreover, their grocery purchases include large amounts of fruit punch, certain brands of peanut butter, and white bread for sandwiches. By pricing one or more of those products as loss leaders, a store can become more price competitive for patronage by large families without cutting its profits on grocery purchases by other customers. As this example illustrates, products purchased primarily by a price-sensitive segment of buyers often make good loss leaders.

The best loss leaders are those that meet both of these criteria: They are purchased frequently and primarily by price-sensitive shoppers.

Product-line interactions noticeably affect a firm's pricing in relation to competitors with narrower product lines. Supermarkets can profitably offer more loss leaders and larger discounts than can convenience stores because the former have more complementary products to sell to the additional customers that a loss leader attracts.

Similarly, retailers who offer a broad product line tend to price the high end of the line higher and the low end lower than retailers with a narrow line. The former can afford to lose sales at the high end because they offer a lower price product to which many customers will switch rather than go elsewhere. Moreover, because they have a higher-end product that draws the less price-sensitive shoppers, they can profitably use the low-end product to draw more price-sensitive shoppers to the store. Consequently, the range of prices within a single broad line may actually exceed the range across stores that specialize in fewer brands.[4]

A word of caution, however: Researchers have found that conventional industry wisdom exaggerates the traffic-generating capacity of price promotions and that managers and executives overestimate how many buyers actively cross-shop in different stores for special prices. Most promotional purchases were made by buyers who did not visit the store in response to the promotion

Microwave Oven Model	Choice (%)	
	Group 1 (n = 60)	Group 2 (n = 60)
Panasonic II (1.1 cubic feet; regular price $199.99; sale price 10% off)	–	13
Panasonic I (0.8 cubic feet; regular price $179.99; sale price 35% off)	43	60
Emerson (0.5 cubic feet; regular price $109.99; sale price 35% off)	57	27

Source: Itamar Simonson and Amos Tversky, "Choice in Context: Tradeoff Contrast and Extremeness Aversion," *Journal of Marketing Research,* 29 (August 1992), pp. 281–95.

EXHIBIT 10-1   Reference Price Effects of a High-End Product

advertisement. They conclude that retailers should emphasize the use of price promotion as a defensive tool to retain the store's price image in the minds of primary customers rather than as an offensive tool to attract new customers into the store.[5]

Product Line Pricing and Price Perceptions

In Chapter 4 we discussed how customer's *reference price* expectations affected the perceived value of a product or service. A marketer can influence the reference price by selecting the product line to which a potential customer is exposed and by selecting the order in which the customer sees the prices.

Adding a higher-priced product to the top of a line increases the buyer's reference price, making the remaining products in the line appear somewhat less expensive. Adding a lower-priced product to the line reduces reference prices. In one study, subjects were asked to choose among different models of microwave ovens. Half of the subjects were asked to choose between two models (Emerson and Panasonic); the other half where asked to choose from among three models (Emerson, Panasonic I, and Panasonic II) (see Exhibit 10-1). Although 13 percent of the subjects were drawn to the top-end model, the largest impact from adding that model was on sales of the Panasonic I, which gained 17 additional share points as a result of becoming the mid-priced brand. The implications of product-line pricing are clear. Adding a premium product to the product line may not necessarily result in overwhelming sales of the premium product itself. It does, however, enhance buyers' perceptions of the reasonableness of other prices.

On the other hand, adding a lower-priced brand to a line can cause customers to slide sales in the other direction. For this reason, high-end brands often require that they be displayed only beside equally high-end competitors. Department stores, for example, often have two women's clothing departments, one for the higher-priced designer brands and one for the brands that attract more value-conscious shoppers. Grocery stores ultimately learned that they were better off displaying unbranded generics among other grocery items rather than in a separate section. The reason is because the most profitable sales for the grocery chains is their house brands. Although the generics draw customers from the house brands, as the stores had originally feared, their effect on reference price expectations causes even more customers to migrate from the national brands to the house brands. Thus, on net the stores gain.

PRICING AND PROMOTION

Promotion is a firm's effort to inform buyers and persuade them to perceive a product more favorably. Effective pricing complements the most salient forms of promotion: advertising and personal selling. In more subtle forms of sales promotion, price itself often becomes the promotional tool. Recognizing this close association between pricing and promotion, managers who price effectively make their pricing decisions in close consultation and coordination with their advertising agencies and sales management. In this section, we discuss the considerations that need to be taken into account.

Pricing and Advertising

The coordination of pricing and advertising is important because advertising can affect how buyers respond to price differences. How it affects price sensitivity, however, has long been debated by both researchers and managers. At one time, nearly everyone accepted the bromide that advertising artificially differentiates otherwise similar products in the minds of easily manipulated consumers, thus reducing their price sensitivity through a spurious value effect. Quantitative research eventually gave us a much less jaundiced view of advertising's effect on consumers. Advertising is simply communication; its effect depends on the nature of the message communicated.

Most experts agree that advertising increases price sensitivity when it focuses on price explicitly. Grocery ads let shoppers know the prices charged for selected items before they choose where to shop; mail-order discounters advertise their prices to let buyers know just how much they can save by giving up the obvious advantages of dealing with a full-service retailer. Being more aware of their alternatives, buyers are more price sensitive (the substitution effect) when deciding where to shop.[6] Companies using a penetration strategy use advertising to assert the claim that they offer equal value at a lower cost, thus undermining the unique value effect. Such advertising often makes explicit arguments (for example, "Why pay more?") to convince buyers that price should be the most important consideration in their purchase decision. If a firm enjoys a price advantage, it obviously pays to make buyers more sensitive to that aspect of the purchase decision (see Exhibit 10-2).

In contrast, advertising specifically designed to minimize price sensitivity is certainly quite common. The advertising campaigns for Bayer to convince buyers that "All aspirin is not alike" and for Q-Tips that "A swab by any other

EXHIBIT 10-2   Advertising a Price Advantage

Reproduced by permission of 128 Volvo.

name is not the same" are clearly intended to reduce buyers' price sensitivity by enhancing the perception that these products are better than those of the competition. Hammermill's ads for its photocopier paper seek to reduce price sensitivity by reminding buyers that the cost of paper is just a small part of the total cost of the end product (the end-benefit effect). Johnnie Walker's ad for

	Advertising	
Price Change	Low	High
$0.50 to $0.60	−21%	−29%
$0.60 to $0.70	−19%	−33%

Source: Gerald Eskin, "A Case for Test Market Experiments," *Journal of Advertising Research,* 15 (April 1975), p. 27.

EXHIBIT 10-3 Percentage Changes in Sales Due to Price Increases: The Effect of Advertising

Black Label Scotch speaks directly to the price-quality effect: "When you are dealing with something quite extraordinary, price somehow seems irrelevant or even irreverent. Indeed, for those who appreciate fine Scotch, Johnnie Walker Black is priceless." One study of *individual* purchase decisions supports the contention that even "feel good" advertising, without a specific message, can reduce individual price sensitivity.[7] In another study of individual purchase decisions, advertising appeared to increase price sensitivity except at very high levels of advertising exposure, when price sensitivity falls back to the level associated with no advertising.[8]

Regardless of the effect of advertising on the price sensitivity of individual purchasers, marketers are interested in effect on an aggregate level. On this question, research results from several well-known studies are quite consistent, at least for frequently purchased consumer products that dominate the studies; advertising increases the sales volume gain associated with a lower price. In technical terms, advertising appears to increase the price elasticity of market demand for a product.[9] Exhibit 10-3 illustrates this effect in a test market experiment for a frequently purchased convenience food. When price was raised in locations exposed to a low level of advertising, sales declined substantially less than they did when price was increased in locations exposed to about 70 percent more advertising.

How can the effect of advertising on the price sensitivity of market demand differ from its effect on individual purchase decisions? The answer is that advertising changes the composition of a product's demand by attracting new customers. Advertising may not increase the price sensitivity of any individual buyers but, as it increases sales, it apparently also increases the volume gains associated with a *reduction* in price and the volume losses associated with an *increase* in price. The implication is that buyers who are relatively more advertising sensitive are also relatively more price sensitive. The index of sales levels in Exhibit 10-4 illustrates this relationship for three different consumer packaged goods. Using the low-price–low-advertising sales level as a base, the index indicates that a high level of advertising raised sales by 80.7 percent for product A, by 52.5 percent for product B, and by 79.4 percent for product C. The index also indicates, however, that a price increase caused a much greater percentage loss of sales where the sales level was already inflated by advertising.

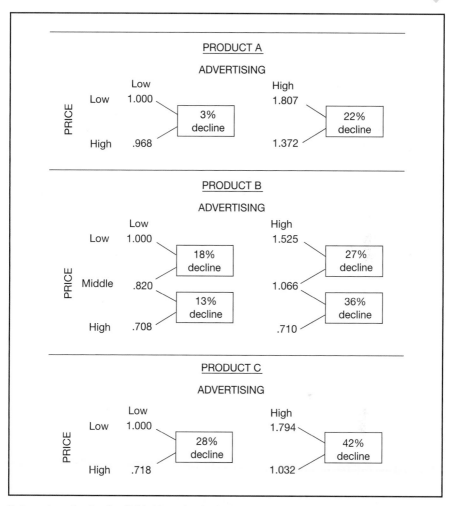

Index = Actual unit sales divided by unit sales in the low price–low advertising condition.

EXHIBIT 10-4   Sales Under Different Price and Advertising Levels

Source: Gerald Eskin and Penny Baron, "Effects of Price and Advertising in Test Market Experiments," *Journal of Marketing Research,* 14 (November 1977), p. 503.

For example, 22 percent of product A's sales were lost following a price increase where advertising was high, but only 3 percent were lost following the same price increase where advertising was high, but only 3 percent were lost following the same price increase where advertising was low.[10]

The implication of this research for coordinating advertising and pricing is that a low price will increase sales more when coupled with a high level of advertising. From a different perspective, it indicates that advertising is more effective when price is set low than when it is set high. Consequently, low prices should be matched with high advertising, when developing strategies for different times and locations. Two notes of caution, however, are in order.

First, research on price and advertising has focused on frequently purchased products in mature product categories. Given that researchers have not examined the interactions between price and advertising for durable goods, services, or products that are genuine innovations, inferences from the current state of research should be taken as only suggestive for those categories. More work is needed to establish or disprove the broader generality of these results.

Second, the conclusion that price elasticity is greater when advertising is high and that advertising is more effective when price is low, applies to a particular brand. *It is not valid for cross-brand comparisons.* For example, it would be entirely incorrect to infer that intensely advertised brands in a category have higher price elasticities than less advertised brands because more than the level of advertising changes when different brands are compared. Highly advertised brands are usually also brands that are highly differentiated and, therefore, have more to communicate than do brands that advertise little. The differentiation value of an intensely advertised brand may make consumers less sensitive to its price than to the price of a generic brand despite its higher advertising. One cannot draw valid inferences about relative price sensitivities and advertising levels among different products.

Pricing and Personal Selling

For most industrial products and for many large consumer durables as well, the major thrust of promotional effort is not advertising but personal selling. The extent of personal selling can vary from a minimally trained person who writes up orders to technically trained experts who spend days or weeks analyzing a customer's needs and explaining how a product could satisfy them. Selecting the right amount of sales effort is an important step toward pricing a product to realize its full profit potential.

Looking at a cross-section of products promoted through personal selling, one can readily classify marketing strategies along a continuum between low price–low effort and high price–high effort, but it is a mistake to believe that any point on such a continuum represents a viable choice for any particular product. Products that are relatively generic in their features, or that are differentiated in ways obvious to a buyer, appropriately adopt low-effort strategies because there is little that a more intense selling effort could communicate. By keeping selling costs low, the seller can offer low prices to attract buyers who wish to spend a minimal amount on a basic product. Products with unique features, however, can realize differentiation values in their prices only to the extent that buyers understand those features. Consequently, such products require a higher level of sales effort to justify their higher prices to buyers.

Unfortunately, firms sometimes develop superior products and then attempt to use price rather than promotion to develop the market. Such a strategy is predictably ineffective. Consider, for example, the classic case study of Dewey and Almy Company with its two-part lithographic printing blanket.[11] The product was vastly superior to competing blankets in its durability, quality of impression, and ease of replacement. To introduce the product, Dewey and Almy chose distributors, usually not a source of strong selling efforts. To give buyers an incentive to adopt the product, however, Dewey and Almy priced it the same as that of competing blankets on a square-foot basis, representing a substantial saving to printers because of the blanket's durability and other advantages.

The problem with Dewey and Almy's strategy was that its product's advantages were not obvious from simple observation. To appreciate them, printers first had to use the blanket—and use it properly. Thus Dewey and Almy's low price looked like a bargain only to printers who already knew of the product's advantages and would have been willing to pay more. It did not serve as an incentive for nonusers to try the product since they did not yet know the features that made the product worth much more than its price.

To develop the market for a product with superior but not obvious advantages, a company needs a sales effort that communicates its product's benefits and then ensures that the buyer realizes those benefits at the time of initial use. Dewey and Almy, in fact, successfully used a high-promotion strategy in its test market. Unfortunately, the company did not follow up with a strong selling effort in actual commercialization. As a result, the blanket suffered a slow rate of acceptance initially, which enabled established competitors to develop copies that captured a substantial share of the market.

The lesson is clear. A low price in relation to product value is no bargain unless buyers can appreciate that value, and a high price in relation to the competition is no deterrent if a strong sales effort can communicate that the product is worth the price. Market penetration on price alone makes sense only when a product's value is already known to buyers. That is usually the case only for established products that buyers have used in the past, products whose unique features are obvious from inspection, and products that offer only the minimal product features that buyers expect it to have. No firm can charge a price that reflects superior aspects of its product, or charge a price less than that amount, and gain rapid market penetration, unless it can first communicate to buyers the true value that the product offers.

A skilled sales force, in addition to explaining a product's features and use, can also provide important augmentations that reduce price sensitivity. A sales expert who understands how a product is used can often identify ways to save buyers money. Sometimes changes in buyers' manufacturing procedures will make the product perform better; sometimes a better ordering system will reduce buyers' inventory needs. When buyers see that skilled sales personnel can save them money, most are willing to share those savings by showing some loyalty in future competition for their business.[12]

Setting the Promotional Budget

In setting a promotional budget for either advertising or personal selling, coordination with pricing is essential.[13] An important factor in deciding the level of promotional spending is the dollar contribution in the price. The greater the profit contribution, the greater the reward for making each additional sale. Consequently, products with higher dollar profit contributions per sale normally justify greater promotional expenditures than those with lower contributions. The rationale is that when a product generates a greater contribution per sale, a firm can justify spending more on promotion to make difficult sales that require extra effort. When the dollar profit contribution is low, however, the additional sales generated by an intense promotional effort are less likely to be worth the cost.

Unfortunately, we frequently encounter companies using wasteful and ineffective criteria to determine advertising and sales-support budgets. A common method is to allocate promotional funding to those brands that "need more" to achieve their sales objectives. The effect of this is to give more promotional spending to weak brands and less to strong brands. Brands that cannot meet their sales objectives are generally weak because competition offers an equal or better value; brands exceeding their sales objectives are generally strong because they offer an exceptional value to their purchasers. Consequently, more money thrown at weak brands is likely to generate few initial sales with low repeat purchases, whereas money spent to promote the advantages of strong brands is likely to generate a much greater increase in both initial and repeat sales. Don't advertise your weaknesses; advertise your strengths.

In general, giving product managers promotional budgets is not recommended. Rather, they should be required to use profitably whatever they spend on promotion. The criteria for any change, positive or negative, in promotional expenditures should be that the expenditure at least pays for itself. As discussed in Chapter 3, any promotional expenditure adds to profitability when it increases sales volume by more than

$$\frac{\text{Change in promotional expenditure}}{\text{Contribution margin (per unit)}}$$

PRICE AS A PROMOTIONAL TOOL

In some cases, price is more than an adjunct to a promotional campaign; it is an integral part of it. Some companies use high prices to enhance the perception of quality. This strategy is most popular for consumables such as premium chocolates (for example, Godiva) and alcoholic beverages (for example, Chivas Regal), but it can be used to promote durable goods as well. Some companies maintain stable prices to complement the images of their products. De Beers, the marketing agent for most gem-quality diamonds, has long recognized the importance of price stability to the image of its product. De Beers promotes its diamonds as gifts that will symbolize forever the purchaser's love for the recipient. Part of that perception is not just that "a diamond lasts forever," but that its value will, too. Consequently, De Beers buys and holds uncut diamonds to keep prices from declining during periods of temporary excess supply and actively counters speculative price increases until it is certain that they can be sustained in the long run. Although these tactics have sometimes required huge financial investments, they have succeeded in creating the expectation among buyers that a diamond's value will never decline.[14]

Occasionally, a seller may even price a product too low as part of a promotional campaign. When new movies premiere in Los Angeles and New York, the theaters charge standard ticket prices, knowing they could fill the theaters at higher prices. They apparently believe that the resulting long lines for tickets (no advance purchases are allowed) generate publicity worth more than the price premium they could charge for the first few weeks. Similarly, developers of multiphase condominium projects will sometimes price the first phase low to make it sell very quickly. The developers hope this tactic will prompt other buyers to commit quickly to purchase units in the later phases. Most promotional pricing, however, is not designed to generate publicity. It is intended to induce buyers to try a frequently purchased product.

For consumer products, price "dealing" has become the most popular form of promotion, increasing from about half as much as advertising budgets in 1980 to over twice as much in 1992. Unlike promotion of regular prices, deals are discounts off the "regular" price. They may take the form of (1) *specially marked packages* that offer a temporarily low price or an extra quantity at the same price, (2) *coupons,* (3) *rebates,* or (4) *trade* (wholesale price) *discounts* that retailers may or may not pass on to the end consumer. The rest of this section concerns the use and abuse of each of these tactics.

Pricing Tactics to Induce Trial

One of the most important strategic uses of pricing, especially when the product is new, is to induce trial. A buyer's first purchase represents more than just another sale; it is an opportunity to educate him or her about the product's attributes.[15] Since only people who are familiar with a product can become loyal repeat purchasers, inducing potential buyers to make their first purchase is a critical step in building sales. Although new products need to build sales quickly, even companies marketing established products face the problem that some educated buyers leave the market, some switch to other brands, and some simply forget what they have learned. Consequently, to maintain a fixed market share, manufacturers must regularly induce trial by new buyers.

One way to accomplish this is to offer the product in a form that minimizes the initial outlay required to try it. Packaged-goods manufacturers sometimes introduce products in small, trial sizes. They have found that many people who would be unwilling to lay out $2.50 to try a ten-ounce package will spend $0.25 for a one-ounce trial package. When marketing some industrial products, companies reduce the initial outlay required for sampling by offering leases. For example, companies introducing new software programs for mainframe computers find business customers reluctant to spend $50,000 on a program that may not work as well as promised. They are more willing to lease the software for $3,000 a month until they find out how well it really works.

A common tactic for inducing trial of repeat-purchase products is a promotional price *deal*. It makes sense for a firm to cut its price, even to an unprofitable level, for a first-time buyer because the firm benefits from a first purchase by much more than the revenue from that sale. A buyer who likes the brand becomes a repeat purchaser at its regular price, thereby beginning a stream of future income for the seller. The price deal is an investment in future sales.

Price deals normally take one of four forms: trial offers, coupons, rebates, or free samples. To understand why manufacturers use these methods rather than simply cut the explicit prices of their products, one needs to understand the objectives of the dealing firm.

- First, the manufacturer wants the promotional price cut to benefit the end customer, not to add to the margin of a distributor. Even in categories with high promotional elasticities, there must be a high likelihood of retailer pass-through, and a low likelihood of forward buying for promotional pricing to be effective.[16]
- Second, the manufacturer wants the end consumer to perceive the price cut as a special, exceptional offer in order to minimize the perception that the product may be of lower quality because it is offered at a lower price.
- Third, the manufacturer wants to direct the price cut to first-time buyers and minimize the extent to which repeat buyers can take advantage of it to make multiple purchases.

An explicit price cut usually fails to achieve these objectives, whereas one of the four common dealing tactics often can.

Trial offers are simple price cuts that the seller makes clear are temporary. Although trial offers are the cheapest way to offer a price promotion, the trick to making them successful is ensuring that the temporary wholesale price cut to the trade, usually in the form of an "off invoice allowance" actually gets passed through to the end consumer and that the end consumer actually perceives the lower price as a special deal. Usually these two objectives are accomplished with special packaging (see Exhibit 10-5). When the package says in banner print "20¢ Off Regular Price" or "Special $1.99," consumer pressure compels the retailer to pass on the promised savings. Consumers are unlikely to interpret the low price as a signal of low quality when it reflects a discount that is clearly temporary. Sometimes, a trial offer can also meet the third objective, excluding repeat buyers. Magazines, for example, offer discount trial subscriptions at rates unavailable to current subscribers. For most products, however, separating new from repeat purchasers is not easy. This is not a major problem for new products, since almost all of their buyers are first-time purchasers. Consequently, trial offers are used most often for products that are new to a market.

EXHIBIT 10-5   Manufacturer Pricing of a Trial Offer

Courtesy of First Brands Corporation.

Coupons meet all three of the objectives effectively, which explains their extreme popularity as a method of dealing.[17] Not only does the consumer receive the discount while seeing clearly that the regular price is higher, the coupon also limits the number of discounted purchases that repeat buyers can make. Moreover, coupons can often be distributed in ways that increase the probability that only first-time users will redeem them. For example, coupons for automatic dishwasher detergent are have been placed inside new dishwashers, and coupons for disposable diapers and other baby products are mailed to new parents.[18] Finally, a coupon makes buyers aware of a deal even when the product is not yet stocked in the store where they shop. Their desire to redeem the coupons can then pressure the store into placing an order.[19]

Coupons do have their drawbacks. Because they are inconvenient, coupon redemption rates are low among families in some demographic groups (those with high incomes or with both spouses working).[20] Moreover, the manufacturer's cost of coupons greatly exceeds the amount of the discount that the consumer receives. In addition to the cost of printing and distributing coupons, retailers must be paid for handling them (at least $0.08), and clearinghouses must be paid for redeeming them (usually $0.02). Finally, a high rate of fraudulent redemption, 20 percent on average but as much as 80 percent in some cases, adds to coupons' cost.[21] Nevertheless, the number of coupons issued attests to the fact that they are often worth these costs. By 1992, the number issued by manufacturers alone had grown to 310 billion with an average face value of $0.59.[22]

Rebates have grown popular in recent years as a substitute for couponing. Rebates can meet all three objectives of dealing, but they have the disadvantage of being more costly to the consumer. The average value of a coupon in 1982 was $0.279. Few people would invest the time and postage to claim a rebate of the same value. Consequently, rebates are effective only when the dollar amount of the discount is large. Companies that sell multiple products, however, can often overcome this problem by requiring the purchase of a number of different products to claim a single large rebate. For example, Richardson-Merrill offered a $2 rebate during the winter of 1980 to consumers who bought any four of its ten cold remedies. In addition to meeting all three of a manufacturer's objectives in dealing, the advantages of rebates are as follows:

- They avoid the problem of coupon counterfeiting and fraudulent redemption by retailers.
- They enable the firm to limit the offer to one per family, thus controlling the benefit to repeat purchasers.
- They often involve lower administrative costs than couponing, particularly when they cover multiple products.
- They enable the firm to develop a mailing list of deal-prone consumers that can be used for future promotions.
- Many consumers buy a product because of the rebate, but then fail to redeem it.[23]

The most effective and most costly deal is the *free sample*. A much larger percentage of consumers will use a free sample than will redeem a coupon, enabling the manufacturer to induce trial far more quickly and with broader coverage of the various demographic groups.

For example, when Lever Brothers introduced its Sunlight dishwashing detergent, it used free samples to gain trial in 70 percent of all households. In contrast, a typical coupon or rebate offer is redeemed by only about 5 percent of the targeted households. Nevertheless, the high cost of free samples makes them a profitable promotional tactic only for products that are repeat purchased very frequently, such as soaps or cigarettes, or those with very high contribution margins, such as computer software.[24]

Defensive Dealing

Over the past two decades, most consumer markets have moved from growth to maturity. Companies with strong brand images and profitable market shares should have recognized the need to change from growth-oriented to value-preserving strategies, as described in Chapter 7. Instead, many companies have offered larger and more frequent deals to sustain sales growth. Both researchers and managers have begun to suspect that such chronic dealing undermines consumer loyalties and increases marketing costs. Moreover, when the dealing is financed at the expense of advertising, the short-term boost to sales is often more than balanced by a long-term loss in brand equity.[25] Recent research suggests that promotions and dealing need to consider the type of product being promoted. For example, one study found that nonmonetary promotions, such as free gifts or sweepstakes, were particularly effective in increasing market share for high-equity hedonic products; the effect was smaller, but positive for low-equity hedonic products and high-equity utilitarian products. By contrast, monetary promotions, such as price cuts or free product, were particularly effective in increasing market share for high-equity utilitarian products; the effect was smaller, but positive, for low-equity hedonic products.[26]

Although dealing is still a useful tactic for new brand introductions in mature markets, it generally does not make sense for established brands to meet the price deals of new competitors. There are three reasons for this: First, only part of an established brand's buyers will actually respond to a dealing firm's inducements to try its brand. Unfortunately, the firm defending an established brand does not know who among its buyers are potentially disloyal. It must offer all of them the defensive price cut in order to neutralize a competitor's deal. This puts the defending brand at a cost disadvantage if the dealing competitor has a smaller market share. Consider the case where the dealing brand has a 10 percent market share and the defending brand has a 90 percent market share, 5 percent of which is disloyal when presented with a deal. The dealing brand must offer the deal on two sales it would have made anyway in order to induce the switch of each additional sale from the established brand. This is because its current market share is twice the additional market share that it can induce to try its brand. In comparison, the defending firm must offer a defensive deal on seventeen sales that it would have made anyway in order to prevent disloyal buyers from trying the competing brand. This is because the loyal market share of the defending firm is seventeen times the share that it would lose if it did not meet the deal. Consequently, the defending firm must give up 8.5 times as much revenue to neutralize a deal as the dealing firm gives up to offer it.

Second, when a product's costs are primarily incremental and avoidable, firms can offer deals on small-share brands at little cost until customers respond to the deal and try the product. The defending firm, however, must bear the cost of a defensive deal each time it offers the deal to retain buyers' loyalty. Consequently, to the extent that costs are incremental and avoidable, a firm marketing a new brand can repeatedly offer attractive deals at little cost until it succeeds, whereas the established firm bears significant cost in repeatedly defending against it.

Third, as mentioned above, frequent dealing can tarnish a brand's image, thus reducing consumers' loyalty. Unless the established brand was already positioned as an economy product, the firm may have difficulty reestablishing its regular price without losing some previously loyal buyers.

Because of these disadvantages, price dealing is generally much more effective for new brands or for those with small market shares to induce trial than for established brands trying to prevent it. One exception to this is defensive end-user inventory tactics that motivate end users to stockpile inventories and thereby remove the end user from the market for a sustained period of time. Packaged-goods marketers frequently use bonus packs, which contain significantly greater quantities of the product for the same price to thwart the price deals of competitors. These bonus packs appeal to already loyal customers, who have less incentive to pay attention to competitive price deals because they will have just stocked up with extra product from their regular brand.[27] Established brands can also use other marketing instruments with which they have a greater advantage. In the beer industry, for example, Heileman, Stroh, and Pabst found couponing an effective marketing tool for entering new geographical markets where their beers were unknown. But Anheuser-Busch and Miller, brewers of the most popular national brands, wisely chose not to respond with deals of their own. Instead, they recognized that they could defend market share more cost-effectively by increasing their advertising and distribution efforts because they enjoyed superior economies of scale in those activities.[28]

Defensive deals are occasionally advisable. Because costs in some markets are overwhelmingly fixed, a new firm offering a promotional deal on a new brand bears costs comparable to those of the defending firm, even if it makes no sales. In many markets, a premium image has so little effect on price sensitivity that the defending firm need not worry about cheapening it. In the airline industry, for example, costs are overwhelmingly fixed and buyers select flights more for convenience and service than for image. As a result, established firms on many routes successfully defend their markets by matching the promotional fares of new entrants.

Defensive dealing may also prove useful as a temporary segmentation technique during recessions. Coupon redemption rates increase during recessions and decline during recoveries.[29] In Chapter 9 on price segmentation, we discuss how coupons offer one way to separate the price-sensitive segment for discounting. Often this can be done very cost-effectively by printing a coupon or rebate certificate on the package for use by consumers willing to take the time to redeem them. Since the price-sensitive segment grows during recessions, these deals can maintain the brand loyalty of customers who are temporarily more price sensitive, without undercutting margins to all customers. Prices can then be increased more easily after the recession simply by dropping the deal.

Trade Dealing

Manufacturers who distribute their products through independent retailers often complement their promotional or defensive pricing with *trade deals*, such as using off-invoice allowances. Traditionally, trade deals were temporary discounts to retailers from a product's regular wholesale price. Beginning in the 1970s, however, manufacturers began using the term to disguise what were actually nothing more than permanent price cuts. They did so in response to three changes in the economy.

First, after being stung by the imposition of price controls in 1970, manufacturers tried to protect themselves against such surprises by setting inflated wholesale prices that they would regularly discount. Later in the decade, constant trade deals were used to solve another problem: declining sales volume due to chronic recessions and competition from generic and house brands. Firms with slow-selling brands camouflaged wholesale price cuts as trade deals because (1) the cuts were then less visible to competitors who might otherwise retaliate, and (2) the cuts were more easily adjusted to reflect the precariousness of a brand's position in different stores and geographical areas.

In the 1980s, large retailers gained substantially more power to extract larger discounts from manufacturers than their smaller rivals. Since giving such discounts would be a blatant violation of the Robinson–Patman Act restrictions on price discrimination, manufacturers offered trade deals that these chains, with their substantial warehousing and distribution capacity, could benefit from disproportionately.

In contrast to such recent practices, the traditional trade deal is a temporary cut in the wholesale price to achieve a specific short-run goal. One such goal is to purchase retailers' favors during a promotional campaign. A packaged-food manufacturer may offer a trade deal in return for a grocery retailer's agreement to feature the product in its newspaper advertising or to display the product at a particularly prominent location with special on-site advertising. Special displays for soft drinks, for example, have been known to increase sales by a factor of six. For new brands that initially have low sales rates and therefore high holding costs for retailers, a discount is often necessary before retailers will allocate any shelf space at all to the product.

Manufacturers also offer trade deals on products that they produce seasonally in order to induce retailers to stock up at the time of production. Canned foods, such as salmon, peaches, and some vegetables, are packed by manufacturers at one time of the year and then must be stored at significant cost for sales in the off-season. If retailers are willing to stock up during the production season in return for a discount less than the manufacturer's cost of holding inventory, such trade deals are a profitable tactic. Retailers are often willing to take advantage of such deals because (1) their inventory holding costs are sometimes lower than those of manufacturers since they fully utilize their storage space by purchasing different products on deal in different seasons, and (2) they can often induce consumers to stock up as well by passing on part of the trade deal as a price promotion of their own.[30]

Occasionally, leading manufacturers also use trade dealing as a defense against the introduction of competing brands. If a temporary trade deal prompts retailers and consumers to load up with inventories of the leading brand, they will be more reluctant to take on still more inventories of a new brand.

Sometimes, however, increased inventory holding by retailers results in an unintended and undesirable effect of dealing. If a manufacturer offers retailers a trade deal to discount and advertise a product for one week, they may order more of the product than they can actually sell that week, enabling them to reduce their purchases in later weeks at the regular wholesale price. In fact, retailers are notorious for effectively converting manufacturers' trial offers and periodic sales into trade deals by ordering more than they can sell during the period of the retail price cut. This "forward buying" unnecessarily raises distribution cost for both retailers and distributors by 1 to 2 percent of sales.

Top management must also be wary of the effect that trade dealing has on incentives for product managers. Trade deals, like price promotions, are sometimes used to meet short-term goals that arguably are not in the firm's long-run interest. When brand managers are rewarded for meeting sales quotas, they may use quick end-of-quarter trade promotions to reach their goals. Although the resulting stocking up by retailers depresses later sales at higher prices, that may be of little concern to some brand managers who may hope to be promoted before the effects of overdealing catch up with them. The money for these trade deals is often diverted from the advertising budget. Although advertising has less of a short-term effect on sales than a trade deal, it probably has a much larger impact on long-term brand equity with consumers. Moreover, as discussed below, the demand "pull" from a manufacturer's advertising reduces a retailer's power to set prices and dictate terms. Such short-run thinking is probably not typical in most firms, but it is sufficiently widespread to cause experts in industry, academe, and government to express alarm.[31]

PRICING AND DISTRIBUTION

The way a product is distributed distinctly affects the way it can be priced. A product's distribution affects the following:

- other products with which it is compared
- images consumers have of it
- ability to differentiate it through augmentation
- ability to segment its market

Since all of these factors are considerations in formulating a pricing strategy, distribution and pricing need to be thoughtfully coordinated. Because of the breadth and depth of this topic, the next chapter is entirely devoted to it.

SUMMARY

Pricing strategy involves more than just setting a price. It also involves product line, promotion, and distribution decisions that affect the firm's ability to capture value in its prices.

The product, probably more than any other element, determines the viability of a price. With all its augmentations, the product determines relative value, indicating the levels at which price can skim, penetrate, and remain neutral in a market. A product's effect on others in the firm's product line requires adjustments to ensure that price maximizes total product-line profit, not only the profit from the individual product being priced. Flanking brands, to meet price competition from slightly differentiated brands or to preclude competition from new brands, plays an important role in maximizing the effectiveness of price competition.

Promotion influences pricing through its effect on price sensitivity. Advertisements can bring to the buyers' attention information that may make price less important in their purchase decisions. Conversely, advertisements can provide information that makes buyers more aware of their alternatives and encourages them to focus on price as an important attribute of choice. Even advertising that does not directly attempt to influence price sensitivity apparently increases it, at least for consumer nondurables. Personal selling, on the other hand, generally reduces price sensitivity by enabling buyers to appreciate the differentiating attributes of unfamiliar brands and by facilitating augmentation.

Price itself is often an effective promotional tool. A high price can signal superior quality, a stable price can signal stability of value, and the excess demand created by a low price can draw attention to a product. A low-price deal can induce buyers to try a product once, and in doing so can educate them about attributes that will prompt them to make future purchases at the regular price. A trade deal can induce retailers to advertise a product, promote it with a special in-store display, or purchase additional quantities for their inventories.

Finally, the choice of a distribution channel should complement a product's pricing. Products priced high to reflect their unique attributes or to ensure exclusivity need channels that will communicate the products' worth. Products designed to sell on the appeal of their relatively low prices need channels that will make consumers aware of their existence but add minimally to their cost.

Notes

1. Rockney G. Walters, "Assessing the Impact of Retail Price Promotions on Product Substitution, Complementarity Purchase, and Interstore Sales Displacement," *Journal of Marketing,* 55 (April 1991), pp. 17–28.
2. See Francis J. Mulhern and Robert P. Leone, "Implicit Price Bundling or Retail Products: A Multiproduct Approach to Maximizing Store Profitability," *Journal of Marketing,* 55 (October 1991), pp. 63–76.
3. See Thomas Nagle and Kenneth Novak, "The Roles of Segmentation and Awareness in Explaining Variations in Price Markups," in *Issues in Pricing: Theory and Research,* ed. Timothy M. Devinney (Lexington, MA: D. C. Heath, 1988), pp. 313–332.
4. Steven M. Shugan, "Pricing When Different Outlets Offer Different Assortments of Brands," in *Issues in Pricing: Theory and Research,* ed. Timothy M. Devinney (Lexington, MA: D. C. Heath, 1988), pp. 289–311.
5. Joel E. Urbany, Peter R. Dickson, and Rosemary Kalapurakal, "Price Search in the Retail Grocery Market," *Journal of Marketing* 60 (April 1996), pp. 91–104; Francis J. Mulhern and Daniel T. Padgett, "The Relationship Between Retail Price Promotions and Regular Price Purchases," *Journal of Marketing,* 59 (October 1995), pp. 83–90.

6. For empirical evidence, see Amihai Glazer, "Advertising, Information, and Prices—A Case Study," *Economic Inquiry,* 19 (October 1981), pp. 661–71.

7. Lakshman Krishnamurti and S. P. Raj, "The Effect of Advertising on Consumer Price Sensitivity," *Journal of Marketing Research,* 22 (May 1985), pp. 119–29.

8. Vinay Kanetkar, Charles B. Weinberg, and Doyle L. Weiss, "Price Sensitivity and Television Advertising Exposure: Some Empirical Findings," *Marketing Science* 11, no. 4 (Fall 1992), pp. 359–71.

9. Lee Benham, "The Effect of Advertising on the Price of Eyeglasses," *Journal of Law and Economics,* 15 (October 1972), pp. 337–52; Gerald Eskin, "A Case for Test Market Experiments," *Journal of Advertising Research,* 15 (April 1975), pp. 27–33; V. Kanti Prasad and L. Winston Ring, "Measuring Sales Effects of Some Marketing Mix Variables and Their Interactions," *Journal of Marketing Research,* 13 (November 1976), pp. 391–96; Gerald Eskin and Penny Barron, "Effects of Price and Advertising in Test Market Experiments," *Journal of Marketing Research,* 14 (November 1977), pp. 495–508; Dick Wittink, "Advertising Increases Sensitivity to Price," *Journal of Advertising Research,* 17 (April 1977), pp. 39–42.

10. Eskin, "A Case for Test Market Experiments."

11. See "Dewey and Almy Chemical Division: Pricing the Polyfibron Blanket," HBS Case No. 9–506–084, Rev. 4/71 (Boston: Harvard Business School, 1961).

12. See Somerby Dowst, "How Top Industrial Salespeople Serve Customers," *Industrial Marketing,* 66 (November 1981), pp. 88–95.

13. See David A. Aaker and John G. Meyers, *Advertising Management,* 3rd ed.

(Englewood Cliffs, NJ: Prentice-Hall, Inc., 1987), chapters 2–3; W. Semlow, "How Many Salesmen Do You Need?" *Harvard Business Review,* 38 (May–June 1959), pp. 126–32; Charles Beswick and David Cravens, "A Multistage Decision Model for Salesforce Management," *Journal of Marketing Research,* 14 (May 1977), pp. 135–44.

14. See Paul Gibson, "De Beers: Can a Cartel Be Forever?" *Forbes,* May 28, 1979, p. 45; John R. Emshwiller, and Neil Behrmann, "How De Beers Revived World Diamond Cartel After Zaire's Pullout," *Wall Street Journal,* July 7, 1983, pp. 1, 12.

15. Of course, this is only true to the extent that a brand actually has differentiating attributes that a buyer can learn by sampling. House brands and generic groceries, for example, do not have price promotions precisely because they lack differentiating attributes that buyers could learn enough about through sampling. Their appeal is their price.

16. Chakravarthi Narasimhan, Scott A. Neslin, and Subrata K. Sen, "Promotional Elasticities and Category Characteristics," *Journal of Marketing,* 60 (April 1996), pp. 17–30.

17. See Russell Bowman, *Couponing and Rebates: Profit on the Dotted Line* (New York: Lebhar–Friedman Books, 1980), pp. 2–3.

18. Checkout coupon systems also, such as Checkout Coupon of Catalina Marketing, automatically issue coupons during supermarket-checkout activities to purchasers of competing products.

19. See William Nigut Sr., "Is the Boom in Cents-Off Couponing Going to Burst?" *Advertising Age,* December 15, 1980, pp. 41–44.

20. Robert C. Blattberg and Scott A. Neslin, *Sales Promotion: Concepts, Methods, and Strategies* (Englewood Cliffs, NJ: Prentice-Hall, Inc., 1990);

William Massy and Ronald Frank, "Short-Term Price and Dealing Effects in Selected Market Segments," *Journal of Marketing Research,* 2 (May 1965), pp. 175–85; David Montgomery, "Consumer Characteristics Associated with Dealing: An Empirical Example," *Journal of Marketing Research,* 8 (February 1971), pp. 118–20; Robert Blattbert et al., "Identifying the Deal-Prone Segment," *Journal of Marketing Research,* 15 (August 1978), pp. 369–77.

21. "Coupon Scams Are Clipping Companies," *Business Week,* June 15, 1992, pp. 110–11.

22. Scott Hume, "Coupons Set Record, but Pace Slows," *Advertising Age,* 64 (February 1, 1993), p. 25; Elliot Zweibach, "Coupon Redemptions Increase 10%," *Supermarket News,* 42 (October 12, 1992), p. 4.

23. See Toni Mack, "Rebate Madness," *Forbes,* February 13, 1984, pp. 76–77.

24. Software suppliers for mainframe computers sell systems for tens of thousands of dollars. They can produce copies, however, for only a few hundred dollars. To enable potential buyers to learn the value of these systems, they sometimes offer free samples of the software, but with a built-in subroutine that destroys the program after a limited time.

25. Charles Hinkle, "The Strategy of Price Deals," *Harvard Business Review,* 43 (July–August 1965), p. 75–85; C. A. Scott, "The Effects of Trial and Incentives on Repeat Purchase Behavior," *Journal of Marketing Research,* 13 (August 1976), p. 263–69; Joe Dodson, Alice Tybout, and Brian Sternthal, "Impact of Deals and Deal Retraction on Brand Switching," *Journal of Marketing Research,* 15 (February 1978), pp. 72–81; John Philip Jones, "The Double Jeopardy of Sales Promotions," *Harvard Business Review,* September–October 1990, p. 146;

David A. Aaker, *Managing Brand Equity* (New York: The Free Press, 1992).

26. Pierre Chandon, Brian Wansink, and Gilles Laurent, "A Benefit Congruency Framework of Sales Promotion Effectiveness," *Journal of Marketing,* 64 (October 2000), pp. 65–81.

27. Kusum L. Ailawadi, Scott A. Neslin, and Karen Gedenk, "Pursuing the Value-Conscious Consumer; Store Brands Versus National Brand Promotions," *Journal of Marketing,* 65, 1 (January 2001), pp. 71–89; Brian Wansink, R. J. Kent, and S. J. Hoch, "An Anchoring and Adjustment Model of Purchase Quantity Decisions," *Journal of Marketing Research,* 35 (February 1998), pp. 71–81.

28. Robert Reed, "Beer Couponing Foams to the Top," *Advertising Age* (February 21, 1983), pp. 10, 71.

29. Scott Hume, "Coupons Set Record, but Pace Slows," *Advertising Age,* 64 (February 1, 1993), p. 25; Zweibach, "Coupon Redemptions Increase 10%."

30. Even when retailers do not receive manufacturer trade deals, they may still offer deals to get consumers to stock up on certain items. This can pay if it reduces a retailer's inventory cost by more than the cost of the deal. See Robert C. Blattberg, Gary D. Eppen, and Joshua Lieberman, "A Theoretical and Empirical Evaluation of Price Deals for Consumer Nondurables," *Journal of Marketing,* 45 (Winter 1981), pp. 116–29.

31. Monci Jo Williams, "The No-Win Game of Price Promotion," *Fortune,* July 11, 1983, pp. 93–102; Robert D. Buzzell, John A. Quelch, and Walter J. Salmon, "The Costly Bargain of Trade Promotion," *Harvard Business Review* (March–April 1990), pp. 141–49; Jakki J. Mohr and George S. Low, "Escaping the Catch-22 of Trade Promotion Spending," *Marketing Management,* 2, 2 (1993), pp. 31–39.

CHAPTER

11

Channel Strategy

Price Management

Distribution channels play a key role in the implementation of pricing strategy. The key to managing pricing strategy through a channel involves seeing the channel as the route to reaching the target customer segment. Careful coordination is required in order to ensure that the pricing strategy is executed through the entire channel. Without this careful coordination, pricing strategy is likely to be poorly implemented or even subverted, with consequent failure to achieve the objectives of the strategy. In this chapter, we will develop the mechanisms for implementing value-based pricing strategies through an extended distribution channel.

Problems in design of the channel network create immense challenges for manufacturers. Compaq built a formidable distribution system with 11,000 retailers and value-added resellers. These channel firms held three to six months of inventories and were the appropriate distribution network when customers needed assistance in buying standardized personal computers. As some customers became more sophisticated in their PC purchases, other channel networks emerged. Catering to buyers who knew what they wanted and were confident in using it, Dell and Gateway began selling directly to consumers. By building computers to order, they also cut out inventory holding costs (significant in a market with falling costs) and retailer margins. That enabled them to profitably undercut Compaq's retail prices.

Compaq could not simply move to alternative channel designs. If it set prices for direct sales the same as for retail, it would not be competitive with Dell and Gateway. If it priced direct sales competitively, it would create conflict with its existing retail network, which could not meet such low prices and still pay for stores, salespeople, and the cost of holding inventories. Ultimately Compaq moved to a direct line, but it offered different models in retail and in the direct channel. If customers saw a model at a retailer, they could not order a customized version directly, nor could they get a retail firm to service a computer purchased on-line.

This chapter is coauthored with George Cressman of the Strategic Pricing Group, Inc.

Further, Compaq's manufacturing and distribution systems were not built to provide order lot sizes of one—necessary for providing customized models. Compaq lost considerable market share to Dell and Gateway, confused consumers about its offerings, and wound up with considerable channel conflict anyway.[1]

Channel systems are undergoing rapid evolution. E-commerce channels are taking larger portions of markets served by more traditional channel firms, and customers are increasingly asking to deal directly and "cut out the middlemen." For example, the recently formed LabPoint has integrated supply for laboratory equipment and supplies, claiming to have brought together 2,300 suppliers of 1.7 million products.[2] LabPoint provides an on-line system to facilitate faster ordering for customers, while providing access to what had previously been a highly fragmented supply stream. Buildersexpress.com lets builders find materials, reduce order delays, and sell excess inventory.[3] USBuild.com has created a buying group for smaller home builders to get volume discounts normally available only to large purchasers. USBuild.com promises "lower prices, automated payments, and more productive trade contractors"[4] in a distribution channel unavailable five years ago. Manufacturers are increasingly being forced to reconsider channel design and its impact on pricing policy.

Channel members make it possible for manufacturers and service providers to reach ultimate customers by providing the following functions:

- Ultimate customers are often a large and dispersed group, while manufacturers and service providers are frequently a more concentrated set. The implication of this disparity in the sizes of groups is that search costs for customers are often expensive. Distribution channels facilitate customers' searches—thus reducing search costs—for required products and services by providing an interface between suppliers and customers. Exhibit 11-1 illustrates this effect. Distribution firms reduce the costs customers incur in supplier search by bringing together multiple suppliers' offerings. Assuming each customer wants to see offerings from each supplier, the introduction of a distribution firm reduces the number of costly interactions from $S \times C$ to $S + C$. As the numbers of customers and suppliers increase, the reduction in interactions created by distribution firms can increase dramatically.

- In order to achieve economies of scale in distribution, most manufacturers ship in large lots—often much more than any individual customer will want to purchase. Channel firms "break bulk" by providing lots of goods and services in the quantities ultimate customers want to buy.

- Again, to achieve economies of scale and to develop the core competencies required to manufacture to the quality level ultimate customers require, manufacturers and service providers "specialize" in providing a limited set of goods and services. Ultimate customers, however, often want to buy a broader assortment of goods and services. Distribution channels help manufacturers and service providers by assembling the required mix of goods and services.

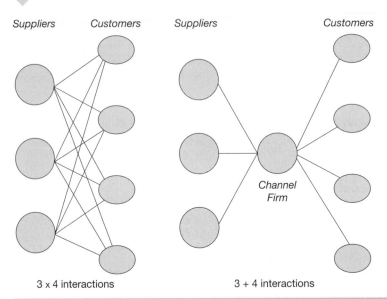

Suppliers   Customers   Suppliers   Customers

3 x 4 interactions   3 + 4 interactions

EXHIBIT 11-1 How Distribution Firms Change Customer Search Costs

- To achieve cost efficiencies and orderly production processes, manufacturers and service providers often desire to manufacture continuously. However, ultimate customers do not buy continuously, they buy at discrete intervals. Distribution channels assist manufacturers and service providers by holding inventory until customers are ready to purchase.

Thus, distribution channels provide a critical linkage to ultimate customers and are an essential element in the implementation of a value-based pricing strategy. The *five Cs* (Comprehend, Create, Communicate, Convince, and Capture) approach to building value-based marketing strategy requires careful integration of channel strategy into pricing strategy. A well-developed pricing strategy may be poorly implemented by the distribution channel, dooming the strategy.

This chapter will explore how to integrate distribution-channel management with value-based pricing. This integration is important because the way products and services are distributed affects both the value perceived by customers and the share of that value that can be captured by the pricing strategy. In particular, distribution-channel policy affects the following:

- The other products and services with which your offering is compared (the reference value defined in Chapter 4)
- The image customers and consumers have of the product/service
- The ability to differentiate through augmentation
- The ability to target and reach desired customer segments
- The ability to implement the desired pricing strategy
- The ability to control the share of contribution among channel members

Since all of these factors are considerations in formulating a pricing strategy, distribution-channel policy and pricing strategy need to be thoughtfully coordinated.

CHANNEL DEFINITIONS

Distribution channels provide a critical linkage for manufacturers: They make it possible for the manufacturer to reach ultimate customers in an effective and efficient manner. Exhibit 11-2 illustrates typical paths from raw-material suppliers to ultimate consumers. Each channel member, except for the last, sells to another channel member. For all of them, however, demand originates not from the ultimate consumers. To develop effective pricing strategy, managers must comprehend the effect of their decisions on pricing and value delivery both to immediate customers and to ultimate consumers.

Markets are a collection of these channels, all competing for the spending power of customers. In order for a firm to be rewarded for its pricing strategy, the entire distribution channel must deliver an effective solution. That is, the channel's solution must be seen as a better value for a consumer than spending the same money on solutions offered by competing channels. This requires firms within a channel to coordinate their activities in such a way that value is increased as solutions move toward ultimate consumers. Value is increased through integration of channel activities, augmenting goods and services to create solutions consumers find attractive for their value delivery.

However, even when a channel creates superior value in its offering to ultimate consumers, "upstream" firms can easily lose out in the internal competition for the rewards. In order for these upstream firms to share in the profits generated by channel success, they must successfully manage the following:

- *Pricing strategy.* Seen in its proper perspective, pricing strategy should move beyond individual firms to encompass the entire channel. The entire channel should engage in the execution of the five Cs framework, concentrating its activities on comprehending, creating, communicating, convincing, and capturing value.
- *Channel efficiency.* Channel efficiency requires management of activities throughout the channel. Activities that do not increase value delivery to consumers, or activities that are redundant, add cost and need to be eliminated.
- *Competitive dynamics management.* As developed in Chapter 5, managing competitive dynamics is key to capturing rewards for value delivery to consumers. Many managers focus competitive strategy on the firms operating at their channel level, but this approach is too narrow to ensure successful reward capture. Managers need to view their entire channel as in competition with other channels. In order to capture rewards for value delivery, managers must act in ways that allow their chosen channel to deliver superior value (i.e., win against other channels), and then manage their chosen channel to ensure rewards flow throughout the channel.

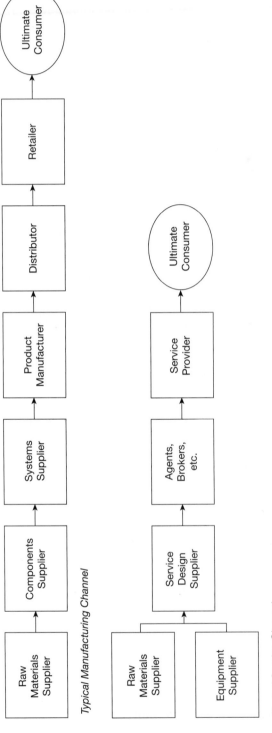

Typical Manufacturing Channel

Typical Service Channel

EXHIBIT 11-2 Distribution Channel Structures

It should be obvious from this discussion that successful implementation of pricing strategy requires careful coordination and integration of the entire distribution channel.

This coordination and integration must recognize sources of power and control in the channel. Channel systems that rely on exclusive arrangements or limited distribution networks are vulnerable to opportunistic moves by channel intermediaries. For example, powerful channel intermediaries may use a supplier's products as "loss leaders" to encourage more store traffic. Other powerful channel intermediaries may block suppliers' attempts to understand the market and create an imagined atmosphere of intense competition. In all of these cases, powerful channel intermediaries may demand price concessions from their suppliers in return for carrying the suppliers' products to ultimate customers. Channel design must include consideration of countering the price demands from these powerful channel firms. Countering tactics are often based in both market communications and product/service design. This chapter will describe some of these countering tactics.

In implementing pricing strategy, the term "distribution channel" should be seen in its broadest context: any means of moving goods and/or services to ultimate customers. From this view, the emergence of e-commerce purchasing is yet one more example of a distribution channel. The e-commerce distribution channel is a means of linking a manufacturer with a segment of customers. The use of e-commerce distribution channels will be further developed later in this chapter.

Distribution channels contain a set of firms that manage the activities mentioned in this chapter's introduction. Historically these firms have been called distributors or retailers, but this term's focus on the logistical function unduly limits the scope of these firms' activities. In this chapter, these channel firms will be called collectively *channel intermediaries*. Channel intermediaries engage in a wide variety of activities, including marketing, finance, operations, and logistics. As developed further in this chapter, the scope of the activities suppliers ask channel intermediaries to perform heavily impacts on pricing strategy.

CHANNEL STRATEGY

As pricing strategy is often internally cost driven, so distribution-channel strategy is often burdened with two significant challenges:

- Distribution-channel strategy is often conceived simply as a means to reach a broad market and is seen as the mechanism to push products and services into the market.
- Distribution-channel strategy is often not integrated into a value-based pricing process.

To deal with these challenges, managers should adopt the process depicted in Exhibit 11-3.

Channel Strategy Development

Channel Strategy Implementation

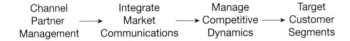

EXHIBIT 11-3 Channel Strategy Development and Implementation

Distribution-channel strategy, like pricing strategy, begins with target customer identification. For both pricing and distribution-channel design, strategy development is founded in comprehending what creates value for the target customers and in creating a set of products and services to provide value for the target customers.

Distribution-channel strategy must next consider the appropriate mix of channel routes:

- *Direct.* In this route, the supplier markets directly to the target customer segment. To the extent the supplier is willing to manage the discrepancies described in the introduction, direct routes are highly desirable. Direct routes give the supplier the highest level of control and increase the probability that a well-conceived pricing strategy will be effectively and efficiently implemented. On the other hand, direct channels increase financial management issues when the target-customer segment has a large number of smaller customers; in such segments, a supplier utilizing a direct route must manage more accounts and is exposed to higher potential for bad-debt losses (although the default of a single account probably incurs a smaller individual loss than the default of a larger distribution account). The cost of managing many smaller accounts and the managing discrepancies of time, lot size, and assortment may make direct routes unattractive.
- *Indirect.* In indirect channel routes, channel intermediaries are used to manage discrepancies of time, lot size and assortment. These indirect routes are particularly attractive in serving target segments where the ultimate customer base is fragmented and widely dispersed. In such markets, channel intermediaries take on the task of reaching the fragmented and dispersed customer base, providing the supplier with fewer and larger accounts. There is a cost to the supplier when using a channel intermediary, and this cost is the analog to price—the discount from list price granted to

the channel intermediary. The channel intermediary uses the markup over its discounted price to cover its cost for managing marketing, financial, and operational activities and earn a profit.

- *Mixes of Direct and Indirect Routes.* Some suppliers choose to employ both direct and indirect channel approaches. In the mixed-channel route, suppliers often market directly to larger customers and require channel intermediaries to market to smaller customers. For the supplier, this approach allows economies of scale in dealing with both larger and smaller customers. The drawback to this approach, however, is that it may accentuate conflict between suppliers and channel intermediaries because channel firms cannot grow profits substantially by marketing to larger customers. Further, channel firms are typically given the smaller customers that frequently are the most costly to serve design.

Seen in the context of the mix of channel route options, e-commerce is an option for direct marketing to target customer segments. E-commerce options offer the potential to reach more dispersed and fragmented customers at lower cost. This potential may encourage more direct marketing through lowering the cost to reach smaller customers.

The channel route decision should be based on responses to the following questions:

- *What is the nature of demand in our target-customer segments?* As individual customers have smaller levels of demand, or are geographically widely dispersed, indirect channel routes are often advisable.
- *How do customers in our target segment(s) prefer to buy?* As customers want to buy a wider assortments of products and services, indirect channels with broadly based channel intermediaries are the preferred route. Likewise, as customer-buying timing becomes more infrequent, indirect routes are often more cost-effective.
- *What are our costs to serve the target-customer segment?* If economies of scale in serving the target customer are significant, then direct routes are advisable if individual customers place large orders. Alternatively, if individual customer orders are small, indirect routes utilizing channel intermediaries are desirable.
- *Are appropriate channel intermediaries available?* If channel intermediaries are not well developed (or the best channel intermediaries are already devoted to competitive offerings), direct approaches are more desirable.

Selecting the optimal channel route by addressing these questions is critical to pricing-strategy development. Defining channel approaches with channel intermediaries (indirect channel routes) means the pricing strategy must deal with discount policies. Further, selecting channel intermediaries that can successfully deploy the pricing strategy becomes essential to the pricing-strategy implementation process.

After channel routes are selected, the next step in channel-strategy design is to assess which channel actions suppliers and channel intermediaries will execute. To some extent, this decision must consider the capabilities of channel intermediaries; if an intermediary is asked to execute an activity it is not capable of doing, the supplier must invest in developing that capability or risk failure of the pricing strategy. Selection of an execution point for channel activities must also consider the cost of execution; activities should be executed where it is least costly to do so.

Suppliers should recognize that the selection of execution points critically impacts pricing strategy. The more activities the supplier asks channel intermediaries to execute, the more the supplier must "pay" for these activities through its price discount policy. In effect, the activity execution point can be viewed as it impacts the suppliers' cost structure. As the supplier chooses to take on more of the execution of the channel strategy (takes on more activities), the cost of these activities resembles a fixed cost to the supplier. Thus, taking on more channel activities increases the contribution margin (see Chapter 2 for a discussion of contribution margin and its role in pricing strategy) of the supplier. As the supplier has channel intermediaries take on more of the execution of the channel strategy, the "cost" of these activities resembles a variable cost to the supplier. This variable cost is really the price discount granted to channel intermediaries.

The final step in channel-strategy design is the selection of appropriate channel-intermediary partners and development of channel policies. Primary to selection of channel-intermediary partners is their ability to reach the target customer segments. Potential channel partners should have the capabilities and geographic presence to serve the target segment(s). Channel partners should also be selected both for their ability to manage the execution of the desired channel activities and for their ability to complement supplier's strategy. Is the manufacturer relying on the channel members to promote or augment the value delivered, or simply to make the product available to the customer when and where they come looking for it?

Based on the desired channel activities (the mix of marketing, financial, operational, and logistical functions) to be executed by the supplier and by the channel intermediaries, a set of channel policies must be developed. These channel policies delineate the desired behavior by all parties. Most important in channel-policy development is the specification of pricing policy. (Channel-pricing policy is developed further below.)

SELECTING AN APPROPRIATE CHANNEL

One important consideration when choosing a channel of distribution is its effect on the product's price. Consider the following examples:

- When the U.S. Time Company developed its inexpensive line of Timex watches, the established channel of distribution was jewelry stores. That was an appropriate channel for watches that competed with one another on their claims of accuracy, the beauty of their designs, and their heirloom qualities. The jewelry stores offered skilled personnel to demonstrate those attributes and the appropriate environment in which to contemplate an expensive purchase. The Timex, however, was not a great timepiece; its attractive attribute was its low price. The sales and service of a jewelry store could do little to improve the perception of its inherent value, but the markups that jewelers expected could have seriously crimped its price advantage. Consequently, the company distributed through drug and department stores—which, although they offered little service, generated maximum visibility while adding relatively little to the product's cost.

- More recently, the development of the Swatch watch followed the Timex strategy at introduction. However, as the strategy evolved to positioning the Swatch as an accessory to complement multiple fashions, distribution was redirected to include fashion boutiques.

- Lenox makes fine-quality china dishes and figurines that carry premium prices. Since the major attributes of china are apparent before purchase and it requires no postpurchase service, Lenox could offer the same physical product through practically any retail channel, but Lenox limits its distribution to high-quality department, jewelry, and specialty stores. The reason is that fine china is a prestige product, displayed for guests or given as gifts. Its image would be tarnished if it were available in stores that discounted its price and lacked luxurious displays.[5]

- Mont Blanc pens are similarly distributed through exclusive shops and retail outlets where less price-sensitive customers are likely to shop.

For a product that attracts buyers with low price, the goal is to obtain low-cost distribution. Such strategies are often coupled with intensive distribution strategies whose goal is to have the product available everywhere it could conceivably be purchased. Bic pens are distributed using such a strategy. For products that attract buyers with superior attributes despite a high price, the goal is to obtain distribution that complements those attributes and makes them salient. Such products are typically distributed in selective or exclusive channels, limiting the availability of the product to outlets that support the pricing strategy.

When a product or service's differentiation value stems from its augmentation, it is risky to rely completely on channel intermediaries. Not only must the manufacturer worry that the product is augmented appropriately, it must also worry that the augmentation might be used to sell competitors' products, eliminating the product's competitive advantage. Thus companies that rely heavily on augmentation often develop distribution routes over which they can exercise at least some control, for example:

- Some companies that manufacture high-priced cosmetics have a unique distribution system. They distribute in high-quality department stores, but they do not sell their products to these stores. Instead, they rent display space and staff it with their own sales representatives. They do so because much of the differentiation value of their products stems from augmentation. Each company's representative is trained as a cosmetologist to help a woman select cosmetics appropriate for her and to teach her how to use them most effectively. At the same time, the cosmetologist makes the connection between the customer's enhanced beauty and the particular brand of cosmetics that is sold.

- Other cosmetic companies employ agents as their sales representatives. Avon and Mary Kay cosmetics are sold by agent "beauty consultants" who consult directly with customers. This approach gives the supplier high levels of control over the distribution channel.
- Caterpillar Tractor is legendary for the quality of its exclusive dealer network. Caterpillar selects its dealers carefully and treats them royally in order to instill a feeling that they are part of a family of Caterpillar employees. This is because Caterpillar's reputation for reliability enables it to charge a substantial price premium. Although that reputation stems in part from the high quality of the physical product, it could be quickly destroyed if a dealer is not quick to come to a customer's aid when inevitable breakdowns occur. Caterpillar dealers, however, view a breakdown as a potential blight on their family name and will go to unusual extremes to correct it. Such commitment is well worth the extra cost to Caterpillar of maintaining its exclusive distribution network.[6]
- Anheuser-Busch treats its distributors similarly. Distributors are granted exclusive territories and are encouraged to behave as respected members of the "A-B family."

The control and loyalty that these manufacturers enjoy are more costly than dealing with completely independent distribution channels, but the cost is justified when augmentations that occur in the channel add substantial value.

When companies use different pricing strategies for different versions of their products, they need to coordinate those strategies with different distribution channels. Despite the success of L'Eggs pantyhose in supermarkets, Hanes continues to sell higher-quality, higher-priced hosiery through department stores. Pitney Bowes continues to sell the bulk of its office equipment through its sales force but uses direct mail to sell its lowest-priced scales and postage meters to small buyers. In each of these cases, low-priced products are appropriately distributed through low-cost channels that preserve their price advantage, whereas higher-priced products justify the higher cost of distribution methods that can enhance perceptions of the product's differentiating attributes.

A clear example of the challenges of not managing these different distribution channels well exists in the PC arena. Suppliers such as Dell and Gateway pioneered the development of direct channels, avoiding or minimizing the use of traditional retail store formats. Other suppliers—heavily invested in retail routes—have tried to play both indirect and direct channel routes. Retailers have become very upset with this split approach and actively encourage price competition among the equipment suppliers for limited retail shelf space.

CHANNEL STRATEGY IMPLEMENTATION

Exhibit 11-3 illustrates the steps in channel strategy implementation. Critical to successful execution of the pricing strategy is careful management of the channel intermediaries chosen as partners in channel-strategy development. The reason why this is important involves development of pricing practice in the distribution channel. As developed below, there are legal constraints on control of price levels in the channel. Without the active management of and cooperation of the channel intermediary firms, pricing strategy is likely to fail.

Equally important to channel-strategy implementation is integration with the market communications process. Success with the pricing strategy requires careful coordination of channel and communication management aimed at supporting the pricing strategy. From a channel-strategy perspective, the objectives of the market communication include the following:

- Informing the target customer segment(s) where they can access the supplier's offerings. For this objective, market communications must consider the buying habits and preferences of the target customer segments, and if necessary, attempt to reposition these habits/preferences to support the channel strategy.
- Supporting and enhancing the image the supplier wants to project around its offerings.

A critical role for channel-strategy implementation involves the management of competitive dynamics. Some pricing strategies fail because channel intermediaries actively encourage competitive price wars. In other cases, channel strategy may not have adequately defined territories, resulting in channel intermediaries warring to grow volume at the expense of other authorized distributors. Pricing-strategy development should envision the effects of channel policies in implementation of the strategy. Scenario planning is a useful tool for forecasting how pricing strategy is likely to play out under different channel-strategy options. (See Schwartz [1991] for a discussion of scenario planning techniques.[7])

MAINTAINING MINIMUM RESALE PRICES

Although manufacturers can always state a suggested retail price for their products, they cannot legally insist that retailers charge that price. Under U.S. antitrust laws, independent resellers must be left free to charge any price they wish. A manufacturer cannot legally refuse to deal with those who do charge another price. Unfortunately, there are times when it is in the interest of some retailers to charge prices lower or higher than a manufacturer would like. Consequently, an important part of pricing through independent channels of distribution is the management of relations with resellers to influence, not dictate, their pricing decisions.

Maintaining a minimum resale price can be essential for the success of products whose perceived value depends not only on the product itself but also on related services offered by the retailer. The time spent by a computer store demonstrating the equipment and helping the customer select the most appropriate software strongly influences both the likelihood that customers will buy and ultimately be satisfied with their purchases. Similarly, most audiophiles will buy stereo speakers only if a retailer offers the service of a listening room, where the sounds of different speakers can be compared. Many first-time purchasers eagerly solicit such retailers to carry their brands, knowing that the high levels of service they offer encourage far more sales than their higher prices discourage.

Unfortunately for manufacturers, retailers have an incentive to provide such services only as long as customers who use the services buy the product from them. If shoppers can see a product demonstrated and learn how to use it from a high-service retailer but purchase it from a low-service retailer at a discount price, the high-service retailer loses. Ultimately, if enough potential customers go to the discounters, high-service retailers either stop promoting the brand or stop carrying it altogether. The value of the product declines and sales suffer.[8]

To avoid this, manufactureres of such products would like to set minimum resale prices, ensuring each reseller a large enough margin to support services that enhance the product's value. Before 1976, manufactures could bind U.S. resellers contractually under the fair-trade laws of individual states not to discount prices.[9] In 1976, the U.S. Supreme Court declared that fair-trade agreements violated the Sherman Act prohibition against "agreements in restraint of trade."

In 1988, however, the Court declared that, while agreements to limit resale prices are illegal, a manufacturure can refuse to supply resellers that fail to comply with a minimum resale prices that it has stipulated unilaterally.[10] The manufacturer can also set other criteria for resellers, such as a requirement to have a minimum display area, excluding mail-order discounters, or the requirement that they provide service or training. Still, retailers who are unwilling to charge the stipulated resale price can often buy wholesale product on the "grey market." This is legal since the resellers has no contractual agreement with the manufacturer about pricing. It is practical since the manufacturer often cannot determine which "legitimate" retailers are secretly reselling product to the discounter.

As an alternative, some manufacturers simply charge wholesale prices that leave low-service retailers with too little margin to discount. Then they pay the high-service retailers generous promotional allowances for specific services such as product displays. They may also supply free training for retailers' salespeople and give them financial-incentive payments for each sale. Of course, these alternatives are administratively more costly, and they run the risk that some retailers will collect payments without providing the services that the manufacturer expects. However, they are the only alternatives when resale prices cannot be practically or legally enforced.

LIMITING MAXIMUM RESALE PRICES

Manufacturers can usually distribute their products much more cheaply through independent retailers than they can directly. A clothing retailer, for example, can distribute the products of many manufacturers at a much lower cost than would be possible if each manufacturer tried to operate its own store. Moreover, buyers are better served when they enjoy the wide assortment that an independent retailer can offer. Balancing these advantages, however, is a potentially significant disadvantage of using independent distribution. Independent distributors sometimes charge excessive resale prices that can make a manufacturer's product less competitive and therefore less profitable.[11] In most markets, competition among retailers limits their ability to overprice. In a few markets, however, the potential for overpricing is great enough to justify special contracts that minimize the problem. In extreme cases, it may even justify vertical integration of manufacturing and retailing within a single firm.

To see why overpricing occurs, consider the hypothetical example in Exhibit 11-4. An independent retailer currently charges $1 for a product bought wholesale from the manufacturer for $0.70. The retailer incurs an additional cost of $0.05 to sell it. Thus, unit profit contribution is $0.25. The manufacturer,

---

EXHIBIT 11-4 Incentives for Overpricing by the Channel

	Total	Per Unit
Independent Retailer's Revenue and Costs		
Sales revenue (price)	$10,000	$1.00
Incremental product cost	7,000	0.70
Other incremental cost	500	0.05
Profit contribution	2,500	0.25
Manufacturer's Revenue and Costs		
Sale revenue (price)	$7,000	$0.70
Incremental costs	2,500	0.25
Profit contribution	4,500	0.45

Breakeven Sales Changes

5% price increase by retailer

$$\frac{-0.05}{0.25 + 0.05} = -16.7\%$$

5% price cut by retailer

$$\frac{-(-0.05)}{0.25 + (-0.05)} = +25.0\%$$

5% price increase by integrated retailer–manufacturer

$$\frac{-0.05}{0.70 + 0.05} = -7.7\%$$

who set the wholesale price of $0.70, incurs an incremental manufacturing cost of $0.25. Thus, its unit profit contribution is $0.45. What is the retailer's incentive to raise or lower the price, and how does it affect the manufacturer?

Chapter 2 illustrated the breakeven sales change needed to maintain profit following a price change. Applying that equation to this example, the retailer would profit from a 5 percent price increase if sales fell by an amount less than 16.7 percent. The retailer would have to increase sales by more than 25 percent, however, to justify a price cut. If the retailer believed that sales would decline by only 10 percent following a 5 percent price increase, raising the price (assuming an initial sales rate of 10,000 units per month) would increase profits by $200.

Note, however, how the retailer's 5 percent price premium would affect the manufacturer. The manufacturer sells the retailer 1,000 fewer units each month. At a profit contribution of $0.45 per unit, the manufacturer would lose $450 each month, or $250 more than the retailer gained, as a result of the price increase. Consequently, if the retailer and manufacturer were one integrated firm, they would not raise price at all. In fact, the integrated firm's breakeven sales change from a 5 percent price increase would be only 7.7 percent, which could actually justify a price reduction.

The independent channel intermediary has the incentive to price higher than would an integrated retailer-manufacturer, because for the independent retailer the entire wholesale price is an incremental cost of doing business. Thus the retailer sees profit contribution as being only $0.25 per unit, or 25 percent of the initial selling price. Since much of the wholesale price goes to cover the manufacturer's fixed costs and profit costs not incremental for pricing, in order to set price to maximize the joint profit from retailing and manufacturing, the manufacturer calculates the profit contribution at $0.70 per unit ($1.00 − 0.05 − 0.25), or 70 percent of the initial selling price. It would therefore judge price cuts as much less attractive, given the same expected changes in sales.

It can clearly pay for a manufacturer to recognize that retailers may have an incentive to price too high and to take steps to alleviate it. The easiest solution is to encourage competition among retailers, thus limiting their ability to charge excessive margins. The evidence is quite strong that a "pull strategy" of heavy brand advertising is the key to maximizing retail competition and minimizing retail margins. Exhibit 11-5 illustrates how dramatic these effects can be. Advertising increases retail competition, thus reducing retailer margins for all brands, but especially for the leading brands in each category. These relationships have been confirmed by other studies across many product categories.[12]

Unfortunately for manufacturers, not all distribution channels are competitive. In fact, manufacturers sometimes deliberately limit competition among those who sell their products. Automobile companies limit the number of dealers in a geographical area so that each dealer has enough sales volume to justify carrying an adequate inventory of cars (there are life-cycle rationales for limiting the number of channel intermediaries; see the discussion below in the life-cycle section). Coca-Cola and Anheuser-Busch grant only one local distributor the exclusive right to sell in a particular territory. This ensures that a

	Average Manufacturing Price	Average Retail Price	Average Retail Margin
Leading Brands			
With heavy advertising	$3.00	$3.95	24%
With light advertising	2.35	4.20	44%
Difference			−20%
Other Brands			
With heavy advertising	$1.70	$2.93	42%
With light advertising	1.96	4.00	51%
Difference			−9%

EXHIBIT 11-5 **Typical Effects of Brand Advertising on Retail Margins**

Source: Robert Steiner, as reported in Mark Albion, *Advertising's Hidden Effects: Manufacturers' Advertising and Retail Pricing* (Boston: Auburn House, 1983), p. 50. Auburn House is an imprint of Greenwood Publishing Group, Inc., Westport, CT. Reprinted with permission.

dealer who promotes the brand in an area and maintains high standards of quality and service will be able to capture the benefits from doing so. Unfortunately, from the manufacturer's perspective, the limited competition also makes it easier for these channel intermediaries to raise prices too high.

Overcoming this problem is difficult when the distribution network is entirely independent. The most straightforward solution—that of a contract between the manufacturer and distributors specifying a maximum resale price—has consistently been found unacceptable under U.S. antitrust laws. However, there are other ways that manufacturers can hold down resale prices. For prepackaged products, manufacturers can limit resale prices by printing on the package a suggested retail price large enough that the retailer cannot easily cover it with a higher-price sticker. They also can advertise the suggested price, leading consumers to complain when retailers try to charge more. Unfortunately, these are all less-than-ideal solutions for many of the products affected by this problem.

The most common method of limiting resale prices is by minimum sales provisions. Many companies, selling everything from fast foods and gasoline to commercial security systems and water-purification equipment, require resellers to sign franchise agreements. These agreements commonly include minimum sales quotas specified as a percentage of the average sales for a typical franchise or as a percentage of the estimated market potential in a particular location. Such contracts cannot legally dictate a specific resale price. Franchisees who set prices too high, however, cannot achieve their minimum sales quotas and can lose their franchises. Short of withdrawing a franchise, there are other ways that manufacturers can enforce minimum sales quotas. Some manufacturers (for example, automobile companies) exert leverage over their channel intermediaries by offering joint advertising programs, preference in receiving models that are in short supply, and other special considerations only to those dealers who maintain sales levels commensurate with the sales potential in their areas.

CONNECTING CHANNEL STRATEGIES TO COMMUNICATION STRATEGY

The third of the five Cs of value-marketing strategies asks managers to communicate the value delivery of their offerings to their target customers. In developing channel strategy, managers have two options to communicate value to their target customers:

- *"Push" strategies.* The focus of communication is on the supplier's next immediate customer. Push strategies are aimed at propelling the supplier's offerings through the channel. For example, some manufacturers of over-the-counter (OTC) drugs and automotive paints do not promote these products directly to ultimate consumers. Instead, they focus on the retailer or auto-repair shops, expecting these channel firms to make the sale to the consumer. Channel firms that carry a variety of competing products may favor push strategies because they permit promoting products that are most profitable to the channel firm (the channel firm's customers frequently do not have strong preconceived preferences). Suppliers often find push strategies less expensive to implement.
- *"Pull" strategies.* The focus of communication is on the end customer or a channel member closer to the end customer. Such strategies are aimed at pulling the supplier's offering through the distribution channel. For example, Intel maintains brand preference by advertising its chips to end consumers with the "Intel Inside®" campaign. The intent is to create a preference for computers with its chips—causing retailers to favor Intel-based computers. Channel members benefit from pull strategies when customers are "presold" for particular brands. Suppliers gain some control over channel firms because it is more difficult for channel firms to switch customers to competing brands.

Push strategies depend on channel intermediaries to carry the value message through the rest of the channel. Pull strategies "presell" the offering to the target customers, who then go to channel intermediaries with brand-specific demands.

Push strategies are essential when the supplier's product and its differential value are not apparent to target customers, or when its value delivery cannot be easily made salient to target customers. For example, most automobile buyers are unaware of the specific machine tools used in the manufacture of their automobile or of the specific brand of paint that covers it. For machine-tool suppliers or automotive-paint manufacturers, convincing manufacturers that their products can make automobiles better or cheaper is more effective than trying to convince consumers to buy vehicles manufactured with a specific brand of machine tool or utilizing a particular paint.[13] The main drawback to push strategies is they depend on the distribution channel to convey the value message to ultimate consumers. In some cases, push strategies may require managers to invest in developing the value-marketing skills of the entire distribution channel or risk having the channel not convey the value theme.

Pull strategies carry the value message directly to target customers. A pull strategy often gives a supplier greater control in communicating value to target customers. Further, pull strategies are often favored by channel intermediaries because they often create "presold" customers, thus reducing the marketing effort required by channel firms. More-exclusive retailers who compete with low-price outlets often prefer suppliers who invest in building brand image. Also, effective pull strategies can provide suppliers insurance against channel intermediaries who try to opportunistically sell competing offerings—customers arrive at the channel firm with strong brand preference.

The choice between "push" and "pull" is usually difficult. Push strategies require both costly incentives for the retail channel partners and limited distribution. In introductory and growth markets, channel intermediaries must invest substantial resources in targeting potential customers and communicating value in return for uncertain sales that may occur considerably later. As a result, suppliers have to share a large portion of their sales price with channel firms as an incentive for the selling effort. In addition, when sales are uncertain or do not follow quickly, manufacturers generally must pay high fees for promotional efforts, such as cooperative advertising and in-store demonstrations.

Given these costs, it would seem that a pull strategy might be preferable, but there are three strong considerations recommending the push approach.

1. *The costs are largely variable*—being proportionate to the amount of sales and the number of retail distribution outlets. This is a big advantage for a product that is starting out small. The cost of an effective advertising campaign could be prohibitive.

2. *The retailers have pretargeted the market.* In markets where demand is diffuse—few people are potential purchasers—the retailer (who may be a catalog or e-commerce company) has already identified them. Either the target consumers already know where to buy or retailers own a highly coveted customer list. For sales of scuba equipment, aids to the physically impaired and to people interested in do-it-yourself home repair, no advertising outlets exist to reach a majority of the potential buyers. All of the potential purchasers, however, will eventually need to visit a retailer or web site, or read a catalog which, given an adequate incentive, can promote the product.

3. *The retailers or others in the chain "augment" the product.* Few people would pay the prices for Mary Kay cosmetics if they were available on a rack in a drug store. The value is in the Mary Kay experience of being "made up" in the privacy

of home. Mary Kay creates that experience with a team of independent distributors who are motivated by, among other things, high margins.

4. *Pull strategies require sophisticated marketing,* expertise that a firm may lack. Managers must know not only who might buy their product, but also understand why. They must connect their offerings to benefits and offerings that these target customers find salient, which may be difficult when channel firms augment the offering in a way that hides the supplier's components, and they must create messages that can be indirectly communicated convincingly in limited space or time.

Still, in most mature mass markets, pull strategies are preferred. They are cost-effective for high-volume, mass-marketed products, and they give the seller control over the message. Moreover, the mass-market channel partners like Wal-Mart, grocery chains, and drugstores prefer pull strategies despite lower margins. They make their money-moving inventory efficiently, not by selling. Moreover, a pull strategy creates a stronger brand identity that increases loyalty.

Pull strategies are an effective counter to brand competition for channel attention. When multiple brand competitors are competing for the same customers, opportunistic channel firms will play them against each other to extract higher margins and fees. Brands that are large enough to support the cost of a pull strategy can undermine the opportunist's ability to do this. Because customers are presold on the supplier's brand, an attempt to switch them to a competing product is more difficult.

Pharmaceutical manufacturers, which traditionally used only push strategies, have in the United States adopted the pull approach for some products. Managed-care practices have encouraged substitution of branded pharmaceuticals with generic products and have discouraged prescribing "quality-of-life" drugs—such as nonsedating antihistamines and drugs for treatment of erectile dysfunction—that have no effect on overall health. The pull strategy educates patients to ask for these drugs by brand name.

Even some suppliers of materials that are not apparent in the finished good have developed "branded ingredient" pull strategies. W. L. Gore, Inc., uses such a strategy to promote Gore-Tex™ apparel, even though W. L. Gore does not manufacture apparel. Similar strategies have been developed by Du Pont (Stainmaster carpet), Intel ("Intel Inside"), and G. D. Searle (NutraSweet in foods and beverages). Branded-ingredient strategies are a special type of pull communication strategy in which a component not immediately transparent to the end user can be linked to benefits and value the target customer highly desires.

The selection of the appropriate channel communication strategy (push or pull) has a strong impact on successful pricing-strategy implementation. This impact is manifested in the ability of suppliers to communicate their value delivery to target customers. Exhibit 11-6 provides some general guidelines on choosing the appropriate value communication strategy.

	Push Channel Strategy	*Pull Channel Strategy*
Manufacturer economics	Deep wholesale discounts and promo fees are "variable" costs, enabling small-volume brands to enter	Heavy advertising and mass marketing create high "fixed" costs that favor high-volume brands
Channel economics	High margins, high fixed costs of sales and service shared across products of different manufacturers	Low margins require making money by efficiently moving volume
Market type, ease of communication	Niche, diffuse markets difficult to target with mass communication	Mass-market appeal, or easily targeted (e.g., 18–24 years old) with mass communication
Value proposition	Complex	Simple
One-site augmentation required by channel	Moderate to high	Low to none
Distribution intensity	Selective, high-service outlets	Intensive, mass retailers
Competitive intensity	Low	High

EXHIBIT 11-6 Push Versus Pull Value Communication Strategies

MANAGING PRICE THROUGH THE DISTRIBUTION CHANNEL

Given the market/channel view of Exhibit 11-3, it should be clear that management's goal should be to develop pricing strategy that is aimed at all channel firms achieving satisfactory profit levels. When a product or service cannot drive adequate margins for all channel intermediaries, the product/service may be in the wrong channel route or perhaps an alternative channel strategy needs to be developed. Channel intermediaries earn profits by three means:

1. Their ability to augment their suppliers' offerings to create more value and to capture it in a higher price.
2. Their ability to achieve higher margins, through negotiating lower prices from their suppliers and capturing higher prices for their own offerings.
3. Driving higher sales volume (referred to as "turns" by many channel intermediaries).

As offerings move through the distribution channel, the ability to manipulate these three elements increases. Successful management of pricing strategy through the distribution channel encompasses all three of these elements simultaneously.

Managing pricing strategy through distribution channels begins with target customer segment selection. As target customer segments are chosen, channel intermediaries should then be selected for the following characteristics:

- Their potential to serve the target segments.
- Their ability to implement the desired pricing strategy.
- Their ability to execute the necessary activities to serve the target segments.
- Their efficiency in providing the necessary activities in serving the target customers.

Channel intermediaries who cannot reach the target customers or who do not have the necessary skills and efficiency to serve the targets are likely to be unable to implement the desired pricing strategy.

In order to achieve the objectives of the pricing strategy, channel firms should be seen as allies in value delivery to target customers. Unfortunately, the channel strategies of many firms encourage conflict rather than partnership in pursuing value delivery. Some channel strategies pit channel intermediaries against each other, forcing channel firms to engage in competitive activities that shift management's focus away from value delivery. Volume-based discounting is a practice that encourages competition rather than value enhancement, especially in mature markets.

As noted in the introduction, the key to managing pricing strategy through a channel involves seeing the channel as the route to reaching the target customer segment. Because suppliers in channels experience derived demand, the ability to successfully implement value-based pricing strategy depends on the following:

- Comprehending the value drivers of target customer segments.
- Coordinating the activities of the channel to create packages of goods and services that deliver value to the target customers.
- Integrating the communication efforts of the entire channel to promote value delivery to the target customers.
- Convincing the entire channel to market the product/service in ways that complement the activities of all channel firms in delivering value to end customers, while managing the costs of delivering this value.
- Integrating the pricing strategies of the entire channel in a way that allows channel members to capture rewards for delivering value.

The focus of this effort is on the integration and coordination of the entire channel's activities.

The Honda Motor Corporation's management of its Acura line of automobiles is a good example of integrated and coordinated channel activity. Honda carefully selects its dealers and employs a selective distribution strategy by granting geographical exclusivity. Dealer locations support the image of a prestige automobile, and dealer sites are constructed to maintain a premium image. Further, Honda trains dealer sales personnel to promote the benefits of Honda ownership and to engage buyers in a value-based selling effort.

MANAGING RETAIL PRICING STRATEGY

In many cases, retailers are the last link in the channel, connecting suppliers to consumers in the market. Large retailers like Wal-Mart, Safeway, and Home Depot control substantial amounts of sales volume in many categories. As such, retailers often significantly affect the implementation of pricing strategies, and in some cases have the power to shape pricing of an entire value chain. For example, automobile dealers working through their independent dealer association forced GM and Ford to abandon plans to market cars directly to consumers through e-commerce channels. Retailers gain pricing strategy leverage in these ways:

- Promoting themselves as the preferred source for products and services.
- Implementing the customer/consumer targeting effort by qualifying potential customers/consumers as part of the desired target segments.
- Providing the final opportunity to communicate the value of the offering to customers/consumers.
- Ensuring the channel convinces the target customer/consumer to pay for delivered value.
- Supporting the channel's activities to capture rewards for delivering value.

Recent research[14] indicates retailer pricing-strategy decisions are driven in large part by an attempt to maintain price consistency across brands being sold. This indicates a desire by retailers to support pricing strategies they can justify to their customers. Clearly, the consistent pricing strategy chosen by a retailer might not be a value-based price. Suppliers should work with retailers to enable them to understand and communicate value delivery, and then manage consistent pricing strategies for this value delivery.

As the channel link to ultimate customers/consumers, retailers represent the final opportunity to communicate value to the market. When implementing a push strategy, suppliers should be very careful to ensure target retailers can support the value-communication effort. This entails selecting the retailers who can communicate benefits and value delivery. For example, Husqvarna, a manufacturer of chain saws, retails these only through a select group of specialty stores. This prevents degradation of the Husqvarna image (and price competition) by mass merchandisers.

Pull strategies are an effective means of controlling value communication to target customers. Procter & Gamble generally sells its products through multiple channels and uses advertising to communicate value propositions directly to end consumers. This reduces the need for channel intermediaries to develop value-selling skills, and reduces the power of channel firms to switch consumers to other products.

Understanding how retailers create revenue flow is an important component of retailer selection. Retailers' revenue flow is driven by two components: the turn rate of each inventory item and the margin for each inventory item.[15] Retailers often make trade-offs between these components, and it is important for suppliers to understand how a particular retailer evaluates inventory turns and margin. Retailers who focus more on inventory turns typically prefer to carry items that are "presold" (encouraging the use of pull strategies) and that are frequently purchased. Suppliers who employ push strategies, with retailers who focus on inventory turns, will need to ensure there is adequate margin to motivate the retailer to communicate value during the sales effort. Even with higher margins available, some retailers who focus on inventory turns may be unwilling to carry products requiring significant selling effort.

Retailers who focus on margin typically prefer to carry items with high levels of differentiation and strongly established images. The absence of a strong image may require too intensive a selling effort for the retailer, even when high margins are available. This image building also often implies the need for suppliers to develop pull strategies.

Suppliers should be aware that retailers have minimum "standards" for margins and inventory turns. For example, recently in the United States there has been a substantial excess of citrus fruit production. Although inventory turns have remained almost constant for grocery stores, some stores are substantially reducing the amount of space allotted to citrus products because margins are so low (resulting in a low-margin on dollars per square foot of shelf space).

As the appropriate retailers are selected, suppliers must then invest in training the retailers to communicate benefits and value, convince customers to pay for the value delivered, and develop consistent pricing strategies that capture rewards for value delivery. It should be obvious that the channel coordination and integration efforts described in the previous section should extend through the retail level.

MANAGING IN E-COMMERCE CHANNELS

As noted in a previous section of this chapter, the emergence of e-commerce channels is best seen as an addition to the channel options available to manufacturers and service providers. These e-commerce channels differ from traditional channels in the following ways:

- E-commerce channels offer the opportunity for ultimate customers to quickly and cheaply acquire information about possible offerings.
- These channels offer the potential for ultimate customers to aggressively pursue price comparisons.
- The development of "reverse auctions" may drive manufacturers and service providers to accelerate bidding wars for customers' business.

All of these aspects of the e-commerce environment make it more important for manufacturers and service providers to carefully construct their pricing strategies. The principles of pricing strategy and tactics developed throughout this text do not change with the emergence of e-commerce. Instead, e-commerce development makes pricing-strategy development and management more important.

For example, recently a sale of ethylene (a chemical used in the manufacture of many other chemicals) was completed in a blind auction on an e-commerce web site named ChemConnect. Suppliers of ethylene believed there would not be any e-commerce deals because the ethylene market is relatively concentrated. But in a January 2000 deal, 10 million pounds of ethylene were sold for $0.02/pound below market prices. Ethylene suppliers initially argued that buyers would ignore this deal because it did not represent the bulk of the market. However, reports indicated that buyers saw this as a new market price, and they used it to push price concessions from suppliers.[16] Suppliers who move products through e-commerce should be aware their pricing moves become public knowledge very quickly. Pricing strategies can be quickly undone by opportunistic moves.

Even channel intermediaries are moving to e-commerce solutions to expand the availability of products and services to customers. For example, Grainger is an industrial distribution firm carrying over 600,000 items in inventory. Grainger launched an Internet-based system in 1995, carrying 200,000 items and reaching $100 million of sales revenue by 1999. Reportedly, customers spend an average of $130 per personal or phone order, but $240 on an Internet order.[17] Grainger has expanded its Internet sites by opening findmro.com, a site devoted to maintenance, repair, and operating (MRO) supplies. This site brings together 12,000 suppliers of 5 million MRO products. Grainger claims findmro.com gives customers all of the following:

- Easy and efficient location of "hard-to-find" MRO products
- Reduced need for customers to search "endless" catalogs and suppliers
- Shorter order cycles
- Reduced number of suppliers[18]

As these e-commerce channels emerge, they improve a customer's ability to compare across offerings (reducing the "difficult comparison effect" described in an earlier channel). This may increase customer price sensitivity at a minimum, but it will also make it easier to find price differences across multiple channels.

Manufacturers must actively manage the pricing moves emerging in the e-commerce arena. By increasing the number of channel options available to ultimate customers, the Internet can heighten channel conflict when prices are very different across the channel options. Suppliers may find their full-service channels are reluctant to support intensive selling when they lose the sale to a lower-priced channel, and Internet channels make it much easier to find these lower-priced channels. Increasingly, customers shop at full-service retailers to gain information about products, and then they buy from a lower-priced discount store or through the Internet. Recently, Whirlpool and Maytag told retailers they will discontinue supplying higher-priced washers and dishwashers to firms selling below the manufacturer's suggested retail price.[19] These firms stated they were trying to protect retailers that provide high levels of customer service. Manufacturers must pay much more attention to pricing deals that create price differentials across multiple channels.

SUMMARY

Successful implementation of value-based pricing requires careful integration and coordination with channel strategy. Like the sales force in direct sales, the distribution channel can make or break any pricing strategy to the extent that their interests are aligned with it.

Channel intermediaries are best seen as allies to reaching the target customers/consumers. As a key component of a marketing strategy, managers must ensure channel strategy enables the entire distribution channel to:

- *comprehend* what drives target customers/consumers.
- *create* offerings through packaging goods and services to deliver value to customers.
- *communicate* the presence of value delivery across the entire distribution channel.
- *convince* target customers/consumers to pay for the delivered value.
- *capture* rewards for delivering value with a consistent set of pricing policies.

In the distribution context, managers must manage the effectiveness of the entire channel to keep the channel focused on delivering value to the target customers. Managers also must deal with the efficiency of the channel so that rewards for delivering value are not wasted with unnecessary and/or redundant channel activities.

Finally, managers must focus their competitive management activities not only on what happens within the distribution channel, but also on competition from alternative solutions between channels. Because suppliers experience derived demand for their products and services, the real competitive battle is waged for the attention (and money) of customers and consumers in the market.

Notes

1. "The Digital Dilemma," *The Economist,* July 22, 2000, pp. 67–68.
2. Bill Schmitt, "Experimenting with Distribution Channels," *Chemical Week,* September 13, 2000, p. 64.
3. Jim Carlton, "Home Builders Learn to Love the Internet," *Wall Street Journal,* February 7, 2000, p. 42.
4. www.usbuild.com/aboutus/index.htm
5. "Rings on Her Fingers, China on Her Table," *Forbes,* February 20, 1978, pp. 76, 81; Claudia Ricci, "Discounters, Alleging Price-Fixing in Their Supplies," *Wall Street Journal,* June 21, 1983, p. 35.
6. Harlan S. Byrne, "A Leaping Caterpillar Is a Wondrous Thing, Even Its Rivals Agree," *Wall Street Journal,* April 19, 1976, pp. 1, 18; and Peters and Waterman, *In Search of Excellence* (Harper & Row, New York, 1982), pp. 171–72.
7. Peter Schwartz, *The Art of the Long View: Planning for the Future in an Uncertain World.* (New York: Doubleday/Currency, 1991).
8. Lester Telser, "Why Manufacturers Want Fair Trade," *Journal of Law Economics,* 3 (October 1960), pp. 86–104.
9. Contracts stipulating minimum resale prices are still enforceable in many other industrialized countries.
10. Fritz Machlup and Martha Taber, "Bilateral Monopoly, Successive Monopoly, and Vertical Integration," *Eonometrica,* 27 (May 1960), pp. 101–119; Steven M. Shugan and Abel P. Jeuland, "Competitive Behavior in Distribution Systems," *Issues in Pric-*

ing: Theory and Research, Timothy Devinney, ed., (D. C. Heath, Lexington, MA, 1988).
11. Robert L. Steiner, "Does Advertising Lower Consumer Prices?" *Journal of Marketing,* 37 (October 1973), pp. 19–26; Paul W. Farris and Mark S. Albion, "The Impact of Advertising on the Price of Consumer Products," *Journal of Marketing,* 44 (Summer 1980), pp. 17–35; Paul W. Farris, "Advertising's Link with Retail Price Competition," *Harvard Business Review,* 59, no. 1 (January–February 1981), pp. 40, 42, 44; Mark S. Albion, *Advertising's Hidden Effects: Manufacturers' Advertising and Retail Pricing,* (Auburn House, Boston, MA, 1983), pp. 185, 199–200.
12. Some firms that have traditionally used push strategies are moving to mixed push-pull strategies using sporting events as the means to communicate with target customers. For example, DuPont's automotive finishes business sponsors a NASCAR driver. Consumers are typically unaware of specific brands of automotive finishes, but because of the popularity of automotive racing, awareness of and preference for DuPont's automotive paints has been increasing.
13. Venkatesh Shankar and Ruth N. Bolton, "Dimensions and Determinants of Retailer Pricing Strategy and Tactics," Working Paper Report No. 99–101, Marketing Science Institute, Cambridge, MA.
14. Retailers often use a productivity measure to represent an item's mar-

gin: margin dollars per square foot of retail space. This measure incorporates the margin component as well as measuring a "return" on the retailer's fixed asset: store space.

15. Larry Terry, "Sellers Rattled by Low-ball Ethylene Deal On-Line," *Chemical Week,* January 19, 2000, p. 13.

16. Douglas A. Blackman, "Selling Motors to Mops, Unglamorous Grainger Is a Web-Sales Star," *Wall Street Journal,* December 13, 1999, p. 22.

17. www.findmro.com/about_us.jsp

18. "Whirlpool & Maytag Nix Discounts on High-End Items," www.consumeraffairs. com/homeowners/appliances.htm. May 19, 2000.

CHAPTER

12

Competitive Advantages

Establishing Foundations for More Profitable Pricing

Previous chapters discussed differences among firms that affect the profitability of different pricing strategies. When discussing costs, we saw how a firm could profit despite relatively low prices because the product represented incremental business that did not need to cover nonincremental fixed costs. When discussing price sensitivity, we saw how the unique value effect of distinctive product attributes could induce buyers to pay a price premium. When discussing competition, we saw how a low-cost position could enable a company to pursue opportunistic pricing. We also saw how a product with attributes uniquely appealing to some market segment could facilitate skim pricing, whereas a product that could be produced at lower cost than competing products could facilitate penetration pricing. These differences among companies, enabling some to implement profitable pricing strategies that others cannot employ, are those companies' competitive advantages. They determine just how profitable even the most effective pricing strategy can be.

Effective pricing fully exploits a product's competitive advantages. Although fraudulent or deceptive pricing may enable an unscrupulous company to profit for a short time, sustainable profits are possible only so long as a company can serve at least one segment of buyers better and/or cheaper than its competitors. There are two types of competitive advantages that can ensure profit in even a highly competitive environment: those that produce lower costs and those that produce a differentiated product offering.

A firm that can produce an equal-quality product at lower cost can profit by capturing sales through opportunistic pricing. Later, it can maintain sales as a cooperative price leader or, occasionally, as a predatory enforcer. As long as a company can sustain its cost advantage, its profits are protected by its competitors' inability to profit by undercutting those prices. A differentiated product offering enables a company to profit as long as the cost of producing that differentiation does not exceed what buyers are willing to pay. The company can sustain profitability in a competitive environment as long as the price does not exceed the value of the product's differentiation. This chapter explains how companies develop the cost and product advantages that provide the foundation for a profitable pricing strategy.[1]

COMPETITIVE COST ADVANTAGES

Controlling costs is an ongoing activity in any successful company. It must be a continuing process because everyone involved with the company has a vested interest in seeing certain costs go up. Employees would like to see their departments increase in personnel or their expense accounts receive less scrutiny. Suppliers think that their service justifies a slightly higher price and that buyers should be more accommodating about scheduling deliveries and holding inventories. Fortunately, even though some employees or suppliers may want the company to let some particular cost rise, they realize that if the company concedes to all such desires, its viability would be threatened. Consequently, cost control is accepted as long as it is perceived that denial is suffered equitably.

It is rare, however, that cost control alone can generate competitive cost advantages for very long. Although tightfistedness might produce a temporary cost advantage, the advantage will soon be lost due to decreases in employee morale and supplier goodwill or to imitation by competitors. Sustainable cost advantages are realized not by constant belt tightening, but by the efficient use of resources.

Internal Cost Efficiencies

There are three different ways that a company can reduce its unit costs through the efficient organization of its internal operations: exploitation of economies of scope, scale, and experience.

1. Economies of Scope

Scope refers to the breadth of a firm's product portfolio. Many firms sell multiple products. The goal of product planning is to compile a synergistic portfolio of products. One important source of synergy, receiving growing attention among marketing practitioners, is the economies that result when different products share a common set of costs. A firm that carefully selects the scope of its product portfolio to maximize shared costs can cut its incremental costs below those of competitors with less efficient portfolios.[2]

Consider, for example, the economies of scope that service stations such as Mobil and Arco gain through their on-site mini-marts. This shared-cost strategy was pioneered by 7-Eleven during the mid-1970s in response to consumers' increased price sensitivity at the pumps. Adding a small convenience store on existing property requires no more labor or rent than operating the service station alone. The same cashier who rings up gasoline sales can ring up sales of beverages, junk food, and cigarettes. Therefore, labor costs—as well as some lesser costs for land, building, and utilities—are not incremental to ancillary sales.[3]

Airlines have captured similar advantages by diversifying into products that share costs. United Airlines trains flight crews for the military, and Delta Airlines services planes for smaller competitors—and both airlines use employees and facilities already established to serve their own needs. American Airlines has also been creative. It established a subsidiary—American Airlines Telemarketing Services—that shares the cost of its telephone reservations system. American contracts to do telephone sales, surveys, fund-raising, and other telemarketing activities at nonpeak hours, when the airline's phones and operators would be otherwise underutilized. American's rates are both highly competitive and profitable because the incremental cost of providing the service is so low.[4]

Developing a new product that can share current costs is more difficult than selecting from products that already exist. Dun & Bradstreet was very successful in developing a new product to generate incremental revenue from its costly credit report database. It learned the types and quantities of products particular companies sought from the credit requests they received about them. It recognized that this information would be valuable to other potential suppliers of those companies. Thus was born a new product, called Dun's Market Identifiers, which shared all the same research but served an entirely different need.

The trick to exploiting economies of scope is to find products that share a common set of costs. The more costs that the products can share the greater the synergy from expanding the scope of a product portfolio. Economies of scope are sometimes limited by a loss in employee efficiency when a firm becomes less specialized, but they are usually limited only by management's entrepreneurial ability to identify products that could share a common set of costs.

2. Economies of Scale

Scale refers to the size of a firm as measured by its long-run, sustainable rate of output. In almost every activity, from purchasing to manufacturing to promotion and distribution, costs tend to decline as output increases. The reasons for economies of scale are numerous:

- A larger scale enables individual employees to work on more highly specialized tasks, increasing their proficiency and reducing the time lost changing tasks.
- Incremental fixed costs, such as those involved in product design, are lower per unit when they can be spread over more units.
- More efficient production processes (for example, assembly lines) are practical only when employed on a large scale.
- Larger sizes of capital equipment can often be built for less than a proportional increase in cost.[5]

Examples of scale economies abound. The British Textile Council noted that output per employee leaped 167 percent when the average run of rayon cloth increased from 3,800 to 31,000 yards. The council's explanation was as follows:

> When staff at all levels can concentrate on the production of a very limited number of products, the smallest details can receive attention and be brought to near perfection ... which would be wildly uneconomic in normal circumstances [but] can be justified if the volume of production is sufficiently great.[6]

Another notable example of scale economies is the automobile industry, where unit output and profitability are consistently correlated. The huge fixed costs in that industry yield a significant advantage to any company that can spread those costs over more units.[7]

Two distinct aspects of scale economies need to be distinguished when formulating pricing strategy: size and extent. These two aspects of scale economies are illustrated graphically in Exhibits 12-1 and 12-2. The *size* of scale economies refers to the percentage difference in unit cost between a small- and large-scale firm. The *extent* of scale economies refers to the minimum market share required to become the low-cost producer. Exhibit 12-3, adapted from a study of twelve American industries, shows scale economies of various sizes and extents. Note that although the size of scale economies for Portland cement is overwhelming, it can be fully exploited with a market share of only 1.7 percent. In contrast, the size of scale economies in refrigerators is only one-fourth that for cement, but the market share necessary to fully exploit these economies is a rather large 14.1 percent.[8]

EXHIBIT 12-1 Scale Economies of Different Size

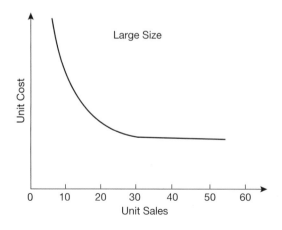

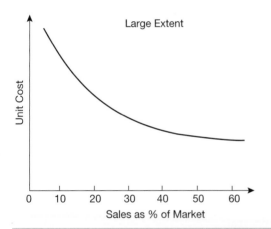

EXHIBIT 12-2 Scale Economies of Different Extent

Unexploited economies of scale offer a risky but potentially rewarding opportunity to establish and maintain a competitive cost advantage. In 1903, Henry Ford recognized that no one had yet fully exploited the scale economies from mass production of automobiles. He showed that by producing on a much larger scale he could profitably sell cars at prices far below his competitors' costs. The strategy involved substantial risk, however, since it depended on a managerial analysis of price sensitivity that could not be tested before going into production. Ford risked a fortune on his belief that tens of thousands of people would buy his standardized black Model T's, lured by the lower price that economies of scale would permit him to charge. If Ford's guess about the number of price-sensitive buyers had been wrong, he could not have achieved the large volumes, and therefore the low unit costs, that enabled him to profit despite the low price that his standardized product could command. Such a

Industry	Minimum Efficient Scale	%Cost Disadvantage of Small Scale Operation*	% Market Share Required to Fully Exploit Economies
Beer brewing	4.5 million (31 U.S. gallon) barrels per year capacity	5.0	3.5
Cigarettes	36 billion cigarettes per year; 2,275 employees	2.2	6.6
Cotton and synthetic broad-woven fabrics	37.5 million square yards per year; 600 employees in modern integrated plants	7.6	0.2
Paints	10 million U.S. gallons per year; 450 employees	4.4	1.4
Petroleum refining	200,000 (42 U.S. gallon) barrels per day crude oil processing capacity	4.8	1.9
Nonrubber shoes	1 million pairs per year; 250 employees on single shift operation	1.5	0.2
Glass bottles	133,000 short tons per year; 1,000 employees	11.0	1.5
Portland cement	7 million (367 pound) barrels per year capacity	26.0	1.7
Integrated steel	4 million short tons per year capacity	11.0	1.6
Antifriction bearings	800 employees	8.0	1.4
Refrigerators	800,000 units per year	6.5	14.1
Automobile storage batteries	1 million units per year; 300 employees	4.6	1.9

*Assumes operation at one-third minimum efficient scale.

EXHIBIT 12-3 Estimated Values of the Minimum Efficient Scale

Source: Reprinted by permission of the publishers from *The Economics of Multi-Plant Operation: An International Comparisons Study* by Frederic M. Scherer, Alan Beckenstein, Erich Kaufer, Dennis R. Murphy, and Francine Bougeon-Massen, Cambridge, MA: Harvard University Press, Copyright © 1975 by the President and Fellows of Harvard College.

guess is not always profitable, as Texas Instruments learned in 1983 after it cut the price of its home computer in a grab for increased scale economies. Unfortunately, during the innovation stage, the home computer market proved insufficiently price sensitive to produce the volumes required. The resulting losses for Texas Instruments forced its ultimate withdrawal from the market. In sharp contrast, increased demand, together with heightened price sensitivity associated with the movement from growth into maturity, have provided the market conditions required to fuel Compaq's move to become the low-cost producer in the home computer market of the mid-1990s.

Cost advantages from scale economies are often particularly attractive because, under the right conditions, they can be sustained indefinitely. The key to sustaining scale economies is *limit-entry pricing*. A limit-entry price is one set low enough to discourage new entrants and smaller competitors from duplicating the company's cost advantage. Whether such pricing makes sense depends upon how low one must go to discourage competition. That depends on the size and extent of the scale economies. Once established companies have achieved scale economies of large size, a new entrant can be cost competitive only if it can quickly gain enough sales volume to also operate at an efficient scale. A new firm cannot afford to let the market gradually learn about its product if a low scale of production forces it to bear significantly higher unit costs. Consequently, where scale economies create a significant cost disadvantage for firms with a small share of a market, new entrants must promote aggressively in order to grow quickly. The higher start-up costs of plant operation and promotion at a small scale provide some degree of competitive protection for companies with an established cost advantage.

The value of such an advantage depends not just on the size of scale economies but also on their extent.[9] If a single company must have more than half of a potential market to achieve the low costs of scale economies, the first company to achieve that scale should be able to limit entry even with a high price. A new entrant would have to price low enough to bring forth all remaining market potential, and to take some sales from the established firm as well, before it could achieve the same scale economies as the established firm. Such a marketing effort would no doubt involve large promotional expenditures and a substantial period of operation at less than efficient scale. On the other hand, if economies of scale are of limited extent, enabling a single company to achieve low costs with only 5 percent of the market, an established firm will be forced to set a very low limit-entry price before it could convince a new entrant not to compete. A new entrant might reasonably believe that it could capture 5 percent of a market quickly and cheaply.[10]

In some markets, frequent technological change by a large-scale producer increases the extent of market share required by a new entrant, thus raising the limit price that the large-scale producer can charge without inviting entry. For example, Intel frequently changes the technology of its microprocessor chips as part of a continuing effort to improve speed and performance. Given Intel's large share, it can recapture the additional fixed investment rather quickly. Its small-share competitors, however, require more time to recapture their fixed investments. The more frequently Intel changes its technology, the greater the minimum share required to recapture fixed investments between each change. Some firms have been accused of withholding new technologies until after competitors have made large investments in old ones.

Economies of scale are often a good source of cost savings and an effective competitive deterrent, but there is a downside risk. Management must be careful when attempting to exploit economies of scale by adopting more capital-intensive techniques. Usually those same techniques not only lower the cost of production when operating at full capacity but also raise the cost of operating far below capacity. In highly cyclical industries (for example, steel, construction, automobiles), the scale economies that some technologies produce at high volumes can be more than overwhelmed by the diseconomies they produce if a recession forces the company to contract.

3. Economies of Experience

Experience economies are reductions in cost that come with increases in the accumulated volume of output, as distinguished from scale economies that depend upon the current volume of output. An old firm and a new one may have an equal volume of output in a certain year, each enjoying the same economies of scale. The older firm, having accumulated more volume from past years of operation, may enjoy lower costs due to greater economies of experience. Experience-cost economies result from learning by doing: The more a company produces, the more it learns how to do so efficiently. For example, in one early study of airplane assembly, the second plane produced took approximately 4,000 labor hours, but the eighth took only 2,600 hours due to learning on the part of employees.

Experience-cost economies do not continually accrue at such a rapid rate. As volume accumulates, costs decline at a decreasing rate, as illustrated by the experience curve shown in Exhibit 12-4. Fortunately, the decrease is surprisingly predictable. In most cases, experience economies generate an equal percentage reduction in unit cost for each doubling of accumulated volume. Thus, if costs decline by 20 percent when accumulated volume increases from 10 to 20 units, they will decline by another 20 percent when volume increases from 20 to 40 units, and decline by the same percentage when volume increases from 40 to 80, 80 to 160, 160 to 320, 320 to 640, and so on.[11]

The existence in manufacturing industries of an experience curve for labor (called a *learning curve*) had been observed by engineers and economists since at least the 1950s.[12] The idea, however, did not begin to influence marketing strategy until further developed and promoted by the Boston Consulting Group (BCG).[13] BCG argued that experience-cost economies affect not just labor costs but also capital, administration, research, and marketing costs. BCG consultants argued that experience effects are not limited to high-technology manufacturing but apply as well to services and simple consumables (for example, margarine and beer).

More important, BCG asserted that experience effects call for an entirely new and daring pricing strategy to establish a sustainable cost advantage. The typical strategy of passively following experience-cost declines with price reductions fails to recognize the opportunities that experience effects engender. A company enjoying experience effects should project its future cost declines

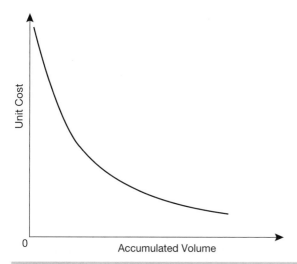

EXHIBIT 12-4 A Typical Experience Curve

and cut its prices in anticipation of those declines, even though such prices may not cover current production costs. Such pricing on the experience curve will enable a company to capture a dominant market share, increase its accumulated volume, and reduce its costs more rapidly than competitors. Moreover, once a company establishes a significant experience-cost advantage over its less quick-footed rivals, it can use that advantage to meet any competitive price, thus maintaining its volume lead and sustaining the advantage indefinitely.

To support its claim that experience effects are of overwhelming and universal importance in pricing, BCG marshalled considerable evidence that costs or prices decline as industries accumulate volume and that firms with dominant market shares are more profitable than their smaller competitors. They were able to cite the notable success of an early client, Texas Instruments, which used pricing on the experience curve to grow rapidly and profitably throughout the 1960s and 1970s. Soon experience curves became somewhat of a fad, touted by most consultants and adopted widely in practice.[14] Like most fads, however, the strategy was often oversold and frequently misused.

The safe and effective use of experience-curve pricing requires thoughtful analysis and judicious application, lest one buy market share with low prices but never collect the future cost savings and anticipated profits. Pricing on the experience curve can be quite profitable under some circumstances, but can fail to pay off for any of the following reasons:

- *Buyers may not be sufficiently price sensitive.* The most damning argument against experience-curve pricing is the notable success of many high-priced firms. Caterpillar dominated the earth-moving equipment market, not by cutting price to buy market share but by supplying services. It is highly unlikely that its competitors could have changed history by cutting their prices more diligently. Buyers whose businesses depend on the reliability, service, and support of earth-moving equipment are just not sufficiently price sensitive for such a strategy to work. Instead, they must be courted with service, even if the service requires a premium price. Unless buyers are primarily price sensitive, pricing on the experience curve will not buy a firm enough additional volume to justify the price reductions.

• *Value added may be too small to justify price-cutting.* Even if buyers are fairly price sensitive and experience effects are large, a firm may still be unable to cut price adequately if its value added is only a small share of the price. Experience economies apply only to costs resulting from a firm's own production processes, not to costs accounted for by raw materials purchased externally. Thus a firm whose gross margin (value added) accounts for just 20 percent of the product's final price must expect a 25 percent reduction in operating costs to justify even a 5 percent reduction in price. Even with large experience effects, such a price cut does not usually generate the required volume to produce an equal reduction in cost.

• *Competitors may not be cooperative.* Pricing on the experience curve to achieve a dominant share assumes that one's competitors will allow it to happen. Before the idea of experience curves became widely known, competitors may have thought that any firm that cut its price below cost would not stay in business very long. Now more knowledgeable competitors, realizing the risk of falling behind in the race for volume, may meet every price cut to maintain their shares. If they do, a battle for market share may ensue from which all firms will emerge as losers.

• *Experience may not be proprietary.* Even when the knowledge gained from accumulated volume lowers one's costs, it will not increase one's profits unless that knowledge can be kept confidential. Otherwise, competitors will also learn how to quickly drive prices down to reflect the cost savings, leaving no reward for the experience-curve pricer. For example, if the knowledge gained from accumulated volume is a cost-saving change in product design, competitors will learn about it as soon as the new design reaches the market. When the knowledge involves a cost-saving production process, competitors have ways of finding out about it. In highly competitive, high-technology markets, companies often hire competitors' key employees to learn of technological advances, and occasionally even resort to espionage to steal competitors' proprietary information. Consequently, unless cost-saving information is known by only a few trusted employees, is patentable, or requires a long lead time to copy, competition may keep the cost savings from ever being converted into profits.

• *Experience may be shared among products.* Cost savings do not actually result from the accumulation of production experience with a product, but rather with a production activity. If many products involve the same production activity, then being the market-share leader in only one of them may not ensure a cost advantage. Apple clearly got a volume jump on all competitors in the personal computer market, but it would have been suicidal for Apple to price on the experience curve. The activities involved in producing personal computers are the same as those involved in producing many other high-technology, microprocessor-based products. Before Apple's competitors had ever sold a personal computer, many had accumulated experience in the necessary production activities to enter with equally low costs.

• *Experience may not be caused by total production volume.* Perhaps the most dangerous misconception of pricing on the experience curve is the idea that accumulated volume causes cost declines when, in fact, the accumulated volume may simply be correlated with cost changes that have another cause. Consider, for example, a company that in past years consistently cut its costs by 15 percent with each doubling of volume. If it continued at its present production rate, it would double its volume again over the next year, cutting its costs again by 15 percent. What happens if this company slashes its prices, thus doubling its sales rate, in order to double its accumulated volume in just six months? The answer, according to advocates of experience-curve pricing, is that 15 percent cost reduction will be reached six months sooner. But will it? It will only if production volume is really the cause of experience-cost savings. What if the cause of cost savings is the experience of a firm's R&D department, which in the past coincidentally accumulated research insights at about the same rate that the company accumulated production volume? Then doubling the production rate through price-cutting without doubling the research budget would cut in half the anticipated cost savings to just 7.5 percent. Or what if the cause of cost savings is the skill that individual production employees accumulate over time? Then doubling the production rate through price-cutting would actually increase unit costs because the firm would have to hire new, inexperienced employees to run a second shift or staff a second production facility.

Clearly, it is not enough to know that one has experience effects; one must also know their cause in order to develop appropriate strategy to exploit them. Sometimes price-cutting to build volume more rapidly will produce a sustainable cost advantage, but not always. The firm whose cost economies come from R&D would do better maintaining its price and doubling its research budget than it would cutting its price and doubling its production rate. The firm whose cost economies come from the experience accumulated by individual employees would do better investing in fringe benefits that reduce employee turnover than it would investing in price cuts to buy market share.

Finally, even when experience effects exist, they are not always worth considering. In mature industries, where firms have already accumulated substantial volume, the rate of cost decline becomes so slow as to become irrelevant. In industries facing the prospect of radical technological change, there is little value in fighting to become the volume leader in a technology that will soon become obsolete. Pricing on the experience curve can be a successful strategy for achieving a cost advantage in some cases, but it is not the universal key to profitable pricing that it was once promoted to be.

External Cost Efficiencies

In addition to internal cost efficiencies, a company can also gain a cost advantage through the careful selection and management of its external relations with customers and suppliers. It can do so by organizing its marketing activities to exploit economies of focus and its purchasing activities to exploit economies of integration.

Economies of Buyer Focus

A company can often gain significant economies by focusing its marketing on one or two products or market segments. One obvious savings is in promotion and selling costs. For example, some suppliers to the automobile industry have essentially no specialized sales forces; their management negotiates annual contracts with as few as one automobile company for all of their sales. This close working relationship gives them not only lower selling costs, but also a better understanding of how to meet their customers' needs.

Exploiting economies of focus is often essential for the small company whose larger rivals are in a position to exploit and sustain cost advantages from greater scope, scale, or experience. The success of Crown Cork & Seal's focus strategy illustrates the point.[15] After years of unsuccessfully competing with larger rivals, Crown recognized an opportunity to achieve cost advantages of focus equal to or greater than the economies of scope, scale, and experience that its rivals enjoyed. It withdrew from a wide variety of packaging markets and focused all of its resources on two segments: cans for hard-to-hold beverages (soda and beer) and aerosol cans.

Crown's focus enabled it to reduce costs and to service its buyers better in the process. By concentrating on a limited market, it developed product improvements (pull tops and two-piece cans) that were highly valued by its customers. Crown built highly efficient production facilities, optimally designed to produce narrow product lines.[16] By locating plants in highly concentrated markets, it reduced transportation costs while providing quicker and more reliable service for its customers. Crown remained a small company compared with its rivals, but Crown's economies of focus produced a return on sales that substantially exceeded the return of its larger, more diversified rivals.

Focus is not always a strategy for companies with small market share. The size and growth of a focused company are limited only by the size and growth of its targeted market. If that segment grows quickly, the targeted company enjoys the inside track to grow with it. In its earliest years, McDonald's was among the most focused of all restaurant chains. The key to the company's early success was mastery of a very limited product line (primarily hamburgers and fries) to serve a very specific segment (suburban families). With such a narrow focus, McDonald's was able to master every detail of the business, perfecting every item (even a special potato for its french fries) and developing a formula for achieving such quality at minimum cost. Since McDonald's was meeting the needs of a rapidly growing market segment, its own rapid growth proved quite consistent with focused marketing. Only later, as the growth of suburban families slowed and competition for the hamburger-and-fries segment intensified, did McDonald's broaden its focus to sustain its own growth.

Focus is a strategy that can produce both low costs and a sound basis for product differentiation, although it does entail the risk of tying one's fortunes to a single market. The Pullman company, for example, profited handsomely from its focus on serving rail passengers, but suffered when its only market was devastated by the development of air travel and interstate highways. The risk of focus is one that a small competitor must bear when it competes with larger rivals that enjoy cost advantages from diversity, size, and accumulated knowledge.

Economies of Logistical Integration

Many companies develop supporting infrastructure in order to gain competitive advantages in sales, operational efficiencies, and operating costs. Companies can achieve these goals by developing internal infrastructure within their own business units or by developing an external infrastructure that facilitates the supplier and distributor relationships.[17] Improved coordination of deliveries can minimize the cost of inventories, better coordination of specifications can minimize the need for further fabrication of a supplier's product, and better coordination of the pricing decision itself can make a company and its suppliers more price competitive and more profitable. Wal-Mart, for example, has lower inventory costs per sale than any other bricks and mortar retailer. It achieves that feat by a system that ties all sales in all stores into a centralized inventory management system. Using that system, the company can quickly redirect excess inventory from one location to another where it is selling well.[18]

International catalog and Internet retailer Land's End relies on a supportive infrastructure that allows it to process 30 percent of its annual orders during the peak holiday months of November and December. In order to support this rash of purchases, Land's End increases its work force by 50 percent, relying largely on busloads of students from nearby colleges. Another advance, not particular to Land's End, is batch picking, which became popular with the barcode scanner. This innovation permits an employee to increase his or her hourly output ninefold, thereby reducing costs and increasing output capabilities (and therefore the company's potential revenues). Prior to batch picking, if there were a 20 percent increase in the number of orders, 20 percent more employees would have to do the picking. With batch picking, Land's End has the ability to grow larger, and to scale up during peak months, without a proportionate increase in employees. Thus Land's End enjoys a competitive advantage over large retailers that lack such a system and smaller rivals that lack the scale to duplicate it.

By creating a net of infrastructural advantages, both internal and external, a company can develop an almost inimitable operational advantage. Dell,[19] considered by many to be a company born of the Internet, actually developed a set of infrastructure advantages that would have propelled it to the top of the personal computer market even without the World Wide Web. One of Dell's major goals was to convert inputs to cash in as short a time period as possible.

To meet this goal, Dell created external infrastructures within the supply and delivery chains, and internal infrastructure with just-in-time (JIT) manufacturing and payment requirements. Dell requires almost all of the components used in its products to be warehoused only fifteen minutes from the factory. Once the product is manufactured, Dell advises UPS what monitor type it needs and UPS picks the monitor from the supplier's stock and ships it to the customer in sync with the shipment of the assembled Dell computer. In an industry where ongoing technological and price declines make holding inventory very costly, this system gives Dell a huge cost advantage.

Internally, Dell developed a JIT process that does not begin assembly (or even parts purchase for that matter) until the order has been placed. At the collection end of the sales process, Dell ensures speed by only accepting electronic or credit card payment. Doing so, Dell can typically convert a sale to cash in less than twenty-four hours. By creating this web of infrastructural capabilities, Dell rose quickly and virtually unchallenged in the PC industry, gaining the number-one position worldwide in 1999 for revenue and market share. This web of logistical efficiencies puts any competitors who cannot immediately duplicate it at a serious cost disadvantage, undermining their ability to compete with Dell on price.

The greatest logistical advantages have come from changing the product itself to facilitate efficient distribution. Most automobile manufacturers hold down inventory costs by offering standardized option packages, a strategy pioneered by the Japanese. In the early 1990s Apple reduced its costs similarly by streamlining its Macintosh product line from six families down to four. Later in the decade it pared its product line even further to the iMac low-end personal computer, a high-speed desktop model, and a laptop model. One supplier of telephones redesigned its product to maintain product variety without bearing the corresponding cost of inventories. The company has standardized the internal mechanisms of its various telephones and ships them to retailers without the outer shells that distinguish styles. The retailers then attach covers to the internal assemblies as needed. This distribution method enabled the company to reduce inventories of internal mechanisms for itself and for its retailers without reducing the number of styles it offers.[20] Wal-Mart is the acknowledged leader in leveraging the economies of logistical integration. Its mastery of distribution and inventory management from raw materials to point of sale has enabled it to decrease costs while increasing profit margins.

Efficiency in Transfer Pricing

All the companies in a chain of production—the suppliers of raw materials, those who make parts, those who do assembly, and those who market the product to the final purchaser—benefit when the entire chain operates efficiently. Inefficient operation by any one member of the chain drives up the price to the end purchaser, thus reducing sales for all the members. Unfortunately, one of the most frequently unrecognized and generally misunderstood sources of inef-

	Current Price, Costs, Sales	*10% Price Cut, 30% Sales Increase*	*Change*
Independent Manufacturing Inc.			
Current unit sales	1,000,000	1,300,00	
Price	$2.00	$1.80	
Variable materials cost	$1.20	$1.20	
Variable labor cost	$0.20	$0.20	
Fixed cost	$0.40	$0.31	
Contribution margin	$0.60	$0.40	
% CM	30%	22%	
Annual pretax profit	$200,000	$120,000	($80,000)
Alpha Parts Inc.			
Current unit sales	1,000,000	1,300,000	
Price	$0.30	$0.30	
Variable cost	$0.05	$0.05	
Fixed cost	$0.20	$0.15	
Contribution margin	$0.25	$0.25	
Annual pretax profit	$50,000	$125,000	$75,000
Beta Parts Inc.			
Current unit sales	1,000,000	1,300,000	
Price	$0.90	$0.90	
Variable cost	$0.35	$0.35	
Fixed cost	$0.40	$0.31	
Contribution margin	$0.55	$0.55	
Annual pretax profit	$150,000	$315,000	$165,000

EXHIBIT 12-5 Inefficiencies in Transfer Pricing

ficiency involves the way independent companies and independent divisions of the same company set the prices of products that pass between them. This problem, known as *transfer pricing,* represents one of the most common reasons why independent companies and divisions are sometimes less price competitive and profitable than their vertically integrated competitors.

Exhibit 12-5 illustrates this often-overlooked opportunity. Independent Manufacturing Inc. sells its product for $2 per unit in a highly competitive market. To manufacture the product, it buys different parts from two suppliers, Alpha and Beta, at a total cost per unit of $1.20. The parts purchased from Alpha cost $0.30 and those from Beta cost $0.90.

Independent Manufacturing conducts a pricing analysis to determine whether any changes in its pricing might be justified. It determines that its contribution margin (price − variable cost) is $0.60, or 30 percent of its price.[21] It then calculates the effect of a 10 percent price change in either direction. For a

10 percent price cut to be profitable, Independent must gain at least 50 percent more sales:

$$\frac{0.10}{0.30 - 0.10} = 50\%$$

For a 10 percent price increase to be profitable, Independent can afford to forgo no more than 25 percent of its sales:

$$\frac{-0.10}{0.30 + 0.10} = -25\%$$

Independent's managers conclude that there is no way that they can possibly gain from a price cut, since their sales will surely not increase by more than 50 percent. On the other hand, they are intrigued by the possibility of a price increase. They feel sure that the inevitable decline would be far less than 25 percent if they could get their major competitors to follow them in the increase.

As Independent's management considers how to communicate to the industry the desirability of a general price increase, one of its major competitors, Integrated Manufacturing Inc. announces its own 10 percent price cut. Independent's management is stunned. How could Integrated possibly justify such a move? Integrated's product is technically identical to Independent's, involving all the same parts and production processes, and Integrated is a company with a market share equal to Independent's. The only difference between the two companies is that Integrated recently began manufacturing its own parts.

That difference, however, is crucial to this story (see Exhibit 12-6). Assume that Integrated currently has all the same costs of producing parts as Independent's suppliers, Alpha and Beta, and expects to earn a profit from those operations. It also has the same costs of assembling those parts ($0.20 incremental labor plus $0.40 fixed per unit). Moreover, Integrated enjoys no additional economies of logistical integration. Despite these similarities, the two companies have radically different cost structures, which respond quite differently to changes in volume and which cause the two companies to evaluate price changes quite differently. Integrated has no variable materials cost corresponding to Independent's variable materials cost of $1.20 per unit. Instead, it incurs additional fixed costs of $0.60 per unit ($0.20 + $0.40) and incremental variable costs of only $0.40 per unit ($0.05 + $0.35). This difference in cost structure between Integrated (high fixed and low variable) and Independent (low fixed and high variable) gives Integrated a much higher contribution margin per unit than Independent's margin. For Integrated, $1.40, or 70 percent of each additional sale, contributes to bottom-line profits. For Independent, only $0.60, or 30 percent of each additional sale, falls to the bottom line. Integrated's breakeven calculations for a 10 percent price change are, therefore, quite different. For a 10 percent price cut to be profitable, Integrated has to gain only 16.7 percent more sales:

	Current Price, Costs, Sales	*10% Price Cut, 30% Sales Increase*	*Change*
Integrated Manufacturing Inc.			
Current unit sales	1,000,000	1,300,000	
Price	$2.00	$1.80	
Variable materials cost	None	None	
Variable labor cost	$0.60	$0.60	
($0.20 + $0.05 + $0.35)			
Fixed cost	$1.00	$0.77	
($0.40 + $0.20 + $0.40)			
Contribution margin	$1.40	$1.20	
%	70%	67%	
Annual pretax profit	$400,000	$560,000	$160,000

EXHIBIT 12-6 Efficiency from Cost Integration

$$\frac{0.10}{0.70 - 0.10} = 16.7\%$$

But for a 10 percent price increase to pay off, Integrated could afford to forgo no more than 12.5 percent of its sales:

$$\frac{-0.10}{0.70 + 0.10} = -12.5\%$$

It is easy to see why Integrated is more attracted to price cuts and more averse to price increases than is Independent. For Integrated, sales must grow by only 16.7 percent to make a price cut profitable, compared with 50 percent for Independent. Similarly, Integrated could afford to lose no more than 12.5 percent of sales (compared with as much as 25 percent for Independent) and still profit from a price increase. How can it be that two identical sets of costs result in such extremely different calculations? The answer is that Independent, like most manufacturers, pays its suppliers on a price-per-unit basis. That price must include enough revenue to cover the suppliers' fixed costs and a reasonable profit if Independent expects those suppliers to remain viable in the long run. Consequently, fixed costs and profit of both Alpha and Beta become variable costs of sales for Independent. Such incrementalizing of nonincremental costs makes Independent much less cost competitive than Integrated, which earns more than twice as much additional profit on each unit it sells.

Independent's cost disadvantage is a disadvantage to its suppliers as well. Independent calculates that it requires a 50 percent sales increase to make a 10 percent price cut profitable. Independent, therefore, correctly rejects a 10 percent price cut that would increase sales by 30 percent. With current sales of 1 million units, such a price cut would cause Independent's profit to decline by $80,000. Note, however, that the additional sales volume would add $240,000 ($75,000 + $165,000) to the profits of Independent's suppliers, provided that they produce the increased output with no more fixed costs. They would earn much more than Independent would lose by cutting price. It is clear why Integrated sees a 10 percent price cut as profitable when Independent does not. As its own supplier, Integrated captures the additional profits that accrue within the entire value chain (Alpha, $75,000; Beta, $165,000) as a result of increases in volume.[22]

Once Independent recognizes the problem, what alternatives does it have, short of taking the radical step of merging with its suppliers? One alternative is for Independent to pay its suppliers' fixed costs in a lump-sum payment, perhaps even retaining ownership of the assets while negotiating low supply prices that cover only incremental costs and a reasonable return. The lump-sum payment is then a fixed cost for Independent, and its contribution margin on added sales rises by the reduction in its incremental supply cost. General Motors does this with auto parts suppliers, bearing the fixed cost of a part's design and paying the supplier for all fixed costs of retooling and set up. Similarly, World Book buys and owns the presses that R. R. Donnelley & Sons use to print World Book's encyclopedias. In these cases, the negotiated price per unit need cover only the supplier's variable costs and profit. As a result, General Motors and World Book earn more on each additional sale and so have a greater incentive to make marketing decisions, including pricing decisions, that build volume.

A second alternative is to negotiate a high price for initial purchases that cover the fixed costs, with a lower price for all additional quantities that cover only incremental costs and profit. Sears sometimes uses this system with suppliers of its house-brand products. Since the lower supply price is the incremental cost of additional sales, Sears can profitably price its products lower to generate more volume. In Independent Manufacturing's case, it might negotiate an agreement with Alpha and Beta that guarantees enough purchases at $0.30 and $0.90, respectively, to cover their fixed costs, after which the price would fall to $0.10 and $0.50, respectively.

Both of these systems for paying suppliers avoid incrementalizing fixed costs, but they do not avoid the problem of incrementalizing the suppliers' profits. They work well only when the suppliers' profits account for a small portion of the total price suppliers receive. Lump-sum payments could be paid to suppliers to cover negotiated profit as well as fixed costs. This is risky, however, since profit per unit remains the suppliers' incentive to maintain on-time delivery of acceptable quality merchandise. Consequently, when a supplier has low fixed costs but can still demand a high profit because of little competition, a third alternative is often used. The purchaser may agree to pay the supplier a small fee to cover incremental expenses and an additional negotiated percentage of whatever profit contribution is earned from final sales.

It is noteworthy that most companies do not use these methods to compensate suppliers or to establish prices for sales between independent divisions. Instead, they negotiate arm's-length contracts at fixed prices or let prevailing market prices determine transfer prices. One reason is that it is unusual to find a significant portion of costs that remain truly fixed for large changes in sales. In most cases, the bulk of costs that accountants label fixed are actually semifixed; additional costs would have to be incurred for suppliers to substantially increase their sales, making those costs incremental. One notable case where costs are substantially fixed is in the semiconductor industry. The overwhelming cost of semiconductors is the fixed cost of product development, not the variable or semifixed costs of production. Consequently, integrated manufacturers of products using semiconductors have often had a significant cost advantage. Bowmar, the company that pioneered the handheld calculator, was ultimately driven from the market precisely because it was not cost competitive with more integrated suppliers and failed to negotiate contracts that avoided the incrementalization of their fixed costs of product development.

Companies that buy computer software to sell as part of their products should note that software, too, is a high fixed-cost product that often represents a substantial portion of the cost of computer-aided equipment. Independent software development houses that price on a per-unit basis should note this as well. By forcing their customers to incrementalize the fixed costs and profit of software development, they will ultimately find that their buyers are not cost competitive with companies that either write their own software or that have different pricing arrangements with their suppliers.

Temporary Cost Advantages

Cost reductions from cost economies and efficiencies are the most desirable sources of cost advantage for two reasons: (1) Cost savings from economies are generally somewhat sustainable once achieved, and (2) cost savings from economies can be achieved without adversely affecting relations with employees or suppliers or undermining product quality. In fact, they often enable a company to differentiate in ways that actually increase the product's value to customers. Mobil customers may be attracted not only by its low prices but also the availability of beverages, junk food, and cigarettes in its on-site mini-marts. Crown Cork & Seal's buyers benefited as much from the quick delivery from Crown's nearby plants as Crown benefited from lower shipping costs.

Although our discussions have focused on ways of achieving sustainable cost economies, one should not underestimate the value of seeking cost reductions that are not sustainable. The benefits from one-time savings often make possible strategic moves that produce more sustainable advantages later on. The labor-cost advantage that the United Auto Workers granted Chrysler Corporation as part of its financial bailout enabled the company to price more aggressively than would otherwise have been possible. Although that advantage was eventually eliminated in later contracts, Chrysler is undoubtedly more profitable today because of that past advantage. The company now enjoys economies of scale because, in those earlier years of recovery, it could price to restore its market share and thereby prove the quality of its new line of cars.

One also must not underestimate the value of cost–quality trade-offs made with careful consideration of buyers' preferences. Some buyers simply do not value certain aspects of product differentiation enough to justify their cost and may willingly forgo some product attributes in order to get a lower price. Liggett & Myers launched its most profitable new product in decades when it introduced generic cigarettes. Some smokers eagerly gave up costly flavorings, advertised images, and fancy packaging to save a few dollars a carton. Discount airlines likewise found that a large segment of travelers would gladly forgo such amenities as meals, baggage handling, and legroom in return for lower ticket prices. Any reduction in quality that buyers willingly accept for a price reduction less than the company's cost saving is a trade-off that adds to a company's profitability and to its competitive position.

COMPETITIVE PRODUCT ADVANTAGES

When a product offers buyers nothing more than its competition, the purchase decision tends to focus on price alone. An undifferentiated product leaves the most important determinant of price sensitivity—the unique value effect—working against the seller. Unless one or more of the other determinants is very favorable (that is, buyers do not know of the substitutes, the expenditure is too small to consider, or they are locked in by complementary expenditures), the resulting price sensitivity creates the potential for intense price competition. Even if cooperation can be maintained to minimize downward pressure on prices, there is little opportunity for growth beyond the growth in total market demand. There is also the constant threat of additional entry by smaller competitors whose interests will not be consistent with cooperative pricing. The kinds of cost advantages discussed can partially shield profits from competitive price-cutting but cannot eliminate the threat itself. The key to disarming the threat is to minimize buyers' price sensitivity through differentiation.

Product Superiority

One way to achieve differentiation is through constant innovation. Some companies—Procter & Gamble, Johnson & Johnson, 3M, Du Pont, Pfizer—seem to possess an uncanny ability to maintain profitable prices by offering a constant stream of new and improved products, one step ahead of the competition. The advantages of product uniqueness are not limited to companies that can develop patentable products in costly research facilities. Even in the most mundane markets, a few companies differentiate their products in ways that enable them to achieve premium prices.

Loctite, a small company just a few years ago, has been particularly successful in making small product changes with big effects on pricing. After six weeks of interviewing product users, it reintroduced a new and improved version of its existing industrial adhesive under the name Quick Metal. Designed to keep broken equipment running until replacement parts arrive, Loctite targeted maintenance engineers who had authorization to purchase whatever they needed to repair broken equipment quickly. The new product was essentially the old one reformulated as a gel (to make it less messy) and repackaged in a tube (to make it easier to apply). Because of the high value of those simple improvements to users, Quick Metal became a runaway success in spite of a price premium of nearly 100 percent.[23]

The key to offering a differentiated product is a clear understanding of the buyers, their product needs, the support they require, and their preferred ways of purchasing. Even when product differentiation is made possible by new technologies, one must first understand buyers' problems in order to recognize how technology might solve them.

The North Face (performance clothing, equipment, and footwear), Cannondale (bicycles), and Marmot (performance outdoor products) are all examples of companies whose success is built on knowledge of the people their products serve and the problems they encounter. Almost any good company has the technical ability to develop product lines such as these companies offer, but few have the necessary understanding of the *needs* that the products are designed to satisfy. These companies cater to the unmet needs of outdoor enthusiasts. Practically everything they sell offers something that the competition does not: extra zippers for easy ventilation, Y-joint sleeves that allow arms to be raised freely without pulling up the jacket, and hoods with cutaway sides for better peripheral vision. Those additional features are worth a lot to their customers when they are facing the elements far from a warm cabin, biking 100 miles, or making an ascent up a sheer cliff.

Product Augmentation

Are some products just inherently undifferentiable? In his classic article "Marketing Success Through Differentiation—of Anything," Theodore Levitt makes a compelling case that any product can, in principle, be distinguished from the commodity mass.[24] The key is recognizing that what buyers purchase is more than just the physical product or particular service exchanged. They buy an entire package—including the ease of purchase, terms of credit, reliability of delivery, pleasantness of personal interactions, fairness in handling complaints, and so on—that is called the *augmented product*. Even when the physical product or service is immutable, the augmented product is invariably differentiable.

Consider Premier Industrial Corporation, whose maintenance division sells a variety of nuts, bolts, lubricants, welding supplies, and other products that people think of as commodities, but these products are not sold or priced as commodities by Premier. When Premier sells oil for heavy-duty truck engines, the buyer can send a sample to the company in a Premier-supplied mailing canister and get a free computer analysis that aids in engine maintenance. At the Indianapolis 500 race, Premier sets up a complete parts shop that not only builds goodwill with influential mechanics and designers, but also lets them see the quality of Premier's products under adverse conditions. What Premier does not do is cut price in this or any of its other divisions. By augmenting its common products to make them uncommon values, it does not have to.[25]

Some companies are able to charge premium prices even when their products are technically inferior because their superior augmentations overcome those deficiencies. Although WordPerfect software may not offer the seamless integration that Microsoft's products possess under Windows®, its outstanding on-line help and customer support help maintain market share in a market dominated by Microsoft Word. To find opportunities for successful augmentation, one must look beyond the obvious. As Levitt states,

> Differentiation is not limited to giving the consumer what he expects. When a securities brokerage firm includes with its customers' monthly statements a current balance sheet for each customer and an analysis of sources and disposition of funds, that firm has augmented its product beyond what was required or expected by the buyer. When a manufacturer of health and beauty aids offers warehouse management advice and training programs for the employees of its distributors, that company too has augmented its product beyond what was required or expected by the buyer.[26]

Similar augmentations have successfully differentiated fertilizer, airfreight, vinyl latex, and, more recently, financial services—all products usually thought of as inherently the same across sellers. Successful augmentations have also enhanced the inherent differences in household kitchen appliances (augmented with cooking classes and magazines), breakfast cereals (augmented with games printed on the box), and retail outlets (augmented with uniquely appealing displays or exceptional service). Given the opportunity to augment, any firm selling any product can offer buyers something extra that will limit price sensitivity or increase differentiation value. Finding that something extra is not easy. It usually requires a total commitment by the entire organization. There is much evidence that such a commitment can produce a profitable augmented product, even where the physical product is at best minimally differentiable.

Sustaining Product Advantages

Unfortunately, product advantages are sometimes short-lived. When a soap company enhances its detergent with a lemon scent, a paper company packages tissues in designer boxes, or a clothing company makes skirts in a new style, competitors imitate the successful improvements within a short time. Unless a company has a unique ability to bring forth a constant stream of such improvements, it often provides little basis for sustained profitability. Some product improvements produce competitive advantages that can be sustained; enabling a company to skim a small market indefinitely or to set prices that are high in dollar terms but are neutral or penetrating when compared with economic value. There are a number of reasons why the first company to improve its product offering may enjoy a *first-mover advantage* that is sustainable against competitive imitation.

Known Supplier

When a product's differentiation involves an attribute that consumers cannot easily observe without first buying the product (such as reliability, cleaning power, or taste), it gains a sustainable competitive advantage as the known supplier. Recall from Chapter 4 that an important determinant of interbrand price sensitivity is the buyer's ability to compare competing brands with ones already known to do the job well (the difficult comparison effect). When comparison among brands is easy, any imitator who offers even a small price discount can be attractive to a large market segment. Why pay more for what is obviously the same thing? When comparison is difficult, imitators must offer a substantial discount to induce buyers to learn that their products are comparable. Hence the first mover with a new differentiation can often sustain its position in spite of a price premium. That premium, however, can be no greater than the cost for buyers to confirm the claims of competitors.

Buyers' Investments

When a company's product requires that buyers make investments, such as in employee training or complementary products, buyers will be reluctant to switch suppliers if it means making those investments again. They will accept a price premium as long as the total premium they spend on the original brand is less than the value of sunk investments (the switching cost effect). Although Microsoft promoted the superior value of its spreadsheet and database software (Excel and Access), most users of Lotus (Lotus 1-2-3) and Borland (Dbase) products remained loyal to their older packages, giving Lotus and Borland time to incorporate the improvements. Although buyers acknowledge the improved performance of the Microsoft packages, the value of that performance did not exceed the sunken investment they made learning their old packages, nor the required investment to learn new ones.

Channel Preemption

The more brands that distributors and retailers carry, the greater their inventory, stocking, and purchasing costs. Like consumers, they will try the first brand simply because it is unique, hoping that it will attract new customers. They are reluctant, however, to carry me-too brands, unless they receive a larger margin to compensate for their trouble. That raises costs for imitators, reducing their ability to undercut the first mover's prices.

Scarce Resource Preemption

The first mover enjoys the first pick of scarce resources. As spring waters became popular, the first movers could buy or lease those springs with the best water and the easiest access. Similarly, the first pay-TV channels contracted for the best reruns, and as discount airlines began to proliferate following deregulation, the first movers got the best choices of available gates at airports.

Niche Marketing

Many products are differentiated to appeal only to a small niche in the marketplace. The product advantage of serving a niche is often sustainable because of economies of scale, even when the extent of those economies is small in relation to the total market. The market may just not be large enough to support many companies serving those same small segments.

Image

The first mover's innovativeness often gives its name a certain cachet with buyers that competitors find difficult to imitate, even when they can imitate the product itself. Because the best auto mechanics all bought Snap-on brand tools when there was no other brand of comparable quality, ownership of Snap-on tools has become a standard by which many garages now judge a mechanic's competence. Even when competitors can easily imitate a first mover's product, images are difficult to duplicate. Moreover, the imitator's lack of image cannot easily be overcome by price-cutting without further undermining buyers' perceptions of their quality (the price–quality effect). Part of what differentiates Perrier from other spring waters is precisely its image as an expensive indulgence.

SUMMARY

The techniques of effective pricing described in this book can only attempt to ensure that a company fully exploits its competitive advantages. How profitable effective pricing is depends upon the competitive advantages that a company enjoys. Competitive advantages are of two general types: cost advantages and product advantages.

Cost advantages may be either internal or external. Internal economies of scope, scale, or experience, and external economies of focus or logistical integration, enable a company to produce some products at a lower cost than the competition. The coordination of pricing with suppliers, although not actually economizing resources, can improve the efficiency of pricing by avoiding the incrementalization of a supplier's nonincremental fixed costs and profit. Any of these strategies can generate cost advantages that are, at least in the short run, sustainable. Even cost advantages that are not sustainable, however, can generate temporary savings that are often the key to building more sustainable cost or product advantages later.

Product advantages can partially insulate a company's pricing from that of its competitors. The most visible and certainly most sustainable product advantages stem from major improvements that are patentable. Some companies spend substantial sums on highly efficient research laboratories, gaining as their reward a constant stream of products that are always a step ahead of the competition. However, product advantages are not limited only to companies with substantial resources, and those of considerable value are often technically very simple. The key to finding such advantages is a clear understanding of buyers' needs. Simple changes in packaging or product design, when they meet real consumer needs, often allow companies to earn significant price premiums.

Even when a product's physical attributes are not readily differentiable, opportunities to develop product advantages remain. The augmented product that customers buy is more than the particular product or service exchanged. It includes all sorts of ancillary services and intangible relationships that make buying the same product from one company less difficult, less risky, or more pleasant than buying from a competitor. Superior augmentation of the same basic product can add substantial value in the eyes of consumers, leading them to pay willingly what are often considerable price premiums.

Unfortunately, unless product advantages are patentable, they are sometimes short-lived. Competitors can observe product advantages and quickly copy them. Imitation by competitors does not always cut short the advantages to the innovator. The first company to improve its product offering often enjoys a first-mover advantage even after other companies have copied the product innovation. This is usually the case when competing products are difficult to compare: when buyers must make sunk investments to use a particular company's product, when the innovator can preempt the best channels of distribution or a scarce resource, when the innovator serves a niche that is not large enough to support multiple competitors, or when purchasing the product generally recognized as best is important to the customer's image.

Notes

1. In *Competitive Advantage* (New York: The Free Press, 1985), Michael Porter offers a detailed procedure for analyzing a company's internal and external activities to create and sustain competitive advantages.
2. For an insightful discussion of the increasing importance of economies of scope in manufacturing, see Joel D. Goldhar and Mariann Jelinek, "Plan for Economies of Scope," *Harvard Business Review,* 61 (November–December 1983), pp. 141–48.
3. Shawn Tully, "Look Who's a Champ of Gasoline Marketing," *Fortune,* November 1, 1982, pp. 149–54.
4. "Now Airlines Are Diversifying by Sticking to What They Know Best," *Business Week,* May 7, 1984, pp. 70, 72.
5. In process industries (for example, aluminum smelting, petroleum refining), engineers use the two-thirds

rule: Any facility can be built with twice the capacity for only a two-thirds increase in cost.
6. As quoted by Frederic Scherer, *Industrial Market Structure and Economic Performance* (Boston: Houghton Mifflin, 1980), p. 82.
7. See "Why Detroit Can't Cut Prices," *Business Week,* March 1, 1982, pp. 110–11.
8. F. M. Scherer and others, *The Economies of Multiplant Operations* (Cambridge, MA: Harvard University Press, 1975), pp. 80, 94.
9. The ideal case for limit pricing, called a *natural monopoly,* occurs where the extent of scale economies is not exhausted even when the firm has 100 percent of the market.
10. The fact that economies of scale are to a small extent relative to the total industry does not mean, however,

that they cannot be exploited for a sustainable competitive advantage. What is relevant is not their size and extent relative to industry sales, but their size and extent relative to the sales in a particular market. Although some industries consist of one large market in which all competitors compete for the patronage of all buyers, most industries are an aggregation of smaller, somewhat independent market segments. Two factors usually determine the existence and size of such submarkets: location and product differentiation. Grocery retailing is one example of a large industry with many locationally distinct submarkets. A single grocery in a small town may satisfy enough of the potential in that market to preclude the entry of any other competition.

11. This is called a *double-log function* because it appears as a straight line when both volume and costs are graphed on a log scale.

12. Harold Asher, *Cost Quantity Relationships in the Airframe Industry*, Rand Corporation Report, Santa Monica, CA, 1956; R. W. Cooper and A. Charnes, "Silhouette Functions of Short-Run Cost Behavior," *Quarterly Journal of Economics*, 68 (February 1954), pp. 131–50; Warner Z. Hirsch, "Manufacturing Progress Functions," *Review of Economics and Statistics*, 34 (May 1952), pp. 143–55; Armen Alchian, "Costs and Output," in *The Allocation of Economic Resources: Essays in Honor of B. F. Huley*, edited by Moses Abramovitz and others (San Jose, CA: Stanford University Press, 1959), pp. 22–40; T. D. Wright, "Factors Affecting the Cost of Airplanes," *Journal of Aeronautical Science*, 3 (February 1936), pp. 122–28.

13. Bruce D. Henderson, *Perspectives on Experience* (Boston: The Boston Consulting Group, 1970); Bruce D. Henderson and Alan J. Zukon, "Pricing Strategy: How to Improve It (The Experience Curve)," in *Handbook of Business Problem Solving*, edited by Kenneth J. Albert (New York: McGraw-Hill, 1980). See also Bruce Robinson and Chet Lakiani, "Dynamic Price Models for New Product Planning," *Management Science*, 21 (June 1975), pp. 113–22; and Robert Dolan and Abel Jeuland, "Experience Curves and Dynamic Demand Models: Implications for Optimal Pricing Strategies," *Journal of Marketing*, 45 (Winter 1981), pp. 52–73.

14. See "Selling Business a Theory of Economics," *Business Week*, September 8, 1973, pp. 85–89; and Michael Porter, "Experience Curve," in "Manager's Journal," *Wall Street Journal*, October 22, 1979, p. 30. Among those firms often cited as practitioners of experience-curve pricing are Black & Decker, Briggs & Stratton, Emerson Electric, Du Pont, 3M, and most firms in the semiconductor industry.

15. Raymond Corey, "Key Options in Market Selection and Product Planning," *Harvard Business Review*, 53 (September–October 1975), pp. 119–28.

16. See Wickham Skinner, "The Focused Factory," *Harvard Business Review*, 52 (May–June 1974), p. 113.

17. Malcolm Gladwell, "Clicks & Mortar," *The New Yorker*, December 6, 1999, pp. 106–115.

18. Gary McWilliams, "Michael Dell: Whirlwind on the Web," April 7, 1997.

19. See Roy D. Shapiro, "Get Leverage from Logistics," *Harvard Business Review*, 62 (May–June 1984), pp. 119–26; and Graham Sharman, "The Rediscovery of Logistics," *Harvard Business Review*, 62 September–October 1984), pp. 71–79.

20. Sharman, "The Rediscovery of Logistics," p. 75.

21. $CM = \$2.00 - \$1.20 - 0.20 = \$0.60$
$\%CM = \$0.60/\$2.00 \times 100 = 30\%$

22. An integrated company does not automatically gain this advantage. If separate divisions of a company operate as independent profit centers setting transfer prices equal to market prices, they will also price too high to maximize their joint profits. To overcome the problem while remaining independent, they need to adopt one of the solutions suggested for independent companies.

23. Bill Abrams, "Consumer-Product Techniques Help Loctite Sell to Industry," *Wall Street Journal,* April 2, 1981, p. 27.

24. Theodore Levitt, "Marketing Success Through Differentiation—of Anything," *Harvard Business Review,* 58 (January–February 1980), pp. 83–91.

25. Susan Fraker, "Making a Mint in Nuts and Bolts," *Fortune,* August 22, 1983, pp. 131–34.

26. Levitt, "Marketing Success Through Differentiation," p. 87. See also, for additional illustrations, Theodore Levitt, *The Marketing Mode* (New York: McGraw-Hill, 1969), pp. 1–27; R. Karl van Leer, "Industrial Marketing with a Flair," *Harvard Business Review,* 54 (November–December, 1976), pp. 117–24.

CHAPTER

Measuring Perceived Value and Price Sensitivity

Research Techniques to Supplement Judgment

E stimates of customer price sensitivity and willingness to pay can sometimes substantially improve both price setting and segmentation. Sometimes research can provide very specific estimates of the impact of
prices on sales volume. Other times estimates provide only a rough indication
of a customer's willingness to pay given a set of circumstances. At their worst,
estimates of price sensitivity fail to reflect the real nature of the buying decision, misleading management into making ineffective pricing decisions. This is
often the case when a research design causes respondents to pay much more
attention to price than real customers would.

There are numerous procedures for measuring and estimating price sensitivity. Each procedure offers particular advantages over the others, so the
choice is not arbitrary. One must think carefully about the appropriate procedure for any particular product before beginning research. In no case
should a manager use a particular technique just because it is cheap, convenient, or fast. Instead, managers need to carefully assess their needs and
adopt techniques that are most appropriate for the given situation. Even if
the cost for those techniques is high, the benefit is often sufficiently large to
justify the expense.

TYPES OF MEASUREMENT PROCEDURES

Procedures for estimating price sensitivity differ on two major dimensions: the
conditions of measurement and the variable being measured. Exhibit 13-1 clas-
sifies the various procedures according to these two dimensions. The conditions
of measurement range from a completely uncontrolled to a highly controlled
research environment. When making uncontrolled measurements, researchers
are only observers. They measure what people actually do, or say they would

do, in a situation not of their making. For example, marketing researchers might collect data on consumer purchases of laundry detergent in a grocery store, but the prices and other variables that influence those purchases are beyond their control. This is often the case in the analysis of historical data of product sales from retail-scanner data.

In contrast, when making controlled measurements, researchers manipulate the important variables that influence consumer behavior to more precisely observe their effect. Researchers conducting an experimentally controlled study of price sensitivity for a laundry detergent could select the prices as well as the advertising and shelf placement of various brands in order to make the data more useful. They might attempt to gain even more control by conducting a laboratory experiment in a simulated store, carefully selecting the individuals whose purchases would be recorded. Participants for the experiment could be chosen to represent various demographic variables (such as race, sex, income, and family size) in proportions equal to those of the product's actual market or to represent a particular group (such as mothers with children) to whom the product was intended to appeal. Controlled research produces more accurate estimates of the effects of the controlled variables on price sensitivity, but it is often costly to implement, given the need for multiple locations and large sample sizes.

The dependent variable for estimating price sensitivity is either actual purchases or purchase preferences and intentions. Actual-purchase studies measure behavior, whereas preference-intention studies measure the intended choices that people claim they would make in a hypothetical purchase situation. Since the ultimate goal of the research is to estimate how people respond to price changes in actual-purchase situations, research that measures actual behavior is generally more desirable, but it is also more costly, time-consuming, and sometimes impractical, given the need to move products to market quickly.

The following discussion summarizes these research techniques and some of the trade-offs of choosing one method over another.

EXHIBIT 13-1 Techniques for Measuring Price Sensitivity

	Conditions of Measurement	
Variable Measured	*Uncontrolled*	*Experimentally Controlled*
Actual purchases	• Historical sales data • Panel data • Store scanner data	• In-store experiments • Laboratory purchase experiments
Preferences and intentions	• Direct questioning • Buy-response survey • Depth interview	• Simulate purchase experiments • Trade-off (conjoint) analysis

Uncontrolled Studies of Actual Purchases

One way to estimate price sensitivity is to analyze past sales data. Naturally, one would expect this to work well in assessing the price sensitivity of customers for existing products in which consumers have prior-use experience. Given the increased use of scanners in supermarkets and mass merchandisers, and the databases maintained on their most frequent customers by hotels, airlines, and Web sites, analysis of historical data is becoming an increasingly important source of information to model customer sensitivity to prices and price deals. Still, changes in (1) the number of brands on the market, (2) how recently competitors offered price promotions, (3) the amount and effectiveness of advertising by each brand, (4) increased price sensitivity of more-educated consumers, and (5) general economic conditions can undermine the ability of historical data analysis to diagnose the true effects of a price change.

There are three types of past sales data from which a marketing researcher might attempt to estimate price sensitivity: (1) *historical sales data*—sales reports from a company's own records or from a sales-monitoring service, (2) *panel data*—individual purchase reports from members of a consumer panel, and (3) *store scanner data*—sales data for an individual retail outlet.

Historical Sales Data

Sales data collected as part of a company's regular operation are cheap and available for all products that have prior sales histories. Given the ability to actually track data on a minute-to minute basis, marketers are able to analyze trends and project future movement of product sales. One needs to be careful in recognizing that, unless the company sells directly to the end user, its sales data reflect shipments to retailers, not actual retail sales during the period. The results may indicate stockpiling to take advantage of short-term promotions on the part of the retailer or in anticipation of increases in demand on the part of consumer. Understanding this, some marketers have direct links with the inventory movement of their retail outlets. While this is generally part of the inventory-management system to facilitate timely replacement of stock, it also provides the marketer with instant data that can be analyzed for important trends in demand.

Good estimates of actual retail sales are available for some products from companies that survey retail stores (for example, A. C. Neilsen).[1] Also, for some factors—such as product reformulations, changes in consumer tastes, and changes in distribution—there is simply no way to take out the effect. For others, such as recessions or changes in the level of advertising, the researcher can statistically control the estimation process to take out their effects.

Another problem with sales data is that it is frequently available only at an aggregated level. In any given week, some stores will charge higher prices than others. Over time, the same store will put the product on sale for a week and then return its price to the regular level. These price variations influence sales and, therefore, could provide useful information about price sensitivity. Unfortunately, data that aggregate sales for all stores over a number of weeks conceal these individual price differences. Given the aggregation in the data, the researcher is forced to explain sales variations by looking at only the average retail price across stores and throughout the time period. Since average prices have less variation and fewer observations than actual prices at individual stores in particular weeks, the data have less statistical power than data on individual purchase prices.[2]

Panel Data

A number of marketing research companies collect individual purchase data from panels of a few thousand households. Each household keeps a daily record of all brands purchased and prices paid or uses a special credit card which tracks purchases. Since products are purchased daily, the data for each household must be aggregated to produce a series on weekly or biweekly purchases. Such data have a number of advantages:

1. One can accumulate observations more quickly with weekly panel data than with bimonthly or quarterly sales data, reducing the problem that other factors may change and reduce the comparability of the data.
2. One can observe the actual price paid, rather than an average of the retail prices that different stores charge, and one can identify sales that were made with coupons or promotions that alter the price actually paid.[3] This captures more price variation in the data, making the effects of price changes easier to detect.
3. One can get data on the sales and prices of competing products (provided someone in the panel bought them), as well as on sales of one's own product.
4. One can correlate price sensitivity with various demographic classifications of consumers and possibly identify opportunities for segmentation.[4]

One potential drawback is that panel data may not be adequately representative of the market as a whole. Of all households invited to join a panel, fewer than 5 percent accept the offer and accurately record their purchases. There is reason to suspect, therefore, that panel members are a biased sample of the population. Moreover, the fact that panel members must record their purchases tends to make them more price aware, and thus more price sensitive. This problem increases the longer a household participates in a panel. Fortunately, technological advances have enabled some research companies to develop panels that do not require consumers to record their purchases.[5] Instead, in-store scanners record purchases automatically whenever panel members identify themselves in the store's checkout line. This vastly simplifies panel membership, increasing the panel participation rate to over 70 percent and attenuating the problem of heightened price awareness. Further, the data tend to be more representative of real purchasing behavior of consumers without the bias that has been problematic in the past.

Given the ever-widening use of scanners and the ability to link scanner data with panel data, increasing numbers of consumer products can be analyzed using this type of analysis. The superiority of panel data estimates over those from aggregate sales data is due to the availability of more observations from a shorter and more comparable time period. With the availability of advertising and other promotional data, researchers are able to estimate price sensitivities for different customer groups with a reasonable degree of reliability (Box 13-1). Since multiple companies share the cost of the same ongoing research, estimates based on panel data are also less expensive than estimates based on an equal number of observations from proprietary research.

Store Scanner Data

An alternate source of actual-sales comes from auditing price transactions and sales at individual retail stores. Modern technologies have made accurate weekly sales and price data available at reasonable cost. Any store that uses scanners can generate such data as part of its normal operations. The weekly frequency of scanner data makes it vastly superior to aggregate sales data. Fortunately, the availability of scanner data, which is used in more than 90 percent of department, grocery, and mass-merchandise stores, provides marketers with almost immediate information on the movement of their product. Some questions have arisen as to the accuracy of pricing information of scanner data, but, for the most part, those inaccuracies have been in less than 10 percent of the cases.[6] Although it lacks the corresponding demographics of consumer panel data, it also costs substantially less. When store scanner data can be combined with panel data that track the demographic and broader behavioral characteristics of consumers, researchers often get huge bonuses in insights into price sensitivity and purchasing behaviors. Scanner data have become a major source of information on the price sensitivity of consumer-packaged goods.[7] Exhibit 4-9 in Chapter 4, which illustrated different price elasticities, was generated from grocery store scanner data.

Analyzing Historical Data

Analysis of historical sales data can involve application of linear regression analysis. This statistical technique attempts to show how much of the historical variation in a product's sales can be explained by each of the explanatory variables, including price, that the researcher includes in the analysis. One should not expect, however, that the researcher will necessarily succeed in identifying the effect of price with such an analysis. If there has been little historical variation in a product's price, then no statistical technique applied to its sales data can reveal the effect of price changes. Moreover, if every time price was changed and some other variable—such as advertising—was also changed, the best one can do is discover the joint effect of such a simultaneous change on sales. Fortunately, the use of more sophisticated analysis of multiple variables, such as time series analysis or Lisrel, permits the development of a structural

BOX 13-1

Using Panel Data to Measure the Impact of Promotion on Choice

In a recent study, the authors asked two important questions: whether consumers are getting more price sensitive and whether the group of price-sensitive consumers is growing. To evaluate these and other questions, they examined more than eight years of usage data from a panel of consumers and were able to compare those data with quarterly advertising data from producers within a household non-food product category. They were able to evaluate three different types of price promotions: temporary price reduction, price feature of the product, or the offering of a coupon. For their analysis, they used a multinomial logit model to evaluate the impact of the promotional (price and nonprice) activities on the consumer's choice of a product. Further, they were able to segment users into loyal and non-loyal segments and compare the price sensitivities of the two groups. The summarized results indicated the following:

Consumer's Sensitivities to:	Average Price Sensitivities	Changes Over Time
1. Loyal segment		
Price	−.28	Increase
Price promotion	.02	Increase
Nonprice promotion	.03	Decrease*
2. Nonloyal segment		
Price	−1.70	Increase
Price promotion	.04	Increase
Nonprice promotion	.09	Decrease*
Nonloyal segment size		Increase*

*Indicates significant at $p<.05$, all else $p<.001$.

The price sensitivities are shown across all of the periods analyzed. Based on the elasticities, the loyal segment showed little price sensitivity, but it did increase over time. The nonloyal, price-oriented segment showed higher price sensitivities that increased over time as well. They did note that the size of the nonloyal segment increased over time, indicating that "an increasing proportion of consumers have become more price and promotion sensitive over time."

Source: Carl F. Mela, Sunil Gupta, and Donald R. Lehmann, "The Long-Term Impact of Promotion and Advertising on Consumer Brand Choice," Journal of Marketing Research, May 1997, pp. 248–261.

equation that includes a number of independent and dependent variables and can provide estimates of their cross-impacts on demand.

In any case, one must be careful to recognize the limits of a successful analysis of historical data. To estimate any equation, the researcher must develop a mathematical form for the relationship between price and sales. To the extent that the assumed form incorrectly specifies the relationship, estimates of price sensitivity may be misleading. Moreover, the researcher's estimate of price sensitivity is valid only over the range of price and advertising levels used to estimate it. There is no reason to believe that the same relationship would necessarily apply to price changes outside that range. Finally, regardless of how well an estimated equation fits past data, its value in predicting the effect of future price changes rests on the assumption that the future is like the past. The more other factors change, the less the past can predict the future. Despite these limitations, if a researcher has a lot of historical data with enough price variation in it, useful estimates of price sensitivity are possible.[8]

Exhibit 13-2 shows the results of research that utilized regression analysis to evaluate the importance of various product attributes to two groups of customers: those who are loyal (more than one year of ownership) and those who are new (less than one year). The categorization of customers as new or loyal was based on input from the managers of the credit-card company who found that people who used their card for at least one year tended to stay users for an extended period of time. Of interest is the marginal increase in price sensitivity as measured by sensitivity to interest rates, for nonloyal customers (attribute importance of .16 compared to .14 for loyal customers) and the very large difference in needs for service.

EXHIBIT 13-2 Use of Regression Analysis

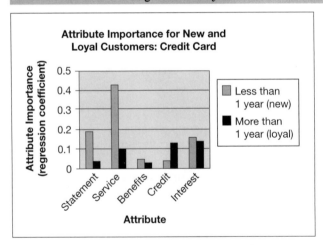

Source: Vikas Mittal and Jerome M. Katrichis, "Distinctions Between New and Loyal Customers," *Marketing Research,* Spring 2000, pp. 27–32.

The researchers were also able to run regression equations for different time periods and determine how attribute importance was changing over time.

Experimentally Controlled Studies of Actual Purchases

A researcher might attempt to estimate price sensitivity by generating experimental purchase data. Such data may come from pricing experiments conducted in a store without the buyers' knowledge or from pricing experiments conducted in a laboratory. Since the researcher controls the experiment, price variations can be created as desired to generate results while holding constant other marketing variables, such as advertising levels and in-store displays, which often change with price variations in uncontrolled sales data. The researcher can examine the effect of a number of different prices quickly and either (1) exclude many unwanted external effects in the laboratory experiment or (2) establish a control for the in-store experiment that will take account of them. Moreover, all this can be done while still *providing* buyers with purchase decisions that are comparable to those they make under normal conditions. As a result, experimental research provides fairly reliable estimates of price sensitivity.

In-Store Purchase Experiments

An in-store purchase experiment relies on actual purchase data collected when buyers are unaware they are participating in an experiment. Although the term *in-store* reflects the fact that most such experiments are conducted in stores, the principles of in-store experimentation are equally applicable to any natural purchase environment. Such experiments are often easier to conduct for products sold through more controlled direct-retail methods, such as mail-order catalogs, than for those sold in traditional retail stores. For example, the researcher can select a subset of the mailing list to receive catalogs with experimental prices that differ from those in the regular catalog. Even in direct sales to business, one can sometimes select a representative sample of customers from one sales area, offer them an experimental price, and monitor the difference between sales to those buyers and to those in other regions where sales are made at the regular price.

The simplest design for an in-store pricing experiment involves monitoring sales at the historical price to obtain a base level of sales and then initiating a price change to see how sales change from that base level. In practice this is a very common experimental design that can yield useful information; however, it fails to exploit one of the major advantages of experimentation: the ability to control for external factors. Without such control, the researcher is forced to make the tenuous assumption that any sales change from the base level resulted from the price change alone, not from changes in other factors.

Fortunately, the addition of an experimental control store (or mail sample or sales territory) can reduce this problem substantially. To establish such a control, the researcher finds a second store in which sales tend to vary over the base period in the same way that they vary in the first store, indicating that factors other than price influence both stores' sales in the same way. The researcher then changes price only in the first store, but continues to monitor sales in both stores. Any change in sales in the control store indicates to the researcher that some factor other than price is also causing a change in sales. To adjust the results, the researcher subtracts from the sales in the experimental store an amount equal to the change in sales in the control store before determining the effect of the price change alone.[9]

One of the greatest benefits of in-store experimentation is the ability to test for interactions between price and other marketing variables that, in historical data, tend to change together. Unfortunately, the cost of such experimentation is very high because each additional factor studied requires the inclusion of more stores. The experimental design with the greatest amount of information, called a *full factorial design,* would require enough stores to match every level tested for each marketing variable with every level of the other variables. Usually, the researcher is forced to use a less-than-perfect experiment, called a *fractional factorial design,* that sacrifices some precision (generally, an understanding of interactions) in order to reduce the number of stores required.[10]

Although many articles illustrate the successful application of in-store experimentation to estimate price sensitivity, the greatest impediment to using in-store experiments is the high cost of monitoring sales, analyzing the data, and securing the cooperation of retailers.[11] Although in theory this is an inexpensive experiment because as few as two stores for one week could constitute a test, accurate tests require many stores and last for months. A large number of stores is necessary to reduce the problem of an external factor influencing just one store and to obtain a representative sample of consumers whose behavior can reasonably be generalized to the market as a whole. It is often necessary to set a long time period for an in-store test in order to get past the short-run inventory effect on price sensitivity that initially masks the long-term effect. Consequently, a good in-store experiment is very expensive. When, for example, Quaker Oats conducted an in-store experiment that focused on the effect of price alone, the study required 120 stores and ran for three months. Such a study can easily cost several million dollars.[12]

In addition to the financial and time cost of in-store experiments, there are other drawbacks. There is the potential loss of consumer goodwill when some buyers are charged higher than others prices. On the other hand, charging prices below normal can become too costly when the product is a large-expenditure durable good such as an automobile or a piece of industrial equipment. An in-store test also involves the very real risk of being discovered by a competitor. If the product is new, a company may not wish to give its competitors an advance look. Moreover, when competitors find out about a test market, they often take steps, such as special promotions or advertising in selected areas, to contaminate the results.[13] Thus, although in-store experiments have the potential for yielding very high-quality estimates, market researchers are more often forced to use alternatives. The closest of those alternatives is a laboratory purchase experiment.

Laboratory Purchase Experiments

Laboratory purchase experiments attempt to duplicate the realism of in-store experimentation without the high cost or the possible exposure to competitors. A typical laboratory experiment takes place in a research facility at a shopping mall. Interviewers intercept potential participants who are walking by and screen them to select only those who are users of the product category being researched. Based on information from a short pretest questionnaire, the researchers can control the proportion of participants in each demographic classification (sex, age, race, income, family size) to ensure that the experimental population is representative of the actual population of buyers. If members of some demographic categories cannot be found in adequate numbers in the mall, telephone interviews may be used to contact such people and offer them an incentive to come and participate in the experiment.

The laboratory researcher can control who participates and can quickly manipulate prices and other elements in the purchase environment (such as shelf location and point-of-purchase displays), all at a single location. Moreover, the researcher can almost entirely eliminate external factors (such as changes in competitors' prices, stock-outs of competing products, or differences among stores) that may contaminate the results of an in-store test. Participants exposed to different prices see exactly the same display at the same location in the laboratory experiment. Even effects associated with the time of day can be controlled by constantly changing prices for each new participant in the experiment. Thus, if testing three different price levels, approximately one-third of the consumers who take the test at any hour can be exposed to each price level. This ability to control the experiment so closely enables the researcher to draw inferences from far fewer purchases in much less time than would be possible with an in-store experiment.

Laboratory research facilities vary greatly depending upon the sophistication of the research organization and the budget of the client company. The simplest facilities may consist of an interviewing room with a display of products from a single product category. The price for each brand is clearly marked, and the participant is invited to make a purchase. In theory, since the consumer is actually making a purchase, or can choose not to buy at all, the purchase decision in a simple laboratory experiment is the same one that the consumer would make shopping in an actual retail store.

In practice, however, that conclusion may not be true. The problem lies in the artificiality of a simple laboratory environment. First, a single display in a laboratory encourages the consumer to give the purchase decision much more attention than would be typical in an actual shopping situation. Research indicates that most grocery shoppers do not even look at most prices when actually shopping in a supermarket. In a laboratory, however, consumers do not want to appear careless. They are, therefore, much more likely to note and respond to price differences. Second, when consumers know they are being watched from behind one-way mirrors, they may act as they think they should rather than as they would in real life. Thus some consumers may buy the low-priced brand just to appear to be smart shoppers, or the high-priced brand so as not to appear stingy. They may also buy something from the category out of a feeling of obligation to the researcher who gave them the money, even though they would not buy from that category in a store.

To overcome these limitations, a few research companies offer highly sophisticated laboratory research facilities. The most elaborate facilities attempt to duplicate as closely as possible the actual conditions under which consumers buy the product. These facilities contain complete simulated stores the size of small convenience stores. Before entering the simulated store, consumers may view reruns of television programs within which are embedded television commercials for the research product, or they may read magazines within which are print advertisements for the product. When consumers finally enter the store, they are invited to do all their shopping, purchasing whatever they want, just as they would on a regular shopping trip. They do not know what products or what product categories are subjects of the research. They use their own money to make their purchases. Their reward for participation is a substantial discount off their total when they check out at the cashier. Box 13-2 describes such a laboratory experiment.

Even the best laboratory experiment is somewhat artificial, introducing some bias into the results. Still, companies that do this research argue convincingly that the problem of bias is not as great as the problems of in-store experimentation and that they can accurately adjust the results of their laboratory experiments, based on their past experience with similar product categories, to take out the effects of any biases inherent in the experimental process.[14] Moreover, one cannot argue with the economics. The cost of even the most sophisticated laboratory experiment is only a small fraction of the cost of in-store testing. As a result, the leading marketers of consumer packaged goods and small appliances rely extensively on this research technique when making pricing decisions.[15]

Uncontrolled Studies of Preferences and Intentions

The most common research technique for directly estimating price sensitivity is the survey of brand preferences or purchase intentions. Companies prefer to measure preferences or intentions, rather than actual purchases, for a number of reasons:

1. Survey data cost much less to collect than purchase data.
2. Survey data can be measured for large durable goods, such as automobiles or photocopiers, for which in-store or laboratory experiments at various prices are impractical.
3. Survey data can be collected even before a product is designed, when the information is most valuable in directing product development.
4. The results can be collected quickly.

BOX 13-2

Measuring Price Sensitivity for a Computerized Clock Radio: A Laboratory Purchase Study

A major Japanese electronics manufacturer was interested in assessing how different advertising and pricing strategies would affect market demand for a new multifunction product (a combination digital clock, AM/FM radio, and cassette player with built-in memory calendar–date book). In addition to being a high-quality clock radio, the product enjoyed several unique features. The clock alarm could activate either a buzzer, the radio itself, or a cassette tape. (A demonstration tape played the old lyric "When the red, red robin comes bob, bob, bobbing along/Get up, you sleepy head/Get up, get out of bed.") Another unique feature was the computer memory, which permitted the user to program up to 500 key dates and/or times. With this system the user could peek ahead in a given month or week to see key dates coming up, and/or wait until the morning of the date when the pre-programmed information would appear on a small screen.

The key questions asked by the manufacturer were twofold. First, how should the product be positioned in television advertising, as an advanced clock radio or as a tabletop time-management computer? Second, should the product be priced at $59 to attract a large share of the high-volume radio market; at $79 to compete with high-quality AM/FM radio-cassette players; or at $99 to signal the product's uniqueness and skim the segment that valued those unique features most highly? To address this problem, the manufacturer contracted with Yankelovich, Clancy, Shulman (now Yankelovich Partners) to conduct a laboratory purchase experiment.

In each of four markets, 300 prospective buyers (men and women, aged eighteen and over) were randomly recruited. They were invited to the company's laboratory facilities for the apparent purpose of previewing a new television program and seeing new home electronic products. The design for the study was very simple. Each participant was randomly assigned to a treatment group for exposure to one of the two possible positionings and three possible prices. Thus, at each location, six groups of the fifty participants each were exposed to a different positioning/price combination.

The groups were first exposed to a new half-hour television program in which was embedded advertising for the new product, for competitive products, and for control products. Following this, participants were invited into an adjoining simulated electronics store where they had the opportunity to see the new product along with many competitive products, priced as they would be at local

(continued)

BOX 13-2 *(continued)*

stores. They could ask questions of store salespeople and read available literature about the products.

All products in the store were for sale at a 30 percent discount off the listed price. Approximately 40 percent of all participants actually made a purchase. The non-buyers were asked a set of questions to estimate what they would have purchased if they had made a purchase.

The results of the study showed significant effects of both positioning and price on demand. Overall, 14 percent of all prospective purchasers were buyers of the new product. Demand varied with positioning and price in the following way:

Percentage of Purchasers Under Different Conditions

Price	Advanced Clock Radio (%)	Time Management Computer (%)
$59	25	20
79	19	11
99	8	1

Source: Provided by Yankelovich, Clancy, Shulman (now Yankelovich Partners), a marketing research, modeling, and consulting firm in Westport, Connecticut. (Although this description is based on an actual study, some details have been masked to maintain confidentiality.)

Unfortunately, the problem with survey research is that many consumers do not provide answers that are a reliable guide to their actual purchase behavior. This is especially true for questions regarding price. In order to solve this problem, some research companies cross-validate the results of one survey with the results of another, often using slightly different methods of data collection and questioning. For example, a firm might collect data using personal interviews and validate the results by telephoning a different group of respondents and asking the same set of questions. The closer the results are from the two samples and methods, the more valid and accurate the final results.

Direct Questioning
Very early in the development of survey techniques for marketing, researchers learned that it was futile to ask consumers outright what they would be willing to pay for a product. Direct questioning sometimes elicits bargaining behavior, with consumers stating a lower price than they would actually pay. Other times, it elicits a desire to please the researcher or to not appear stingy, prompting consumers to state a higher price than they would actually pay. Fre-

quently, it simply elicits a cursory answer that consumers would change were they to give the question the same thought as an actual purchase decision. Consequently, uncontrolled direct questioning as a research technique to estimate price sensitivity should never be accepted as a valid methodology. The results of such studies are at best useless and are potentially highly misleading.

Buy-Response Surveys

A slight variant of the direct-question survey involves showing consumers a product at a preselected price and asking if they would purchase at that price. Surprisingly, although directly asking consumers what they would pay usually yields meaningless answers, asking them if they would buy at a preselected price yields answers that are at least plausible. When the answers given by different consumers for different price levels are aggregated, they produce what looks like a demand curve for market share, sometimes called a *purchase probability curve* (Box 13-3). Presumably, questioning willingness to buy generates better responses simply because it is structured more like an actual purchase decision than as an open-ended question about what the consumer would pay. Also the consumer has no opportunity to bargain with the researcher.[16]

Attribute Positioning

Another method for evaluating price sensitivity is to include price as one of the attributes describing a product or a purchase situation. Consumers rate the importance of each attribute using a variety of scaling techniques. Those scales can be a 1 to 5 or a 1 to 10 importance rating or simply an evaluation of the percent of respondents mentioning the attribute as being important.[17] This approach is problematic because responses tend to be offhand and overly positive, due to halo effects, where respondents tend to not carefully discriminate among listed attributes and give similar ratings or responses to many attributes, especially those adjacent to each other.

Depth Interviews

A depth interview is a "semistructured" method that is used to elicit responses from customers on how they use products and services, from which the research infers value rather than asking about value directly. The interview is often conducted one on one with a respondent and lasts for one to two hours. In a consumer environment, it is used to understand how individuals and families use products and how they might value different features or positioning approaches. In a business-to-business environment, the interview attempts to understand how businesses gain revenues or reduce costs by using a specific product or service. Depth interviews in pricing research are useful in (1) understanding which product or service features and benefits are important to a customer; (2) assessing the monetary or psychological value of these features and benefits that a customer receives as a result of using the product or service; and (3) assessing roughly what a customer might be willing to pay to obtain these features and benefits. Depth interviews are also used to develop economic-value models of how much a customer could gain in monetary terms

BOX 13-3

Purchase Probability Curves: A Simple Buy-Response Study — Opportunity for a Higher Price

A software firm developed a product for law firms that would easily produce high-quality legal documents and would manage document storage and billing of time for both small and large offices. The original estimates of price were $500 per unit. Chadwick Martin Bailey, Inc., conducted a national study to measure price sensitivity for the product. It began the process by conducting extensive exploratory research, including focus groups and semistructured interviews. This phase of the research initially indicated that prices in the range of $6,000 might be perfectly acceptable to a large segment of attorneys. A random sample of 603 attorneys was contacted by telephone and asked the likelihood of purchase at either $2,000, $4,000, $6,000, or $8,000, yielding about 150 responses per price point. Probability of purchase was measured using a 0–10 likelihood of purchase scale, and all responses in the 8–10 range were used as a basis for assessing price sensitivity. At $2,000, 49 percent of the firms would have bought the package. Demand was found to be very inelastic for higher prices, as shown in Figure A. Movement from $4,000 to $8,000 in price made little difference in the proportion of law firms willing to buy the product, but produced large differences in revenue from sales, as shown in Figure B.

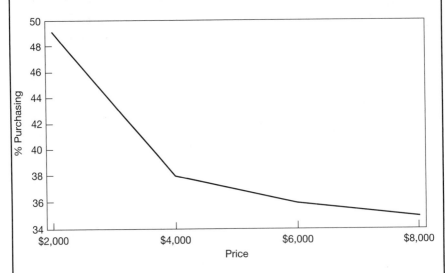

Figure A
Purchase Probability Curve
Source: Chadwick Martin Bailey, Inc.

FRONTIER
A I R L I N E S

NAME ALCORN/BARRYA

DATE 21FEB

FQTV 1010618813

FLIGHT F9   720

E-TICKET

GATE   SEAT

A31   9D

DEP DEN   420P

ARR DCA   930P

BOX 13-3 (*continued*)

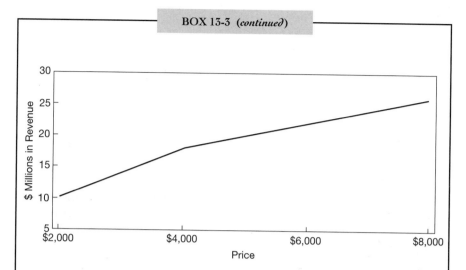

Figure B
Total Revenue Estimates
Source: Chadwick Martin Bailey, Inc.
This study was provided by Chadwick Martin Bailey, Inc., a planning and market research firm located in Boston, Massachusetts.

One cannot, however, treat buy-response data as directly comparable to or directly predictive of the sales that would actually occur at the corresponding prices in a store. Most problematic is the fact that consumers' answers depend on their recollection of the actual prices of competing products. To the extent that they overestimate or underestimate competing prices, they will misjudge their willingness to buy. Even with this form of the question, some consumers will still want to please the researcher, or will fear appearing stingy, and so will falsely claim a willingness to buy the brand over competing brands regardless of the price.

Nevertheless, such research is useful (1) as a preliminary study to identify a range of acceptable prices for a new product and (2) to identify changes in price sensitivity at different points in time or place, assuming that the biases that affect these studies remain the same and so do not affect the observed change. For example, recall that in Chapter 4 (Exhibit 4-4), we saw a buy-response survey for a new food product that showed no difference in consumers' willingness to buy at different prices when they knew only the product concept, but a significant difference after they had tried the product. In interpreting the study, one would not want to take the absolute percentage

(*continued*)

BOX 13-3 *(continued)*

of consumers who claimed they would buy as an accurate prediction of the percentage of consumers who would actually buy at the different prices. However, differences in the stated probability of purchase before and after trial may reliably predict the change in price sensitivity caused by the product trial.

Intention measurement is also sometimes used successfully to predict actual purchases when researchers have past experience that allows them to adjust for the bias in subjects' stated intentions. Typically, purchase intentions are measured by asking people to indicate which of the following best describes their likelihood of purchase:

Definitely would buy
Probably would buy
Might/might not buy
Probably would not buy
Definitely would not buy

The leading survey research firms have asked such questions of millions of buyers for thousands of products. Consequently, they are able to develop adjustments that reflect the average bias in these answers for various product classes. Thus, an experienced researcher might expect that only 80 percent of people answering "definitely would buy," 50 percent answering "probably would buy," 25 percent answering "might/might not buy," and 10 percent answering "probably would not buy" will actually purchase.

---

from purchase of the product. The model then becomes part of a promotional campaign to increase customers' willingness to pay. Such models work well for business customers, where most benefits can be translated into additional revenues or costs saved. It works well in consumer markets where the benefit is a cost saving (e.g., the value of buying a more-efficient refrigerator).

Similar to a focus group, (Exhibit 13–3) a depth interview is relatively unstructured and is usually conducted by an experienced interviewer who has a specific interview guide and objective, such as to quantify the value of differentiating features. Depth interviews are used less frequently in market research due to the need for highly specialized interviewers, the expense per interview, and the small sample size.[18] This is especially true for consumer pricing research for mass-market products and services. However, for more complex business-to-business pricing research, the quality of information obtained with regard to customer value and willingness to pay often yield much more fruitful insights and analysis.

For example, depth interviews enable the interviewer to probe customer needs: unique problems, customers experiences (e.g., running a manufacturing line at close to maximum-capacity utilization), how they attempt to deal with problems (e.g., consequently paying workers overtime wages, or hiring tempo-

Effectiveness of Focus Groups vs. Depth Interviews

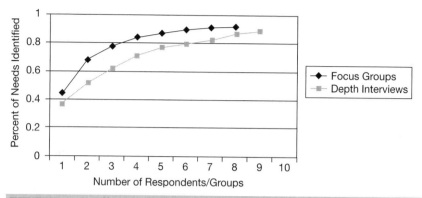

EXHIBIT 13-3 Effectiveness of Focus Groups vs. Depth Interviews

Source: Jonathan Alan Silver and John Charles Thompson Jr., "Understanding Customer Needs: A Systematic Approach to the 'Voice of the Customer,'" Master's Thesis, 1991, Cambridge, MA, Sloan School of Management, Massachusetts Institute of Technology.

rary employees at premium wage rates), how the supplier's products or services could solve these problems, and the value to the customer of the consequent savings or gains they would realize from using the firm's products or services.

Depth interviews do not ask customers directly how much they would be willing to pay. Instead, the interview focuses on the financial benefits to the customer that a product or service could influence. It is also possible to get a sense of perceived value by identifying other items that the customer buys to achieve the same benefit. For example, one method used successfully in business-to-business markets, *evoked anchoring,* asks respondents to identify items in their budget that they might consider a trade-off in order to obtain the value and benefits promised by a supplier's proposed product or service solution. For example, when helping a software client to price relationship-management software, we identified that one benefit was reduced customer turnover. By asking potential buyers of the software to identify the costs to acquire new customers, we could infer the value to retain them.

Depth interviews enable marketers to understand not only what someone might perceive their product or service to be worth, but also why it is worth that much. The depth interview attempts to understand the needs that the product addresses and how the product or service addresses them. The process often uncovers ways that suppliers can enhance their current product or service offerings and, in doing so, provide the basis for creating more differentiated products that can be sold at higher prices. It also exposes who in the buying organization has goals that are likely to benefit from purchase of the product.[19]

The interview must be conducted outside the context of a selling opportunity or a negotiation, since customers are unlikely to reveal value at such times. However, the data garnered often form the basis of a value-based selling approach in which salespeople, armed with an understanding of how their products differ from those of competitors and how those differences create value for customers, can justify their pricing to the customer and to themselves. Companies often can use the information gained from depth interviews to develop "value case histories." These case histories describe the experience of a particular customer in using a firm's products and the specific value that the customer received. These case studies eventually become a sales support tool.[20]

The depth interview is an excellent method for developing a better understanding of how different product and service features create value for customers, especially customers in a business-to-business environment. It is especially useful in moving beyond the core product and understanding how different service and support elements can create incremental value for a user and provide insights into how a product might be priced to capture that value. It often identifies similar service and support characteristics that can successfully differentiate what are often thought of as commodity products.[21] A common concern is that customers won't provide the data. However, our experience is that most customers are quite willing to share insights and data that will help suppliers serve them better.

Experimentally Controlled Studies of Preferences and Intentions

To solve some of the problems of bias and extraneous factors when measuring preferences and intentions, researchers try to exercise some control over the purchase situation presented to respondents.

The questions must be designed to make the survey respondents consider the questions in the same way they would consider an actual purchase decision. The extent to which that can ever be fully accomplished is still an open question, but marketing researchers, recognizing the potential value of accurate survey information, are certainly trying.

Simulated Purchase Experiments

Many researchers believe that the best way to get consumers to think about a survey question and to respond as they would in a purchase situation is to simulate the purchase environment as closely as possible when asking the survey questions. With this type of research, the researcher asks the consumers to imagine that they are on a shopping trip and desire to make a purchase from a particular product class. Then the researcher shows the consumers pictorial representations or descriptions—concepts—or sometimes actual samples of brands along with prices and asks the consumers to choose among them, given various prices. Since actual products need not be used, this technique enables one to test pricing for new product concepts, as part of a general concept test, before the concepts are actually developed into products.

The primary difference between such a simulated purchase experiment and a laboratory purchase experiment is that participants only simulate the choice decision to purchase a product and so do not get to keep their choices.[22]

The simulated purchase experiment is a widely used tool in pricing research that overcomes two important drawbacks of other types of surveys. If it is structured as a choice task among alternative brands, a consumer's thought process should more closely approximate the process actually used when making a purchase. Also, since consumers have no way of knowing which brand is the one of interest to the researcher, they cannot easily think of the choice as a bargaining position or as a way to please the researcher. Thus, simulated purchase experiments can sometimes predict price sensitivity reasonably well.[23]

While any type of research is prone to bias, the simulated purchase experiments can often be an acceptable method for gaining quick and low-cost information on the buying behavior of consumers. If, for example, a company wants to estimate the price sensitivity of a product sold nationally, the cost of hundreds of in-store experiments throughout the country would be prohibitive. If the company conducted both an in-store experiment and a simulated purchase experiment in a few locations and found them reasonably consistent, it could confidently use the latter to cover the remaining locations and to conduct future research on that product class. Even if the experiment showed a consistent tendency to be biased, simulated purchase experiments could still be used successfully after the results had been adjusted by the amount of that previously identified bias.

Trade-Off Analysis

An experimental technique, called trade-off (or conjoint) analysis, has become popular for measuring price sensitivity as well as sensitivity to other product attributes.[24] The particular strength of trade-off analysis is its ability to disaggregate a product's price into the values consumers attach to each attribute. Consequently, trade-off analysis can help a company identify the differentiation value of unique product attributes and, more important, design new products that include only those attributes that consumers are willing to pay for as well as how much they are likely to pay for the entire product and service package. Currently, trade-off analysis aids in the design of a range of products, from automobiles and office equipment to household cleaners and vacation packages.

The basic data for trade-off analysis are consumers' answers to questions that reveal not their directly stated purchase intentions, but rather the underlying preferences that guide their purchase intentions. The researcher collects such data by asking respondents to make choices between pairs of fully described products or between different levels of just two product attributes. The data are usually collected with a questionnaire but can also be collected online with a personal computer.

After obtaining a consumer's preferences for a number of product or attribute pairs, the researcher then manipulates the data to impute the value (called *utility*) that each consumer attaches to each product attribute and the relative importance that each attribute plays in the consumer's purchase decision.[25] With that data, the researcher can predict at what prices the consumer would purchase products containing various combinations of attributes, including combinations that do not currently exist in the marketplace. The researcher can also estimate how much of one attribute the consumer is willing to trade off in order to obtain more of another attribute—for example, how much more price a consumer is willing to trade off in order to obtain more fuel efficiency in a new automobile.

With similar data from a number of consumers who are representative of a market segment, the researcher can develop a model to predict the share of a market that would prefer any particular brand to others at any particular price. Since the researcher has collected data that reveal underlying preferences, consumers' preferences can be predicted, or interpolated, even for levels of price and other attributes not specifically asked about in the questionnaire, providing the attributes are continuously measurable and bounded by the levels that were asked about in the survey. Box 13-4 provides an example of such a process. Readers should note how the basic features were varied along with price in order to develop a relationship between features and value, here termed "feature *utility*." Segmentation in the sample of respondents is needed to understand how some groups of individuals have higher values for some attributes than others. In this study, those segmented ratings were used as the basis for successfully predicting the probable market share for a new hotel, given careful analysis of how existing hotels matched the needs of different consumers. Failure to segment the respondents into high- and low-value groups often hides the true nature of price and value sensitivity in the population.

Of all methods used to estimate price sensitivity from preferences or intentions, trade-off analysis promises the most useful information for strategy formulation. The researchers can do more than simply identify the price sensitivity of the market as a whole; they can identify customer segments with different price sensitivities and, to the extent that those differences result from differences in the economic value of product attributes, can also identify the specific product attributes that evoke the differences. Consequently, researchers can describe the combination of attributes that can most profitably skim or penetrate a market. The economic value of a product can also be identified even when the product is not yet developed by presenting consumers with different experimental product combinations in the form of pictorial and descriptive product concepts, or new product prototypes. Moreover, trade-off analysis can do all this for hundreds of different product variations for no more than the cost of a simulated purchase experiment to evaluate just one product.

With the use of more-advanced modeling techniques, researchers are able to use an adaptation of conjoint analysis, discrete choice analysis, in which consumers are given either a limited number of choices or a wide range of choices of different product packages from different competitors, all often at different prices. Based on the analysis of their choices, researchers are then able to form segments by grouping consumers based on the similarity of their responses and develop estimates of market share based on the size and responsiveness of the different segments (Box 13-5). Given internal costs and external promotions, the models can predict likely levels of profitability given those customer and competitive responses.

BOX 13-4

A Conjoint Study: New Hotel's Best Price and Attributes

The Greater Southern Development Authority of Western Australia commissioned a conjoint study into the feasibility of building a new resort hotel in Australia's southwest region. The objective of the study was twofold: (1) to verify whether the demand was adequate to justify the project and (2) to determine the optimal features that the hotel should offer. Important hotel attributes—*cost per night, site* (view), *town center* (nearness to town)—and feasible "levels" of those attributes were identified by reviewing current hotels and developer proposals for new hotels and by interviewing possible users of the proposed facility.

Using these attributes levels, sixteen feasible hotel profiles were developed and consumer preferences for them were tested. Telephone interviews were used to identify tourists likely to visit the area. A questionnaire was mailed to 300 potential tourists who were asked to rate the sixteen alternative hotel configurations. Eighty-one percent of the questionnaires were returned and included in the analysis.

Respondents rated the alternative configurations using an eleven-point "likelihood of purchase" scale. Average scores for each attribute level were compared to determine their overall value in the purchasing decision. The initial results of the analysis included an evaluation of the importance of each attribute and the value or utility that each of the attribute levels had relative to one another. Those utility values were then interpreted relative to the utility of the price of the hotel room in order to develop a dollar (Australian) value for the non-monetary attributes. Table A lists the results for the attributes reported here. Because of the high negative utility associated with higher price points, the data suggest the market is too price sensitive for a high-priced resort hotel.

Unfortunately, many analysts using conjoint data would stop at this point. In fact, Table A shows only the price sensitivity for a mythical "average" consumer who may be unlike any in the marketplace. Different consumers often have very different price sensitivities for various products and their attributes. To understand these differences, the data for this study were analyzed by applying cluster analysis to individual utilities. This analysis resulted in the identification of four customer segments, each with differing values for the product attributes (see Table B).

Only when the attribute values of the individual segments are evaluated can we find a segment of "active water seekers" for whom price is relatively unimportant. Once this segment was found, the data were analyzed to predict the market share that the "ideal" hotel

(continued)

BOX 13-4 (*continued*)

TABLE A Importance, Utilities, and Value for Attribute Levels

Attribute and Levels	Importance	Utility	Value*
Cost per night	56		
40*		1.86	
60		0.28	
80		−0.45	
100		−1.99	
Site	6		
View		−0.01	$−0.16
Harbor		−0.19	−2.96
Mountains		−0.07	−1.09
Beach		0.25	3.89
Town center	7		
Short walk		0.05	$0.78
5 minutes		0.21	3.27
20 minutes		−0.26	−4.05

*Values are in Australian dollars.

TABLE B Attribute Importance and Utilities for Different Hotel Segments

Attribute and Levels	Convenience Seekers		Basics Seekers		Active Water Seekers		Passive Viewers	
	Impor-tance	Utility	Impor-tance	Utility	Impor-tance	Utility	Impor-tance	Utility
Cost per night	31		73		14		41	
40*		0.87		3.14		0.09		1.44
60		0.35		0.89		−0.05		0.64
80		0.15		−1.15		0.23		−0.12
100		−1.27		−3.89		−0.09		−2.17
Site	16		3		29		14	
View		0.16		−0.04		−0.35		0.19
Harbor		0.01		−0.10		0.22		0.31
Mountains		0.37		0.07		−0.30		0.31
Beach		0.28		0.14		0.30		0.47
Town center	18		1		3		9	
Short walk		0.15		0.01		0.04		−0.03
5 minutes		0.39		0.04		−0.02		0.26
20 minutes		−0.74		−0.05		−0.02		−0.34

*Values are in Australian dollars.

Source: Chadwick Martin Bailey, Inc., a planning and market research firm located in Boston, Massachusetts. The results of this study were reported in complete form at the Second International Conference on Marketing and Development, Budapest, July 10–13, 1988, in a paper entitled "Regional Planning for Resort Hotels: A Conjoint Application" by John Martin and David Blackmore.

BOX 13-4 (*continued*)

could obtain for this segment. The results: A hotel on the beach and a short walk to the town center could capture a 16.4 percent market share at a price of A$80, with most of the potential customers coming from the active water seekers segment. The fact that most of the customers in this market would deem this hotel a poor value is irrelevant.

BOX 13-5

Profitability Optimization Model Using Discrete Choice Survey

Alltel, a telecommunications provider, was trying to determine the appropriate bundles of offerings and prices for a broad range of telecommunications services. They used an outside market research firm to develop a model from conjoint-like data that allows scenario testing for specific product/service offerings in terms of price, product features, and packaging of those features.

The research firm needed to model the complex elements of the wireless industry (access, per minute fees, roaming, toll, and features), wireline (access, interstate toll, intrastate toll, optional call plans, and features), and several others. They knew that prices in all sectors would continue to decline quickly and that they could expect a response to any move by all of the competitors in each area. The business questions they faced were these: (1) Would consumers choose Alltel over the dominant local provider? (2) Would they want bundles rather than individual services and at what price? (3) What prices would optimize Alltel's market share/sales/contribution? (4) What would happen when competitors responded?

The market researcher surveyed a large number of potential customers using the survey instrument in Table A. Analysis of the data revealed six very distinct segments in the respondent population, so a separate model was developed for each segment that analyzed expected demand, price elasticity for each product/service, cannibalization of existing products, and possible competitive responses. The resulting model permitted the real-time input of competitive prices (Table B) and provided expected market share, sales volume, and subsequent profit contribution for the client and its competitors (Table C).

This research was performed and provided by SDR Consulting, a market research/modeling firm located in Atlanta, Georgia.

(continued)

BOX 13-5 (continued)

TABLE A   Research Instrument

Please indicate which individual services or packages you would prefer.

Individual Services	Alltel	Bell South	AT&T	Cable Provider	Regional Bell	Other
Wireless (Cellular/Mobile) Service						
No free local minutes	$14.95	$19.95	$19.95	$14.95	$19.95	$19.95
200 free local minutes	n/a	$39.95	$39.95	$39.95	$39.95	$39.95
400 free local minutes plus 5 calling features*	$49.95	$49.95	$49.95	$49.95	$49.95	$49.95
1,000 free local minutes plus 5 calling features*	$89.95	$99.95	$99.95	$89.95	$89.95	$89.95
Wireline (Local) Service						
Single-line basic service	n/a	$22.95	n/a	n/a	n/a	n/a
Single line with all calling features*	n/a	$28.95	$26.95	$26.95	$29.95	$28.95
Single line with all calling features plus Voice Mail	$34.95	$34.95	$31.95	$31.95	$31.95	$33.95
Second line, no features	$19.95	$13.95	$12.95	$12.95	$19.95	$13.95
Long Distance						
Wireline	$0.08	$0.13	$0.13	$0.13	$0.10	$0.13
Wireless	$0.09	$0.15	$0.15	$0.15	$0.13	$0.15
Internet						
Unlimited on-line access	$19.95	$19.95	$21.95	$34.95	$19.95	$21.95
		OR				
Packages	1 year contract	1 year contract	1 year contract			
Bronze*	$49.95	$79.95	$79.95			
Silver*	$109.95	$114.95	$114.95			
Gold*	$149.95	$209.95	$209.95			

*See handout for explanation of Bronze, Silver, and Gold packages, along with special calling features.

BOX 15-5 (continued)

TABLE B Market Response Simulator

	Alltel	Local Bell (ILEC)	AT&T	Cable Provider	Regional Bell	Other
Wireless						
No free local minutes	$14.95	$19.95	$19.95	$14.95	$19.95	$19.95
200 free local minutes	$29.95	$29.95	$29.95	$29.95	$29.95	$29.95
400 free local minutes	$49.95	$49.95	$49.95	$49.95	$49.95	$49.95
1000 free local minutes	$89.95	$99.95	$99.95	$89.95	$89.95	$89.95
Local Service						
Single-line basic service	n/a	$22.95	n/a	n/a	n/a	n/a
Single line w/features	n/a	$28.95	$26.95	$26.95	$29.95	$28.95
Single line w/features plus Voice Mail	$34.95	$34.95	$31.95	$31.95	$31.95	$33.95
Single w/features plus second line	$19.95	$13.95	$12.95	$12.95	$19.95	$13.95
Long Distance						
Wireline	$0.10	$0.13	$0.13	$0.13	$0.10	$0.13
Wireless	$0.13	$0.15	$0.15	$0.15	$0.13	$0.15
Internet						
Unlimited on-line access	$19.95	$19.95	$19.95	$19.95	$19.95	$21.95
Packages						
Alltel	1 year contract	1 year contract	1 year contract	1 year contract	1 year contract	
Bronze	$44.95	$69.95	$69.95	$62.95	$69.95	n/a
Silver	$99.95	$99.95	$99.95	$99.95	$99.95	n/a
Gold	$179.95	$184.95	$184.95	$179.95	$179.95	n/a

(continued)

BOX 13-5 (continued)

TABLE C Market Response Simulator Summary Output

Customer Share *Total Model*	Alltel *Test*	Local Bell (ILEC) *Test*	AT&T *Test*	Cable Provider *Test*	Regional Bell *Test*	Other *Test*	Total *Test*	
Wireless	46.8%	9.8%	11.7%	6.8%	0.8%	8.8%	84.7%	Shows the provider's customer share of each service and percentage of customers buying packages
Local service	3.3%	52.4%	23.6%	2.5%	0.8%	2.0%	84.7%	
Long distance	16.4%	7.4%	45.7%	2.8%	4.3%	8.1%	84.7%	
Internet	7.8%	31.7%	9.1%	1.6%	1.4%	8.2%	59.8%	
Packages	15.3%	0.0%	0.0%	0.0%	0.0%	n/a	15.3%	

Total Annual Dollars (million $) *Total Model*	Alltel *Test*	Local Bell (ILEC) *Test*	AT&T *Test*	Cable Provider *Test*	Regional Bell *Test*	Other *Test*	Total *Test*	
Wireless	$49.47	$13.19	$14.42	$7.02	$1.36	$10.45	$95.91	Shows the provider's total annual revenue for each service and package offering
Local service	$6.05	$78.15	$36.76	$3.93	$1.39	$3.30	$129.58	
Long distance	$15.02	$8.58	$51.84	$3.25	$3.75	$9.32	$91.75	
Internet	$6.64	$27.10	$7.81	$1.38	$1.21	$7.71	$51.85	
Packages	$74.58	$0.00	$0.00	$0.00	$0.00	n/a	$74.58	
Total	$151.76	$127.02	$110.83	$15.58	$7.70	$30.78	$443.67	

Total Annual Contribution (million $) *Total Model*	Alltel *Test*	
Wireless	$31.76	Shows Alltel's total contribution (revenue–cost) for each service and package offering
Local service	$2.41	
Long distance	$3.31	
Internet	$1.90	
Packages	$21.10	
Total	$60.47	

As a result of these promised advantages, the use of trade-off analysis by both market research firms and internal research departments has grown rapidly, but the promises of trade-off analysis are only as good as its ability to predict actual purchase behavior. There are, however, a number of reasons why a prudent manager might suspect the reliability of this technique for some markets. Trade-off analysis is an experimental procedure that introduces bias to the extent that it does not simulate the actual purchase environment. The respondent taking a conjoint test is encouraged to focus much more attention on price and price differences than may occur in a natural purchase environment. Thus, while trade-off analysis is still useful for studying nonprice trade-offs, it should not be trusted in situations where there is little evidence that the purchaser evaluates prices when actually making a decision. For example, research companies have compared the predicted effects of price on physicians prescribing decisions with data on the actual price of the pharmaceuticals they prescribed. The conjoint tests predicted much higher price sensitivity than in fact was the case. Also, if respondents have little experience with the product as is usually the case with innovative product categories, the technique poorly predicts the trade-offs that customers will make.

Because trade-off analysis measures underlying preferences, the researcher has the ability to check if an individual consumer's responses are at least consistent. Consumers who are not taking the survey seriously, or who are basically irrational in their choice processes, are then easily identified and excluded from the sample. Even more comforting are three separate studies that show a high degree of consistency, or reliability, when subjects are asked to repeat a trade-off questionnaire a few days after having taken it initially.[26] Since the subjects are unlikely to remember exactly how they answered the questions in the earlier session, the consistency of the answers over time strongly suggests that they do accurately reflect true underlying preferences. More comforting yet is the result of a study showing that the exclusion from the questionnaire of some product attributes a subject might consider important does not bias the subject's responses concerning the trade-offs among the attributes that are included.[27] Although trade-off analysis is more costly than a simple survey, it also provides much more information. Given its relatively low cost and the fact that it has met at least some tests of reliability, it certainly warrants consideration when seeking to develop a product with features that can be priced most profitably.

USING MEASUREMENT TECHNIQUES APPROPRIATELY

Numerical estimates of price sensitivity can either benefit or harm the effectiveness of a pricing strategy, depending on how management uses them. This is especially true when respondents have considerable experience with the use and purchase of a product. If managers better understand their buyers and use that knowledge to formulate judgments about buyers' price sensitivity, as discussed in Chapter 4, an attempt to measure price sensitivity can be very useful.

It can give managers new, objective information that can either increase their confidence in their prior judgments or indicate that perhaps they need to study their buyers further.

Integrating soft managerial judgments about buyers and purchase behavior with numerical estimates based on hard data is fundamental to successful pricing. Managerial judgments of price sensitivity are necessarily imprecise while empirical estimates are precise numbers that management can use for profit projections and planning. However, precision doesn't necessarily mean accuracy. Numerical estimates of price sensitivity may be far off the mark of true price sensitivity. Accuracy is a virtue in formulating pricing strategy; precision is only a convenience.

No estimation technique can capture the full richness of the factors that enter a purchase decision. In fact, measurements of price sensitivity are precise specifically because they exclude all the factors that are not conveniently measurable. Some estimation techniques enable the researcher to calculate a confidence interval around a precise estimate, indicating a range within which we may have some degree of statistical certainty that the true estimate of price sensitivity lies. That range is frequently wider than the interval that a well-informed manager could specify with equal confidence simply from managerial judgment. Unfortunately, researchers often do not (or cannot) articulate such a range to indicate just how tenuous their estimates are. When they do, managers often ignore it. Consequently, managers deceive themselves into thinking that an estimate of price sensitivity based on hard data is accurate because it is precise.

Fortunately, a manager does not have to make the choice between judgment and empirical estimation. Used effectively, they are complementary, with the information from each improving the information that the other provides.

Using Judgment for Better Measurement

Any study of price sensitivity should begin with the collection of information about buyers—who they are, why they buy, and how they make their purchase decisions—since those are the essential inputs in the formulation of judgment. At the outset, this information should come from open-ended, qualitative, or exploratory research that enables managers to discover facts and formulate impressions other than those for which they may have been specifically looking.[28] In industrial markets, such research may consist of accompanying salespeople to observe the purchase process. After a sale, managers might follow up to ask how and why the purchase decision was made. In many cases, managers can interview important customers and intermediaries by telephone to gain their impressions about a variety of price and marketing issues.[29] In consumer markets, such research may consist of observing consumers discussing their purchase decisions in focus groups or depth interviews as previously discussed. Insights generated from such informal observation could then be confirmed with more formal research in the form of a survey administered to a larger number of buyers.

In addition, managers can learn much about their buyers from secondary sources of data. In industrial markets, the Census of Manufacturers, the Survey of

Industrial Buying Power, and numerous other governmental and private sources[30] can tell sellers the types of businesses their buyers engage in and the share of the total market each accounts for, the average size of their purchases in major product classes, and their growth rates. In consumer markets, consumer panel surveys are widely available to tell managers the demographics of their buyers (income, family size, education, use of coupons) as well as those of their closest competitors. Other companies, such as SRI International, develop complete psychographic profiles of buyers that go beyond just demographics to delve into the innermost psychological motivations for purchase. These are relatively inexpensive sources of data from which management can form judgments about price sensitivity.

Having formed judgments about buyers based on qualitative impressions developed from observing them, a manager will often find it practical and cost-effective to expand this understanding through original primary research that attempts to measure certain aspects of buyer behavior, such as price sensitivity. That attempt is far more likely to produce useful results, to the extent that management already understands the way buyers make their purchase decisions and uses that information to help structure the attempt at measurement. There are a number of ways that managerial judgment can, and should, guide the measurement effort.

1. For experimentally controlled data estimation, managerial judgment should determine the focus of the research on certain target demographic groups and provide guidance for generalizing from those groups to the population as a whole.
   - Management may know that 80 percent of its product's buyers are women who are employed full-time. That information is important if the researcher plans to measure price sensitivity with an in-home survey or an experiment in a shopping center. On a typical day between 9:00 A.M. and 5:00 P.M., few of the experimental subjects at home or in the shopping center would be representative of that product's buyers. To get a representative sample, the researcher might need to conduct the in-home survey in the evenings or the experiment only during the lunch hour at locations near where many women work. He or she might also ask a pre-screening question (are you employed full-time?).
   - If management also knows that different demographic groups buy the product in different quantities, that information can be used to scale the survey results differently for different subjects in the sample to reflect their relative impact on the product's actual sales.

2. For historical data estimations, the intervention of informed managerial judgment into the analysis is even more essential, since the lack of any experimental control invariably results in data that are full of potential statistical problems. Managerial judgment should be used to reduce random error and solve statistical problems.
   - The effect of price changes tends to get overwhelmed in historical purchase data by the amount of sales variation caused by other factors,

which may not be obvious to the researcher but may be to managers who know their buyers. For example, a researcher analyzing many years' worth of data on the sales of a frozen seafood product could substantially improve the estimation of price sensitivity if management pointed out that many buyers purchase the product as part of their religious observance of Lent, a Christian holiday that shows up at a different time every year. That one bit of information about why consumers buy would enable the researcher to eliminate a substantial amount of random variation in the data that would otherwise yield a biased estimate of price sensitivity if it were not included.

- The researcher using historical data is also often confounded by the problem called *colinearity,* where different explanatory variables change together. Perhaps, at the same time that a firm offers a promotional price deal, it always offers retailers a trade deal in return for a special product display. Without additional input from management, the researcher cannot sort out the effect of the price deal from that of the display. If, however, management knows that buyers of the product are like those of another product that is sometimes sold on special displays without a price deal, the researcher could use sales data from that other product to solve the colinearity problem with this one. Alternatively, if managers are confident in making a judgment about the effectiveness of special displays (for example, that they account for between one-third and one-half of the total sales change), that information can likewise help the researcher to narrow an estimate of the effect of price on sales.[31]

3. Managerial judgment should also be used to select the appropriate structure for an experiment or survey, and the appropriate specification of a statistical equation for analysis of historical data.
- A manager who has studied buyers should know the length of the purchase cycle (time between purchases) and the extent of inventory holding, both of which will govern the necessary length of an experiment or the number of lagged variables to include when analyzing historical data. Failure to appropriately specify the purchase cycle could cause a researcher to grossly miscalculate price sensitivity by ignoring the longer-term effects of a price change.
- Management may have much experience indicating that an advertisement affects buyers differently when the advertisement focuses on price rather than on other product attributes. If so, the researcher should separate those types of advertising in an experiment or in historical data analysis. The researcher might also treat price advertising as having an effect that interacts with the level of price, and nonprice advertising as having an independent effect.

4. For survey research, managerial judgment should guide the preparation of product descriptions, to ensure that they include the variables relevant to buyers and that they describe them with the appropriate connotations.

- For an automobile survey, management can point out that the amount of time required to accelerate to 65 mph is an important attribute to include when describing a sports car, but not when describing a family car.
- For a survey on radios, managers can point out that the word "knob" in a description will carry a connotation much different from the word "control," which may influence buyers' perceptions about other attributes such as reliability and state-of-the-art technology.
- The common failure to use this type of managerial input (or the failure of management to know buyers well enough to provide it) is no doubt one reason why research to measure price sensitivity is often disappointing.

When measurement embodies managerial judgment, it is much more likely to provide useful information, but even then the results should never be taken uncritically. The first question to ask after any marketing research is "Why do the results look the way they do?" The measurement of price sensitivity is not an end result but a catalyst to learn more about one's buyers. If the results are inconsistent with prior expectations, one should consider how prior judgment might have been wrong. What factors may have been overlooked, or have been given too little weight, leading to the formulation of incorrect expectations about price sensitivity? One should also consider how bias might have been introduced into the measurement process. Perhaps the measurement technique heightened buyers' attention to price or the sample subjects were unrepresentative of the product's actual buyers. Regardless of the outcome of such an evaluation, one can learn more about the product's buyers and the factors that determine their price sensitivity. Even when one concludes that the measurement technique biased the results, the bias reveals information (for example, that the low level of price sensitivity that management expected is substantially due to buyers' low attention to price in the natural purchase environment, or that a segment of people who do not regularly buy the firm's product has a different sensitivity to price).

Using Internet-Based Techniques

With the rapid growth of the Internet and e-commerce, market researchers and their clients are increasingly using this forum for gathering customer and market data. On-line research is often far less expensive and much faster than traditional research methods—for example, you avoid the costs of mailing or telephone staff. It tends to obtain better response rates because it is less intrusive and more convenient to simply click a "respond" button in an e-mail. However, on-line research may yield biased results because of sampling bias— on-line respondents are not necessarily representative of the broader target population. Minorities, lower-income households, rural residents, and older people, for example, are less likely to be represented among on-line samples. Nonetheless, online research can be particularly effective for identifying very specific or specialized subgroups to target for research. Esearch.com, for example, sends out qualifying questionnaires to many on-line respondents to find those with specific product or service needs, and then follows up with that smaller pool of respondents with more in-depth research. Eli Lilly, an Es-earch.com client, used this on-line qualifying process to identify people with obscure ailments for which the company is developing treatments.[32]

Selecting the Appropriate Measurement Technique

The choice among measurement techniques is not arbitrary. Each is more appropriate than another under certain circumstances. Information about one determinant of price sensitivity, the unique value effect, is most valuable when a company is developing new products or improving old ones. The value that buyers place on differentiating attributes should determine which ones the final product will include. Clearly, since one cannot use historical data or a purchase experiment to test undeveloped products, one must turn to research on preferences and intentions that require only product descriptions or experimental prototypes. Given the lack of realism in such research and the fact that it often predicts actual price sensitivity rather poorly, one may be skeptical of its value in the product development process. Surveys of preferences and intentions yield poor predictions of actual price sensitivity partly because they fail to capture some important factors in the actual purchase environment, such as price awareness and knowledge of substitutes. At the time of product development, however, those are not factors about which management is concerned. Product development focuses on efforts to enhance the unique value effect. Even when survey research accurately measures only the effect of product attributes on price sensitivity, it is a useful tool for product development, although it may be inadequate for actually setting prices later on.

Once a product is developed, management would like to have measurements that capture as many of the different determinants of price sensitivity as possible. In-store or sophisticated laboratory purchase experiments are definitely the first choice for frequently purchased, low-cost products. With few exceptions, such products are bought by consumers who have low price awareness and give the purchase decision little attention. Consequently, surveys to estimate price sensitivity for such products focus much more attention on price in the purchase decision than would occur naturally, thus distorting the estimates. The cost of in-store experiments, however, may make them impractical for testing on a large scale. In that case, management might best do a few in-store experiments with matched simulated purchase surveys. If the amount of bias in the latter is stable, the survey could be used for further research and adjusted by the amount of the bias.

When the fully developed product is a high-cost durable such as a television set or a photocopier, an in-store experiment is generally impractical. A laboratory purchase experiment may be practical since experimental control permits inferences from fewer purchases but will be too costly for many products. Fortunately, high-value products are also products for which consumers naturally pay great attention to price. In fact, they may give all aspects of the purchase careful thought because it involves a large expenditure. Consequently, a simple laboratory experiment or a simulated purchase survey may be reasonably accurate in predicting price sensitivity for these types of products. Even a buy-response survey may be useful to identify the range of prices that potential customers might find acceptable for such products, although the exact estimates of sales at various prices should not be treated with much confidence.

Once a product has been on the market for awhile, historical data become available. Such data are most useful when managers are willing to implement marketing decisions in ways that can increase the research value of the resulting sales data. For example, sales data become more useful if price changes are sometimes accompanied by a change in advertising and other times not, enabling marketing researchers to isolate their separate effects. A log of unusual events that cause distortions in the actual sales data (for instance, a strike by a competitor's truckers may be causing stock-outs of the competitor's product and increased sales of yours) is also extremely useful when the time comes to adjust the historical data. Moreover, as managers talk with and observe buyers, they should keep questions in mind that would aid the researcher using historical data: What is the length of the purchase cycle? To what extent do buyers purchase extra for inventories when price is expected to rise in the future? Even if historical data are so filled with random variations that no conclusions can be drawn from them with confidence, they may still point toward possible relationships between price and sales or other marketing variables that would be worth examining with another research technique.

SUMMARY

Numerical estimation of price sensitivity is no shortcut to knowing a product's buyers—who they are, how they buy, and why they make their purchase decisions. Numerical estimates are an important source of objective information that can supplement the more subjective observations that usually dominate managerial judgments about price sensitivity. As a supplement, they can substantially improve the accuracy of such judgments and the effectiveness of a firm's pricing.

Measurement techniques differ in the variables they measure and in the conditions of measurement. The variable measured may be either actual purchases or preferences and intentions. Since the ultimate goal of research is to predict customers' actual purchases, research based on actual purchase data is generally more reliable than research based on preferences and intentions. Unfortunately, collecting and analyzing actual-purchase data cost more, require much more time, and are entirely impossible for products that are not yet fully developed and ready for sale. Consequently, most research on price sensitivity infers purchase behavior from questions potential customers answer about their preferences and intentions.

Pricing research studies range from those that are completely uncontrolled to those in which the experimenter controls almost completely the alternative products, their prices, and the information that customers receive. Although research techniques that permit a high degree of experimental control are more costly than uncontrolled research, the added cost is usually worth it. Uncontrolled data on actual purchases are plagued by too little variation in prices and too many variables changing at once. Uncontrolled data on preferences and intentions are biased by people's untruthful responses and by their inability to recall competitive prices. In contrast, controlled in-store experiments and sophisticated laboratory purchase experiments often predict actual price sensitivity well. Even experiments using preferences and intentions seem to warrant confidence when they are highly controlled. In particular, trade-off analysis is proving highly useful in predicting at least that portion of price sensitivity determined by the unique-value effect.

The appropriate technique for numerically estimating price sensitivity depends on the product's stage of development. When a product is still in the concept or prototype stage, research measuring preferences or intentions is the only option. Trade-off analysis is especially useful at this stage because it can identify the value of individual product attributes, thus helping to decide which combination of attributes will enable the firm to price the product most profitably. When a product is ready for the market, in-store or laboratory purchase experiments are more appropriate because they more realistically simulate the actual purchase environment. After a product has been on the market for a while, actual purchase data can be an inexpensive source of estimates, provided that management monitors sales frequently and makes some price changes independently of changes in other marketing variables. Even when actual purchase data cannot provide conclusive answers, they can suggest relationships that can then be measured more reliably with other techniques.

Regardless of the technique used to measure price sensitivity, it is important that managers not allow the estimate to become a substitute for managerial judgment. The low accuracy of many numerical estimates makes blind reliance on them very risky. They always should be compared with a manager's own expectations, based on his or her more general knowledge of buyers and their purchase motivations. When inconsistencies occur, the manager should reexamine both the measurement technique and the adequacy of his or her understanding of buyers. The quality of numerical estimates depends in large part on the quality of managerial judgment that guides the estimation process. Managers who know their buyers can get substantially better estimates of price sensitivity when they use that knowledge (1) to select a sample of consumers that accurately represents the product's market, (2) to identify and explain extraneous changes in sales that might camouflage an effect, (3) to provide information to sort out the effects of price from other variables that tend to change with it, (4) to identify an appropriate equation or experimental structure, and (5) to properly describe the product for survey research.

Notes

1. A. C. Neilsen conducts a bimonthly product audit of retail sales and retailer inventories for many types of frequently purchased products, including foods, household products, health and beauty aids, tobacco products, photographic products, writing instruments, small electrical appliances, and

some automotive products. The Neilsen audit is based on a probability sample of all types of stores in which the product might be sold.

2. Use of Bayesian statistics enables a researcher to quantify a manager's prior beliefs and to reestimate equations using them. Unfortunately, such a formal marriage of prior belief and data is complicated, requiring the special skills of researchers trained well in statistics. For the clearest explanation of the practical application of Bayesian techniques, see Edward E. Leamer, *Specification Searches: Adhoc Inferences with Nonexperimental Data* (Wiley, New York, 1978).

3. Actually, the researcher observes only the price that the consumer reports having paid. There is some risk of erroneous reporting, which weakens the data but does not bias it. Fortunately, this problem is being solved by technologies that enable consumers to avoid the task of reporting.

4. See Ronald E. Frank and William Massy, "Market Segmentation and the Effectiveness of a Brand's Dealing Policies," *Journal of Business*, 38(April 1965), pp. 186–200; Terry Elrod and Russell S. Winer, "An Empirical Evaluation of Aggregation Approaches for Developing Market Segments," *Journal of Marketing*, 46(Fall 1982), pp. 65–74.

5. The companies are Information Resources Inc. (headquarters in Chicago) and Burke Marketing Research (headquarters in Cincinnati, Ohio).

6. The increased usage of scanner data in both applied and academic research results from the widespread availability of such information. Researchers should be aware, however, that research continues to point to the inaccuracy of some of the data available. An excellent study on this subject is "UPC Scanner Pricing Systems: Are They Accurate?" by Ronald C. Goodstein, *Journal of Marketing*, April 1994.

7. See K. Wisniewski and R. C. Blattberg, "Response Function Estimation Using UPC Scanner Data," *Advances and Practices of Marketing Science*, 1983, ed. F. Zufryden, pp. 300–11; Kenneth Wisniewski, "Analytical Approaches to Demand Estimation," *1983 Proceedings of the Business and Economic Statistics Section, American Statistical Association* (ASA, Toronto, 1983), pp. 13–22; and David R. Bell, Joengwen Chiang, and V. Padmanabhan, "The Decomposition of Promotional Response: An Empirical Generalization," *Marketing Science*, 18,4,1999, pp. 504–526.

8. For a brief introduction to regression analysis, see Thomas C. Kinnear and James R. Taylor, *Marketing Research: An Applied Approach*, 4th ed. (McGraw-Hill, New York, 1991), pp. 626–628; or Mark L. Bereson and David M. Levine, *Basic Business Statistics: Concepts and Application* (Prentice-Hall, Englewood Cliffs, NJ, 1992), Chapter 16.

9. In practice, of course, there are always some external factors that will affect only one store's sales, undermining the effectiveness of the control. For example, the control store may run out of a competing brand. One can reduce the distorting effect of such factors by increasing the number of both experimental and control stores, but at a corresponding increase in cost.

10. For guidance in the proper design of either a field or laboratory experiment, see Thomas Cook and Donald T. Campbell, "The Design and Conduct of Quasi-Experimental and True Experiments in Field Settings," in *Handbook of Industrial and Organizational Psychology*, ed. Marvin Dunnette (Rand McNally, Chicago, 1976), pp. 223–35.

11. William Applebaum and Richard Spears, "Controlled Experimentation in Marketing Research," *Journal*

of Marketing, 14(January 1950), pp. 505–17; Edward Hawkins, "Methods of Estimating Demand," *Journal of Marketing,* 21(April 1957), pp. 430–34; William D. Barclay, "Factorial Design in a Pricing Experiment, " *Journal of Marketing Research,* 6(November 1969), pp. 427–29; Sidney Bennet and I. B. Wilkinson, "Price-Quantity Relationship and Price Elasticity Under In-Store Experimentation," *Journal of Business Research,* 2(January 1974), pp. 27–38; Gerald Eskin, "A Case for Test Marketing Experiments," *Journal of Advertising Research,* 15(April 1975), pp. 27–33; Gerald Eskin and Penny Baron, "Effect of Price and Advertising in Test Market Experiments," *Journal of Marketing Research,* 14(November 1977), pp. 499–508.

12. Barclay, "Factorial Design in a Pricing Experiment," p. 428.

13. Paul Solman and Thomas Friedman, *Life and Death in the Corporate Battlefield* (Simon and Schuster, New York, 1982), p. 24.

14. Each company develops its own adjustment factors, which are often closely guarded trade secrets.

15. Several good discussions of the increased use and application of laboratory test markets (called Simulated Test Marketing by the authors) can be found in Kevin J. Clancy and Robert S. Shulman, "Simulated Test Marketing: A New Technology for Solving an Old Problem," in *A.N.A./The Advertiser,* Fall 1995, pp. 28–33; and also by Kevin J. Clancy and Robert S. Shulman, "Test for Success: How Simulated Test Marketing Can Dramatically Improve the Forecasting of a New Product's Sales," in *Sales and Marketing Management,* October 1995, pp. 111–14.

16. One might well argue that buy-response surveys should be included with the experimentally controlled studies since the researcher does exercise control over the price asked. That observation is correct. The reason that buy-response questioning is better than direct questioning is precisely because the researcher introduces a bit of control. Still, the amount of control that the researcher can exercise in these studies is slight. No attempt is made to control the respondents' perception of competitive prices, exposure to promotion, or demographics.

17. Henry Assael, *Consumer Behavior and Marketing Action,* 2nd ed. (Boston, Massachusetts, Kent Publishing, 1983).

18. For a good discussion on the application of and difference between focus group and depth interviews as unstructured/uncontrolled data-collection techniques, see Thomas C. Kinnear and James R. Taylor, *Marketing Research: An Applied Approach,* 4th ed., (McGraw Hill, Inc., New York, 1991).

19. Abbie Griffin and John R. Hauser, "The Voice of the Customer," *Marketing Science,* 12,1,Winter 1993,pp. 1–27.

20. F. James C. Anderson and James A. Narus, "Business Marketing: Understand What Customers Value," *Harvard Business Review,* November–December 1998, pp. 53–65.

21. For and excellent discussion on the types of value drivers and how to uncover those value drivers in both consumer and business-to-business research, read Ian C. MacMillan and Rita Gunther McGrath, "Discovering New Points of Differentiation," *Harvard Business Review,* July–August 1997, pp. 133–45.

22. D. Frank Jones, "A Survey Technique to Measure Demand Under Various Pricing Strategies," *Journal of Marketing,* 39 (July 1975), pp. 75–77.

23. John R. Nevin, "Laboratory Experiments for Estimating Consumer Demand," *Journal of Marketing Research,* 11 (August 1974), pp. 261–68.

24. The first article on trade-off analysis to appear in the marketing literature was Paul E. Green and Vithala R. Rao, "Conjoint Measurement for Quantifying Judgemental Data," *Journal of Marketing Research,* 8 (August 1971), pp. 355–63. For a nontechnical discussion of applications specifically to pricing, see Patrick J. Robinson, "Applications of Conjoint Analysis to Pricing Problems," in *Market Measurement and Analysis,* ed. David B. Montgomery and Dick R. Wittink (Cambridge, MA: Marketing Science Institute, 1980), pp. 183–205.

25. The following articles describe data manipulation procedures for conjoint analysis: J. B. Kruskal, "Analysis of Factorial Experiments by Estimating Monotone Transformations of the Data," *Journal of the Royal Statistical Society,* Series B (1965), pp. 251–63; Dove Peckelman and Subrata Sen, "Regression Versus Interpolation in Additive Conjoint Measurement" (ACR, 1976), pp. 29–34; Philip Cattin and Dick Wittink, "Further Beyond Conjoint Measurement: Toward Comparison of Methods," 1976 Association for Consumer Research Proceedings (ARC, 1976), pp. 41–45.

26. Franklin Acito, "An Investigation of Some Data Collection Issues in Conjoint Measurement," in 1977 Proceedings American Marketing Association, ed B. A. Greenberg and D. N. Bellenger (Chicago: AMA, 1977), pp. 82–85; James McCullough and Roger Best, "Conjoint Measurement: Temporal Stability and Structural Reliability," *Journal of Marketing Research,* 16(February 1979), pp. 26–31; Madhav N. Segal, "Reliability of Conjoint Analysis: Contrasting Data Collection Procedure," *Journal of Mar-keting Research,* 19 (February 1982), pp. 139–43.

27. McCullough and Best, "Conjoint Measurement," pp. 26–31.

28. Bobby J. Calder, "Focus Groups and the Nature of Qualitative Marketing Research," *Journal of Marketing Research,* 14 (August 1977), pp. 353–64.

29. Johnny K. Johansson and Ikujiro Nonaka, "Marketing Research the Japanese Way," Harvard Business Review (May/June, 1987).

30. The Census of Manufacturers is a publication of the U.S. Department of Commerce. For other federal sources, see the Commerce Department publication entitled *A Guide to Federal Data Sources on Manufacturing.* The "Survey of Industrial Buying Power" is published annually as an issue of *Sales and Marketing Management* magazine. Other useful sources of information about the demographics and motivations of buying firms can be obtained from the buying firms' trade associations (for example, Rubber Manufacturers Association, National Machine Tool Builders Association) and from privately operated industrial directory and research companies (for example, Predicasts, Inc., Dun & Bradstreet, Standard & Poors).

31. For the reader trained in classical statistics, these suggestions for adjusting the data with managerial judgment may seem unscientific. But it is important to keep in mind that the purpose of numerical measurement of price sensitivity is to derive useful estimates, not to objectively test a theory. If managers have strongly held beliefs, in light of which the historical record of sales could yield much better estimates, it is simply wasteful to ignore those beliefs simply because they may not be objective. See Edward E. Leamer, "Let's Take the Con Out of Econometrics," *American Economic Review,* 73 (March 1983), pp. 31–43.

32. "Survey Your Customers—Electronically," from *Harvard Management Update,* April 2000, pp. 3–4, Harvard College, Cambridge, MA.

CHAPTER

14

Ethics and the Law

Understanding the Constraints on Pricing

When making pricing decisions, the successful strategist must consider not only what is profitable, but also what will be perceived as ethical and legal. Unfortunately, good advice on both of these issues is all too often unavailable or misleading. Attorneys who do not specialize in antitrust law tend to be overly conservative—advising against activities that are only sometimes illegal or that could trigger an investigation. In fact, benign changes in questionable pricing policies are often all that is necessary to make them both profitable and defensible. On the other hand, product and sales managers eager to achieve quarterly objectives will sometimes fail to consider these constraints at all, resulting in costly condemnations of their companies in courts of law or public opinion. This chapter is intended to raise awareness of the issues and educate you enough to question the advice you receive.

ETHICAL CONSTRAINTS ON PRICING

"Perhaps no other area of managerial activity is more difficult to depict accurately, assess fairly, and prescribe realistically in terms of morality than the domain of price."[2] This oft-quoted assessment reflects the exceptional divergence of ethical opinions with respect to pricing. Even among writers sympathetic to the need for profit, some consider it unethical to charge different prices unless they reflect differences in costs, while others consider pricing unethical unless prices are set "equal or proportional to the benefit received."[3] Consequently, there is less written on ethics in pricing than on other marketing issues, and what is written tends to focus on the easy issues, like deception and price fixing.[4] The tougher issues involve strategies and tactics for gaining profit.

This text is intended to help managers capture in the profits they earn more of the value created by the products and services they sell. In many cultures, and

This chapter is coauthored with Eugene F. Zelek, Jr., a Partner in the Antitrust and Marketing Law Group of Freeborn & Peters,[1] a Chicago law firm.

among many who promulgate ethical principles, such a goal is morally reprehensible. Although this opinion was once held by the majority, its popularity has generally declined over the last three centuries due to the success of capitalism and the failure of collectivism to deliver an improvement in material well-being. Still, many people, including many in business practice and education, believe that there are legitimate ethical constraints on maximizing profit through pricing.

It is important to clarify your own and your customers' understanding of those standards before ambiguous situations arise. The topology of ethical constraints in pricing illustrated in Exhibit 14-1 is a good place to start. Readers should determine where to draw the line concerning ethical constraints—for themselves and their industry—and determine as well how other people (family, neighbors, social groups) might view such decisions.

Most people would reject the idea of zero ethical constraints, where the seller can dictate the price and terms and force them on an unwilling buyer. Sale of "protection" by organized crime is universally condemned. The practice of forcing employees in a one-company town to buy from the "company store" is subject to only marginally less condemnation. Even when the government itself is the seller that is forcing people to purchase goods and services at a price (tax rate) it sets, people generally condemn the transaction unless they feel empowered to influence the terms. This level of ethical constraint was also used to condemn the "trusts" that, before the antitrust laws, sometimes used reprehensible tactics to drive lower-priced competitors out of business. By denying customers alternative products, trusts arguably forced them to buy theirs.

Ethical level one embodied in all well-functioning, competitive market economies, requires that all transactions be voluntary. Early capitalist economies, and some of the most dynamic today (for instance, that of Hong Kong), condone any transaction that meets this criterion. The legal principle of caveat emptor,

EXHIBIT 14-1 When Is a Price Ethical?

Ethical Constraints

Level	The Exchange Is Ethical When	Implication/Proscription
1	The price is paid voluntarily	"Let the buyer beware."
2	. . and based on equal information.	No sales without full disclosure (used-car defects, risks of smoking).
3	. . . and not exploiting buyers' "essential needs."	No "excessive" profits on "essentials" such as life-saving pharmaceuticals.
4	. . . and justified by costs.	No segmented pricing based on value. No excessive profits based on shortages, even for nonessential products.
5	. . . and provides equal access to goods regardless of one's ability to cover the cost.	No exchange for personal gain. Give as able and receive as needed.

"Let the buyer beware," characterized nearly all economic transactions in the United States prior to the twentieth century. In such a market, people often make regrettable purchases (for example, expensive brand-name watches that turn out to be cheap substitutes, and stocks in overvalued companies). On the other hand, without the high legal costs associated with meeting licensing, branding, and disclosure requirements, new business opportunities abound even for the poor—making unemployment negligible.

Ethical level two imposes a more restrictive standard, condemning even voluntary transactions by those who would profit from unequal information about the exchange. Selling a used car without disclosing a known defect, concealing a known risk of using a product, or misrepresenting the benefits achievable from a product are prime examples of transactions that would be condemned by this ethical criterion. Thus, many would condemn selling land in Florida at inflated prices to unwary out-of-state buyers, or selling lottery tickets to the poor, since the seller could reasonably expect these potential buyers to be ignorant of, or unable to process, information needed to make an informed decision. Since sellers naturally know more about the features and benefits of products than most consumers do, they may have an ethical duty to disclose what they know completely and accurately.[5]

Ethical level three imposes a still more stringent criterion: that sellers earn no more than a "fair" profit from sales of "necessities" for which buyers have only limited alternatives. This principle is often stated as follows: "No one should profit from other people's adversity." Thus even nominally capitalist societies sometimes impose rent controls on housing and price controls on pharmaceutical costs and physicians' fees. Even when this level of ethical constraint is not codified into law, people who espouse it condemn those who raise the price of ice during a power failure or the price of lumber following a hurricane, when the demand for these products soars.

Ethical level four extends the criteria of ethical level three to all products, even those with many substitutes and not usually thought of as necessities. Profit is morally justifiable only when it is the minimum necessary to induce companies and individuals to make decisions for the good of "less-advantaged" members of society.[6] Profit is ethically justifiable only as the price society must pay to induce suppliers of capital and skills to improve the well-being of those less fortunate. Profits from exploiting unique skills, great ideas, or exceptional efficiency (called "economic rents") are morally suspect in this scenario unless it can be shown that everyone, or at least the most needy, benefits from allowing such profits to be earned, such as when a high-profit company nevertheless offers lower prices and better working conditions than its competitors. Profits from speculation (buying low and selling high) are clearly condemned, as is segmented pricing (charging customers different prices to capture different levels of value), unless those prices actually reflect differences in cost.

Ethical level five, the most extreme constraint, is inconsistent with markets. In some "primitive" societies, everyone is obliged to share good fortune with those in the tribe who are less fortunate. "From each according to his ability, to each according to his need" is the espoused ethical premise of Marxist societies and even some respected moral philosophers. Those that have actually tried to put it into practice, however, have eventually recoiled at the brutality necessary to force essentially self-interested humans "to give according to their abilities" without reward. Within families and small, self-selected societies, however, this ethical principle can thrive. Within social and religious organizations, members often work together for their common good and share the results. Even within businesses, partnerships are established to share, within defined bounds, each other's good and bad fortune.

For each level of ethical constraint on economic exchange, one must determine the losses and gains, for both individuals and societies, that will result from the restriction. What effect does each level have on the material and social well-being of those who hold it as a standard? Should the same standards be applied in different contexts? For example, is your standard different for business markets than it is for consumer markets? Would your ethical standards change when selling in a foreign country where local competitors generally hold a higher or lower ethical standard than yours? In assessing the standards that friends, business associates, and political representatives apply, managers must ask themselves if their personal standards are the same for their business as well as for their personal conduct. For example, would they condemn an oil company for earning excess profits as a result of higher crude prices, yet themselves take excess profits on a house that had appreciated substantially in a hot real estate market? If so, are they hypocrites or is there some justification for holding individuals and firms to different standards?

Although we, the authors of this text, certainly have our own beliefs about which of these ethical levels is practical and desirable in dealing with others, and would apply different standards in different contexts, we feel that neither we nor most of the people who claim to be experts on business ethics are qualified to make these decisions for someone else. Each individual must make his or her own decisions and live with the personal and social consequences.

Regardless of one's personal ethical beliefs about pricing, it would be foolish to ignore the legal constraints on pricing. Antitrust law in the United States has developed over the years to reflects both citizens' moral evaluations of companies' actions and companies' attempts to get laws passed that protect them from more efficient or aggressive competitors. As the summary below illustrates, the meaning of these laws changes over time as courts respond to changing social attitudes and the placement of judges with differing political views.

THE LEGAL FRAMEWORK FOR PRICING

When making pricing decisions, the strategist must consider not only what is profitable, but also what is lawful. Since the late nineteenth century, the United States has been committed to maintaining price competition through establishing and enforcing antitrust policy. Statutes, regulations, and guidelines, as well as countless judicial decisions, have defined what constitutes anticompetitive pricing behavior and the rules under which the government and private parties may pursue those who engage in it.

For more than a hundred years, U.S. antitrust law has responded to a complex and dynamic marketplace by being both of these things, resulting in policies that are always being scrutinized and questioned and sometimes stretched and revised. The overall trend in the United States for the last several decades has been to move away from judging behavior based on economic assumptions toward focusing on demonstrable economic effect, something that has fostered a great deal of contemporary pricing freedom. Of course, a necessary companion to evolving policies, as well as the lag time sometimes necessary for the law to catch up with the marketplace, is ambiguity. In return for some uncertainty, there is more latitude for businesses to cope creatively with both new and old challenges.

This chapter discusses key aspects of the law of pricing, focusing primarily on that of general applicability at the federal level.[7] Due to the long history of U.S. law in the pricing area, it has served as a model for other parts of the world, including the European Union (EU) and Japan. For example, EU antitrust law historically prohibited such things as territorial restrictions on intermediaries that interfered with cross-border trade, but a safe harbor became effective in 2000.[8] That, much like the change in the U.S. view that occurred more than twenty years earlier, recognizes a supplier's legitimate interest in controlling how its products are resold under certain circumstances.

In the United States, the antitrust laws are enforced by both government and private parties. The Department of Justice is empowered to bring criminal and civil actions, although the former is reserved primarily for price fixing and hardcore cartel activity.[9] At the same time, the Federal Trade Commission (FTC) may bring civil actions,[10] as can private parties. Often, civil plaintiffs pursue injunctions to stop certain conduct and, in the case of private parties, they may also or alternatively seek three times their actual economic damages (something known as "treble damages"), as well as their legal fees and court costs.[11] While the volume of private antitrust litigation dwarfs that brought by the government, private suits often follow significant government cases.

PRICE FIXING OR PRICE ENCOURAGEMENT

In an effort to reduce or avoid market risks, businesspeople have long been interested in setting prices with their competitors or dictating or influencing the prices charged by their downstream intermediaries, such as distributors, dealers, and retailers. Over the years, U.S. law has taken a rather dim view of this behavior. At the same time, it is now clear that there is some flexibility in what competitors—which collectively affect market prices—can do, but the biggest changes are in the area of distribution channels, where price setting is lawful if done properly.

There are two types of price fixing: horizontal and vertical. In the former, competitors agree on the prices they will charge or key terms of sale affecting price. In the latter, a supplier and a reseller agree on the prices the reseller will charge or the price-related terms of resale for the supplier's products. However, where an intermediary, such as an independent sales representative, does not take ownership of the supplier's products and acts only as the supplier's agent, there cannot be any vertical price fixing because the law views the sale as taking place directly between the supplier and the end user, with the intermediary serving as a conduit. Consequently, the supplier is only setting its own prices and terms of sale.[12]

The primary law in this area is Section 1 of the Sherman Act, an 1890 statute that prohibits "[e]very contract, combination . . . or conspiracy in restraint of trade."[13] The contract, combination, or conspiracy requirement necessarily means that there must be an agreement between two or more individuals or entities. As a result, the law does not reach unilateral behavior.[14] Moreover, the Sherman Act does not ban merely imitating a competitor's pricing behavior (something called "conscious parallelism").[15]

Sometimes, there are written contracts or other direct evidence of price fixing conspiracies. Far more often, evidence of agreement must be inferred from the actions of the parties involved. Although conscious parallelism by itself is not enough to establish an agreement, when uniform or similar behavior is coupled with one or more "plus factors," courts have found concerted activity. Perhaps the most powerful of these factors is if the conduct in question would be against the self-interest of each party if it acted alone, but consistent with their self-interest if they all behaved the same way, such as the uniform imposition of unpopular restrictions or price increases in the face of surplus.[16] Another factor is the opportunity to collude (often shown by communications between or among the parties), followed by identical or similar actions, although the probative effect of such opportunity or communications can be undercut by legitimate business explanations.[17]

Once concerted action has been found, the next step is to evaluate it. Case law has further refined Section 1 of the Sherman Act to require two levels of proof, depending on the nature of the alleged offense. Some offenses are considered to be "per se" illegal, while others are analyzed under the "rule of reason." Per se offenses require that the presence of the objectionable practice be proven and that there be antitrust injury and damages, while offenses subject to the rule of reason add a third element—that the practice at issue be unreasonably anticompetitive. In general, it is easier to prove a violation under the per se test and more difficult to do so under the rule of reason, because the latter requires detailed economic analysis and a balancing of procompetitive and anticompetitive effects. Of course, the rule of reason also provides defendants with the opportunity to justify their behavior; something denied under the per se rule.

Historically, all arrangements affecting price were presumed to be unreasonably anticompetitive on their face and, therefore, per se illegal. However, during the last twenty-five years or so, the U.S. Supreme Court has placed more emphasis on showing demonstrable economic effect rather than relying on assumptions, so there has been an erosion of per se application to both horizontal and vertical pricing issues.

Horizontal Price Fixing

In the horizontal arena, direct price fixing—competitors in the stereotypical smoke-filled room agreeing to set prices or rig bids—remains per se illegal. The same treatment is accorded to indirect price fixing, where there is an ambiguous arrangement between competitors that a court has determined constitutes illegal price fixing after conducting a detailed factual review or market analysis.[18]

However, when a restriction on price is merely the incidental effect of a desirable procompetitive activity (sometimes referred to as "incidental price fixing"), it is now clear that the more forgiving rule of reason applies. This point is illustrated by *National Collegiate Athletic Association v. Board of Regents,* where the U.S. Supreme Court applied the rule of reason and noted that rules covering athletic equipment and schedules were appropriate, but those that limited the television exposure of member football teams were an unreasonable restriction on output that unlawfully increased prices.[19]

RESALE PRICE FIXING OR ENCOURAGEMENT

Vertical Price Fixing

Vertical price fixing always has been considered per se illegal, but recent Supreme Court cases have narrowed the application of the per se rule. In late 1997, the Supreme Court in *State Oil Co. v. Khan* unanimously overturned the precedent in a twenty-nine-year-old case to hold that the rule of reason, rather than the per se test, applies to vertical agreements that set maximum or "ceiling" resale prices, because purchasers are not always harmed by such arrangements and, indeed, may be benefited by them to the extent they hold down prices.[20] However, the use of maximum resale pricing is relatively rare, occurring, for example, when the supplier wishes to limit reseller margins for a hot, new product or to facilitate national or regional price advertising.[21] From a business point of view, the desire to set minimum ("floor") or exact prices (each usually designed to address discounting) is far more common, but doing so by agreement remains illegal on face.

However, the Supreme Court's *Monsanto* and *Business Electronics* decisions in the 1980s make it clear that setting maximum, minimum, or exact resale prices without an agreement (i.e., unilaterally) is not illegal price fixing prohibited under the Sherman Act.[22] As a result, a supplier may announce a price at which its product must be resold (i.e., establish a ceiling, floor, or exact price policy) and refuse to sell to any reseller that does not comply, as long as there is no agreement between the supplier and its reseller on resale price levels.[23] Even when resellers follow the supplier's resale price policy, there is no unlawful agreement. With this latitude after *Monsanto* and *Business Electronics,* many manufacturers of desirable branded products have successfully discouraged the discounting of their products in such diverse industries as consumer electronics, furniture, appliances, sporting goods, luggage, handbags, agricultural supplies, and automotive replacement parts.

A frequent justification given for minimum or exact resale price policies is to permit resellers sufficient margin to provide a selling environment that is consistent with the supplier's objectives for its products, including brand image. For example, the supplier may want knowledgeable salespeople, showrooms, substantial inventory, and superior service. Of course, such policies also may help support higher supplier margins. Sometimes, the imposition of such policies is sought by resellers to insulate them from price competition. As long as there is no agreement on price levels, such requests, even if acted upon by the supplier, are not unlawful.

Pricing policies may be used broadly or selectively to cover everything from a single product to all of those in a supplier's line. Similarly, they can be used in certain geographic areas and with specific channels of distribution in which price erosion is a problem, or they can be used throughout the country. In any event, a policy violation typically requires that the supplier stop selling the offending reseller the products involved, although it also is permissible to pull a product line or all of the supplier's business.[24] When and if the supplier wishes to resume selling is the supplier's unilateral decision, although some cases suggest that warnings, threats, and probation short of termination are unacceptable, apparently because they support the inference that some form of prohibited agreement has been reached.

To make such a policy stick, the supplier must generally have brand or market power. Otherwise, resellers simply won't bother to follow the policy, as there are plenty of substitutes available. Ironically, it is those highly desirable products that are most susceptible to discounting anyway, so the requisite power is typically present. In addition, it is important to note that resale price policies have a vertical reach that is limited to one level down the distribution channel. If all resellers buy directly from the manufacturer, this restriction poses no problem, but if a significant amount of sales are made through multiple levels of distribution, a policy will be too porous to be effective. In other words, a manufacturer can control a direct-buying retailer's sell price, but it can't reach that of a retailer that buys from a wholesaler. To address this problem, the manufacturer may "jump over" the wholesaler by making a sales directly to the retailer, or it may convert the wholesaler into an agent for the purpose of such sale.

Resale price policies are potent, but the rules for managing them within the law are necessarily picky. Careful implementation keeps otherwise lawful programs from going astray. This means that any form of agreement regarding resale prices must be avoided. There must be no resale pricing contracts, no assurances of compliance, and no probation. Because this area can be a legal minefield, it's crucial to carefully train supplier personnel. At the same time, many companies have adopted such programs with considerable success.

Direct Dealing Programs

Another way to control the prices charged to end users is for the supplier to sell them directly or, constructively, by the use of agents. When the supplier agrees with the end user on price, but the latter cannot handle delivery of large quantities or maintain sufficient inventory to justify direct shipments from the supplier, some suppliers look to a reseller to fill the order out of the reseller's warehouse. This can be done by consignment or by the supplier buying back inventory from the reseller immediately prior to its transfer to the end user, so, in either event, the sale runs directly from the supplier to the end user. The reseller becomes the supplier's warehousing and delivery agent and is compensated by the supplier for performing only these functions.

When the supplier has negotiated the price to the end user, but the reseller has or retains the title, the supplier has another alternative. Under the "reseller's choice" approach, the reseller may either choose to sell the product to the end user at the price set by the supplier or tell the supplier to find someone else to do so. Even if the reseller agrees to sell at the contracted price, there is no per se illegal price fixing, as this practice is seen as voluntary and therefore subject to the rule of reason.[25]

Resale Price Encouragement

Instead of dictating a resale price by agreement, policy, or direct sale, some suppliers encourage desirable resale pricing behavior by providing financial or other incentives, such as advertising allowances to promote certain prices. Although these practices are judged under the rule of reason because participation is not mandatory, the provision of incentives is subject to the prohibitions in the Robinson-Patman Act against price and promotional discrimination.[26]

In the area of price advertising, a common practice is to use a Minimum Advertised Price (MAP) program, although the underlying concept could also be used for maximum or exact prices. Under this approach, the reseller receives an advertising allowance (often in the form of co-op advertising funds) in return for adhering to the appropriate price in advertising, in a catalog, or over the Internet.[27] Some companies pay an explicit allowance (such as a percentage rebate on purchases), while others employ an implicit allowance stating that failure to follow program requirements results in the loss of the allowance and an increase in price. The latter is found in consumer electronics.

A variant on MAP programs is group or shared-price advertising, where a supplier sponsors an ad, but resellers can be listed in it only if they agree to sell at the promoted price during the period indicated. Again, resellers that wish pricing freedom may decline to be in the ad, and, because of the voluntary nature of this approach, there is no per se illegality.

Another alternative is target-price rebates. Here, the supplier rewards the reseller with financial incentives the closer its resale prices are to the target set by the supplier. This practice requires point-of-sale (POS) reporting, typically easier to get in the consumer area due to the widespread use of scanners, but becoming more common in the industrial marketplace.

PRICE AND PROMOTIONAL DISCRIMINATION

Although economists maintain that the ability to charge different prices to different customers promotes efficiency by clearing the market, U.S. law on that issue has focused on maintaining the viability of numerous sellers as a means to preserve competition. Consequently, while price discrimination has been unlawful since 1914, the Robinson-Patman Act amended existing legislation in 1936, so this entire area is commonly referred to by the name of the amendment.[28]

This complex, Depression-era legislation was enacted to protect small businesses by outlawing discriminatory price and promotional allowances obtained by large businesses, while exempting sales to government or "charitable" organizations for their own use. At the same time, the emergence of contemporary power buyers through internal growth or consolidation (like Wal-Mart or W. W. Grainger), as well as supplier efforts to make discounts and allowances provided to customers more efficient, have forced or encouraged sellers to provide lawful account-specific pricing and promotions by creatively finding ways through the Robinson-Patman maze. This trend is likely to continue, as further consolidation and evolving distribution channels (brought on by e-commerce, among other things) will demand and reward more sophisticated differentiation.

As is the case with the other antitrust laws, the Department of Justice, the FTC, and private parties may each bring Robinson-Patman cases, although the enforcement agencies have not focused on this area for some time. Indeed, the Justice Department has criminal powers in this area that have gone unused for many years, while the FTC today brings few significant cases in this area after being particularly active through the 1970s. Private suits on behalf of businesses (consumers have no standing to sue under the statute) account for most of the enforcement activity.[29] Successful plaintiffs are entitled to the same remedies as those available under the antitrust laws discussed previously (injunctions, treble damages, attorneys' fees and costs).

Price Discrimination

Keep in mind that discrimination in price is not always unlawful. In order to prove illegal price discrimination under the Robinson-Patman Act and assuming that the supplier sells in interstate commerce, each of five elements must be present:[30]

1. **Discrimination.** This standard is met simply by charging different prices to different customers. However, if the reason for the difference is due to a discount or allowance made available to all or almost all customers (like a prompt payment discount), but some customers choose not to take advantage of it, the element of discrimination drops out, ending the inquiry. This is known as the "availability defense."

2. **Sales to Two or More Purchasers.** The different prices must be charged on reasonably contemporaneous sales to two or more purchasers—a rule that permits price fluctuations. In other words, it is inappropriate under the statute to compare two widely separated sales in a highly volatile market. Yet if prices typically change annually or semiannually, a sale made in January may be compared with one made in March.

In addition, offering different prices is not enough. Actual sales or agreements to sell at different prices must exist. For example, if two electrical supply distributors seek special pricing from the manufacturer to bid on a construction job or an integrated supply contract that only one will get, the manufacturer may, if it is careful, give one a better price than the other, because in doing so, it is providing two offers, but making only one sale.[31]

3. **Goods.** Robinson-Patman applies to the sale of goods only ("commodities" in the statute), so services—such as telecommunications, banking and transportation—are not covered.[32] When a supplier sells a bundled offering, such repair services that include parts or computer hardware that includes maintenance services, Robinson-Patman is relevant only if the value of the goods in the bundle predominates. Also, it is possible to turn goods into services if the manufacturer procures raw materials and produces and stores the products on behalf of the customer, with the customer owning the inventory every step of the way and bearing the risk of loss.

4. **Like Grade and Quality.** The goods involved must be physically or essentially the same. Brand preferences are irrelevant, but functional variations can differentiate products. In a key case, the Supreme Court stated that a branded product and its physically and chemically identical private-label version must be priced the same by the manufacturer.[33] While the distinctions drawn in the case law sometimes appear arbitrary, meaningful functional or physical variations can result in different products that legitimize different prices. For example, two air conditioners that have significant differences in cooling capacity are distinct products, even if they otherwise are physically identical.

5. **Reasonable Probability of Competitive Injury.** The law generally focuses on injury at one of two levels. The first, called "primary line," permits a supplier to sue a competitor for the latter's discriminatory pricing. But here the law also requires that the supplier's discriminatory pricing be below its cost, something designed to drive its rival out of business or otherwise injure competition in the market as a whole (called "predatory intent"), rather than to merely take some incremental market share. Moreover, the structure of the market must be such that the discriminating supplier can raise prices after it disposes of the targeted competitor or that market injury otherwise is threatened through reduced output.[34] Not surprisingly, there are few contemporary primary-line cases due to this high standard.

Far more common is "secondary line" injury, where a supplier's disfavored reseller or end-user customer may sue the supplier for price discrimination. However, the law is clear that only competing customers must be treated alike. To the extent that customers do not compete due to their locations or the markets they serve, different prices are appropriate under the Robinson-Patman Act. Significantly, if these distinctions do not occur naturally, they may be introduced or formalized by contract or policy through the use of vertical nonprice restrictions.[35]

Defenses to Price Discrimination

Even if all five price-discrimination elements are present, there are three defenses that may be used to avoid what otherwise is unlawful discrimination.[36]

1. **Cost Justification.** This defense permits a price disparity if it is based on legitimate cost differences. For example, freight is usually less expensive on a per case basis for a truckload shipment. However, while there is no requirement to pass on any savings, if the supplier does so, the law states that some or all of the actual savings may be passed on to the customer, but not a penny more.

One common problem area is volume discounts, particularly those that are stair-stepped with large differences between levels. Perhaps this structure reflected real cost differences many years ago when it was adopted by the supplier, but, unless the underlying cost analysis is regularly updated, the discounts probably do not track today's costs. Indeed, the dynamic nature of business and the precision required to support this defense make it difficult to apply successfully, although the sophistication of activity-based costing holds a great deal of potential. Some manufacturers keep profit-and-loss statements on their customers and adjust their pricing accordingly.

2. **Meeting Competition.** Under this defense, discrimination is permissible if it is based on a good-faith belief that a discriminatory price is necessary to meet the price of a competitive supplier to the favored customer or to maintain a traditional price disparity.[37] Most managers are familiar with the application of this defense on the micro level, that is, when a buyer tells the seller that the seller's competitor offered a lower price. However, meeting competition may also be used on the macro level to justify things like volume discounts that are so institutionalized in the industry that adjusting them to reflect true cost savings would result in the loss of business.

Of course, it is at the micro level where this defense is most often used. Unfortunately, this means relying on the purchaser for competitive pricing information when the buyer has every incentive to lie.[38] Some companies provide their salespeople with detailed meeting-competition forms that require competitive invoices and other documentary evidence. While this sort of evidence is helpful, it is not essential, as long as the seller has a reasonable basis at the time of the decision to believe that the competitive price described by the buyer is legitimate, even if it turns out to be wrong later. Nevertheless, a written or electronic record of why the otherwise discriminatory price was provided is useful.

Because meeting competition is a defense, there is no obligation to provide the special price to anyone other than the customer that asked for it. Of course, smart buyers will attempt to secure "most favored nations" clauses in their contracts or purchase orders to automatically get the benefit of a lower price elsewhere, regardless of whether they would otherwise be entitled to them. Such clauses may cause tension between a supplier's Robinson-Patman responsibilities and those under the law of contract.

3. **Changing Conditions.** Special prices may be provided to sell perishable, seasonal, obsolete, or distressed merchandise, even though the full price had been charged up to the point of offering the special prices.

Promotional Discrimination

The Robinson-Patman Act also bans promotional discrimination in an effort to deny an alternative means of achieving discriminatory pricing. The distinction between price and promotional discrimination is an important one because different legal standards apply and, while the standards in certain respects are tougher for promotional discrimination, there is ultimately more flexibility.

Price discrimination covers the sale from the supplier to the reseller or to the direct-buying end user, while promotional discrimination usually relates only to the reseller's sale of the supplier's products.[39] Historically, promotional discrimination was largely the purview of consumer goods marketers, as industrial goods sellers concentrated on such things as volume discounts subject to price discrimination standards. However, the need for creative account-specific marketing and the desire to make supplier incentives work harder have caused many industrial sellers to face the same issues. Both consumer and industrial suppliers are now focusing on how their resellers sell their products (promotional discrimination), rather than only on how they buy them (price discrimination).

As was the case with price discrimination, each of several elements must be present to violate the law:

1. **The Provision of Allowances, Services, or Facilities.** Here, the supplier grants to the reseller advertising or promotional allowances (like $5 off per case to promote a product) or provides services or facilities (such as demonstrators or free display racks), usually in return for some form of promotional performance.

2. **In Connection with the Resale of the Supplier's Goods.** As is the case with price discrimination, the law regarding promotional discrimination does not reach service providers. In addition, promotional discrimination generally applies only to resellers. Typically this does not cover purchasers that use or consume the supplier's product in making their own. Also, it usually does not cover

the incorporation of a product, such as, sugar used in baked goods, cutting tools used to make machine castings, or sound systems installed at the automotive factory. However, these purchasers are resellers for promotional discrimination purposes if they receive allowances or other benefits from the supplier for promoting the fact that the finished goods were made using the supplier's product or contain it, such as an ice cream producer that advertises the use of a particular brand of chocolate chip or a manufacturer that promotes the use of an axle brand in its heavy-duty trucks.

3. **Not Available to All Competing Customers on Proportionally Equal Terms.** Once again, not all of the supplier's customers need to be treated alike, only those which compete. In addition, the services or facilities offered or the performance required to earn the allowances must be "functionally available," i.e., usable or attainable in a practical sense by all competing resellers, something that may require alternatives. In other words, if a reseller could take advantage of a promotional program, but chooses not to do so, the supplier is off the legal hook.[40] For example, if a warehouse club chain could advertise in newspapers, but it decides not to do so, the supplier is under no legal obligation to offer an alternative to a newspaper-advertising allowance. On the other hand, if the supplier pays for advertising on grocery carts, but some of its retail customers can't have them due to the size of their stores, the supplier must make available an alternative means of performance, such as a poster or window sign in lieu of cart advertising.

The flexibility available under promotional discrimination standards is based on the fact that competing customers do not have to receive the same level of benefits, something contrary to the implicit mandate to do so under price discrimination rules. Instead, the promotional discrimination requirement is one of "proportional equality," and there are three ways to proportionalize what is provided: (1) on unit or dollar purchases (buy a case, get a dollar—something that lawfully favors larger resellers that buy more); (2) on the cost to the reseller of the promotional activity (a full-page ad in a national trade magazine costs more than that in a regional newsletter); or (3) on the value of the promotional activity to the supplier (salespeople dedicated exclusively to the supplier's brand have more value than those who are not).[41]

Competitive Injury, Defenses, and Indirect Purchasers

There also are other, somewhat less attractive differences between price and promotional discrimination. First, no competitive injury is necessary for illegal promotional discrimination, making it more like a per se rule.[42] Second, meeting competition is the only defense, as cost justification and changing conditions are irrelevant. Third, if the supplier provides promotional allowances to direct-buying resellers, it must also furnish them to competitive resellers that buy the promoted product through intermediaries, something accomplished with ultimate reseller rebates or mandatory pass-throughs.

USING NONPRICE VARIABLES TO SUPPORT PRICING GOALS

Vertical Nonprice Restrictions

Under the standards for price and promotional discrimination, the Robinson-Patman Act requires that only competing reseller and direct-buying end-user customers be treated similarly. For this reason, or to be consistent with other price-related or marketing objectives, the supplier may wish to control the degree to which its resellers compete with each other, something known as "intrabrand competition." In 1977, the Supreme Court's *Sylvania* decision provided suppliers with considerable flexibility in this regard, by holding that vertical nonprice restrictions are subject to the rule of reason and that intrabrand competition could be reduced to promote "interbrand competition," or the rivalry between competing brands.[43]

As a result, suppliers may impose vertical restraints on resellers to help manage distribution channels and to provide considerable leeway in pricing design, using the carrot approach (financial incentives), the stick approach (contractual requirements), or some combination of the two.[44] Historically, industrial sellers have favored the use of vertical restrictions and the more selective distribution that goes with them, while many consumer goods suppliers (except those who sell durables) have been more interested in widespread distribution without the same sort of restrictions. However, the challenges of Internet sales and other factors have focused more attention on limiting how products may be resold.

Broadly speaking, there are three types of vertical nonprice restraints, each subject to the rule of reason:

1. **Customer Restrictions.** Rather than selling to any customer, the reseller is restricted only to particular customers or is prohibited from selling to certain customers. For example, in the industrial area, the reseller could be required to sell only to plumbing contractors or to stay away from accounts that are reserved to the supplier or another reseller. On the consumer side, the reseller could be limited to customers who order over the Internet or prohibited from selling to such customers at all.

2. **Territorial Restrictions.** Although generally designed to prevent or discourage selling outside of a geographic area, these can also be thought of as market restrictions. An "exclusive distributorship" is actually a restraint on the supplier, as it agrees that a particular reseller will be the exclusive outlet in the latter's territory or market (however defined) for some or all of the supplier's products. When the reseller is required to sell inside only a particular territory or market, it is subject to "absolute confinement." By combining an exclusive distributorship with absolute confinement, the result is known as an "airtight territory." In other words, if a supplier promises a dealer that the latter will be the only outlet in Oregon for a particular product, it has granted an exclusive distributor-

ship. If the dealer is limited to selling in that state, there is absolute confinement and, when it is combined with an exclusive distributorship, the reseller has an airtight territory.

Due to some flip-flopping on the part of the Supreme Court, vertical non-price restrictions were per se illegal from 1968 until the *Sylvania* decision in 1977. In response, a number of so-called "lesser restraints" were established that may not be as helpful in pricing as other restraints, but still can be useful. The first of these is an "area of primary responsibility" that permits sales outside a reseller's territory, but expects the reseller to focus its efforts on its designated geographic area.[45] The second is a "profit passover" that allows the reseller to sell anywhere, but, to neutralize the "free-rider effect," the reseller must split revenue or profit for sales outside its territory with the reseller in the area encroached upon. The third is a "location clause" that restricts the reseller to approved sites only. While this last approach is ineffective if sales are made over the Internet or by phone or fax, it can be useful where a physical presence in the territory is necessary, especially in an environment where resellers are consolidating.

3. **Product Restrictions.**
   - *Designated Products.* Suppliers have no legal obligation to sell their reseller or end-user customers any of their products, except in two instances—when the supplier has a contract to do so or in the relatively rare situation when the supplier is a monopolist with excess capacity.[46] In other words, the supplier may generally determine what products, if any, it sells to its reseller or direct-buying end-user customers. In this way, it may limit intrabrand competition or other conflicts by restricting what can be purchased by whom.

   - *Exclusive Dealing.* Here, the reseller or the end user is not permitted to purchase particular products or services or types of products or services from another supplier. Alternatively, it may be discouraged from doing so through financial or other incentives, often called "loyalty programs." Judged under the rule of reason, the test is whether competing suppliers are unreasonably foreclosed from the market. As long as such suppliers have reasonable access to the market through other resellers or other means, exclusive dealing is permissible.

   - *Tying and Full-Line Forcing.* In some respects, tying is the other side of the coin from exclusive dealing, with the same effect.[47] In its most extreme form, tying requires that in order to purchase a desirable product or service, the customer must also buy another product or service that is less desirable. Although tying is often described as per se illegal, the analysis necessary to prove a violation is more akin to that required by the rule of reason.[48] Bundling is not illegal tying, as long as the products or services are available separately, even at a somewhat higher, but reasonable, cost.

Full-line forcing, judged under the rule of reason, is a variation on tying that requires a reseller to carry the supplier's entire line or a specified assortment to avoid the customer's cherry-picking of the more desirable products. Note that tying and full-line forcing can effectively crowd competitive products off the shelf.

Nonprice Incentives

To motivate desired behavior, a supplier may provide a favored reseller or end user with certain nonprice benefits, such as first access to new products or enhanced technical support. Due to their nonprice nature, this type of discriminatory reward is not covered by the Robinson-Patman Act, although the other antitrust laws still apply.[49] At the same time, anything that the supplier does to assume or subsidize an expense that normally would be incurred by the customer raises Robinson-Patman Act concerns.

OTHER PRICING ISSUES

Predatory Pricing

Chapter 5 introduced the concept of a predatory price, a price set so low that the firm harms its own profitability in an attempt to do greater harm to a competitor. The purpose of such behavior is either to discipline a competitor for competing too intensely or to drive it from the market and thus eliminate its competition entirely.

Long-term aggressive pricing that is below marginal cost (or its measurable surrogate, average variable cost) can be attacked as monopolization or attempted monopolization under Section 2 of the Sherman Act, and by the FTC under Section 5 of the FTC Act.[50] However, in 1993, the Supreme Court ruled that a successful prosecution requires proof that the price-cutting seller could likely recoup its losses with higher prices later on.[51] This heavy burden of proof severely limits claims of predation and favors the presumption that price-cutting is procompetitive.

Price Signaling

The practice of a supplier communicating its future pricing intentions to its competitors is known as "price signaling." It is usually done to facilitate price parallelism through such means as supplying advance notice of price changes to customers or the media. In *Du Pont,* the court of appeals overturned an FTC decision that such behavior violates the antitrust laws, ruling that consciously parallel pricing is not unlawful unless it is collusive, predatory, coercive, or exclusionary.[52] While signaling raises questions about the possibility of collusion, it can have legitimate business purposes as well. According to the court, signaling serves the legitimate business purpose of aiding buyers in their financial and purchasing planning.[53]

SUMMARY

The development and implementation of pricing strategies and tactics that do not violate the law is an important aspect of pricing. In addition to the risk of legal actions initiated by the government, a company can be sued by private parties, usually its competitors or its customers. If the Justice Department can prove that the company's pricing violated the criminal provisions of the antitrust laws, the company is subject to fines and its managers may face both fines and imprisonment. In successful civil cases brought by the Justice Department or the FTC, the company may be enjoined from certain conduct, while in civil actions filed by private parties, defendants that lose may also be enjoined and have to pay treble damages and the attorneys' fees and court costs of the plaintiff. Even if antitrust claims are successfully defended, their defense is usually disruptive to the business and expensive in terms of monetary and management costs, as well as the effects on reputation.

At the same time, it is obvious that the law is rarely black and white, particularly in the area of pricing. Over the last several decades, U.S. courts have placed more emphasis on showing demonstrable economic effect, rather than relying on assumptions to find antitrust violations. Indeed, once the business objectives are clear, contemporary antitrust law provides considerable flexibility to develop alternative strategies and tactics, which are usually compatible with the degree of legal and trade-relations risk a business wishes to assume. While there often are no easy answers, in most cases the ends are achievable with some modification of the means.

Notes

1. Eugene F. Zelek, Jr. wrote "The Legal Framework for Pricing" section of this chapter. He is a partner in the Antitrust and Marketing Law Group of the Chicago law firm of Freeborn & Peters. The author wishes to thank his partner, William C. Holmes, and his sometime co-author, Professor Louis W. Stern of the Kellogg School of Management at Northwestern, for their comments and suggestions.
2. Clarence C. Walton, *Ethos and the Executive* (Englewood Cliffs, NJ, Prentice-Hall, 1969), p. 209.
3. William J. Kehoe, "Ethics, Price Fixing, and the Management of Price Strategy," in *Marketing Ethics: Guidelines for Managers,* eds. Gene R. Laczniak and Patrick E. Murphy (Lexington, MA, D. C. Heath, 1985), p. 72.
4. Kehoe, "Ethics, Price Fixing," p. 71.
5. Manuel G. Velasquez, *Business Ethics,* 3rd ed. (Englewood Cliffs, NJ, Prentice-Hall, 1992), pp. 282–83.
6. Tom L. Beaucamp and Normal E. Bowie, *Ethical Theory and Business,* 4th ed. (Englewood Cliffs, NJ, Prentice-Hall, 1993), pp. 697–98.
7. Specialized or industry-specific statutes are outside the scope of this discussion. However, federal and state laws of general applicability tend to be consistent. For antitrust issues (particularly in pricing), it is wise to have the assistance of knowledgeable legal counsel. This chapter is not a substitute for such help.

8. See 1999 O.J. (L 336) 21 (the safe harbor is available to the supplier if its market share is 30 percent or less). The U.S. approach does not establish a numerical market-share threshold, but instead looks at economic effects as a whole under the "rule of reason" discussed in the next section. (Territorial restrictions and other nonprice restraints in the United States are examined in "Using Nonprice Variables to Support Pricing Goals" below.) For an even more significant difference between U.S. and EU antitrust law, see note 23 infra.

9. Criminal violation of the Sherman Act, the country's principal antitrust statute, is a felony punishable by a $10 million fine if the perpetrator is a corporation or other entity and a $350,000 fine or three years in prison or both if the violator is an individual. 15 U.S.C. § 1. Application of the Comprehensive Crime Control Act and the Criminal Fine Improvements Acts, 18 U.S.C. § § 3571-3572, permits an even greater financial penalty by allowing the fine to be increased to twice the gain from the illegal conduct or twice the loss to the victims, while the Federal Sentencing Guidelines can also impact the penalties imposed. See United States Sentencing Commission, 1991 Sentencing Guidelines.

10. The FTC has no authority under the Sherman Act and relies on other antitrust statutes, including Section 5 of the Federal Trade Commission Act, 15 U.S.C. § 45.

11. Since the 1980s, state attorneys general also have been active in civil antitrust enforcement at the federal level, suing on behalf of the citizens of their states and often coordinating their efforts through the National Association of Attorneys General (NAAG).

12. Similarly, vertical price fixing does not apply to the sale of services through intermediaries when the services are performed by the supplier for the end user (such as cellular telephone services), because ownership of the services never passes to the intermediaries. Indeed, the role of the intermediaries is that of selling agent on behalf of the supplier.

13. 15 U.S.C. § 1.

14. This also is why sales through agents are not subject to the price fixing prohibitions of the Sherman Act's Section 1 nor are consignment sales where the supplier retains title to the goods in the reseller's possession until they are sold to the end user. These are unilateral activities on the part of the supplier, because ownership flows directly to the end user from the supplier.

15. For a discussion of "price signaling," a practice that facilitates conscious parallelism, see "Other Pricing Issues" below.

16. *See Interstate Circuit, Inc. v. United States,* 306 U.S. 208, 222 (1939)(restrictions); *American Tobacco Co. v. United States,* 328 U.S. 781, 805 (1946)(price increases). Of course, if the challenged conduct is consistent with rational individual behavior or there is little reason for the defendants to engage in a conspiracy, it is more difficult to find one.

17. See *e.g., In re Baby Food Antitrust Litig.,* 166 F.3d 112 (3d Cir. 1999). Moreover, the validity of the purported reasons for engaging in the conduct under examination is a consideration, but even a pretext for doing so does not alone establish a conspiracy.

18. For a case illustrating direct price fixing, see *United States v. Andreas,* 216 F.3d 645 (7th Cir. 2000)(Archer Daniels Midland executives). For a situation involving indirect price fix-

ing, see *United States v. Container Corp.,* 393 U.S. 333 (1969).

19. 468 U.S. 85 (1984). This case validated the Court's decision in *Chicago Board of Trade v. United States,* 246 U.S. 231 (1918), which upheld an exchange rule that after-hours trading had to be at prices at which the market most recently closed. Such a rule was supportive of the free-for-all competition that occurred during the trading day and, therefore, was reasonable even though it set prices among members.

20. 522 U.S. 3 (1997).

21. Not surprisingly, most customers of the reseller don't care if it sells below an advertised price.

22. *Monsanto Co. v. Spray-Rite Service Corp.,* 465 U.S. 752 (1984); *Business Electronics Corp. v. Sharp Electronics Corp.,* 485 U.S. 717 (1988).

23. The modern cases build on *United States v. Colgate & Co.,* 250 U.S. 300 (1919), the first Supreme Court decision that permitted this conduct, and unilateral vertical price fixing is said to apply the "*Colgate* doctrine." Strictly speaking, the supplier is not "setting" prices. It is only "suggesting" or "recommending" them, but the result is the same if the supplier's unilateral price policy is effective. Note that vertical price fixing of any sort (maximum, minimum, or exact) by agreement is illegal in Canada and in the EU, and there is also nothing analogous to the *Colgate* doctrine in either place.

24. The flexibility under antitrust law notwithstanding, pulling all of the supplier's business may trigger reseller protective statutes at the federal or state level that are usually industry-specific (covering automobile dealers or beer wholesalers, for example), although some states have more general protections. See, e.g.,

Wisconsin Fair Dealership Law, Wisc. Stat. § 135. Also, unless the deletion of one or more products is allowed by the applicable agreement, doing so under an otherwise lawful price policy could still constitute breach of contract.

25. For example, this approach is common in the area of disposable medical products. Interestingly, the supplier-negotiated sell price to a large hospital chain may be below the reseller's buy price from the supplier. However, after proof of such a sale is provided to the supplier, it rebates the difference, along with additional funds to provide the reseller with a margin.

26. 15 U.S.C. § 13. This statute is discussed in the next section. Until 1987, the FTC classified price restrictions in promotional programs as per se illegal, but then changed its mind. See 6 Trade Reg. Rep. (CCH) ¶ 39,057 at 41,728 (FTC May 21, 1987).

27. Of course, practices that go too far are still subject to attack, as was the case of five major suppliers of consumer audio recordings that, faced with an FTC enforcement proceeding alleging the effective elimination of price competition, agreed to drop their MAP programs as part of a consent order. See *Sony Music Distribution, Inc.,* [1997–2001 FTC Complaints and Orders Transfer Binder] Trade Reg. Rep. (CCH) ¶ 24,746 (August 30, 2000).

28. 15 U.S.C. § 13. Price discrimination is covered by Section 2(a) of the Act, while promotional discrimination is addressed under Sections 2(d) and 2(e). *Id.* § § 13(a), (d)-(e). States tend to have laws that are comparable to that at the federal level. Canada also has a statutory prohibition on economic discrimination. See Competition Act, Paras. 50(1)(a)-(b).

29. For example, certain pharmaceutical companies paid more than $700 million to settle a consolidated lawsuit brought by thousands of drug resellers who allege that health maintenance and managed care organizations received preferential pricing in violation of the Robinson-Patman Act and as part of a price fixing conspiracy. *In re Brand Name Prescription Drugs Litig.,* No. 94 C 897, 1999 WL 639173, at *2 (N.D. Ill. Aug. 17, 1999). Other companies fought the suit and succeeded in getting essential portions of it thrown out. *In re Brand Name Prescription Drugs Litig.,* 1999-1 Trade Cas. (CCH) ¶ 72,446 (N.D. Ill), *aff'd in part,* 186 F.3d 781 (7th Cir. 1999).

30. For structuring purposes, there is no violation if one or more of the elements are missing. Often overlooked is that resellers selling to other businesses in interstate commerce are required to follow the Robinson-Patman Act with respect to their selling activities. Buying activities by resellers or end users are covered by Section 2(f) of the Act, 15 U.S.C. § 13(f). See note 38 infra.

31. In this situation, many companies insist on treating both resellers the same, a somewhat more conservative approach that avoids the trade relations risk of the disfavored reseller finding out what occurred, as well as the legal risk that a sale will be made at the special price for the project and another of the identical goods and quantity at a higher price will be made to a second reseller at about the same time. By the same token, a supplier's clearly articulated policy that each piece of bid business is discrete from everyday sales for inventory may avoid the legal issue if the manufacturer wishes to favor some distributors over others in bid situations.

32. This distinction between a good and a service is not always obvious. For example, printing, advertising, and land are all services, even though something tangible is involved. In addition, off-the-shelf software is a good (much like a book or a music CD), while customized software is most likely a service. The courts have split as to whether electricity is a good or a service, a particularly important distinction in the era of deregulation. While service sellers are free from the Robinson-Patman Act, economic discrimination on their part may give rise to other antitrust claims or violate industry-specific statutes. Moreover, state law can cover discrimination in service pricing, such as in California. See Cal. Bus. & Prof. Code § 17045 (West 1999).

33. *FTC v. Borden Co.,* 383 U.S. 637 (1966)(evaporated milk). Although this result is counterintuitive, if brand preferences translate into different costs to produce or sell, these costs may be taken into account in pricing the otherwise identical products by relying on the defense known as "cost justification," which will be discussed later in the chapter.

34. Consistent with its modern focus on actual economic effect, the Supreme Court substantially raised the bar in this area in *Brooke Group v. Brown & Williamson Corp.,* 509 U.S. 209 (1993). See the discussion of "Predatory Pricing" below.

35. See "Vertical Nonprice Restrictions" below.

36. Note that a defense shifts the burden of proof from the plaintiff to the defendant, so recordkeeping on the part of the defendant takes on added importance.

37. Sometimes a supplier provides a trade discount to a purchaser that is

based on the latter's role in the supplier's distribution system and that reflects in a generalized way the services performed by the purchaser for the supplier. For example, a wholesaler may receive a lower price than a direct-buying retailer for such functions as warehousing and taking credit risk. There is no requirement or blanket Robinson-Patman exemption to differentiate between distribution levels, so if it is done, the differences may be cost-justified or legitimized as meeting competition. If either of these defenses is not available, a functional discount may still be lawful if it reflects reasonable compensation for the services provided. *Texaco Inc. v. Hasbrouck,* 496 U.S. 543 (1990). Danger areas include: (1) the use of intermediaries controlled by the ultimate customer to disguise discounts and (2) situations in which the intermediary makes some sales as a wholesaler and others as a retailer, but the supplier provides it with the wholesaler discount on all purchases.

38. Section 2(f) of the Robinson-Patman Act, 15 U.S.C. § 13(f), prohibits buyers from knowingly inducing discriminatory prices, but this provision is largely toothless, as the FTC is not as jealous in its enforcement as it once was and suppliers almost never sue their customers.

39. While it is possible that an industrial consumer of the supplier's products could be covered under the promotional-discrimination provisions of the Robinson-Patman Act in certain situations (such as where it promotes the use or inclusion of the supplier's products), it is far more common for these provisions to apply only to resellers. (See the discussion that follows "In Connection with the Resale of the Supplier's Goods.") For consistency in this section, the party that purchases from a supplier will be referred to as the "reseller," unless otherwise noted.

40. Of course, the supplier may still face trade relations issues.

41. In its Guides for Advertising Allowances and Other Merchandising Payments and Services, 16 C.F.R. § 240, the FTC endorses the first two approaches and purposely ignores the third, although there is case support for it. Fortunately, the Guides do not carry the force of law.

42. As is the case with price discrimination, it is illegal for buyers to knowingly induce discriminatory promotional allowances, but, due to a drafting quirk, only the FTC can chase lying buyers here. See 15 U.S.C. § 13(f).

43. *Continental T.V., Inc. v. GTE Sylvania Inc.,* 433 U.S. 36, 51–52 (1977).

44. While vertical restrictions are often used with product resellers, certain restraints may also be useful in dealing with sales agents, the provision of services, and direct-buying product end users. For example, with respect to direct buyers, see the discussion of Product Restrictions below.

45. The best area-of-primary-responsibility contract or policy language requires that a quantitative goal be attained before outside sales are permitted. The worst provision uses a meaningless "best efforts" clause that requires the reseller to use its best efforts to sell the supplier's products in the reseller's area. Note that if the supplier does not have written contracts with its resellers, it may use written policies to impose vertical restrictions.

46. The same rule applies to noncustomers who want to become customers and request certain products.

47. Both exclusive dealing and tying may be challenged under Section 1 of the Sherman Act, 15 U.S.C. § 1 (goods or services); Section 3 of the Clayton Act, *id.* § 14 (goods only); and Section 5 of the Federal Trade Commission Act, *id.* § 45 (goods or services).

48. The elements of unlawful tying are (1) two separate products or services; (2) the sale of one (the "tying product") is conditioned on the purchase of the other (the "tied product"); (3) there is sufficient economic power in the market for the tying product to restrain trade in the market for the tied product; (4) a not insubstantial amount of commerce in the market for the tied product is affected; and (5) there is no defense or justification available, such as proper functioning or trade secrets.

49. Under certain distributor, dealer, or franchisee protective laws at the state level, suppliers may be required to treat all intermediaries more or less the same in all business dealings, or, as in Wisconsin, not change their "competitive circumstances" without cause. See Wisconsin Fair Dealership Law, Wisc. Stat. § 135.

50. 15 U.S.C. §§ 2, 45. Monopolization requires (1) monopoly power in the relevant market and (2) the willful acquisition or maintenance of that power, while attempted monopolization consists of (1) predatory or exclusionary conduct; (2) specific or predatory intent to achieve monopoly power in the relevant market; and (3) a dangerous probability that the defendant will be successful. The presence of a conspiracy to engage in predatory pricing can violate Sections 1 and 2 of the Sherman Act. Id. §§ 1, 2.

51. *Brooke Group v. Brown & Williamson Corp.,* 509 U.S. 209 (1993).

52. *E. I. Du Pont de Nemours & Co. v. FTC,* 729 F.2d 128, 139-40 (2d Cir. 1984).

53. *Id.* at 134. Of course, not all types of price signaling fare as well. Eight airlines and their jointly owned data collection and dissemination company settled a price fixing case brought by the Justice Department over a computerized system that was used to communicate fare changes and promotions in advance to the participants and permitted later modification or withdrawal of such announcements. *United States v. Airline Tariff Publishing Co.,* 1994–2 Trade Cas. (CCH) ¶ 70,686 (D.D.C. 1994)(all defendants, except United Air Lines, Inc. and USAir, Inc.); 836 F. Supp. 12 (D.C.C. 1993)(United and USAir). In the government's view, the nonpublic nature of this data exchange and its method of operation were tantamount to the airlines having direct discussions in the same room.

Name Index

A

Aaker, David A., 276-77
Abrams, Bill, 331
Acito, Franklin, 369
AGFA, 186
Ailawadi, Kusum L., 277
Airlines, 152
Albion, Mark, 293, 303
Alcaly, Roger E., 117
Alchian, Armen, 330
Amazon.com, 91, 126
American Airlines, 181
American Hospital Supply, 209
Anderson, F. James C., 368
Anderson, Jr., M.J., 198
AOL.com, 90, 124-26, 180
Applebaum, William, 367
Aramco, 124
Asher, Harold, 330
Assael, Henry, 368
AT&T, 125, 136

B

Barclay, William D., 368
Barron, Penny, 276, 368
Bass, Frank M., 198
Beaucamp, Tom. L., 387
Beaujon, George J., 34
Beer industry, 125
Behrmann, Neil, 276
Bell, David, 117, 118, 367
Benham, Lee, 276
Bennet, Sidney, 368
Bereson, Mark L., 367
Berss, Marcia, 145
Beswick, Charles, 276
Best, Roger, 369
BF Goodrich, 194
Blackman, Douglas A., 304
Blattberg, Robert C., 276–77, 367
Blattbert, Robert, 277
Bolton, Ruth N., 303
Bonoma, Thomas V., 226

Borden, James P., 34
Boring, R.A., 116
Boston Consulting Group (BCG), 312–13
Bowie, Normal E., 387
Bowman, Russell, 276
Brandenburger, Adam, 145
Buzzell, Robert D., 277
Byrne, Harlan S., 303

C

Calder, Bobby J., 369
Campbell, Margaret C., 118
Campbell, Donald T., 367
Carlton, Jim, 303
Carpenter, Gregory S., 198
Cassady, Jr., Ralph, 252
Caterpillar Corporation, 163–64
Cattin, Philip, 369
Celeron, 129
Chakravarthi, Narasimhan, 251, 276
Chandon, Pierre, 277
Channel Tunnel, 238
Charnes, A., 330
Chiang, Jeongwen, 118, 367
Churchill, Neil, 34
Clancy, Kevin J., 176, 367
Compaq, 185, 278–79
Consumer Reports, 89
Cook, Thomas, 367
Cook, Victor, 198
Cooper, Arnold C., 199
Cooper, Robin, 34
Cooper, R.W., 330
Corey, E. Raymond, xix, 14, 115, 176, 330
Cravens, David, 276
Cuisinart, Inc., 182

D

Davidow, David, 176
Day, George, 198
Dean, Joel, 176

Dell, 13, 185, 278–79
Della Bitta, Albert J., 116
Desiraju, Romarao, 251
Devinney, Timothy M., 275, 303
Dhalla, Nariman, 198
Dickson, Peter, 117, 275
Dodson, Joe, 277
Dolan, Robert J., 252, 330
Doob, A., 116
Dowst, Somerby, 276
Dressmart.com, 180
Drucker, Peter F., 14
Dunnette, Marvin, 367

E

eBay, 126
Elrod, Terry, 367
EMC, 183
Emshwiller, John R., 276
Enis, Ben, 116–17
Eppen, Gary D., 252, 277
Eskin, Gerald, 276, 368
E-Trade.com, 90
Exhibit 13–4: A Conjoint Study: New Hotel's Best Price and Attributes, 353–55
Exhibit 13–5: Profitability Optimization Model Using Discrete Choice Survey, 355–58

F

Farris, Paul W., 303
Firestone, 193
Flint, Jerry, 117
Ford Motors, 5–6
Fraker, Susan, 331
Frank, Ronald E., 277, 367
Freemarkets.com, 161
Friedman, Thomas, 368
Fruhan, Jr., William E., 198
Fuld, Leonard M., 146

Subject Index